New Perspectives in German Studies

General Editors: Professor Michael Butler, Head of the Department of German Studies, University of Birmingham and Professor William Paterson, Director of the Institute of German Studies, University of Birmingham.

Over the last twenty years the concept of German studies has undergone major transformation. The traditional mixture of language and literary studies, related very closely to the discipline as practised in German universities, has expanded to embrace history, politics, economics and cultural studies. The conventional boundaries between all these disciplines have become increasingly blurred, a process which has been accelerated markedly since German unification in 1989/90.

New Perspectives in German Studies, developed in conjunction with the Institute for German Studies at the University of Birmingham, has been designed to respond precisely to this trend of the interdisciplinary approach to the study of German and to cater for the growing interest in Germany in the context of European integration. The books in this series will focus on the modern period, from 1750 to the present day.

Titles include:

Peter Bleses and Martin Seeleib-Kaiser
THE DUAL TRANSFORMATION OF THE GERMAN WELFARE STATE

Michael Butler and Robert Evans (*editors*)
THE CHALLENGE OF GERMAN CULTURE
Essays Presented to Wilfried van der Will

Michael Butler, Malcolm Pender and Joy Charnley (*editors*)
THE MAKING OF MODERN SWITZERLAND 1848–1998

Paul Cooke and Andrew Plowman (*editors*)
GERMAN WRITERS AND THE POLITICS OF CULTURE
Dealing with the Stasi

Wolf-Dieter Eberwein and Karl Kaiser (*editors*)
GERMANY'S NEW FOREIGN POLICY
Decision-Making in an Interdependent World

Jonathan Grix
THE ROLE OF THE MASSES IN THE COLLAPSE OF THE GDR

Margarete Kohlenbach
WALTER BENJAMIN
Self-Reference and Religiosity

Charles Lees
PARTY POLITICS IN GERMANY
A Comparative Politics Approach

James Sloam
THE EUROPEAN POLICY OF THE GERMAN SOCIAL DEMOCRATS
Interpreting a Changing World

Ronald Speirs and John Breuilly (*editors*)
GERMANY'S TWO UNIFICATIONS
Anticipations, Experiences, Responses

Henning Tewes
GERMANY, CIVILIAN POWER AND THE NEW EUROPE
Enlarging Nato and the European Union

Maiken Umbach
GERMAN FEDERALISM
Past, Present, Future

New Perspectives in German Studies
Series Standing Order ISBN 0–333–92430–4 hardcover
Series Standing Order ISBN 0–333–92434–7 paperback
(*outside North America only*)

You can receive future titles in this series as they are published by placing a standing order.
Please contact your bookseller or, in case of difficulty, write to us at the address below with
your name and address, the title of the series and the ISBN quoted above.

Customer Services Department, Macmillan Distribution Ltd, Houndmills, Basingstoke,
Hampshire RG21 6XS, England

Party Politics in Germany

A Comparative Politics Approach

Charles Lees
Lecturer in Politics, University of Sheffield

First published in 2005 by
PALGRAVE MACMILLAN
Houndmills, Basingstoke, Hampshire RG21 6XS and
175 Fifth Avenue, New York, N.Y. 10010
Companies and representatives throughout the world.

PALGRAVE MACMILLAN is the global academic imprint of the Palgrave Macmillan division of St. Martin's Press, LLC and of Palgrave Macmillan Ltd. Macmillan® is a registered trademark in the United States, United Kingdom and other countries. Palgrave is a registered trademark in the European Union and other countries.

ISBN-13: 978–1–4039–9742–5 hardback
ISBN-10: 1–4039–9742–X hardback

This book is printed on paper suitable for recycling and made from fully managed and sustained forest sources.

A catalogue record for this book is available from the British Library.

Library of Congress Cataloging-in-Publication Data

Lees, Charles.
    Party politics in Germany : a comparative politics approach / Charles Lees.
       p. cm. – (New perspectives in German studies)
    Includes bibliographical references and index.
    ISBN 1–4039–9742–X (cloth)
     1. Political parties – Germany. 2. Political parties. I. Title. II. New perspectives in German studies (Palgrave Macmillan (Firm))

JN3971.A979L44 2005
320.943'09'04—dc22   2005045254

10 9 8 7 6 5 4 3 2 1
14 13 12 11 10 09 08 07 06 05

For Kirsten

Contents

List of Tables

List of Figures

Foreword

The idea of writing a volume such as this first came to me during a conversation with Willie Paterson at the 2001 meeting of the American Political Science Association in San Francisco. We were talking about the wealth of comparative politics panels to be found at APSA and of how single-country scholarship, broadly defined, might benefit from a more reflexive use of comparative models, frameworks and data. Four years later I hope that this study goes some way to tap into the potential we both felt was inherent in such an approach.

A more detailed rationale for the book is included in Chapter 1 so I will not indulge the temptation to pre-empt the arguments here. All I will say at this point is that I have found completing this study an illuminating and rewarding exercise that has made me think more deeply about what I do in research terms – and why I do it. It has also been invaluable to be able to bounce ideas off colleagues as the manuscript developed and I thank them for their input and inspiration throughout the process. In particular I would like to thank Willie Paterson, the series editor; Martin Smith, Ian Bache and my colleagues at the Department of Politics in Sheffield (who have waited some time for this book to appear); Paul Taggart, Dan Hough and former colleagues at Sussex; Alison Howson and Guy Edwards at Palgrave Macmillan; Alan Ware, Gordon Smith and Steven Padgett for help and advice; and an anonymous referee for a very thorough and constructively critical report on the draft manuscript. I would also like to thank Vidhya Jayaprakash and staff at Newgen Imaging Systems for their painstaking work on the manuscript. However, the person I wish to thank the most for her quiet patience and encouragement is my wife Kirsten. This book is dedicated to her.

CL.
Sheffield

1
Germany in Comparative Context

1.1 Introduction

This book examines the phenomenon of party politics in the Federal Republic through comparison across time and space. In other words the book is both a diachronic and synchronic study and, as a result, draws upon two distinct literatures that crosscut the disciplines of political science, political sociology and political history. The first tradition is the German-language and Anglophone literature that focusses specifically on German politics and society. The second is a predominantly (but by no means exclusively) Anglophone comparative politics literature that eschews the depth and specific focus of the single country studies in favour of a broader lens that is capable of defining and explaining patterns of political development and behaviour across cases. By-and-large these cases are to be found in the advanced industrial democracies of Europe, North America and South-East Asia, but it will become apparent to the reader as the book unfolds that useful comparisons can also be drawn with political systems and phenomena in the developing world as well.

The broad purpose of this exercise is two-fold. First, by drawing on a wider literature than is generally found in single-country studies the book will shed new light on political phenomena and suggest new nuances or even explanations to students of German politics (and perhaps country specialists more generally). Second, it is also intended that the book will allow students of the comparative method to apply some of the key concepts, models and approaches with which they are familiar to the rich context of a single-country study. In performing both functions it is hoped that the book will problematise the trade-off in such a study between depth and breadth, micro-and macro-level explanation, rich description and abstraction, inductive and deductive reasoning, and so on. These are quite ambitious aspirations and it is up to the reader to decide how successfully the book fulfils them.

More specifically, however, the reader will discern that the book has two strands of debate – one empirical and the other theoretical in nature.

The dominant and recurring empirical debate problematises the balance between (1) the singularities of the German *Sonderweg*, or 'special path', by which the reasons behind the (often uniquely tragic) course of German social and political development can be 'read off' against the warp and weft of German history, culture and norms; and (2) the commonality of characteristics shared by Germany and other nations. The balance between the two strands goes to the core of the book's purpose – for if we can find robust explanations for the way party politics works in Germany today simply by referring back to some notion of the *Sonderweg*, then there is very little rationale for a comparative study such as this. It follows, therefore, that this book starts from the assumption that the *Sonderweg* narrative is a necessary but not sufficient condition for the analysis of party politics in Germany. More specifically, the study aims to make greater use of more comparative data, more often than has been the norm in single-country studies of this type.

Now our discussion of the rationale for the use of comparative data leads us to the second, theoretical, strand to the study. Once again, this relates back to the balance between the narrative of the *Sonderweg* and the need for comparison. For if we can construct robust explanations using the logic of the *Sonderweg* alone, then we are essentially working in the realm of 'thick description' in which, although theory is often used to great effect, it is not always essential. If, however, we are to use the comparative method then the abstractions of theory become central to our study – in order to impose order upon – and harness the explanatory power of – an often diverse set of data. These points are returned to later in the chapter, but first let us return to our motives for using the comparative method in this study and explore in greater detail the potential benefits from using a comparative politics approach.

1.2 Why compare?

Having read the previous two paragraphs the reader might be forgiven for asking whether using the comparative politics approach is not making life harder than it really needs to be. Why not work solely within the single-country format? It is clear that there is already a rich German politics literature available, primarily written in German but augmented by Anglophone scholars in the United States and United Kingdom, for instance. It is not necessary to name names at this point but a quick glance at the bibliography to this book will give the reader some idea of the fine scholarship to be found in this field of study. Moreover this book is only about party politics and as such the literature cited is only a sub-set of a much wider canon. But it is for this very reason that the book attempts to offer a slightly different perspective to the German politics mainstream – an approach that is designed to be complementary to it, has its own reasons for existence, and brings its own benefits.

And what are those reasons? Landman suggests that there are four of them (Landman, 2000: 4). First, that the comparative method provides 'contextual description' that allows us to deepen and widen our understanding of the political world. Second, it is a driver of classification, in that we are forced to render the political world less complex through the refinement of our classificatory schemes. Third, the generation of comparative data is a powerful tool for hypothesis-testing. Finally, the process of comparison and generalisation generates predictions that can be tested on other countries and datasets. The benefits that are generated are also four-fold. First, the comparative method makes social science more accessible and relevant to more people both within and outside the academy. Second, comparison helps explain and generalise findings across a range of settings. Third, it stimulates the process of hypothesis-building and refinement. Finally, when done well it has a positive impact on the researcher. In particular, it can challenge and break down the residual ethno-centrism of the researcher and force her to re-assess her understanding of the political world – not just in other countries but also on her doorstep. It is perhaps something we should all engage in from time to time.

1.3   Rationale of the study

It was noted earlier that the book has two strands – one empirical and the other theoretical. Let us begin with the dominant empirical strand. Broadly speaking there are five different techniques of comparison. These are, first, global statistical analysis; second, case studies; third, focussed comparisons; fourth, diachronic studies; and finally, pooled comparative research (Lijphart, 1971). These can be divided into two categories of comparison – 'large n' and 'small n' studies. Large n studies are quite simply studies that rely on a large number of observations, as a rule of thumb 50 or more (Sartori, 1970). The word 'observation' is used advisedly as we are not necessarily talking about cases or countries, although in comparative politics this is very often the case. For practical reasons – in other words, the need to frame, order and make sense of such a large number of observations – data generated by such studies is generally quantitative in nature and is often used to derive some form of statistical inference about the relationship between variables. Thus, large n studies tend to work at a relatively high level of empirical abstraction. By contrast, small n studies rely on fewer observations and work at a lower level of abstraction but make up for this with a more culturally specific (and culturally sensitive) strand of 'thick description' intended to draw out the nuances of a given political phenomenon. Such studies are more reliant on qualitative data but not exclusively so.

In practice, however, a great deal of comparative research does not fall neatly into such taxonomical categories but rather combines methods. By-and-large there are two reasons for this. On the one hand, restricting one's research to one particular method may not allow the researcher to address all aspects of the research question, whilst on the other, the use of multiple methods allows one to enhance the validity of the research – because each method serves as a check on the other (Read and Marsh, 2002: 237; see also Hopkin, 2002). For these reasons a great deal of comparative research deliberately combines different types of data or even distinct methods in order to achieve a 'triangulated perspective' (Denzin, 1970). Thus this book explicitly triangulates between quantitative and qualitative data and between the five techniques of comparison noted above. In terms of quantitative data the book draws upon primary data from recent Bundestag elections, as well as secondary data including statistical analyses of voter choice, value orientation, and other socio-economic data. In terms of qualitative data the study uses primary data from recent party publications and other official documents – including election manifestos and coalition agreements – as well as secondary data from the two literatures discussed earlier in the chapter. Moving on to techniques of comparison it will become apparent to the reader that the book uses all five techniques. It will be recalled that the purpose of the study is to examine party politics in Germany through comparison across time and space in such a way that will (1) add value and augment the German politics literature and (2) provide a single-country study with which to apply and test models and approaches from comparative politics. In order to fulfil the first objective the book uses the diachronic technique as well as the synchronic techniques of global statistical analysis, focussed comparisons, and pooled comparative research. And it will become apparent to the reader that the specific mix of the two techniques of comparison varies from chapter to chapter, as appropriate to the focus of study. But in order to fulfil the second objective the dominant research design is that of the case study – in this case party politics in Germany, as a sub-set of the wider phenomenon of party politics.

Sartori draws a distinction between case studies as a comparative method *per se* and as a method with some merit within the context of a wider comparative analysis (Sartori, 1994: 23). By this he means that case studies can only be regarded as a good method of comparison if a well-defined and operational theoretical framework informs them. This is echoed by Rose, who argues that it is the presence of such an operational framework – capable of application across cases – that makes a study comparative (Rose, 1991: 449).

Lijphart divides case studies up into five ideal types. These are (1) interpretative case studies using existing theory; (2) hypothesis-generating case studies; (3) case studies used to interrogate or test a theory; (4) studies used to confirm a theory; and (5) so-called 'deviant' studies (Lijphart, 1971: 691–3). Again, this is a useful taxonomical exercise but such classifications do not always apply in practice. In particular, as Mackie and Marsh observe, Lijphart's first category of case study is not strictly comparative anyway and the other four ideal types are not necessarily comparative either. They can only be considered comparative if 'they use and assess the utility of concepts developed elsewhere ... test some general theory or hypothesis, or generate concepts to be of use elsewhere' (Mackie and Marsh, 1995: 177). As will become apparent, this study does just that – using and testing the utility of concepts developed elsewhere and covering three out of the five categories. Obviously the use of existing models and approaches to comparative politics is interpretative rather than comparative, in keeping with Lijphart's first classification, but the study also conforms to the third ('theory informing') and fourth ('theory confirming') ideal types. This discussion is returned to in the conclusion to the book.

It must be remembered, however, that the triangulation of data in the manner described above means that the study uses different levels of analysis and poses two questions that must be resolved. On the one hand it raises the possibility that the study is vulnerable to the problem of individualist and/or ecological fallacies. As Landman point out, this occurs 'when inferences are drawn about one level of analysis using evidence from another' (Landman, 2000: 49). In order to resolve this problem the book uses the 'principle of direct measurement' (Scheuch, 1969). This means that conclusions about individual-level phenomena such as partisan orientation are only drawn from individual-level data, such as sample surveys and censuses, and those relating to ecological-level phenomena such as political culture or the degree to which a state is authoritarian are only drawn from ecological-level data, such as aggregate data from electoral districts, sub-national tiers of government, and so on. This principle is all the more important given that the book draws upon such a diverse secondary literature. As a result much is made of 'non-editorialised' data from tables and figures that are re-interpreted by the author.

The debate above leads us to the second question that must be resolved, namely the underlying ontological and epistemological position of the book. And obviously this leads us to a discussion of the second, theoretical, strand of the study. The consequences of one's chosen mix of micro-political analysis, using individual-level data, and macro-political analysis, using more ecological data, are part of the so-called 'structure–agency' debate (Hay, 1995). Studies that adopt micro-level explanations are implicitly making claims about the primacy of agency in explaining political phenomena, whilst those that use predominantly macro-level data tend to be focussed on the role of structure. Although not universally considered to be important, some scholars make very strong claims about the need to have a consistent position in this regard and make it explicit (see Marsh and Furlong, 2002). In principle they are right, but in practice it is not always possible to make one's position as explicit as one would wish. This is because the type of explanation one makes is to a great extent driven by the type of data available. Thus, the underlying position of the book is that political agency lies at the heart of political phenomena, but that political agents are constrained by the institutional setting within which they operate. Therefore, where possible the book uses individual-level data from Germany and further afield but, as is discussed in Chapter 2, those elements of diachronic analysis in the book are heavily reliant on macro-historical accounts, most notably the work of Lipset and Rokkan (1967). Similarly the book is grounded in the idea of rational action on the part of individuals (voters and non-voters, party members and members of elites) and uses models and approaches (post-materialism, economic voting, political elites, deductive models of coalition behaviour, and so on) appropriate to this position. At the same time, however, the idea of institutions as constraints upon political agency includes structural variables (such as political culture, socio-economic development and class structure, etc.) and therefore draws upon work (for instance, relating to cleavage structures and voter alignments) that are appropriate in that respect. In other words, the approach of the book is in line with the idea of Weale's concept of 'idioms of analysis' (Weale, 1992). As Weale observes, one's choice of 'idiom' depends upon the extent to which it 'provide(s) a way of talking about, and therefore understanding, political processes'. In contrast to Marsh and Furlong's position, Weale argues that not only are such idioms not mutually exclusive but that their internal components are often only loosely related to each other. As a result, Weale suggests that the analyst may have to draw upon a quite heterogeneous literature, given that 'there sometimes is no canonical source to which one can go' (Weale, 1992: 38). It will become clear to the reader that in the case of this study there is certainly no canonical source on which the book draws. In the end, the study is carried out in the knowledge that what is important is that one is aware of and makes explicit the underlying epistemological tensions inherent in its approach and makes sure one does not compare apples with oranges.

Having said that, however, we do need to impose some form of loose theoretical framework upon the study in order to make clear what it is we are examining, why we consider it to be important and what specifically we are trying to say about it. In other words, we need some form of heuristic theoretical device that will knit together our diverse models and data into a coherent narrative. But what kind of theoretical framework are we looking for and what are our ambitions for the framework? Moreover, can we find a framework that satisfies our theoretical ambitions and yet is able to stand up empirically?

A good starting point would be to consider trying to embed our account of party politics in Germany within the narrative of normative democratic theory. Ware (1987a) provides a thorough account of how this has been done elsewhere in the literature (and, incidentally, also highlights how the empirical study of party politics has become somewhat disinterested in the normative dimension of party activity over the last 40 or 50 years). Although by no means identical to this study, Ware's book addresses many of the theoretical and empirical issues that are engaged with in this volume and therefore the next few pages draw heavily upon his original discussion.

Ware's analysis was built around three questions. First, what are the different elements of democracy? Second, what are political parties? And third, how have theorists seen the role of parties in facilitating or constraining democracy in society? (ibid: 7). Let us deal with each in turn.

In terms of the first question, Ware argues that the debate between political theorists can be framed within three elements – (1) interest optimalisation; (2) the exercise of control; and (3) civic orientation. Beyond that, however, there is little agreement over the relative importance of these elements and how they should relate to each other. In terms of the first element, Ware uses the assertion of Thompson that the key to democratic legitimacy is the ability of the state to 'satisfy the interests of the greatest possible number of citizens' (1970: 41) as a starting point but observes that this leaves open the question of what are citizens interests and how can they be satisfied? Some theorists would argue that it is the 'outputs' of the political process that are important, focussing for instance on the distribution of resources in society (Irish and Prothro, 1971) or the degree of match between individual preferences and collective choice (Arrow, 1951). Others would argue that it is the procedural or 'input' side of the equation that is important and that all that is required is 'some degree of freedom of communication and organisation ... (as a) ... necessary condition for the formation, expression and aggregation of political preferences' (Barry, 1979: 156–7). Thus, although there must be some link between procedures, preferences and outcomes, the process and outcomes of collective choice in complex democracies will not necessarily – indeed cannot in practice – accurately reflect the distribution of preferences (Riker, 1982). This leads us to the second element of democracy, namely the exercise of control over the government and ancillary organisations by the people – and again, we find that theorists disagree on *what* and *the degree to what* can be controlled by citizens. At what we might label the minimalist (some might use the word pessimist) end of the spectrum we find scholars such as Riker (1982), Sartori (1962) and Schumpeter (1943) who argue that a democracy needs little more than the minimum requirement that citizens are able if they so wish to remove governments at periodic elections. In most cases this would imply electoral competition but taken at face value Sartori at least would argue that this is not necessary as long as individual leaders can be removed. A more elaborate (or optimistic) view of democracy would argue that mechanisms must exist that enable citizens to exercise other forms of participation and control. But again there is disagreement about the nature of preferences and whether these mechanisms exist to reflect existing preferences or – in their more participatory manifestations – to actually help form and enhance the nature of citizens' preferences (Ware, 1987a: 9–10). Which leads us to the third element, that of civic orientation – or in other words what kind of objectives should citizens be pursuing in the field of the 'political'? Here it is possible to follow in the footsteps of Rousseau and argue that participation is the means by which individuals'

Weltbild becomes less self-regarding and acquires an other-regarding character. Alternatively, one might argue the classic liberal case and assert that the nature of individuals' preferences is of little or no interest and that it is the ability of individuals to express and promote their preferences, subject to certain restrictions on the externalities of these actions, which is important. Crudely put, therefore, the debate about civic orientation can be seen as a choice between 'the general will' and 'life, liberty and the pursuit of happiness' – with the former approach attaching more weight to the participatory element of the democratic process.

Let us now move on to Ware's second question, what are political parties? As Ware rightly points out, this is not an easy question and he reminds us that there is a danger of setting too narrow a definition – and thus excluding certain organisational forms – or coming up with something that is so wide and amorphous that it is of little or no analytical value. Ware uses Janda's definition of political parties as 'organisations that pursue a goal of placing their avowed representatives in government positions' (Janda, 1980: 5) in order to demonstrate this problem. As Ware observes, not all parties want to place their members in government and, even if we relax the assumption to mean merely to 'exercise control' over government, then organisations that are not parties, such as the Christian militias in Lebanon of the 1980s, would fall into this category. Alternatively, we might want to specify a certain set of means by which political parties pursue control over government – thus discriminating between, say, the IRA and Sinn Fein (admittedly a distinction that has at certain times and places been somewhat blurred). On the one hand we can see how this specification would work. On the other, however, Ware demonstrates that this would exclude the Chinese Communist Party during its period of conflict with the Kuomintang in the 1920s and 1930s when, although its operational posture was overwhelmingly military, it never ceased to be regarded by itself and others as a political party. Under conditions of repression, moreover, political parties are often forced to eschew many orthodox political-party activities and operate more like a 'sect', using secrecy and a restricted membership to maintain their activities. Paterson (1976) for instance describes how the German Social Democratic Party (SPD) survived the Third Reich in this way and how, after the collapse of National Socialism in 1945, party members queued up with their membership cards to bring their subscription cards up to date. Indeed, some even dug up party banners that had been buried in back gardens and allotments during the Nazi years. Buttressed by a provisional leadership in exile, the SPD was clearly a party that maintained a continuity of existence between 1933 and 1945 – albeit not in the form that would have been the case under democratic conditions – and any global definition of political party must be able to encompass this. Finally, Ware makes it clear that, although control over government within a specific state might be the immediate objective of a political party, for some parties this is more of a means rather than an end.

Thus, before the fall of the Soviet Union, national Communist parties saw themselves as part of a wider internationalist revolutionary project, of which taking control of the nation-state in which they found themselves was just a part. Similarly, according to Ware, the German Greens 'conceives itself as the German wing of a wider movement' (Ware, 1987a: 18).

We now move on to third of Ware's three questions – how do parties advance democracy? It should be pointed out at this juncture that this question is especially important in the German context. There are three reasons for this. First, in the Federal Republic there was until relatively recently a strong sense that German democracy had shallow roots and that the German state was compelled to harness all means possible in order to protect and nurture them. This manifested itself in the constitutional doctrine of 'militant democracy'. Second, and more specific to this study, the Federal Republic is the first fully – fledged party democracy in German history in which parties have been placed at the centre of the state and society – in a manner that was not the case under previous constitutional settlements. Finally, because of both the doctrine of militant democracy and the central role afforded to political parties, the collective fortunes of both the parties and the state itself are seen as inextricably linked (see Paterson, 1987). As a result any lack of legitimacy or sub-optimal performance on the part of political parties is regarded by elites as a potential threat to the democratic settlement and even of the German state itself. These arguments are returned to and examined in more depth elsewhere in the book.

Leaving the German case to one side, then, what are Ware's arguments in relation to the role that political parties play in enhancing democracy? Let us start with the first element of democratic practice – the optimalisation or aggregation of interests. Focussing in on those approaches that consider interest aggregation as the key element of democratic practice, Ware identifies three distinct strands of thought (ibid: 23). First, scholars working within the New Right or neo-liberal tradition and who advocate as small a state as possible would regard organised political parties, and sometimes even the wider mechanisms of representative democracy itself, as antithetical to the workings of the market by which individual preferences are most efficiently satisfied. Thus parties act as intervening institutions that distort the aggregation of individual preferences and serve to undermine the process of collective choice. Moreover, once in power, elected politicians find it hard to resist the temptation to manipulate the political economy in order to secure re-election – thus further skewing the market clearing of interests (see Tufte, 1978, for instance). Second, we find the pluralist and neo-pluralist schools that argue that political parties perform a useful role in structuring the vote, but that the principal organisational platform for articulating preferences within the polity is the interest group (Truman, 1951; Dahl and Lindblom, 1953; Dahl, 1956, 1961). Third, there is the school of thought that would argue that it is the electoral process itself that is central to the aggregation of preferences and that the party system(s) and the individual parties play a crucial role in structuring voter choices, eliminating irrelevant alternatives and thus preventing electoral cycling and instability (Shepsle, 1979; see also Weale, 1984; Shepsle and Weingast, 1989). In these accounts it is the number of parties within the party system that is often crucial and, in keeping with the idea of 'responsible' party government, two-party majoritarian systems tend to be favoured over multi-party systems because (1) they offer clearer alternatives to voters; and (2) there is a more transparent link between the aggregation of voters' choices and governmental outcomes. As will become apparent elsewhere in this study, the German party system does not conform to this ideal type and governmental outcomes tend to be determined in the 'smoke-filled rooms' of coalition negotiations rather than on election day. Thus, they are only tangentially linked to the aggregation of voter choice.

We now move on to the second element of the democratic process, namely the exercise of popular control by citizens over the government. In theory there are two ways in which political parties might help or hinder this process. On the one hand they might drive 'their' governments on to exceed their remits and pursue unpopular policies, whilst on the other they can provide a buffer between government and the electorate, thus providing the breathing space for government to do its job. In more recent years, however, focus has shifted to the degree to which the internal decision-making processes of parties serve as a check on governmental power (see Katz and Mair, 1995; also Lees, 2001) and a normative strand of theory has emerged that advocates 'weak' party structures in order to prevent the 'capture' of party organisations by unrepresentative groups. In particular, there has been a fear that the bureaucratisation and professionalisation of political parties have made them vulnerable to capture by groups with an interest in the extension of state power (Brittan, 1975). Once again, it will become clear to the reader that this is an issue that is highly pertinent to conditions in the Federal Republic where, as already noted, the penetration of the state by political parties is part of the post-1949 constitutional settlement.

Finally, let us consider Ware's third element of the democratic process – that of civic orientation. Amongst scholars who consider this element of democracy to be crucial, we find a division between those who consider political parties to be unnecessary and divisive barriers to individual participation and development and those who regard political parties as crucial conduits for participation and the development of other-regarding values and behaviour. In particular, this latter school regards political parties as also performing a disciplinary role in educating the public about societal interests and the limits of personal preferences. As will become apparent later in this study, this disciplinary/educative function is central to the theory and practice of democracy in the Federal Republic, where political parties were used overtly in the post-war years to inculcate and consolidate democratic values and practice after the fall of the Third Reich.

So, having discussed in general terms the role of political parties in the democratic process, what approach does this study take? In the broadest terms the approach is as follows. First, the book places greatest emphasis on the 'input' side of the equation and examines the role by which political parties, operating within a multi-party system, articulate and aggregate citizens' preferences within a complex modern industrial democracy such as Germany. It goes without saying, therefore, that it is assumed that individual preferences matter and that, although there are undeniably strong intervening variables associated with socio-economic location, voters are not 'cultural dupes'. As a result, therefore, a substantial amount of the book is dedicated to examining voter behaviour and related issues such as partisan identification, post-materialism and economic voting. In other parts of the book, however, a more macro-historical approach is taken but it is made clear that this is used (1) because the lack of individual-level data makes it impossible to draw many conclusions about individual preferences and (2) as it is a useful device for exploring the social and institutional variables generated by the course of German historical development and the constraints they impose upon the political marketplace. At no time, however, is it assumed that voters in this historical context are not reflective and capable of evaluating parties on the basis of their programmes. Nevertheless, it is reasonable to assume that voters' preferences were less individualistic and more group-oriented than today and that the information available to them in exercising party choice was less and more likely to be filtered through the lens of socio-economic location and the institutions (Trade unions, churches, etc.) associated with that location.

This leads us back to our assumption that political parties respond to voters' preferences. And here it will be made clear that, although in an ideal world parties should be highly responsive to – and be held to account by – voters, the reality is that parties are only partially responsive and tend to do as much as is necessary to avoid an electoral backlash from their voters. In this sense political parties can be regarded as firms that compete with one another to sell their product (party programmes and, where appropriate, records in government) in the marketplace (the party system) to potential customers (the voters). It is assumed that the first objective of these firms is survival in the marketplace and that participation in government, whilst highly desirable, is secondary to this. In other words these are firms that often 'satisfice' (Simon, 1965) rather than maximise market share – not least because the institutional and normative environment within which they operate constrains them in this regard. At the same time, however, these same institutions and norms also constrain entry into the political marketplace and therefore create oligopolistic market conditions. Such market conditions make it easier for established firms to pursue their first objective of survival and give them more leeway vis-à-vis their customers. For their part, customers are not given unrestricted choice but rather often have to choose between a number of sub-optimal alternatives. It is assumed that in multi-party systems such as Germany's there are more alternatives on offer than in two-party majoritarian systems but, nevertheless, it is in this restriction of choice that paradoxes and cycles are avoided and voters are 'educated'. Thus, the output issue of civic orientation is touched upon in the study, but by-and-large as an externality of political competition. And in addition to political competition, the often normal practice of coalition governance in multi-party systems such as Germany's means that parties must sometimes co-operate in order to achieve their secondary objective of participation in government. They will also occasionally co-operate to exclude new competitors from the market. Finally, beyond the issue of civic orientation, the output side of the equation is considered to be part of the product offered to voters by parties of government. Thus policy outcomes are important if political parties are to maintain credibility with their customers.

The epistemological basis of the market metaphor that drives this study can be traced back to Anthony Downs' (1957) analogy of party systems as markets, with parties as firms competing with each other for voters who, in turn are analogous with consumers. However, its use in this study is somewhat more heuristic than the rigidly deductive approach laid out by Downs and, in as far as the deductive approach remains, some of the a priori assumptions as to how the political marketplace works have been modified. In the Downsian universe, the policy dimension is laid out uni-dimensionally along a single left/right continuum (although later models have often supplemented this with an additional dimension, based on, for instance, a authoritarian/libertarian or materialist/post-materialist dimension). Under normal circumstances, it is assumed that the individual voter will have one ideal position along the continuum and that voters' preferences are fairly evenly distributed along it. Theoretically, the distribution of these preferences in normal party systems resembles a classic bell-curve, with the aggregate reaching an equilibrium (and thus effectively a consensus) around the median of the distribution. Downs assumed that it is around this point, occupied by the 'median voter' that office-seeking parties will manoeuvre in order to maximise votes. The median voter, who has an equal number of voters on each side, is in a privileged position because he/she can vote down alternatives to both the right and the left. The ideal point of the median voter is the equilibrium outcome under majority rule – and it is expected that parties that form governments will be representative of the preferences of the median voter and thus the majority of voters' preferences. However as will become clear in this study, although some political parties do seem to mobilise the median voter, others do not and are content to carve out a niche position along the bell-curve – which is why office-seeking is assumed to be secondary to survival.

Moving on to the political marketplace, party systems display various degrees of differentiation: defined in such terms as the degree of concentration or deconcentration, partisan alignment or dealignment, dominant or cross-cutting cleavages. Moreover, the opportunity costs of entry into the party system differ across time and space, not only because the appeal of a given political product differs, but also due to system attributes such as voting rules (plurality versus proportional systems), barriers to representation (such as the five per cent hurdle at the Federal level in Germany), laws regulating internal party democracy, and so on. Thus it is important to note that party systems are constrained arenas, and cannot be likened to conditions of perfect competition.

This last point is important because although neo-classical economic theory often assumes the existence of perfect competition within markets, in practice this is rarely if ever the case. As is assumed to be the case in this study, markets are often oligopolistic and in some instances they are characterised by the presence of cartels – groups of firms that co-operate together in order to rig the market and shut out potential competitors. The analogy of the oligopolistic market is easily applied to the German party system – especially at the Federal level. In the three decades after the inception of the Federal Republic in 1949 the political marketplace became increasingly dominated by a limited number of parties. Elsewhere I have called this state of affairs a 'party oligopoly' (Lees, 2001). However, the last two decades have been marked by two systemic junctures that have served to undermine this party oligopoly to some extent. The first, in 1983, took place when the Greens entered the Bundestag following the federal elections of that year. The second, in 1990, took place after the first all-German Federal elections, when the PDS entered the Bundestag. Thus the development of the party-political marketplace in the Federal Republic over the last half century or so has been one of (1) party oligopoly, dominated by the two big *Volksparteien*, and (2) two systemic junctures which have served to break down this party oligopoly and shift the centre of gravity within the party system towards the political left. This account will become more apparent to the reader as the book progresses – and is returned to in some detail in the conclusion to the study.

1.4   Book structure

So let us now examine how the book does progress. As discussed, the book is framed within the idea of party systems as political markets, but with institutions and norms acting as constraints upon political agency. It builds up from the social basis of party politics to the more formal institutions that are the arenas for political action and interaction between political agents, most notably political elites. Each chapter is to some extent freestanding and includes an initial discussion of the theoretical approaches used to frame the data. Chapter 2 draws upon the social cleavage literature and examines the development of political cleavages in Germany through a primarily diachronic lens. The chapter is divided into four sections. First, there is a general discussion of the social cleavage literature. This is followed by a further discussion of Lipset and Rokkan's (1967) account of the development of cleavage structures in Western Europe, with an emphasis on Germany where appropriate. Third, the chapter moves on to an analysis of social and political cleavages in Germany in a comparative perspective. This approach is extended into Chapter 3, which provides a diachronic account of the development of social and political cleavages in Germany from the Reformation, through the Second Reich, and on to the Weimar Republic. The chapter starts with an account of the development of political cleavages in the Second German Reich (1871–1919), which established a pattern of party competition that persisted into the early years of the Federal Republic. Second, there is a discussion of the social base of party politics in the Weimar Republic (1919–33) – Germany's first ill-starred experience of popular democracy, which ended in the horror of Nazism.

By contrast, Chapter 4 plots the erosion of social and political cleavages in post-war Germany and assesses the impact of this process on party politics in the modern Federal Republic. As a result, it signals a shift from macro- to micro-level data. The chapter opens with an account of the re-emergence of political cleavages after the Second World War and examines how these cleavages stabilised and structured the party system during the first 20 years of the Federal Republic. The chapter then moves on to the period 1969–90, leading up to the unification of Germany, with an emphasis on how the impact of secularisation and economic change eroded social cleavages and led to greater electoral instability and partisan dealignment. This is followed by an account of the social base of party politics in post-unification Germany, as well as an up-to-date analysis of the social base of contemporary German party politics, drawing on data from the 2002 Bundestag elections.

Chapter 5 takes a different tack and explores some of the key models of voting behaviour and their impact on party politics. Thus we return more explicitly to the idea of the voter as a reflexive individual – and therefore with individual preferences. It starts with an examination of the idea of partisan identification and the account it provides of support for political parties over time, before looking at the concept of value-orientation and value-change as the drivers of political choice. The chapter then provides an assessment of the economic voting literature, which serves both as a critique of the psychological and sociological approaches and also as a framework for empirical research. All three approaches are used widely in studies of voting behaviour in the Federal Republic and use some of the most developed technological and methodological tools in political science (Schultze, 1997: 603). All allow for more complex and potentially less deterministic accounts of the interaction between social structures and party politics than that provided by the social cleavage literature, but are reliant on the wealth of data that is only widely available in advanced democracies, and even then only really since the Second World War.

Having established the social basis or setting for party politics, Chapter 6 moves on to the arenas in which political agency takes place. The chapter examines the impact of three institutional structures on the political marketplace in Germany and in a comparative perspective. These are, first, the structure of the state; second, the electoral system(s); and, third, the party system(s). This is followed in Chapter 7 by an analysis of the key political agents within the realm of party politics, the political parties themselves. Because of this, Chapter 7 is possibly the most explicitly comparative of the chapters. It starts with a review of the political parties literature and the problems associated with establishing a single classificatory scheme that is able to function both in a comparative perspective and in a way that is appropriate to the German context. The chapter then moves on to such a single scheme, primarily based on degrees of variance in the extent or 'thickness' of party organisation. This is followed by the bulk of the chapter, in which this classificatory scheme is used to frame a discussion of the main parties in the German party system in a comparative perspective.

Chapter 8 then goes on to examine the patterns of action and interaction between the firms in the political marketplace, in this case that of competition and co-operation between political parties. The chapter first looks at competition between parties in Germany and in a comparative perspective and focusses on parties' programmes, in other words the parties' 'product', and the campaign strategies used to promote the product, namely the 'message'. At the same time, the chapter discusses some of the theoretical and empirical claims that underpin the literature associated with this field of research. The chapter then goes on to look at the antithesis of party political competition, that of co-operation, and places a strong emphasis on coalition politics at the national and sub-national levels, in Germany and in a comparative perspective. It is at this point that the book places more emphasis on the output side of the political equation. It should be noted that both sections of the chapter, and the second section in particular, include new data on 'Red–Green' coalitions between the SPD and Greens, both in the *Länder* and at the Federal level.

Finally, Chapter 9 concludes the book by discussing the empirical and theoretical implications of the study. In empirical terms it concentrates upon the balance between the singularities of the German *Sonderweg* and the commonalities shared by German party politics and similar phenomena in comparative perspective. In theoretical terms it returns to the analogy of the political marketplace discussed above. Both the empirical and theoretical strands are used to assess the amount of 'added-value' the use of the comparative method (defined in terms of both data and theoretical framework) brings to the study of German party politics specifically and single-country studies more generally.

2
The Development of Social and Political Cleavages in Germany before 1945

2.1 Introduction

Political cleavages are the fundamental lines of political conflict that structure political competition and (along with electoral systems and electoral laws) determine the shape of party systems. In other words they are fundamental structural attributes within the political marketplace. But how do these lines of conflict arise and how do they become institutionalised into structural attributes over time? There are two main approaches within the comparative politics literature. On the one hand, there is the school of thought that argues that political cleavages are underpinned by more embedded social cleavages, around which parties mobilise (see Lipset and Rokkan, 1967; Rose and Urwin, 1969, 1970; Allardt and Rokkan, 1970; Rokkan *et al.*, 1970; Rose, 1974). On the other, there is a revisionist school that argues that party politics are more uncoupled from social structures, with lines of conflict that are contingent on strategic decisions made by political elites (see Loewenberg, 1968; Converse and Valen, 1971; Berglund and Lindstrom, 1979). As Claggett *et al.* observe, the two approaches are often driven by the availability of data. Thus, most accounts of pre-1939 party systems rely on historical documents and adopt the Lipset and Rokkan approach, whilst accounts of more contemporary party systems are able to draw upon more sophisticated survey data and are better able to examine individual vote choices and value-orientations (Clagget *et al.*, 1982: 644). This allows for a more complex and less deterministic account of the interaction between social structures and party politics.

The tension between these two approaches returns us to the 'structure–agency debate' discussed in Chapter 1 and a long debate on the respective merits of the two approaches is beyond the scope of this chapter. However, it is clear that both structural and agency-based factors have contributed to the development of competitive party systems as we know them today. Paradoxically perhaps, given this study's epistemological position, the relative absence of micro-level data on voters' preferences before 1939 means that Chapter 2 concentrates on the macro-historical social cleavage literature and uses it to establish the context in which the underlying dynamics of political mobilisation in Germany developed. It is, however, critical of such approaches where appropriate. The chapter is divided into four sections: first, a discussion of the social cleavage literature in general terms; second, a further and more specific discussion of Lipset and Rokkan's (1967) account of the development of cleavage structures in Western Europe, with an emphasis on Germany where appropriate; third, an analysis of social and political cleavages in Germany in a comparative perspective; and finally, a brief summary of the chapter's arguments.

2.2   Cleavage theory

Macro-historical accounts of party system development hold that the social base of party politics is grounded in groups and associations engaged in collective action. In the nineteenth century de Toqueville identified four groups that had the potential to impact on the political process: (1) churches, (2) leisure associations; (3) interest organisations; and (4) neighbourhood associations (de Toqueville, 1990). Twentieth-century political sociology developed the concept of cleavages to describe the social structures that underpin these groups. Implicit within cleavage theory is the idea that cleavages represent social fragmentation, which has the potential to create political conflict (see Almond, 1956, for instance). Actual political conflict arises when political parties actively mobilise around one or more social cleavages, transforming them into political cleavages. Thus, whilst social cleavages lend themselves to a structural interpretation of politics, the development of political cleavages is not just the product of impersonal social forces but involves agency on the part of political elites.

Cleavage theory is now part of the vernacular of the study of party politics and is used in both comparative and single-country studies. However, there are four main pitfalls evident in some of the literature that should be avoided. First, conflation of and imprecision in use of categories and terms. The term 'cleavage' is often used in quite an elastic fashion to denote social cleavages, political cleavages mobilised around social cleavages, and more diffuse ideological conflicts with little or no connection to social structures. More appropriate categories or terms for many of these conflicts would be voter preferences or value orientations, and these are examined separately in Chapter 4. Second, there is a tendency in some single-country studies to examine the development of social cleavages in a given country as discrete phenomena rather than as part of a wider pattern of state-building and democratic development that took place across Western Europe. This can lead to the third pitfall, the extrapolation of small- or single-*n* studies to build more general models of the social base of politics. A good example of this is what Dogan calls the 'fallacious model' of class-based voting (Dogan, 2001: 98). Dogan refers to instances in which scholars in predominantly Protestant countries such as the United States, the Scandinavian countries and Britain (see Butler and Stokes, 1969; Pulzer, 1975; for example) over-stressed class as the primary political cleavage. This not only fails to tally with empirical studies of countries with strong religious and/or ethnic cleavages but is also questionable in the countries in which these models were originally generated (see Lijphart, 1968; Rokkan, 1969; Rose and Urwin, 1969; Rogowski, 1981; Inglehart, 1990). Finally, the failure of small- or single-*n* studies to examine social and political cleavages at the country level in a comparative context can mask the degree to which the *particular* pattern of political cleavages in that country are the result of political agency rather than impersonal social forces. Inevitably and rightly, cleavage theory owes a great deal to Marxian analysis but in this study we will attempt to avoid the overt social and economic determinism of 'vulgar Marxism'.

Lipset and Rokkan (1967) provide the seminal account of how cleavages shape party systems and party competition in advanced West European Democracies. They adopt a diachronic approach to demonstrate how the growth of industrial society and state-building in Western Europe created a pattern of political competition that, although different from country to country, allows for meaningful comparison between them. Key similarities include (1) mass politics; (2) universal suffrage; (3) secret ballots; and (4) the open competition for votes by parties mobilising around social cleavages. Key differences depend on (1) representation criteria; (2) election rules; and (3) the pattern of cleavages in a given country. So the following assertions are held to be true across all cases:

- West European states are created by 'nation builders', attempting to create a centralised state and erode local power arrangements and traditional loyalties;
- political parties reflect the cleavage structure of the country concerned;
- West European polities and party systems are similar because they are grounded in the same historical conditions;
- West European polities and party systems are different because of (1) different sequencing of historical development and (2) different strategies adopted by political elites;
- the resolution of one set of conflicts shapes the resolution of all subsequent conflicts; and
- all major cleavages in contemporary politics were generated before the 'political arrival' of the working class and mass political mobilisation.

Subsequent work by Rokkan (1970) refined this model and set out a schematic of cleavage types around which parties mobilised during the process of democratisation. These are grounded in four historic junctures: (1) the Reformation; (2) the 'national revolution' leading to the ascendancy of the centre over local/regional power; (3) the 'industrial revolution' leading to

Table 2.1   Rokkan's types of cleavage and political conflict

Cleavage	National/Centre	Local/Regional/Periphery
Interest/Economy	1A	1B
Ideology/Culture	2A	2B

Source: Adapted from Lane and Ersson, 1999: 40.

the erosion of land-owning power and religious power; and (4) the 'international revolution' leading to the Communist seizure of power in Russia in 1917. In the original Lipset–Rokkan model, this fourth juncture was added in a more tentative manner (Lipset and Rokkan, 1967: 47). Rokkan's types of cleavages and associated political conflicts are set out in Table 2.1.

Rokkan argues that there are four basic cleavage-based conflicts: (1) 1A: workers versus owners; (2) 1B: primary versus secondary economy (3) 2A: church(es) versus government; and (4) 2B: the cultural/ideological clash between centre and periphery. These can be grouped into two 'families'. The first family of cleavages are generated by the industrial revolution and relate to questions of labour exploitation or control over the means of production (1A) as well as the proper balance of tariffs, quotas and taxes (1B). The second involves supranational versus national religion, national languages versus Latin etc. (2A) as well as national language versus local dialects, and national versus particularist loyalties (2B).

Rokkan's work with Lipset and others provides the benchmark for cleavage theory. However, it is not uncontested (see Pesonen, 1973; Zuckerman, 1975). The key questions are, first, how many cleavages are there and where do we draw the line? and, second, how generalisable are our theories? At the most generalisable level, Rae and Taylor identify three types of cleavage that can apply across cultures. These are 'ascriptive' (race, caste), 'attitudinal' (ideology, preference) and 'behavioural' (voting, organisational membership) (Rae and Taylor, 1970: 23). In a more 'Eurocentric' vein, Daalder argues that the core dividing lines are those of class or sectional interest, religion, geography (urban/rural; centre/periphery), nationality(ism), and regime (status quo versus reform, revolutionary versus counter-revolutionary) (Daalder, 1966). Using a similar European frame of reference, Flanagan develops an alternative typology of three wider categorisations: 'segmental' (racial, religious, linguistic), 'cultural' (young/old, urban/rural, traditional/modern, libertarian/totalitarian), and 'economic-functional' (class, status and role). By contrast, Dunleavy and Husbands (1985) concentrate primarily on political (rather than social) cleavages in Britain and argue that the key conflict lines shaping party competition are 'sectoral cleavages', particularly 'production' (public/private sector) and 'consumption' (council or private tenant/homeowner) cleavages.

All of the models discussed above have their strengths and weaknesses. Dunleavy and Husbands' account provides a powerful analysis of voting behaviour in 1980s Britain, but is arguably less useful today. More importantly, its focus on British politics makes it too specific for the purposes of this book. Rae and Taylor, on the other hand, are truly comparative but are perhaps too global for our purposes. Daalder provides a nuanced typology for the study of multiple cases but, in the context of a study of Germany as a single case, raises the classic comparative politics problem of 'too many cases and not enough variables'. Finally, Flanagan conflates the ideas of cleavage and issue orientation/ideology, which the book deals with separately.

Chapter 2 is therefore structured around Lipset and Rokkan's original model. The Lipset–Rokkan model assumes that party competition in Europe is primarily driven by four cleavage conflicts: (1) centre/periphery; (2) religion (church/state and inter-church); (3) urban/rural; and (4) social class. Of these, the dominant conflicts are those of class and religion. As in other West European countries, the precise pattern that these cleavages assumed in Germany depended on the extent to which these three cleavages were (1) latent (present within society but not mobilised by political parties) or (2) manifest (explicitly mobilised by political parties). The distinction between latent and manifest cleavages are useful for the purposes of this study because it allows us to retain some conception of political agency throughout our account of the historical development of the political marketplace in Germany and elsewhere.

Cleavages have two 'directions'. 'Vertical' cleavages, such as those around religion, ethnicity, or centre/periphery, divide society across socio-economic groups. The accommodation of such cleavages by political agents can lead to consociation or 'pillarised' institutional arrangements such as are found in the Netherlands. 'Horizontal' cleavages, such as involving landowners, urban entrepreneurs or industrial workers, are associated with groups' productive capacity or relationship to the means of production. Two observations should be made at this point. First, horizontal conflicts are generally easier to 'pacify' (Landman, 2000: 129) than vertical conflicts. Thus in Germany – as in all West European democracies – rising prosperity and the development of the Welfare State meant that class conflict has lost much of its salience and social class alone is no longer a reliable indicator of voter preferences (see Chapter 3). Second, the voting behaviour of individuals is affected by more than one cleavage: the typical example of such 'cross-cutting' cleavages is that of class and religion. Moreover, such cleavages can be reinforced by auxiliary structures such as church organisations or trade unions. Under normal conditions cross-cutting cleavages bring stability to democracies and prevent one dominant cleavage from splitting society along religious, ethnic or class lines. However, under abnormal conditions cross-cutting cleavages can paralyse the political centre. A paradigmatic example of this was the failure of 'democratic' forces in the Weimar Republic to overcome class and confessional divisions and fight off the threat of National Socialism.

The Lipset–Rokkan model argues that European party systems were 'frozen' in the dominant configuration of cleavages present at the introduction of universal male suffrage. In Germany, this took place at the foundation of the Second Reich in 1871, although Lipset and Rokkan date the freezing of European party systems to the 1920s. It is generally accepted that the 'frozen party system' hypothesis held true for most European democracies until the 1970s, when the cumulative effect of embourgoisement and social mobility became apparent. Since then political scientists have noted the pacification of traditional cleavages, leading to partisan de-alignment (see Chapter 3). The political space created by the erosion of class loyalties in particular created a political opportunity structure (Kitschelt, 1986; Tarrow, 1994) for the rise of the 'new politics'. The timing and extent of these changes varied from country to country depending on local conditions (Dalton *et al.*, 1984).

The impact of social cleavages takes place on three levels: (1) society; (2) party system; and (3) government (Lane and Ersson, 1999: 41). Nevertheless, we return to the assumption that the resolution of one set of conflicts shapes the resolution of all subsequent conflicts. In other words, although the processes discussed above are common to all West European democracies, the unique pattern in which they impacted upon Germany was the result of the specificities of local history, political culture, institutions, and – crucially – the strategies adopted by political agents.

2.3   The Lipset–Rokkan model

Lipset and Rokkan point to three critical junctures of the Reformation and Counter-Reformation, the National Revolution, and Industrial Revolution. The first juncture, the Reformation and Counter-Reformation, took place in the sixteenth and seventeenth centuries and created the religious cleavage. It left three types of countries: (1) Protestant; (2) Catholic; and (3) 'divided' countries. In explicitly Protestant countries, such as England and Sweden, national churches were set up and the state's supremacy over them established, thus neutralising religion as a significant source of political conflict. In Catholic countries, such as France and Spain, the church retained its power, leading to later church–state conflicts and a manifest clerical/anti-clerical cleavage. Divided countries, to which we will refer from now on as 'Group 3' countries, such as the German Reich, Switzerland and the Low Countries, suffered worst: experiencing Protestant/Catholic conflicts as well as later church/state conflicts.

The second critical juncture was the National Revolution, which generally took place in the late eighteenth and early nineteenth centuries and 'forced ever-widening circles of the territorial population to choose sides in conflicts over values and cultural identities' (Lipset and Rokkan, 1967: 19). This created two types of cleavage: centre/periphery and church/state. Driven on by the French Revolution, political elites across Europe worked towards the establishment of standardised modern states and the spread of democratic values. As a result, centre/periphery conflicts arose out of the resistance of groups on the periphery to the nation-building process. These conflicts focussed on issues of territorial, linguistic, cultural and religious difference. At the same time, Catholic and divided countries also experienced a manifestation of the church/state cleavage as secular and religious elites struggled over control of issues such as education.

Finally, the Industrial Revolution of the late eighteenth to early twentieth century generated two further cleavages: urban/rural and social class. The urban/rural conflict manifested itself in two ways. First, it was apparent in conflicts between landed and industrial commercial interests, focussed on the commodity market. In Prussia for instance, this involved a conflict between agricultural tariffs and free trade. Second, it appeared in terms of a more cultural struggle between the 'real' (rural) nation and the 'cosmopolitanism' of the cities. The social class cleavage pitted owners and employers against tenants and workers. The level of bitterness in this conflict was partly determined by the relative openness of the society and political system in each country.

How this sequence of events took place in any given country depended on two factors. First, the nature of alliances between nation-builders, churches, landowners, urban industrialists and entrepreneurs, and peripheral groups. Second, how each state dealt with the four problems: of (1) legitimation of protest; (2) incorporation of new groups into the political arena; (3) representation of groups in political institutions; and (4) majority rule. The outcome of these developmental sequences are eight ideal types of 'alliance–opposition structure' (AOS) that are shaped by and, in turn, shape the sequencing and speed of development of party competition in individual states.

In the Catholic countries of Southern and Central Europe, the success of the Counter-Reformation re-established the position of the Catholic Church and established a symbiotic relationship between a transnational Church and the *ancien regime*. The nature of this relationship made both Church and State inimical to modernising and nation-building forces. As a result, these countries were characterised by patterns of political conflict between a Catholic-traditionalist 'right' with a predominant rural/landed base and a national, radical, secular 'left' with strong support among the emergent urban bourgeoisie. The balance struck within these countries between landed and urban interests determined the relative significance of the religious, urban/rural, and centre/periphery cleavages in the patterning of political competition. In the Protestant states, such as Britain and the Scandinavian countries, the settlement of the Reformation pacified any latent conflict between the established churches and nation-builders. As a result, the political 'left' was made up of dissenters, non-conformists, and fundamentalists in both the periphery and, particularly in Britain, among the urban middle classes in provincial cities such as Birmingham (Uglow, 2002). Again, the relative commitment to landed or urban interests determined the pattern of political conflict. The class cleavage is significant in all of these countries. However, the centre–periphery cleavage is much stronger in the Scandinavian countries, where nation-builders were predominantly urban, than in Britain, where nation-builders were supported by landed interests. Finally, in the Group 3 countries the potential existed for all of the cleavages noted above. Group 3 countries responded to these divisions in different ways, but a common theme was that nation-builders opted for 'weak state' models, based on ideas of consociationalism, 'pillarisation' and federalism, in which accommodation between ethnic or religious groups could take place at the elite level. As will be discussed later in the chapter, the outcome of elite strategies in these different countries led to different patterns of political cleavage over time.

2.4   Germany in comparative perspective

The use of Germany as a paradigmatic example is a common thread throughout the cleavage theory literature. This is unsurprising given the size, economic development and geo-political importance of Germany. Nevertheless, it provides a useful contrast to the school of literature that concentrates on the special circumstances and particularities of the German *Sonderweg*. In *Anna Karenina*, Tolstoy observed that 'all happy families are happy in the same way, but each unhappy family lives its own unhappiness in a unique and unmistakable way' and sometimes country specialists use the same logic in the analysis of nation states. Whilst the more routine political phenomena lend themselves to systematisation, it is tempting to regard political upheavals such as the October Revolution in Russia, the Spanish Civil War, or the rise of National Socialism in Germany as examples of nations' 'unique and unmistakable unhappiness'. By contrast cleavage theory adds an explicitly comparative systems-level analysis to otherwise country-specific narratives.

As already noted, Germany, like Switzerland and the Low Countries, suffered two types of religious cleavage. These were generated through, first, the conflict between German Protestants and Catholics in the Thirty Years War, which crippled the nation-building process, and, second, the Church/State conflict made manifest in the party system through the *Kulturkampf*, Bismarck's campaign against the Catholic church. This is explored in greater depth in Chapter 3. At the same time, as Lipset and Rokkan make clear, although nations may be categorised in this way, the specific manner in which nations in this category adapted to social divisions within their territory depended on (1) the nature of alliances between nation-builders, churches, landowners, urban industrialists and entrepreneurs, and peripheral groups; as well as (2) how each state dealt with the four problems of (i) legitimation of protest; (ii) incorporation of new groups into the political arena; (iii) representation of groups in political institutions; and (iv) majority rule. Switzerland and the Netherlands, for example, opted for 'weak state' models, based on ideas of consociationalism and 'pillarisation', in which accommodation between ethnic or religious groups took place at the elite level via leaders of peak associations.

Theoretically the Second Reich's federal structure was also a 'weak state' model, but in practice the relative weight of Prussia within the federation, the power of the executive – dominated as it was by Bismarck – combined with Bismarck's nation-building instincts increased the steering capacity of the state. As is discussed in Chapter 3, this was further enhanced by the alliance of 'Iron and Rye' and the co-opting of the 'national liberals' into the dominant coalition. Thus, the Second Reich was a hybrid of the type-III (favouring landed interests) and type-IV (favouring urban interests) ideal-types set out in the Lipset-Rokkan model. Bismarck's coalition was dedicated to economic, rather than social, modernisation, and external tariffs and protectionism (Stöss, 1976), with the aim of challenging Great Britain as the predominant European power. The coalition served to pacify the urban/rural and centre/periphery cleavages, but Bismarck's parallel persecution of the SPD through the *Sozialistengesetz* sharpened the economic cleavage (Pappi, 1985). As a result, by the end of the nineteenth century the German party system was patterned by the two dominant cleavages of religion and class.

Germany's pattern of political cleavages relative to other advanced democracies is set out in Figure 2.1. Two aspects of the dominance of the religious and class cleavages in Germany are worthy of note. First, not all of the Group 3 countries identified in the Lipset–Rokkan model are characterised by the persistence of strong vertical and horizontal cleavages. Belgium and Austria do have similar patterns, although Belgium is divided by ethnic and linguistic differences rather than religion, and in Austria the confessional cleavage does not have the territorial dimension that is found in the Federal Republic. In addition, although party politics in the other Group 3 countries of Switzerland and the Netherlands are patterned by the strong vertical cleavages of ethnicity and linguistic affiliation (Switzerland) and religion (the Netherlands), the horizontal class cleavage is relatively weak. Empirically, these differences are evidence that nations' fates are not pre-determined and that convergence/divergence between states is dependent on the strategies of, and coalitions between, elites discussed above. Second, this method of comparative analysis does, ironically, provide empirical support for the narrative of the German *Sonderweg*. Germany is part of a group of 12 democracies with strong vertical cleavages, and eight with strong horizontal cleavages. However, only three countries – Germany, Austria, and Belgium – are cross-cut by strong horizontal and vertical cleavages. Theoretically, cross-cutting cleavages like this should bring stability but, as discussed in Chapter 2,

Vertical cleavages

		Strong	Weak
Horizontal cleavages	*Strong*	Germany Austria Belgium	Britain Sweden Finland Denmark Norway
	Weak	France Italy Netherlands Spain Portugal Switzerland Northern Ireland Canada USA	Ireland Greece

Figure 2.1   Strength of vertical and horizontal cleavages in Western Europe
Source: Adapted from Dogan, 2001: 98.

this was not the case in Germany until the foundation of the Federal Republic. Conversely, there is a literature that problematises a link between political instability and Catholicism (Tawney, 1938; Samuelson, 1961; Weber, 1965), based on the premise that Protestant countries provide more of the preconditions for the successful development of liberal democracy. Again the German case defies this logic. Unlike the failed Second Reich and Weimar Republic, both of which were dominated by bourgeois Protestantism, the success of the Federal Republic in the post-war years was underpinned by a more even confessional mix and a model of political economy that owed much to Catholic social theory.

Let us examine the relative position of Germany along the dimensions of the religious and class cleavages. Tables 2.2 and 2.3 set out the confessional structure and levels of religious fragmentation in Western Europe over the last century. Three observations should be made about the data. First, the

Table 2.2 Confessional structure in Western Europe (%)

	1900				1995			
	RC	Prot.	Orth.	Other/Non	RC	Prot.	Orth.	Other/Non
Austria	91.8	02.7	02.3	03.3	78.0	04.9	00.0	17.2
Belgium	98.8	00.2	00.0	01.0	90.0	00.0	00.0	10.0
Denmark	00.2	99.4	00.0	00.4	00.0	88.2	00.0	11.8
Finland	00.0	98.3	01.7	00.0	00.0	86.7	00.0	13.3
France	97.1	02.2	00.0	00.7	73.9	00.0	00.0	16.1
Germany	36.1	62.5	00.0	01.5	35.3	40.2	00.0	24.4
Greece	01.8	00.1	83.3	14.8	00.0	00.0	97.6	02.4
Iceland	00.0	100.0	00.0	00.0	00.0	92.1	00.0	07.9
Ireland	89.4	10.5	00.0	00.1	93.1	00.0	00.0	06.9
Italy	99.6	00.1	00.0	00.3	83.1	00.0	00.0	16.9
Luxembourg	98.7	00.8	00.0	00.4	94.2	00.0	00.0	05.8
Netherlands	35.5	61.0	00.0	03.6	33.0	23.0	00.0	44.0
Norway	00.1	99.8	00.0	00.0	00.0	87.9	00.0	12.1
Portugal	99.9	00.1	00.0	00.0	94.5	00.0	00.0	05.5
Spain	100.0	00.0	00.0	00.0	94.9	00.0	00.0	05.5
Sweden	00.1	98.8	00.0	01.2	00.0	88.2	00.0	11.8
Switzerland	41.0	58.4	00.0	00.6	46.1	40.0	00.0	13.9
UK	06.6	90.8	00.0	02.5	13.1	72.0	00.6	14.3

Source: Adapted from Lane and Ersson, 1999: 46.

secularisation process that has taken place in Germany over the last century is part of a process that has hit some European countries harder than others. By-and-large all religious denominations have lost active members over the last 100 years, especially among the various Protestant churches, but much of this is masked by the self-reporting of respondents surveyed. In the Scandinavian countries the presence of a Lutheran state church means that Protestants who no longer practice strict religious observance nevertheless self-report as Protestant. This is an artefact of the Reformation settlement, which pacified the religious cleavage. As a result, anti-clericalism is not a salient issue and secularised Protestants are happy to adhere to the dominant form of 'cultural Protestantism' despite no longer being religiously observant. By contrast, the latent salience of the religious cleavage (and perhaps the existence of church taxes for declared religious observers) in Germany means more secularised individuals from the Protestant milieu self-report as having no religious affiliation. As a result, Germany has the second-highest level of this category (22.3 per cent) after the Netherlands (39 per cent), another country with a strong religious cleavage. By contrast, the number of self-reporting German Catholics remained remarkably stable over the time-period. This is an artefact of the mobilisation of Catholic milieus as a result

Table 2.3 Religious fragmentation index in Western Europe

	1900	1970	1995
Austria	0.16	0.19	0.38
Belgium	0.02	0.15	0.18
Denmark	0.01	0.08	0.21
Finland	0.03	0.07	0.23
France	0.06	0.33	0.42
Germany	0.48	0.59	0.66
Greece	0.28	0.05	0.05
Iceland	0.00	0.05	0.14
Ireland	0.19	0.09	0.13
Italy	0.01	0.17	0.28
Luxembourg	0.03	0.12	0.11
Netherlands	0.50	0.59	0.68
Norway	0.00	0.03	0.21
Portugal	0.00	0.07	0.10
Spain	0.00	0.05	0.10
Sweden	0.02	0.41	0.21
Switzerland	0.49	0.52	0.61
UK	0.17	0.41	0.45
Mean score	0.14	0.23	0.29

Source: Adapted from Lane and Ersson, 1999: 46. I have added mean scores to the data.

of the anti-Catholic *Kulturkampf* and has ensured the resilience of a minority 'cultural Catholicism' in Germany. The second point to be made about the data is that more than 300 years after the Reformation – despite the process of secularisation discussed in this and earlier chapters – Germany remains the Group 3 country identified by Lipset and Rokkan, Switzerland and the Netherlands also remain in this category, demonstrating the remarkable persistence of the religious cleavage in West European countries. However, in Germany the impact of secularisation in the traditionally Protestant new federal states means that, even after unification, the roughly even confessional balance that characterised the 'old' Federal Republic is retained.

This leads us to the third point to be made from the data. Table 2.3 sets out indices of religious fragmentation in West European countries at three points (1900, 1970 and 1975) over the last 100 years. The figures for each country denote the probability of two individuals belonging to different religions, with zero denoting the lowest probability and one the highest. There are three trends of religious fragmentation within the data. First, the concentration of religious affiliation – and thus the pacification of the religious cleavage – in Greece. This represents the progressive homogenisation of religious observance around the Greek Orthodox Church in the years following the collapse of the Ottoman Empire. Second, the reversal of trends of concentration/deconcentration over the run of data. Thus, in Ireland there was a concentration of religious observance around the Catholic Church in the first half of the twentieth century followed by a deconcentration between 1970 and 1995. In Sweden, the reverse process took place. Finally, a more general trend of deconcentration of religious observance over the run of data. Interestingly, although Germany has the second highest score of fragmentation after the Netherlands, the rate of deconcentration has been much higher in other countries such as France (up from 0.06 in 1900 to 0.42 in 1995), Norway (0.00 to 0.21), and Finland (0.03 to 0.23). As a result, we see a slow convergence of levels of religious fragmentation with the mean score for all nations doubling from 0.14 to 0.29 over the run of data. However, levels of religious fragmentation in Germany remain high in absolute terms, despite this long-term trend of convergence.

So the data in Tables 2.2 and 2.3 demonstrate the slow 'normalisation' of Germany in terms of the religious cleavage, albeit with special characteristics that are an artefact of the country's historical development. What is also clear from the comparative politics literature is that in Western Europe the religious cleavage has conditioned the class cleavage as well (Dogan, 2001: 104–8). Thus, the religious cleavage remains a better indicator of voter preferences than the class cleavage, especially when the latter is uncoupled from trade union membership. Nevertheless, religious observance has reduced and as individuals' preferences became increasingly uncoupled from religious affiliation this had a spill-over effect along the dimension of the class cleavage. Again, Germany is cited as a paradigmatic example of this process. As is discussed in Chapter 4, the key change that took place in the Federal Republic over the post-war period was the decline in the reluctance of some Catholics to vote for the SPD (Linz, 1967; Noelle-Neumann and Kocher, 1993). However, the German case is just the most pronounced and most well-researched example of a process that has also taken place in countries such as the Netherlands (Dekker, 1994), Italy and France (Dogan, 2001), Spain (Orizo, 1983; Diaz, 1991) and Portugal (Nataf, 1985).

As is also discussed at greater length in Chapter 4, the other key variable that impacts on the class cleavage in Germany is trade union membership, which buffers left parties from the impact of partisan dealignment. But how does this compare with other West European countries? Table 2.4 sets out levels of trade union density in Western Europe at three points (1970, 1980, 1990) over the period that is generally accepted as marking the onset of partisan dealignment (see Chapters 4 and 5). Again, we see three main trends over this period. The first trend, restricted to the Nordic countries (Sweden, Finland, Iceland), is of a steady increase in the level of trade union density of the period. The second trend, seen in six countries (Austria, France, the Netherlands, Portugal, Spain and Switzerland) is that of reductions in levels of trade union density. Some of these, such as Portugal (down 29 per cent) and Spain (down 16.4 per cent) have experienced precipitous reductions, albeit from a relatively high baseline in the case of Portugal. Germany conforms to the third trend within the data: that of a steady rise in the period 1970–80 followed by a drop-off in membership between 1980 and 1990. In some instances, the percentage changes over the period are quite marked. Italy, for instance, saw a rise of 13 per cent up to 1980 followed by a fall of 10.5 per cent in the following decade. Others, such as Greece, saw changes that were barely significant. The pattern in Germany (up 2.6 per cent/down 2.7 per cent) puts it at the low end of volatility in levels of trade union density. However, it should be noted that throughout the period 1970–90 levels of density in Germany were significantly lower – around 13 per cent – than the mean score for the 18 countries in the table.

Table 2.4 demonstrates that levels of trade union density *per se* do not positively equate to the relative salience of the class cleavage. Countries with high levels of trade union density, such as Austria, Finland, Sweden, Denmark and Norway, do have strong class cleavages. But so does Germany, despite relatively low levels of trade union density. So why is there no clear pattern at the European-level? One obvious factor is the degree of institutional linkage between trade unions and parties of the left, particularly Social Democratic parties. At one end of the scale, countries with strong corporatist

Table 2.4 Trade union density in Western Europe (%)

	1970	1980	1990
Austria	62.2	56.2	46.2
Belgium	45.4	55.9	51.2
Denmark	60.0	76.0	71.4
Finland	51.4	69.8	72.6
France	22.3	17.5	09.8
Germany	33.0	35.6	32.9
Greece	35.8	36.7	34.1
Iceland	68.1	75.2	78.2
Ireland	53.1	57.0	49.7
Italy	36.3	49.3	38.8
Luxembourg	46.8	52.2	49.7
Netherlands	38.0	35.3	25.5
Norway	51.4	56.9	56.0
Portugal	60.8	60.7	31.8
Spain	27.4	25.0	11.0
Sweden	67.7	79.7	82.5
Switzerland	30.1	30.7	26.6
UK	44.8	50.4	39.1
Mean score	46.4	51.1	44.8

Source: OECD, 1994.

arrangements, like Austria, have co-opted indigenous labour movements into formal mechanisms of interest aggregation. Trade unions are explicitly linked with re-distributionist policies championed by left parties in government (see Schmitter and Lehmbruch, 1979; Lehmbruch and Schmitter, 1982; Schmitter and Grote, 1997). As such, corporatist countries are characterised by high levels of trade union density and strong correlations between union membership and preferences for left voting. At the other end of the scale, countries such as France and Spain have low levels of trade union density and weak class cleavages. These countries are also characterised by the lack of a single unified trade union peak association. France, for instance, has three major labour organisations: the pro-Communist CGT, anti-Communist FO, and the more right-wing Catholic CFDT. Thus, membership of a trade union does not necessarily equate with support for left parties. Finally, we see a group of countries with relatively low levels of trade union density, but with relatively strong class cleavages. The two paradigmatic examples of this are Germany and the United Kingdom, both of which are characterised by unified trade union peak associations with strong links to Social Democratic parties. In the case of Britain, the Labour Party was founded by trade unions, many unions are affiliated to the party, and union leaders retain constitutional powers within it. In addition, the unions' peak association (TUC) is relatively united and exercises considerable influence over party debate. In the case of Germany, the SPD is formally independent from the trade unions but individual union leaders and the unions' peak association (DGB) are very influential over party policy. As such, the trade union movements in both countries are explicitly linked to Social Democracy – albeit via different institutional configurations – and we see a positive relationship between union membership and voter preference for left parties.

The other reason for the lack of a general Europe-wide pattern is because socially embedded political cleavages across Europe have less leverage over voter preferences and the pattern of party competition. Up to around 20 years ago, there was a consensus among scholars that the class cleavage was important in most West European democracies, and that class was a reliable indicator of voter preferences (Lane, 1965; Goldthorpe *et al.*, 1969; Rose and Urwin, 1969; Korpi, 1983). However, economic modernisation, social change and the subsequent process of partisan dealignment has blurred this picture of class-based voting; and with it, the consensus amongst scholars has broken down. Three schools of thought can be clearly identified in the literature. First, there is the argument that class has become more salient, albeit in fora outside mainstream party politics: such as labour movements (Matheson, 1979). Second, as already discussed, some researchers argue that as class is a horizontal conflict it has been easier to pacify than vertical conflicts such as religion or ethnicity. Thus, the process of economic modernisation and, crucially, the development of the Welfare State have had a specific impact on the class cleavage in a manner that has not happened with other cleavages (Lenski, 1966; Cutright, 1967). Finally, there is school of thought that argues that although the salience of class has reduced noticeably it is part of a wider process that is decoupling voter preferences from individuals' social location. This may be symptomatic of the 'end of ideology' (Tingsten, 1955; Aron, 1957; Di Palma, 1973) or, alternatively, due to the growth of new ideologies of value orientations such as post-materialism and environmentalism (Inglehart, 1990; Talshir, 2002).

These arguments are explored in more detail in later chapters. What is clear from this chapter is that over time both class and religion have become less reliable indicators of voter preferences in Germany. But how does Germany compare with other democracies? Table 2.5 sets out the relative strength of association between party preference, employment status, and religious affiliation in a group of democracies, over the period 1990–93. The higher the figure for each country, the stronger the association between voter preference and the variable the figure denotes. The table uses a different 'basket' of countries than in the previous three tables, and draws comparisons with the new democracies of East-Central Europe as well as Australia and the United States. The East-Central European comparison is especially useful because it enables us to examine the old and new federal states separately and compare patterns in the new federal states with those

Table 2.5   Strength of association between party preference, employment status and religious affiliation in a basket of democracies, 1990–93

	Predictor variable							
	White collar	**uc**	**Manual**	**uc**	**Farmer**	**uc**	**Religious affiliation**	**uc**
Poland	0.04	s	0.01	s	0.04	s	0.03	s
Czech Rep	0.01	s	0.01	so	0.02	s	0.06	s
Slovakia	0.01	s	0.01	so	0.01	so	0.08	s
Hungary	0.01	s	0.00	ns	0.01	s	0.05	s
Australia	0.00	s	0.01	s	–	–	0.01	s
USA	0.01	s	0.01	ns	0.00	ns	0.01	ns
Ireland	0.00	ns	0.01	ns	0.01	s	0.01	s
N. Ireland	0.01	s	0.01	ns	–	–	0.02	s
Great Britain	0.04	s	0.04	s	–	–	0.02	s
Norway	0.01	s	0.01	s	0.03	s	0.08	s
(West) Germany	0.00	ns	0.01	s	0.01	s	0.05	s
(East) Germany	0.01	s	0.01	s	0.00	ns	0.02	s
Italy	0.00	ns	0.01	s	–	na	0.05	s

Notes: uc: uncertainty coefficient; ns: not significant; so: significant at the 0.05 level in at least one of three datasets; s: significant on the 0.05 level in each dataset.

Source: Adapted from Tóka, 1996: 116.

found in other former Warsaw Pact countries. Three trends are revealed in the data. First, there are three countries – Poland, Britain and Norway – in which there is a reasonably strong association (0.03 or above) between employment status and voter preferences. However, only in Britain can this be regarded as evidence of a 'pure' class cleavage. In Poland, there are strong levels of association among manual workers (0.04) and agricultural workers (0.04), but less so among white-collar employees (0.01). However, we know that Polish voter preferences are strongly influenced by a centre–periphery cleavage and workers in Poland's large agricultural sector are especially attracted to the particularist agenda of the Polish peasant parties (Tóka, 1996: 112). Norway registers quite a high level of association among agricultural workers (0.03) but less of an association (0.01) among manual workers or white-collar employees, indicating again that electoral preferences among agricultural workers are also influenced by the cross-cutting centre–periphery cleavage discussed earlier in this section of the chapter. Britain, by contrast, registers relatively high levels (0.04) of association among both manual workers and white-collar employees (there are no data for agricultural workers).

The second trend is that of a stronger association (0.05 or above) between voter preferences and church attendance. This is found in the Czech Republic (0.06), Slovakia (0.08), Hungary (0.05), Norway (0.08), (West) Germany (0.05), and Italy (0.05). Again, this suggests that the religious cleavage is more robust and persistent than the class cleavage. On the basis of these figures Germany appears to be at the low end of the scale, compared with, say, Norway. However, what matters is the strength of association in relation to levels of religious fragmentation in the countries concerned. It will be recalled that the data in Table 2.2 and Table 2.3 indicate that Norway is a far more religiously homogenous country than Germany. The population of Norway is 87.9 per cent Protestant, with a tiny Catholic population, and has a fragmentation score of 0.21. By contrast, Germany has a much larger Catholic minority (35.3 per cent) and a fragmentation score of 0.66. Following the logic of the Lipset–Rokkan model, it is the presence of significant confessional minorities that provides the raw material for political agents to make the religious cleavage manifest in the political process and this is the reason why it is stronger in Germany than it is in Norway.

The final trend is that of no significant association (0.02 or less) between social location and voter preference. This is found in the data for Australia, USA, Ireland, Northern Ireland and East Germany. Thus, taken in a comparative perspective the kind of decoupling of politics from traditional social cleavages that we find in East Germany is not an unusual case. Moreover, the particular weakness of the class cleavage in the new federal states seems to be consistent with the pattern in other former Warsaw Pact countries such as the Czech Republic, Slovakia and Hungary. This is consistent with the atomisation of traditional social ties associated with Communist rule.

Taken in the round, the comparative data on the pattern and impact of cleavage structures on voter preferences demonstrates two things. First, in certain respects the narrative of the German *Sonderweg* is an appropriate one. Germany is relatively unusual in that it is cross-cut by both vertical (religious) and horizontal (class) cleavages. As is discussed in the next two chapters, although such cross-cutting cleavages are normally assumed to enhance the stability of party systems this has not always been the case in Germany – especially during the latter period of the Weimar republic when the mainstream parties failed to defend the political system against the rise of National Socialism. Moreover, the 40-year division of Germany meant that after unification the Federal Republic was characterised by two distinct party systems, with different cleavage dynamics. This, by any standards of comparison, is unusual. The second point to make, however, is that notwithstanding the disasters of National Socialism and division, in terms of the impact of cleavage structures on contemporary party politics Germany is not *sui generis*. The 'west German' party system is in many ways a paradigmatic example within the literature and even the 'east German' party system conforms to the pattern observed in other former Warsaw Pact countries.

2.5 Summary

The chapter uses the social cleavage literature to establish the context in which the underlying dynamics of political mobilisation in Germany developed. The first section provided a broad discussion of the social cleavage literature and the rationale for concentrating on the Lipset–Rokkan (1967) model. The second section utilised this model and provided an account of the development of cleavage structures in Western Europe, with an emphasis on Germany. Finally, the third section examined the structure of social and political cleavages in Germany in a comparative perspective.

Amongst other things, the chapter raises four issues that are worth returning to. First, that for obvious reasons Germany is very often used as a paradigmatic example of a country cross-cut by social and political cleavages. Second, that despite this paradigmatic status, Germany is not alone in having such cross-cutting cleavages and that the specific pattern of class and confessional cleavages is shared by other 'Group 3' countries such as Belgium and the Netherlands. Third, that despite these commonalities Germany's institutional and cultural development – and its almost uniquely tragic historical legacy – can be used to support the discourse of the German *Sonderweg*. Finally that, although the Lipset–Rokkan model does provide a robust, historically grounded and context-sensitive framework for comparative analysis for pre-1939 political systems, its explanatory power wanes when examining more contemporary political systems. This is reflected in the structure of the next three chapters, which – although grounded in the cleavage structure literature – begin to problematise that literature as we move towards the modern model of post-Fordism and consumer capitalism that we are familiar with today. And as more micro-level data become available the idea of the voter as a customer with individual preferences is made more explicit.

3
Social and Political Cleavages in the Second Reich and Weimar Republic

3.1 Introduction

This chapter uses the Lipset–Rokkan (1967) model of social cleavages to provide a historical perspective of the development of social and political cleavages in Germany from the Reformation, through the Second Reich, and on to the Weimar Republic. Because of the lack of micro-level data, the idea of the voter as analogous to a customer with individual preferences remains underplayed at this point in the study. However, it is possible to retain a strong sense of political agency on the part of political agents such as Bismarck. The chapter is divided into three sections. First, an account of the development of political cleavages in the Second Reich (1871–1919): establishing and structuring a pattern of party competition that persisted into the early years of the Federal Republic. Second, a discussion of the social base of party politics in the Weimar Republic (1919–33): Germany's first ill-starred experience of popular democracy. Finally, the chapter ends with a brief summary of the data and arguments.

3.2 Development of political cleavages in the Second Reich

During the period up until the end of the seventeenth century, whilst England and France were nation-building, the First German Reich collapsed into a patchwork of principalities and Free Cities. At this time there were no manifest cleavages. Germans displayed strong local loyalties that were only slowly undermined by the Reformation, which brought a degree of uniformity to written German, through Luther's translation of the Bible into High German. On the one hand, this slowly undermined the parochialism of political elites, as they gradually accepted a uniform written style of the language that was not contingent upon geographical location. On the other, however, the rise of Protestantism made manifest the religious cleavage and prompted the Thirty Years War, which set back the process of nation-building for generations.

The Thirty Years War ended with the signing of the Peace of Westphalia in 1648. As a result of Westphalia, and under the aegis of France and Sweden, power passed from the centralising Hapsburgs down to the local princes and notables and, as a result, Germany lapsed into feudalism and particularism. This was at a time when most of the other leading European states were emerging from feudalism and slowly developing recognisable urban- and capitalist-oriented structures and cultures. Thus what remained of the First Reich lagged behind, lacking a strong central state, a significant middle class to offset the old landowners, or any form of secular culture.

Nevertheless, as A.J.P. Taylor observes, Westphalia 'was not the cause of German decline and weakness, but the result' (Taylor, 1982: 13). Moreover, it paved the way for the emergence of Prussia, which from the seventeenth century onwards began to expand its territory and political influence. Up until this time, Prussia had been little more than a somewhat backward colonial outpost, at the north-eastern edge of German territory and abutting Slavic lands to the east. But Westphalia was the first German 'year zero', and the ensuing vacuum was filled by this aggressive state under the leadership of the Hohenzollern Frederick II, King of Prussia, and his successors. The Prussian expansion of the seventeenth and eighteenth centuries was buttressed by a strong administrative structure that inevitably exercised centralising tendencies, and was given intellectual coherence through a robust Protestantism that would drive the development of the confessional cleavage that underpins the German political marketplace to this day. In addition, the French Revolutionary Wars accelerated the process of centralisation in three ways. First, Napoleon's defeat of Prussia and Austria led to the collapse of the Reich in 1806 and the territorial simplification of the German states. Second, this drove the smaller and less belligerent German states into the Prussian camp, dissolving the smallest principalities and merging them into larger administrative units. Third, the French brought with them the ideologies of liberalism and nationalism, which took root amongst the still very small urban middle classes.

The Congress of Vienna in 1815 established a new German Federation. The number of German states was now brought down to 39, of which only two – Austria and Prussia – had the size, military power and economic clout to assume the leadership of the new confederation of German states. Austria was focussed on the Austro-Hungarian Empire and the mantle of nation-building fell to Prussia.

Although the territorial dimension of nation-building continued apace, political modernisation did not. One reason for this was the need to contain French imperialism. As Carr observes, 'respect for legitimate rights was perfectly compatible with a viable balance of power in Italy and Spain but not in Germany ... security won the battle against legitimacy in the councils of the Great Powers' (Carr, 1991: 1). This had the effect of marginalising local notables in the myriad of tiny principalities that had existed before, thus strengthening the centre against the periphery. But the political void left by the decline of local notables was not filled by the emergence of a recognisably liberal democratic culture. Social reforms enacted by Napoleon in the Rhineland remained in place, but were not matched by political reforms. Some political rights were granted in the southern German states but Prussia did not follow suit.

The failure of Prussia to democratise was important because developments in the nineteenth century – the foundation of the German Customs Union (*Zollverein*) in 1834, the defeat of the liberal uprisings of 1848, and victories over Denmark in 1864, Austria in 1866 and France in 1870 – served to enhance Prussia's dominance of the confederation. As a result, when Germany unified in 1871, the Second German Reich was made in Prussia's image and lagged behind other relatively advanced industrial countries in the development of its political culture. As already noted, the Lipset–Rokkan model stresses two factors that determine the sequencing of the development of democratic politics in West European countries. These are, first, the nature of alliances between nation-builders, churches, landowners, urban industrialists and entrepreneurs, and peripheral groups, and, second, how each state dealt with the problems of legitimation, incorporation, representation and majority rule. In Germany, elites eventually forged a 'bourgeois alliance' between nation builders, a substantial segment of the fragmented liberal middle classes, landowners and industrialists (the latter two in the alliance of 'Iron and Rye'). However the process of nation-building came to a relatively late conclusion and the problems of legitimation, incorporation, representation and majority rule remained thorny issues until after the Great War.

In the new unified German state, activity within the political marketplace was highly constrained by the Second Reich's constitutional settlement. The Kaiser appointed the Chancellor, who was the head of government yet responsible to the Kaiser rather than parliament. In turn, the Chancellor appointed his cabinet ministers, although the key policy domains of defence and foreign affairs remained the province of the Kaiser and Chancellor. Parliament was bicameral, made up of the directly elected lower house (the Reichstag) and the upper house (the Bundesrat), the latter made up of delegates from the *Länder*. The legislature was able to exercise some control over defence and foreign affairs, through its power of appropriations, but this could be over-ruled by the Kaiser.

So how did underlying social cleavages impact upon party politics in the Second Reich? Broadly speaking, the party system in Wilhelmine Germany comprised eight party 'families'. These are set out in Table 3.1. The table demonstrates a paradox within the political marketplace. On the one hand, as already noted, activity within the marketplace was highly constrained – with real power retained within a hard core of the state executive. At the same time, however, entry into the marketplace was relatively unconstrained and the data reveals an immature party system, displaying very little

Table 3.1   Party 'families' in Wilhelmine Germany, 1871–1912 General Elections

Family	Dates	Party
Conservatives	1871, 1874	'Conservatives'
	1877–1912	'German Conservatives'
German Reich	1871, 1874	'German Empire Party'
	1877–1890	'German Empire Party and Independent Conservatives'
	1893–1907	'German Empire Party'
	1912	'German Empire Party and Independent Conservatives'
National Liberals	1871, 1874	'Liberal Empire Party' + 'National-liberals'
	1877, 1878	'Liberals, except National Liberals and Progressives' + 'National Liberals'
	1881(a)	'Liberals, except National Liberals, Liberal Union and Progressives' + 'National Liberals' + 'Liberal Union'
	1881(b)	'Liberals, except National Liberals, Liberal Union and Progressives' + 'National Liberals'
	1884	'National Liberals and Moderate Liberals'
	1887–1912	'National-Liberals'
Progressives	1871, 1874	'Progressive Party' + 'People's Party'
	1877–1881(a)	'German Progress Party' + 'People's Party'
	1881(b)	'German Progress Party' + 'People's Party' + 'Liberal Union'
	1884, 1887	'Progressive Liberals and German Free Thinkers' + 'People's Party'
	1890	'Progressive Liberals and German Free Thinkers' + 'People's Party and Democrats'
	1893	'Free Thinker's Union' + 'Free Thinking People's Party'
	1898–1912	'Free Thinker's Union' + 'Free Thinking People's Party' + 'German People's Party'
Social Democrats	1871–1912	SPD
Centre	1871–1912	'Centre'
Anti-Semites	1871–1912	'Anti-Semites'
Particularists	1871–1912	'Polish Party', 'Alsace-Lorraine Party', 'Bavarian Farmer's Union', 'Peasants' Union', 'the Danes', 'Hanoverian Guelphs' etc.

Source: Amended data from Claggett *et al.*, 1982: Appendix.

party system concentration. This deconcentration is all the more notable, given the fact that the Reichstag was made up of 387 constituency MPs, elected by a Simple Majority system. In such a fragmented party system, parties' selective mobilisation around one or two cleavages serves to simplify and sharpen the lines of political conflict. Bismarck used this device in order to shore up the legitimacy of the new Reich, polarise the Reichstag, and secure a stable right-of-centre majority in support of the Chancellor's policies. As a result the Second German Reich's party system crystallised into a three-bloc (*Dreilagersystem*) system, made up of Catholic, socialist, and nationalist blocs (Rohe, 1997: 49). In addition to the three blocs, the progressive or left liberals occupied political space adjacent to the SPD. Finally, the party system was flanked by a heterogeneous group of protest parties: the Anti-Semites and various particularist parties, such as the Polish Party, the Bavarian Farmers' Union, and the Peasants' Union. The presence of such particularist parties is a distinct aspect of the early German party system that would persist into the early years of the Federal Republic.

The Catholic bloc was represented by the Centre party (*Zentrum*), which attempted to mobilise Catholic voters regardless of class or social strata. Beyond the common bond of Catholicism, the Centre's social base was heterogeneous – made up of workers, farmers, artisans, shop owners, white-collar employees, civil servants, professionals, entrepreneurs, aristocrats and members of the church hierarchy. However, both party membership and support were characterised by the over-representation of farmers, agricultural workers and the old middle class (Ritter, 1990: 34–6). As a result, the Centre performed well in rural and small-town Germany but made less of an impact in urban areas (Anderson, 1981).

The Catholic and Socialist blocs competed for sections of the electorate. Despite – or because – of similarities in social policy with the Centre, the SPD competed against it along the economic cleavage. This became pronounced after the repeal of Bismarck's 'anti-socialist law' (*Sozialistengesetz*) in 1890, which opened up the opportunity for the SPD to court urban working class Catholics. Over the period of the Second Reich, the SPD became increasingly successful at mobilising the party's working class support: between 1871 and 1912 its vote-share in Reichstag elections rose from 3 per cent to 35 per cent. The success of SPD mobilisation was enhanced by the party's unique ability to field candidates throughout the Reich, making it the only national party in Germany (Bartolini, 2000: 438). However, the party's share of parliamentary seats lagged behind its share of the votes. There were two reasons for this. First, the distribution of electoral districts in the Reich failed to reflect the rapid industrialisation of the late nineteenth century, which meant that urban areas of Germany were under-represented in the Reichstag. Second, the potency of the class cleavage meant that other parties often formed alliances to ensure the defeat of SPD candidates at the second ballot stage (Smith, 1986: 12). Despite these structural and political disadvantages, the SPD grew in influence over the period of the Second Reich, buttressed by tight party discipline and a mass membership that grew to over a million by the start of the Great War.

The national bloc was made up of 'national' liberals and the more authoritarian Conservatives. This heterogeneity arose from conditions specific to Wilhelmine Germany. Unlike in other countries, such as Britain, there were few meaningful links between liberals and socialists (although the SPD and the left liberals did co-operate in the 1912 elections). The abdication of German liberalism as a socio-economic or political reform force (Breuilly, 1985) was partly due to the split between socio-economic and national liberals that took place in the period from 1848 to 1871, as well as its lack of a clear social profile: involving conflicts of interest between a new entrepreneurial bourgeoisie and older interests hostile to modernity and trade liberalisation. This latter divide also had a territorial dimension, with socio-economic liberals strong in the Hanseatic cities but less so elsewhere. Bismarck exploited these splits during the period of the Cartell (1884–90),[1] which saw the centre of gravity shift permanently in the direction of the political right. The failure of the liberal political project was reflected in a steady decline in the liberal parties' share of the vote: from just under 50 per cent in 1874 to just over 20 per cent by 1912. That is not to say that the Conservatives were numerically dominant within the bloc. Between 1878 and 1912 the Conservative parties' share of the vote also fell from around 25 per cent to just over 13 per cent. This decline reflected the decline in the social base within which the parties were embedded: a milieu of landowners from the areas of the Reich east of the Elbe, in Prussia and Mecklenburg, as well as farmers, artisans and small shopkeepers. The transition to mass politics, combined with rapid industrialisation, presented a challenge to the Conservative parties. However, their over-representation in the Prussian Diet – where they regularly won around 45 per cent of the seats – provided an effective electoral and institutional power base which offset the parties' decline elsewhere (Ritter, 1990: 40–1). Taken in the round, the fragmentation of the liberal parties and the territorial strength of the Conservatives constituted an anti-socialist coalition in which the class, confessional, and – to a lesser extent – urban/rural cleavages were conflated into a 'nationalist' discourse centred on the political economy and institutional configuration of the new unified German state.

The very limited data available on voting behaviour during this period demonstrates how deliberate political mobilisation by political elites around the class and religious cleavages led to the *Dreilagersystem*. Using regression analysis of voter preferences in general elections over the period 1871–1912, Claggett *et al.* (1982) argue that three political cleavages can be identified. Two of these cleavages – religion and economics/class – conform to the *Dreilagersystem* thesis, in addition to which Claggett *et al.* identify a third cleavage arising around the existence of the Cartell. However the Cartell cleavage was more ephemeral in that it was not socially grounded, and over time it was gradually subsumed into the economic cleavage. The other two political cleavages are much more socially embedded and their salience increases over time as elites mobilised around them.

Because of the dominance of Protestant Prussia within the Reich, the religious cleavage encompassed both inter-religious and church/state dynamics.

But its manifestation as a political cleavage is very weak at the beginning of the period. For instance, in the 1871 elections only one third of German Catholics voted for the Centre. At the same time, roughly 10 per cent of Protestants voted for the party, which was seen as a defender of traditional social values and thus an alternative to the Conservatives and German Reich Party. Nevertheless, over time we see a polarisation of electoral support along religious lines. By 1874, 60 per cent of Catholics voted Centre, whilst Protestant support had virtually disappeared altogether (Clagget *et al.*, 1982: 654–7). This coincided with the 'cultural struggle' (*Kulturkampf*) between the Catholic Church and the new German state, which served to make the religious cleavage manifest within the party system (Metje, 1994). The *Kulturkampf* served to disproportionately mobilise Catholics: in the 1874-Reichstag elections voter turnout in predominantly Catholic areas was over 70 per cent compared with around 50 per cent in Protestant areas (Ritter, 1990: 32). In addition, it distanced the Centre from potential allies amongst the liberals, who were overwhelmingly Protestant. As a result, the Centre became marginalised within the political process, and remained an explicitly 'Catholic' party for the remainder of the period.

At the same time the alliance of 'Iron and Rye' served to neutralise the urban/rural social cleavage and settle most arguments about Free Trade and Tariffs between capitalists and landowners. As a result, any political cleavage focussed on economic matters inevitably coalesced around issues of social class and workers' rights, although the tactical alliance between the SPD and the German Free Thinkers over opposition to the alliance's policy of external tariffs and protectionism (Stöss, 1976: 30) conforms to Rokkan's (1970) type 1B conflict (involving the urban/rural cleavage). The analysis of the economic cleavage by Claggett *et al.* reveals a similar dynamic to that observed with the religious cleavage. The SPD was the major party that explicitly identified with the working class and, as a result, was generally shunned by the bourgeois parties over the course of the period. In the first few elections, class does not appear to be a particularly strong indicator of voting behaviour. Indeed, the data indicates that at this time the SPD's avowal of a 'positive' role for the state and opposition to Bismarck made the party a credible second choice for Conservative voters. But the legacy of the *Sozialistengesetz* sharpened the economic cleavage (Pappi, 1985). It served to mobilise the working class and build the SPD's mass membership whilst, at the same time, isolating the Social Democrats within a political marketplace and party system that had begun to line up along the familiar left-right dimension that remains dominant today (Claggett *et al.*, 1982: 657–9).

So why did the class and religious cleavages develop so quickly and to the exclusion of other latent cleavages? On the one hand, it is true that institutional factors served to subdue the urban/rural and centre/periphery cleavages. The 'Iron and Rye' alliance took the heat out of the urban/rural cleavage, whilst the Reich's federal constitution allowed for the territorial dimension of politics to be incorporated by the Bundesrat and thus dissolved many centre/periphery conflicts. But it takes more than a benign political opportunity structure to explain why the left-right and religious cleavages became ascendant at that time. One also has to focus on the strategic decisions of elites, and in particular those of Bismarck himself. In terms of the left-right polarisation, the period of the 'Red-Scare' and the subsequent *Sozialistengesetze* served to open up a political gulf between the SPD and the bourgeois parties, just as the *Kulturkampf* raised the salience of religion both amongst the electorate and within the party system.

Faced with growing opposition, including from the Kaiser himself, Bismarck abandoned the *Kulturkampf* in 1876 (Carr, 1991: 128) and subsequently normalised relations with the Catholic Church. By contrast, and despite growing levels of electoral support, the SPD remained isolated within the party system (although the *Sozialistengesetze* was not renewed after 1890). Yet once made manifest, both the class and confessional cleavages would outlast the Second Reich itself and persist as the two main social bases of political conflict well into the second half of the twentieth century (Gluchowski and von Wilamowitz-Moellendorff, 1997: 182–3). It would take the twin forces of economic development and secularisation in the decades following the Second World War to finally erode the power of class and confession as indicators of voter preference.

3.3   The Weimar Republic

With the defeat of Germany in 1918, the Kaiser abdicated and – following a period of revolutionary turmoil – a Republic was declared at Weimar in 1919. The last years of the Great War had seen economic dislocation and shortages at home and the resultant civil unrest eventually forced the German high command to sue for peace, in order to allow them to crush the forces of insurrection at home. The Armistice was signed in November 1918 and the defeated Germany turned on itself. It was the second German 'year zero'.

On 30 September 1918, in an attempt to avoid out-and-out revolution, the Kaiser dismissed Chancellor Hertling and issued a proclamation establishing a parliamentary government. On the first of October, Prince Max of Baden – a moderate Conservative – was asked to form a new government. However, by now events were out of control and, on 9 November 1918, the Kaiser was informed that he no longer enjoyed the full loyalty of the Armed Forces High Command. Max of Baden appointed the right wing SPD leader Friedrich Ebert as the new 'Imperial Chancellor' and General Groener, the Chief of Staff of the Armed Forces promised him the army's support in return for a commitment to pursue a moderate course. This moderate course would involve the use of the army to suppress the revolutionary left.

The deal with the army aggravated the ideological and cultural split within the SPD that had emerged the previous year. In 1916 the SPD leadership had forcibly taken over control of *Vorwärts*, the party newspaper, in order to suppress growing left-wing criticism of the leadership's pro-War stance. This was accompanied by a campaign of expulsions of left-wingers, many of whom attended a meeting at Gotha over Easter 1917 at which they formed the new Independent Social Democratic Party, or USPD (Paterson, 1976: 216–17). The majority of SPD members opposed the split and sided with the leadership (see Stöss, 1976: 32–3), but the loss of what Paterson calls the 'articulate critical left' (Paterson, 1976: 217) was a blow to the SPD. For its part the USPD stood in the 1919 and 1920 elections but was absorbed into the new Communist Party (the KPD) after 1920.

Ranged against the left, on the other side of the political spectrum, was the Free Corps, made up of de-mobilised soldiers, students and white-collar workers. In January 1919, members of the Free Corps murdered Rosa Luxemburg and Karl Liebknecht, as well as many of the KPD's followers, following the Spartacist uprising. The following month, the leader of the Independent SPD, Kurt Eisner, was assassinated and, following the declaration of a Soviet Republic in Bavaria in April 1919, the Free Corps and the Army crushed the left there as well.

At this point, the main political division was between pro- and anti-regime forces, not all of which operated within the party system itself. But as revolutionary conditions subsided and the Weimar Republic stabilised itself, the old *Dreilagersystem* – and the class and confessional cleavages that underpinned it – re-emerged. The main difference was that the 1917 Russian Revolution and the later Treaty of Versailles were to result in the 'creation of two powerful anti-system parties of left and right which posed a permanent threat to the established parties' (Paterson, 1987: 158) and, it would become apparent, the democratic system itself. Table 3.2 demonstrates the degree of continuity and change between the pre-1914 party system and the system that emerged after the Great War.

The first Weimar elections took place on 19 January 1919, with the election of a new constituent assembly. All of the non-socialist parties re-constituted themselves with new names, but with the old personnel and objectives (Carr, 1991: 252). In the Catholic bloc, the Centre re-named itself the Christian People's Party (but soon reverted to the Centre) and distanced itself from much of the rural particularism of its pre-1914 incarnation. Some years later the Catholic bloc was augmented by the Bavarian People's Party (BVP). In the national bloc the liberal left formed the German Democratic Party, whilst the National Liberals kept the name of the German People's Party (or 'Populists'). Further to the right, the conservative Free Conservatives

Table 3.2 Continuity and change in the German party system, 1914–20

1914	Centre		SPD	FVP	NLP	DRP	DKP
1920	Centre	KPD	SPD	DDP	DVP		DNVP

and German Conservatives merged to form the German National People's Party, but remained representative of the old alliance of 'Iron and Rye' and were suspicious of the new Republic. Finally, the socialist bloc was divided two ways between the majority-Socialist SPD and a cluster of USPD members. Arranged on the left-right scale, the 1919 elections saw the Independents win 22 seats, the majority-Socialists 165, the Centre 91, the German Democratic Party 75, the German People's Party 19, and the German National People's Party 44.

The establishment of the Weimar Republic appeared to signify Germany's coming of age as a liberal democracy. But the Weimar Republic only survived for 14 years and was chronically weakened by economic difficulties. The first serious crisis was the Great Inflation of 1923. The roots of the Great Inflation lay in the Armistice Terms, which were announced in 1921. The terms were excessively punitive, and involved Germany paying reparations to the Entente powers, particularly France. Germany had already lost Alsace Lorraine, West Prussia, Upper Silesia, Posen, her few colonies and had to accept the establishment of a Polish Corridor that separated East Prussia from the rest of Germany. Taken in the round, these terms served to inflame the already militant sentiments of the Far Right and undermine the efforts of the authorities to re-establish economic stability. The Germans experienced currency problems and defaulted on payments to France in 1923, with the result that the French occupied Germany's industrial heartland in the Ruhr. The German currency tumbled and hyperinflation took hold. Savings were wiped out and segments of the German middle classes ruined. This led to many in the middle classes withdrawing what had always been contingent support for the Republic and increasingly taking refuge in the propaganda of the Far Right. The first political casualty of this development was what was left of German liberalism: between 1919 and 1932 the two liberal parties' share of the vote fell from 23 per cent to 2.9 per cent.

The keystone of right-wing propaganda was the myth of the 'stab-in-the-back' (*Dolchstosslegende*). The *Dolchstosslegende* arose from evidence given by Hindenburg in November 1919 to a parliamentary enquiry in to the causes of Germany's defeat in the Great War, in which he claimed that a British General had exonerated the German army from any blame in Germany's defeat. On the contrary, he claimed, defeat came from the stab-in-the-back given to the Army by the 'November traitors': the coalition parties that undermined the war effort, overthrew the monarchy, and sued for peace. Of these, the prime culprits were the SPD.

The *Dolchstosslegende* was a nationalist myth that provided comfort to many in a wounded and disoriented Germany. However, the targeting of the SPD also made it a tool for mobilisation around the class cleavage. The class and religious cleavages remained highly salient throughout the period of the Weimar Republic and political parties showed little or no willingness to move beyond narrow sectional interests. As a result, the formation and

Table 3.3   Continuity and change in the German party system, 1920–33

1920	Centre	KPD	DDP	DVP	DNVP	
		SPD				
1933	Centre	KPD	DDP/DSP	DVP	DNVP	NSDAP
		SPD				

maintenance of coalition governments was a difficult process, with twenty governments formed between 1919 and 1933, of which only four lasted more than a year (Roberts, 1997: 7). Nevertheless, the mid-1920s were a period of relative stability and affluence for the Weimar Republic in which the underlying polarisation of party politics along class and confessional cleavages was masked to a certain extent by rising living standards. But the Wall Street Crash of 1929 sparked a world recession in which American investment and loans to Germany ceased and unemployment soared. By 1933, there were six million unemployed in Germany, fanning the flames of the extremism that the fragile Weimar party system could not contain.

The economic misery of the late 1920s and early 1930s had a centrifugal effect on the party system, with voters deserting the political middle ground. Interestingly, two of the three blocs – the socialists and Catholics – remained relatively stable during this period (Rohe, 1997: 56), although the SPD saw considerable slippage of support to the KPD. By contrast, the nationalist bloc moved sharply to the right. Table 3.3 demonstrates how the social base of the German party system structured party competition in the early 1930s, compared with 1920.

The largest beneficiary of the collapse of the *Dreilagersystem* was the National Socialist German Workers' Party (NSDAP), which saw its vote share rise from 810,000 votes in 1928 to six-and-a-half million in 1930. This gave the party 103 votes and made it the second largest party in the Reichstag (Carr, 1991: 297). The NSDAP was founded in 1919 in Munich, as one of many radical nationalist and *völkisch* (racialist) parties that sprang up in the post-war era. However, the NSDAP would probably have remained insignificant had it not been for Hitler, who took control of the party and transformed its tactics. The failed 'Beer hall' Putsch of 1923 convinced Hitler that the NSDAP had to come to power legally if the party was to secure the support of the bureaucracy, the Army and the judiciary. Oddly, the decision to move away from a revolutionary strategy coincided with a move to the right in terms of economic policy. In the early years the party displayed a curious mix of socialist and nationalist sentiments. The party's 1920 programme was heavily influenced by its 'left-wing', led by the ideologue Strasser and the SA Chief Röhm, and argued for an anti-capitalist, classless society (*Volksgemeinschaft*), based on a co-operative economic order (*Genossenschaften*). During the 1920s Hitler distanced the party from this 'socialist' agenda and began to emphasise the nationalist strand of NSDAP thinking. Slowly, the NSDAP set about gaining the support of all members of the public, particularly those marginal groups in German society that had either done badly out of the chaos of the immediate post-war years or had suffered in the aftermath of the 1929 crash, with what Brozcat has described as 'a Catch-all, a hodgepodge of ideas' that could be trimmed in order to exploit the issues of the day (Brozcat, 1981: 32). Hodgepodge or not, the NSDAP's appeal cross-cut the dominant class and confessional cleavages and appealed to small shopkeepers, artisans, unemployed university graduates and other marginalised or aggrieved groups with a potent mix of national renewal, rearmament, revision of the hated Versailles Treaty, and economic and social reform (see Smith, 1986: 30–3).

The NSDAP's cross-class and (to a lesser extent) cross-confessional appeal meant that the party's social base resembled that of a post-1945 Catch-all party, to the extent that Falter has described the NSDAP as 'the first German *Volkspartei*'. Using correlation and regression analysis of election data from all counties of the Weimar Republic, Falter (1990: 72–5) has plotted what he calls the 'social correlates' of all political parties' electoral support in Reichstag elections over the period 1928 to 1933. Falter's data demonstrates that the NSDAP was unique amongst the Weimar parties in lacking a clear social profile, but rather relied on a base of support that was broad and diffuse. Although there was some variance between different social groups (for instance, Catholics were less likely to vote NSDAP than their Protestant neighbours) and within social groups over time (agrarian workers and the self-employed became increasingly likely to vote NSDAP) the NSDAP's strategy of political mobilisation transcended the manifest cleavages of class and confession. It also acknowledged that voters were not cultural dupes but rather had individual preferences that might be satisfied by a somewhat incoherent but malevolent mix of policy proposals.

Of course, the neutralisation of social cleavages is consistent with the *völkische* ideology of the NSDAP, with its emphasis on the organic unity of the German nation. In March 1933, after Hitler became Chancellor, the NSDAP set about eliminating all political opposition with the passing of the Enabling Act, which suspended the parliament and constitution. In the years that followed, the NSDAP set up institutions – such as the German Workers' Front – that were explicitly designed to pacify social conflict. This *Gleichschaltung*, or co-ordination, of all areas of German life to the Nazi ideal temporarily buried social and political cleavages under the 'National Socialist Bulldozer' (Mintzel, 1983: 245). It would be another 12 years, and a catastrophic World War, before these cleavages would once more re-emerge amongst the rubble of German military defeat.

3.4 Summary

Chapter 3 uses the Lipset–Rokkan (1967) model of social cleavages to provide a historical perspective of the development of social and political cleavages in Germany. The underlying rationale of the Lipset–Rokkan model is that all Western European countries underwent similar processes of historical development from the Reformation onwards. In Germany, this process eventually resulted in the Weimar Republic, Germany's first experiment in popular democracy.

Lipset and Rokkan argue that all European democracies are characterised by mass politics, universal suffrage, secret ballots, and the open competition for votes by parties mobilising around social cleavages. However, they note that there are significant differences across West European countries in terms of representation criteria, election rules, and the pattern of cleavages in a given country. As discussed in Chapter 2, these differences can be attributed to two factors: (1) the nature of alliances between nation-builders, churches, landowners, urban industrialists and entrepreneurs, and peripheral groups, and (2) how each state dealt with the problems of legitimation of protest, incorporation of new groups into the political arena, representation of groups in political institutions, and majority rule. This chapter demonstrates that in Germany the alliance of 'Iron and Rye' served to pacify the urban/rural cleavage, and create a majority consensus that sustained protectionism at the expense of the urban proletariat, as well as split German liberalism between socio-economic and 'national' liberals. At the same time, Bismarck's *Kulturkampf* and *Sozialistengesetze* served to sharpen confessional and class cleavages and make them manifest as political cleavages within the Second Reich's party system. The salience of these two cleavages persisted into the Weimar Republic, making it difficult for political parties to move beyond narrow sectional interests. As a result, the Weimar Republic was characterised by a number of short-lived and unstable governments. This instability was made worse by the economic crises that rocked the Weimar Republic, as well as the *Dolchstoßlegende*, which was both a symptom and a cause of the German right's ambiguity to the new democratic order. Eventually, the shallow roots of democracy in the Weimar Republic were exposed by the failure of the established parties to defend the Republic from the threat of National Socialism. The NSDAP's *völkische* ideology and belief in the organic unity of the German nation made it hostile to party politics and the organisational expression of cleavage-based conflict. As a result, political parties, trade unions, churches, and other social associations were suppressed or persecuted.

Any analysis of the development of German party politics over this period is faced with a choice. On the one hand, despite Germany's difficult history we can identify many of the variables common to other West European democracies that are discussed in the Lipset–Rokkan model. Thus it is clear that the conceptual tools of mainstream political science can structure a historical narrative of the development of party politics in Germany. In this sense, one can say with some confidence that Germany is not *sui generis*. On the other hand, the late development of the German nation-state, and its unique mix of economic and military development combined with social and political backwardness, make it tempting to fall back into the exceptionalism of the German *Sonderweg*. As the next chapter demonstrates, even the foundation of the Federal Republic and the restoration of popular democracy in 1949 would not make Germany a 'normal' case of competitive party politics.

4
Social and Political Cleavages in the Federal Republic, 1945–2002

4.1   Introduction

Chapter 4 builds on the historical account of social and political cleavages provided in previous chapters and examines the extent to which these cleavages persisted in the Federal Republic of Germany. At the same time, however, we can begin to make use of more sophisticated methods of data collection and analysis – including micro-level data – in order to construct a more nuanced picture of individual voter behaviour and preferences, how this has changed over time, and how political parties have responded to this. The chapter is divided into six sections: first, an account of the re-emergence of political cleavages during the period of Allied occupation, 1945–49; second, an analysis of how these cleavages stabilised and structured the party system during the first 20 years of the Federal Republic, 1949–69; third, an examination of the period 1969–90, leading up to the unification of Germany, with an emphasis on how the impact of secularisation and economic change eroded social cleavages: leading to greater electoral instability and partisan de-alignment; fourth, an account of the social base of party politics in post-unification Germany and the effects of the 'grafting on' of a second party system characterised by significantly different social cleavages and patterns of partisan identification; fifth, an up-to-date analysis of the social base of German party politics, drawing on data from the 2002-Bundestag elections; and sixth, a summary of the main issues raised in the chapter. Throughout this account the reader will be aware of how, after an initial period of consolidation and routinisation of party politics in Germany, political parties have been confronted by increasingly fluid and unpredictable conditions in the political marketplace within which they operate. In particular, the ability of political parties to structure the vote and eliminate irrelevant alternatives has been eroded as voters increasingly display a significant level of impatience and disillusionment with the party political process.

4.2   The re-emergence of political cleavages: 1945–49

May 1945 was the third and, one hopes, final German 'year zero'. After the capitulation of the Nazi regime in that month the Allies divided Germany into four zones of occupation. It was out of these zones that two new states were created. The Federal Republic arose out of the British, American and French zones, whilst the German Democratic Republic emerged out of the Soviet zone. Both states were formally established in 1949.

It is a paradox of German history that the Third Reich served to create the conditions whereby liberal democracy could finally and permanently take root on German soil. Because of its totalising nature, and also because of the dislocation caused by the war, the sectional and regional loyalties that had hampered the creation of a democratic identity during the Weimar years had been eroded. This was illustrated by the rapid emergence of, for the first time in German political history, a cross-confessional conservative party: the Christian Democratic Union (CDU), and its Bavarian sister-party the Christian Social Union (CSU). The CDU/CSU was a 'loose conservative coalition under a non-sectarian label' (Chandler, 1988: 61) that would go on to transcend sectional loyalties in a manner that the Centre never succeeded in doing.

Political activity was first allowed in the Soviet zone. In June 1945, the Russians allowed the KPD, SPD, CDU, and a new liberal party – the LDPD – to organise there. The Allies responded to this by allowing these parties to organise in their zones as well, although in the western zones the main liberal party was to change its name to Free Democratic Party (FDP). In 1946 the Soviet Union forced the merger of the KPD and the SPD in their zone, to form the Socialist Unity Party (SED). However, the forced merger (*Zwangsvereinigung*) of the two parties was resisted by the SPD in the Allied zones, with the result that in the west a rival SPD remained in existence under the leadership of Kurt Schumacher. The *Zwangsvereinigung* was one of the first political manifestations of a process that would eventually lead to the division of Germany. Even at this early stage, it set a pattern of separate political development that would drive the process of division forward. In January 1947, the British and US zones merged to form 'Bizonia', and set up two institutions – an Economic Council and Executive Council – which became the main arena for party politics during the period of Allied occupation. In June 1947 delegates from state parliaments were appointed to the new Economic Council. The distribution of seats is set out in Table 4.1. The distribution of seats in the Economic Council represents the aggregate of party competition in the individual German states. As such, it provides a good snapshot of the shape of the emerging party system under Allied rule. What is clear is that, despite the impact of National Socialism, this emerging party system was still underpinned by the manifest social cleavages of confession and class (Schmidt, 1990: 181), with the residual effects from the

Table 4.1   Distribution of seats and social base of party competition in the Economic Council, June 1947

Workers' parties		Bourgeois parties				
KPD	SPD	Centre	CDU/CSU	FDP etc.	NLP/DP	WAV
03	20	02	20	04	02	01
Total	23					29

centre/periphery cleavage manifesting itself through the existence of a separate Bavarian wing of Christian Democracy, the CSU.[2]

But how did these cleavages impact on the party system? As Dahrendorf points out, Germans in the western zones reacted to the totalitarianism of the Third Reich with a 'counter-revolution' in which 'as part of the search for reliable fixed points of social structure, (society chose) in quite a few areas, the return to pre-modern structures' (Dahrendorf, 1967: 435). As part of this process the long-established strategy of the Catholic milieu was resurrected. Confessional schools, banned by the Nazis, were re-opened and the Catholic Church's auxiliary organisations were re-constituted along pre-war lines (Gotto, 1983). But the renewal of the Catholic subculture was not matched by the re-emergence of a distinctly 'Catholic' political party. In the new Economic Council, the old Centre party gained only two seats, compared with 20 for the CDU/CSU, which not only drew support from Catholics but also from those elements of the Protestant community (particularly Lutherans) that had been politicised by their experiences of the 'struggle with the churches' (*Kirchenkampf*) under National Socialism. From now on the religious cleavage did not just manifest itself as a conflict between Catholics and Protestants, but also as a conflict between the religious and secular elements of the population (Wolf, 1996). But Catholic support for the CDU/CSU remained higher than that of Protestants as a proportion of the total population. Most of this support was a form of 'cultural Catholicism' and in as far as this skewed support was an indicator of the religious cleavage it was because religious traditionalists were over-represented amongst Catholics (Pappi, 1984: 18).

By contrast, the Cold War and emerging division of Germany temporarily raised the salience of the class cleavage and brought about a division of the party system into two camps: with the workers' parties (KPD and SPD) on the left and the bourgeois parties (Centre, CDU/CSU, FDP, National Liberal Party (NLP)/DP, Economic Development and Unification (WAV)) on the right. Given the antipathy between KPD and SPD, as well as the ideological distance between bourgeois parties such as the Centre and the right-wing German Party (DP), this was a false dichotomy. Nevertheless, the SPD did rely on manual workers – especially those organised in trade unions – for the core of its support. Whether inevitable or not at this point in German history, the polarisation of the party system between socialist and bourgeois blocs was used by the CDU/CSU to isolate the SPD and set the course for the future Federal Republic. Thus the CDU/CSU formed a centre–right coalition with the FDP and DP, under the leadership of the CDU's Konrad Adenauer. The coalition elected the free-marketeer Ludwig Erhard as Director of Economics. Adenauer would become the first Chancellor of the Federal Republic in 1949, with Ludwig Erhard its first Economics Minister. Erhard would preside over the post-war Economic Miracle and eventually succeed Adenauer as Chancellor in 1963.

Despite Schumacher's belief that only the working class and its party the SPD had the moral right to lead Germany's in the aftermath of the Third Reich (Bark and Gress, 1993: 108–9), the SPD played a constructive role during this period. Schumacher was determined not to further isolate the SPD and, to that end, saw the need to reach out beyond the working class for electoral support. Although by no means a right-winger, Schumacher recognised that if the SPD was to become a people's party then it must involve a rejection of Marxism as the ideological compass of the party (Paterson, 1976: 224–5). Shorn of the certainties of Marxism, the SPD's opposition to the emergent political-economic settlement was one of objection to the details rather than rejection of its entire trajectory. But where the SPD under Schumacher did part company with the CDU/CSU in a more fundamental manner was in matters of external policy. Here the party took a more neutralist – or even nationalist – line that manifested itself in its opposition to Adenauer's closeness to the Western allies and in his support for the Korean War.

From the distance of over half a century it is tempting to take for granted the success in establishing a stable and democratically grounded party system in the Western zones, in what was a relatively short period of time. But it was a remarkable achievement, not least when it is compared with the disasters that overwhelmed the Weimar Republic. So how and why did the 1945–49 process succeed when democracy in the Weimar Republic so conspicuously failed? Two key factors can be identified. The first was the role of the Allies. Unlike in 1918, Germany was occupied in 1945 and, as a result, most if not all of the key 'high politics' issues were beyond the competence of the emerging political class. In what Kirchheimer has called a 'protected party system' (Kirchheimer, 1966) a democratic culture was able to emerge and develop within the political lagoon created by the Allies' benign authoritarianism. This was a far more propitious environment than had been the case in 1918–19 where, although free of foreign occupation, the small crew of democrats found themselves upon the open sea and forced to try and navigate the ship of state through uncharted waters, amid the storms of political and economic upheaval. The second factor, however, was the capacity of the domestic political class to grasp the opportunity presented to them. In Germany's first democratic experiment too few of the Weimar Republic's political class were committed to the idea of democracy in the abstract. Democratic institutions were invested with the power of the state, but the contingent nature of elite support for them meant that it lacked the equivalent degree of authority to go with it. Thus the Weimar Republic's political settlement, in as far as there was one, was ill-equipped to survive the crises that overwhelmed it. By contrast, the disaster of Nazism had served to undermine the legitimacy of the Lutheran-inspired 'authoritarian state' (*Obrigkeitsstaat*) and, as a result, there was a greater will to take the democratic road. That is not to say that it was a *collective* will. By-and-large the popular instinct was to withdraw from the political arena and concentrate on the business of survival in the difficult material conditions of the late 1940s. It was left to individuals of sufficient calibre – such as Adenauer, Schumacher, Kaiser and Reuter – to take the first steps down the road.

4.3   The Federal Republic: 1949–69

In many ways the new Federal Republic was made in the CDU's image and the SPD was forced to adapt. The new Republic was a Federal State, whereas the SPD favoured a unitary solution, and under Erhard's tutelage the CDU/CSU pursued the goal of a 'Social Market' economy, at a time when the SPD favoured a larger role for state planning. Significantly, however, the social base of party politics had also shifted to the disadvantage of the SPD.

The key change was in the confessional balance. From 1871 to 1949 Germany was predominantly Protestant and the party system reflected this dominance, with the Centre isolated by what was then a strongly manifest confessional cleavage. Territorially, the distribution of the Catholic population was skewed towards the south and west of the country. But the division of Germany on east-west lines meant that Catholics now made up 45 per cent of the population of the new Federal Republic. For a segment of the population that had, since the *Kulturkampf*, never been totally at ease within the political process, the new Federal Republic provided the opportunity to feel politically at home. For Protestants, who still made up the majority of the population but whose political mobilisation – despite the *Kirchenkampf* – was not as strong as Catholics, the new settlement put them on the defensive. The protestant church leader Martin Niemöller articulated this feeling when he described the new Republic as a 'Catholic state conceived in Rome and born in Washington' (*New York Herald Tribune*, 14/12/49).

In a sense, Niemöller's description of the early Federal Republic was right. The CDU remained in office until 1969 and was supported overwhelmingly by Catholics. By contrast, the SPD had lost its Prussian heartland and lagged behind the CDU in its ability to appeal to voters across the class and confessional cleavages. Nevertheless, these cleavages cross-cut each other, and the relationship between social class and voting behaviour became more complex as the economic structure of the Federal Republic became more differentiated. Thus Pappi's (1984) study of the German party system demonstrated that up until 1969 the religious cleavage remained a good indicator of voting behaviour and that Catholics were far less likely to vote SPD than CDU. Similarly, Catholics were also more likely to vote CDU than FDP. By contrast, social class is a much more complex indicator and its relationship to voting behaviour harder to operationalise empirically. Pappi's own preference was to compare data on the electoral preferences of manual workers with those of the self-employed rather than with white-collar employees. For Pappi, the conflictual relationship between workers and white-collar employees is more one of social status, which is likely to also reflect differences in value-orientation, rather than the more visceral zero-sum conflict over economic resources that plays out between manual workers and the self-employed (Pappi, 1984: 18–19). Pappi's observations reflect a more complex relationship between social class and partisan identification that became apparent in the late 1960s and was to gather pace in the 1970s and 1980s. It was also indicative of voters' increasing sophistication and independence from traditional social and economic cues (Paterson, 1987: 161).

4.4   De-alignment and electoral instability: 1969–90

Gordon Smith has observed that 'of all West European societies, Germany was perhaps the most open to the impact of rapid economic and industrial change, a susceptibility which was promoted by the changes wrought by National Socialism and increased by the dislocation of German defeat' (Smith, 1986: 128). Thus, whilst Dahrendorf was right in noting the need of Germans to retreat into the social and institutional structures of the pre-Nazi era, the post-war decades inevitably unleashed a wave of technical change that was to have substantial impact on the social base of party politics. The extraordinary levels of growth of the German 'economic miracle' (*Wirtschaftswunder*) saw the Federal Republic's Gross National Product grow from DM 98.1 million in 1950 to DM 679 million by 1970. Over the same period, per capita income rose from DM 1588 to DM 8725, whilst the effects of migration and the initial post-war 'baby boom' meant that the population increased from just over 46 million to a little under 62 million. Similarly, the number of Germans living in villages of less than five thousand people fell from around 30 per cent to under 10 per cent, thus marginalising latent urban/rural and centre/periphery cleavages. Finally, growing affluence and the need for a better-educated workforce meant that more Germans enjoyed access to a good education. In the 1940s only about 10 per cent of the relevant age group went to the equivalent of Grammar School (*Gymnasien*), but by the late 1980s this would rise to 30 per cent (Statistisches Bundesamt). This inevitably meant that many more Germans were given the opportunity to go to University. These social changes had three main effects on the social base of party politics. First, it led to the growing secularisation of German society. Second, it led to the blurring of class identity and loyalties. Finally, the 'cohort effect' of these changes on the younger age groups led to a 'generation gap' within the electorate, with younger voters displaying a significantly different value-orientation to older voters. The class and religious cleavages continued to structure the pattern of party politics, although there was increasing evidence that the class cleavage was weaker than, and conditioned by, the religious cleavage (Dogan, 2000: 105). Nevertheless, the net effect of social change was growing partisan de-alignment, greater electoral instability, and the growth of the 'new politics' (see Chapter 5).

The impact of social change had its effect on the composition of party membership as well. In the 20 years from the late 1950s until the late 1970s the proportion of working class party members declined across all of the mainstream parties. At the same time, party membership for all of the parties became more middle-class, albeit with a skew towards the self-employed among the 'bourgeois' parties. Crucially, the decline in the proportion of working class party members affected the SPD as much as the other parties. Over the period, the centre of gravity among the SPD's membership shifted from manual workers to white-collar employees – mirroring the party's attempts to move beyond its core working class base and compete with the CDU/CSU as a catch-all party. Civil servants also become more numerous within the party over the period (Chandler, 1988: 59). This also reflected the SPD's embeddedness in *Land* government (the level of government in the Federal Republic where most civil servants are employed), the growth of the welfare state, and the cumulative impact of the Federal Republic's 'party state' (*Parteienstaat*) ethos, which encouraged the partial politicisation of the civil service. These developments are examined in more detail in Chapter 6, but they do seem to bear out Brittan's (1975) fear that professionalised political parties were vulnerable to capture by groups with an interest in the expansion of state capacity.

With social change came secularisation, which gathered pace in the 1960s and 1970s. In the 1950s, more than 40 per cent of the population attended Church at least once a week but, by 1987, this had dropped to just over 25 per cent. The apparent impact of secularisation was further aggravated by the practice of claiming no religious affiliation in order to avoid Germany's church taxes but, nevertheless, the figures are quite stark. Within the Catholic subculture attendance dropped from 54 to 32 per cent (Conradt and Dalton, 1988: 7). Changes within the Catholic Church had an effect as well, with the Second Vatican Council bringing about a temporary moderation of the Church's ideological position and a more long-term relaxation of its relationship with the SPD (Schmidt, 1990: 187). By the same token, the Catholic Church's relationship with the CDU/CSU became more contingent on questions of policy, to the extent that it was 'no longer possible to regard Church organisations as the natural reserve army of the CDU' (Kühr, 1982: 97).

Nevertheless the CDU retained the electoral support of most Catholics, regardless of the strength of their religious beliefs. At the same time, the party continued to garner high levels of support amongst religious traditionalists of both denominations. In 1990, 78 per cent of Catholics and 65 per cent of non-Catholics with strong religious ties voted for the CDU/ CSU. The SPD continued to mobilise around the secular side of the religious cleavage but here as well it was subject to competition from the CDU. Whereas in 1953 only around 25 per cent of CDU/CSU voters were secularised, this had risen to around 70 per cent by the 1980s. Thus, despite immense social change, the CDU/CSU managed to retain its cross-confessional support amongst practising Christians, sustain its core Catholic electorate, and compete with the SPD amongst the secularised electorate (Forschungsgruppe Wahlen, 1994: 639–48).

More profound change took place around the class cleavage. Economic growth and the growing differentiation of modes of production in the post-war period created a significantly more complex occupational profile. Between 1950 and 1991 the traditional industrial working class declined in size from around 51 per cent to fewer than 39 per cent, with a similar drop in levels of trade union membership. Nevertheless, trade unions remained the key auxiliary organisation of the 'worker' side of the class cleavage and continued to exercise an independent impact on voting intentions during this period. Thus, trade union membership was a key indicator of an increased likelihood to vote SPD rather than CDU/CSU, regardless of whether voters were manual workers, white-collar employees or civil servants. Amongst manual workers – who were more likely to vote SPD anyway because of their social status – the margin of increased support for the SPD ranged from 9 per cent in 1980 to 22 per cent in 1983. However, the impact of union membership on voting intentions among white-collar employees and civil servants was even more pronounced and increased over the period, with the margin between members and non-members increasing from 18 per cent in 1976 and 1980, to 22 per cent in 1983 and, finally, 25 per cent in 1987 (Forschungsgruppe Wahlen, 1976–87).

Interestingly, the spikes in the margins for both employment categories take place in the mid- to late-1980s when the SPD was in opposition and under-performing electorally. This indicates that SPD support among members was not as elastic as that of non-members, which was more contingent upon perceptions of the party's policy profile and general performance (Feist and Liepelt, 1987). In other words, during the electorally 'lean years' of the 1980s, the SPD became more reliant on the loyalty of its core unionised support among both employment categories. At the same time the interests of unionised manual workers and union members of the white-collar salariat and civil service were not the same, and presented the SPD with a strategic dilemma in how to reconcile the interests of traditional social democracy with those of the so-called 'teachers' SPD', increasingly dominated by the public-sector white-collar employees and civil servants (Betz, 1999).

One other point is worth noting – data from the 1980s and early 1990s indicate that union membership did not appear to have had a persistent effect on the likelihood of voters to favour either the FDP or the Greens. This was particularly true of the FDP, despite the party's bourgeois nature. Support for the FDP appeared to be more contingent on the party's coalition behaviour than voters' trade union membership status. Thus, support for the FDP among all manual workers was higher in the 1976 and 1980 Bundestag elections than in the 1983 and 1987 elections. In the 1976 and 1980 elections the FDP were in coalition with the SPD and these higher levels of support among manual workers are indicative of SPD-supporting manual workers giving their second vote (*Zweitstimme*) to the FDP, to support the party's role as 'liberal corrective' within the coalition. After the FDP switched support to the CDU/CSU in 1982, this level of support amongst manual workers was reduced. Similarly, there is a pattern of trendless fluctuation in support for the FDP among white-collar employees over the period. The only exception to this was the 1983 election, in which support for the FDP amongst members and non-members dipped to 4 per cent (the same thing happened among manual workers, as well). 1983 was the first election after the FDP's switch of allegiance support from the SPD to the CDU/CSU and this dip in support is indicative of SPD voters who had previously given their *Zweitstimme* to the FDP 'punishing' the party for breaking up the social–liberal coalition (Forschungsgruppe Wahlen, 1976–87).

As for the Greens, electoral data from the period reveals an interesting paradox. Over the period, support for the Greens among non-unionised voters was higher in both employment categories. Among manual workers, support from union members averaged 2.5 per cent compared with 2.75 per cent among non-members. Similarly, support among white-collar employees and civil servants averaged 4 per cent among union members and 5.5 per cent among non-members. So taken at face value, membership of a trade union appeared to be a negative indicator of support for the Greens. However, union membership among white-collar employees and civil servants seemed to stabilise levels of support for the Greens from one election to the next. Thus in a similar fashion to the impact of union membership on SPD support, support for the Greens among unionised white-collar workers and civil servants is less elastic than that found among non-members (Forschungsgruppe Wahlen, 1976–87). This is indicative of the relatively small, but stable, constituency of support for the Greens found amongst specific public sector employees such as teachers and care workers (see Lees, 1998).

At the same time as trade union membership dropped, the proportion of self-employed within the workforce also fell from 28 to 9.5 per cent (Schäfers, 1995: 192). Thus, using Pappi's definition, the parameters of the most salient dimension of the class cleavage shrunk significantly over the period. Meanwhile, the bourgeoisie became larger and more diverse. In addition to the traditional groups of capitalists and petty bourgeoisie, the post-war period saw the emergence of the 'new middle class' of civil servants and salaried white-collar employees. Over the period the old middle class of the self-employed, farmers and professionals declined from 28 to 12 per cent, whilst the new middle class grew from 21 to 48 per cent (Conradt and Dalton, 1988: 459). The new middle class was important for two reasons. First, its sheer size meant that it was to become the key social group within the electorate. Second, the lack of a clear pattern of partisan identification amongst the new middle class meant that the support of members of the new middle class for political parties was more contingent on the parties' policy positions.

In the 1960s and early 1970s, the initial benefactor of this development was the SPD, with 50 per cent of the new middle class voting SPD in the 1972 Bundestag elections. In mid-1970s the CDU/CSU overhauled the SPD and, apart from a brief spike in SPD support in the late 1970s and early 1980s, support for the CDU/CSU remained a little higher amongst the new middle class until the late 1980s. However the key point to note is that neither of the two big catch-all parties managed to establish a decisive electoral advantage amongst this social group, and both parties' support fluctuated between 40 and 50 per cent. For its part, the FDP's share of the vote hovered between 10 and 15 per cent until the early 1980s, when the party came under increasing electoral pressure from the Greens (Gluchowski and Wilamowitz-Moellendorff, 1997: 190).

The growth of the Greens was also symptomatic of the cohort effect of a new generation of voters that had been socialised during the period of change in the post-war years. Thus, the impact of secularisation, growing affluence, better education, and greater social mobility meant that this cohort of voters had only weak links to the traditional social cleavages around which the mainstream political parties mobilised their core support. In turn, this led to an erosion of the cognitive links of loyalty and identification between younger voters and political parties, which had three effects. First, the Federal Republic experienced much higher levels of electoral volatility than had been the case since the mid-1950s. Second, there was more 'split-ticket' voting, in which voters gave their first vote (*Erststimme*) for one party and their *Zweitstimme* for another. Finally, the impact of higher levels of education and the growth of sectors of the economy reliant on intellectual capital (rather than money capital or productive capacity) led to the growth of a 'post-materialist' value-orientation amongst younger generational cohorts (Inglehart, 1990). This development is discussed at greater length in Chapter 5. The emergence of this new value-orientation meant that the dominant left-right dimension of conflict was cross-cut by a 'materialist/post-materialist' dimension. The subsequent growth of the 'new politics' reflected an emphasis on 'quality of life' issues and a rejection of the hierarchical and authoritarian nature of the traditional parties and their auxiliary organisations.

The main effect of this process of partisan de-alignment was a decline in the overall vote for the two catch-all parties. This changed the way political scientists talked about the Federal Republic's party system, in particularly its reputation for hyper-stability (see Crewe, 1985). As Conradt observed 'the volatility of a generally stable electorate and party system also prompted some analysts to perceive a crisis in the system as a whole' (Conradt, 1990: 35). Voters appeared to be increasingly instrumental in their party choice and there no longer seemed to be a clear link between economic performance and party popularity (Kirchgässner, 1986; cited Padgett, 1993: 43). As a result, it became harder for the established political parties to identify and articulate the interests of the voters, which, in turn, increased voter alienation and volatility. By the end of the 1980s, the entire social basis of party politics in the Federal Republic appeared to be in flux. The seismic impact of German Unification, in 1990, 'injected new uncertainty into this already fluid political environment' (Dalton *et al.*, 1992: 55).

4.5   Post-unification Germany: 1990–2002

The unification of Germany on 3 October 1990 grafted onto the Federal Republic a population and social structure which, although as 'German' as the 'old' Federal Republic, had undergone a profoundly different historical development over the post-war years. Both Germanys inherited the legacy of National Socialism, but in the former East Germany the effects of Nazi dictatorship had been compounded by 40 years of Communist rule. Thus it is no surprise that the party politics in the former GDR was grounded in different social dynamics to that found in the 'old' Federal Republic.

Writing in the 1960s, Dahrendorf argued that the GDR was 'the first modern society on German Soil'. In this he meant that the social ties of kinship and privilege had been systematically eroded in ways that have not been the case in the Federal Republic. As Dahrendorf observed, 'while a few faithful churchgoers, some old people, the rare self-employed who have so far been forgotten by successive waves of nationalisation may for a while resist the onslaught of co-ordination, the comrade has already won the day, and the new society is complete'. Dahrendorf identified three ways in which the co-ordination of society had been achieved. First, by the establishment of 'positive' social rights: to a comfortable old age, to sickness benefit, to reasonable welfare treatment and so on. Second, by the political direction of education, which was explicitly designed to create a cohort effect over time that would erode sectional loyalties within the populace. Finally, by the systematic dismantling of all intermediate ties embedded within civil society in order to '(tear) people out of their inherited loyalties and (force) them into an equal basic status, which frequently enough contradicts their own wishes and intentions'. According to Dahrendorf the changes associated with the social co-ordination of the GDR were profound and irreversible (Dahrendorf, 1967).

From the perspective of 40 years on, Dahrendorf's prediction about the permanent effects of 'real existing Socialism' now looks a little over-pessimistic. Nevertheless, after unification political scientists trying to explain the strange quality of political life in the former GDR remarked upon the lack of traditional social ties. Communist social engineering had atom-ised the patterns of civil society that was the basis of party identification in the Federal Republic and survey data indicated that only 4 per cent of voters in the 'new States' of the former GDR admitted to 'strong ties' to a particular party (Dalton *et al.*, 1992: 71). In addition, the wider institutions of civil society, particularly interest associations, were not indigenous to the new federal states but rather imposed upon them from the old Federal Republic (Wielgohs, 1996). Table 4.2 sets out the class composition of voter prefer-ences in the East German 'People's Chamber' (*Volkskammer*) elections of March 1990. The 1990 *Volkskammer* elections were the first – and last – democratic elections to take place in the GDR. As such, it was the first oppor-tunity for political scientists to examine the political preferences of the East German population before its absorption into the Federal Republic in October of that year. What is clear from this data is that in 1990 the 'normal' class cleavage found in West Germany had effectively turned through 180 degrees in East Germany. The 'inverted social profile' of the electorate was most evident in the figures for support for the SPD, CDU and, to a lesser extent, the FDP. Table 4.2 demonstrates that the CDU had a clear lead of 68 per cent over the SPD among industrial workers. Moreover, even the FDP polled more than three times as many votes among this group than the SPD. Conversely, the SPD polled much better than the CDU and FDP among non-manual workers. Thus, the logic of the class cleavage spelt out by Pappi (1984) and others was turned on its head.

The effect of this obvious inversion of voter preferences and the general lack of socially grounded patterns of partisan identification among East Germans was to challenge some of the initial assumptions about the social base of politics in post-unification Germany. Table 4.3 provides data on the class and confessional structures in the 'old' and 'new' states of the Federal Republic in the early years of post-unification Germany. The data demon-strates the clear differences in the balance of social cleavages between the east and west. In terms of class structure, the table shows a substantially higher percentage of manual workers in the new federal states (42.2 per cent) and slightly more salaried employees (49.1 per cent) compared with the old (35.9 and 45.4 per cent respectively). Conversely, there are significantly lower levels of civil servants (2 per cent) and the self-employed (6.5 per cent) than in the old states (7.9 and 9.2 per cent respectively). More interesting are the figures for religious affiliation. On the one hand the data demonstrates a clear difference in the balance between Catholics and Protestants, with the much larger proportion of Protestants in the new federal states in keeping with the pattern that prevailed in the Second Reich and Weimar Republic.

Table 4.2   Voting preference by party, 1990-Volkskammer elections (%)

Occupation	PDS	B'90	SPD	Lib.	DBD	Other	DSU	NDPD	CDU	Non-voters	Total
Industrial	00.4	00.5	03.2	10.1	00.3	02.7	08.9	00.2	71.3	02.2	100
Crafts	00.9	02.0	07.6	03.7	00.2	06.1	16.9	00.1	61.1	01.6	100
Building	40.9	02.3	32.2	00.1	00.5	05.8	00.0	00.2	05.3	12.7	100
Agriculture	07.8	00.1	28.9	02.8	19.6	03.6	01.0	01.9	32.2	02.2	100
Transport	39.2	03.6	37.2	00.0	00.4	03.8	00.0	00.2	01.0	14.6	100
Commerce	35.0	06.6	36.6	00.0	00.1	04.9	00.0	00.1	01.3	15.2	100
Other manual	26.0	18.6	27.7	00.1	00.2	05.0	01.0	00.1	05.0	16.4	100
Non-manual	38.3	05.4	39.3	00.0	00.1	03.5	00.0	00.1	01.7	11.5	100
Retired	02.8	01.6	14.1	06.7	01.2	03.3	11.9	00.4	54.3	03.7	100
	15.3	02.7	20.5	04.8	2.1	03.6	05.9	00.4	38.2	06.6	100

Source: Berglund, 1994: 139.

Table 4.3   Class and confessional structures in post-unification Germany, 1993 (%)

	New federal states	**Old federal states**
Employment status		
Manual worker	42.2	35.9
Salaried employee	49.1	45.4
Civil servant	02.0	07.9
Self-employed	06.5	09.2
Religious affiliation		
Catholic	06.0	40.0
Protestant	25.0	43.0
No affiliation	69.0	17.0

Sources: *Statistisches Bundesamt* 1995; Gluchowski and von Wilamowitz-Moellendorf, 1997: 197.

On the other hand, the percentage of eastern Germans claiming no religious affiliation is disproportionately high compared with the figures for the old federal states. This is consistent with the outcome of social engineering, characterised by the erosion of traditional ties, in the GDR described by Dahrendorf 30 years earlier.

As already noted, the division of Germany in 1949 along east-west lines meant that the balance between Catholics and Protestants in the Federal Republic was far more equal than had been the case in the Second Reich or Weimar Republic. This shift in the confessional balance was seen to have benefited the CDU/CSU and disadvantaged the SPD. By implication, the reintegration of the eastern states, including the territory that used to constitute the SPD's former heartland of Prussia, should have tipped the electoral scales in favour of the SPD. In addition, one might have expected that the relatively high levels of manual workers in the former GDR would have compounded this relative advantage. But the first all-German Bundestag elections, which took place on 2 December 1990, proved these assumptions wrong. In as far as one could define any clear pattern of cleavage-based voter choice on the basis of one election, the situation in the new federal states was broadly the same as in the Volkskammer elections earlier that year: an inversion of that of the old federal states. Thus, the CDU enjoyed disproportionate support amongst manual workers compared with its overall share of the vote: polling 49.8 per cent compared with 41.8 per cent overall (and 24.8 per cent for the SPD). In addition, the CDU not only led the SPD amongst Catholic voters but also commanded a majority of voters with affinity to the Protestant church (Padgett, 1993: 39–41). The only section of the population in which the SPD was ahead of the CDU was amongst those sections of the electorate that claimed no religious affiliation. However, even here the SPD found itself under pressure from the Greens and the post-communist PDS.

The 1990-Bundestag elections took place during the initial period of post-unification euphoria and returned the incumbent CDU/CSU-FDP coalition to power. Given these circumstances, it might be expected that the CDU/CSU in particular benefited from a sense of optimism and gratitude on the part of voters in the eastern federal states. Data from the 1994 Bundestag elections demonstrate that the 'inverted social profile' found in the new federal states still existed but in a more moderated form: indicating that the class cleavage in the new federal states had begun to converge with the pattern long established in the old Federal states. The CDU remained ahead of the SPD in terms of support from manual workers but the margin between the two parties in 1994 (4 per cent) was far less than in 1990 (when the margin was over 10 per cent). Moreover, the CDU's overall share of the vote of manual workers in the new federal states was only 6 per cent higher than its share amongst the same social group in the old Federal Republic, implying that social groups in the eastern states were returning slowly to what Padgett has described as their 'natural political home' (Padgett, 1995: 87). Conversely, the confessional cleavage remained significantly strong in the new federal states. This took two forms. First, the small group of Catholic voters in the east were much more likely to vote for the CDU in preference to the SPD than their counterparts in the old Federal states. Second, Protestant voters in the east were far more likely to vote CDU rather than SPD. This represented a strong religious/secular cleavage between religious traditionalists and those with little or no religious affiliation (Gluchowski and von Wilamowitz-Moellendorf, 1997: 199). In one sense, this is similar to the religious/secular cleavage that emerged in the old Federal Republic in the late 1940s and early 1950s. However, the cleavage that initially structured the pattern of political competition between the CDU/CSU in the 1950s emerged before the impact of secularisation. As a result, the CDU was able to mobilise the entire

Catholic sub-culture and retain the support of Catholics with weak religious affiliations even after secularisation set in. In the case of the new federal states in the 1990s, secularisation had already taken place on a scale much larger than that which had taken place in the old Federal Republic. Thus although the CDU enjoyed the support of nearly all practising Protestants in the new federal states (as opposed to West Germany in the 1950s, when the party drew most of its Protestant support from Lutherans), the impact of secularisation in the new federal states meant that it was mobilising a comparatively small segment of the population. As a result, the CDU's support amongst these groups did not have the scale or persistence of impact on the pattern of party competition as had been the case in the early years of the old Federal Republic.

Despite the lack of embeddedness of the CDU/CSU's lead among Catholic and traditionalist Protestant voters in the new federal states, the party retained its advantage over the SPD amongst these groups at the aggregate level of Germany as a whole. This was demonstrated by the party's performance in the 1998-Bundestag elections.

Table 4.4 demonstrates the division of the popular vote in the 1998-Bundestag elections by employment status and religious affiliation. The CDU/CSU lost the elections in the face of a strong SPD Chancellor candidate and a concertedly centrist electoral campaign. Yet the table demonstrates that in the old federal states the CDU/CSU continued to outperform the SPD amongst the self-employed (by a margin of 24 per cent) and Catholics (11 per cent). In addition, the remnant of the urban/rural cleavage was demonstrated by the CDU/CSU's 65 per cent advantage among the relatively small group of agricultural workers. Conversely, the SPD enjoyed a clear advantage among manual workers (22 per cent) and secular voters (25 per cent). The SPD also performed well among the new middle class of white-collar employees (9 per cent) and Protestant voters (16 per cent). In the new federal states these clear cleavage-based differentials were generally less pronounced, although the SPD's clear lead over the CDU/CSU among secular voters (23 per cent) and the emergence of a preference for the SPD among manual workers (12 per cent) indicate some degree of 'normalisation' of cleavage-based politics in the new federal states.

Taken in the round, the 1998-elections demonstrated high levels of stability within cleavages at the national level. As Gibowski observes, despite the SPD's electoral gains 'prior structures were preserved in the various social milieus. The SPD did not manage to encroach on typical CDU/CSU structures' (Gibowski, 1999: 31). In other words, the SPD outperformed the CDU/CSU nationally but long-established differentials of support for the SPD or CDU/CSU in the various social groups remained broadly the same. The lack of strong partisan ties in the new federal states amplified the national swing towards the SPD but, ultimately, 1998 was not a re-aligning election.

The 1998-Bundestag elections re-confirmed two aspects of the social base of party politics in the unified Germany that had become clearer with every subsequent Bundestag election during the 1990s. First, that despite the process of partisan de-alignment that has taken place, the social base of party politics in the old federal states remains a significant factor. Table 4.4

Table 4.4 Class and confessional cleavages and voter preferences in the 1998-Bundestag elections (%)

	CDU/CSU	SPD	FDP	Greens	PDS	Others
Old Federal States						
Employment status						
Agricultural	75	10	09	02	01	03
Self-employed	46	22	17	10	01	04
Civil servant	41	37	07	11	02	02
White-collar employee	34	43	08	09	01	05
Manual worker	31	53	03	04	01	08
Religious affiliation						
Catholic	47	36	06	06	01	04
Protestant	32	48	08	07	01	04
No affiliation	22	47	07	13	04	07
New Federal States						
Employment status						
Agricultural	43	35	08	03	08	03
Self-employed	43	35	08	03	08	03
Civil servant	34	35	04	10	15	02
White-collar employee	24	35	04	07	25	05
Manual worker	27	39	03	02	17	22
Religious affiliation						
Catholic/ Protestant	42	38	–	–	08	12
No affiliation	18	41	–	–	26	15

Please note that because of the small *N* of eastern Catholics in the dataset, eastern Catholic and Protestant voters have been conflated. Similarly, the small *N* of eastern Green and FDP voters divided by religious orientation has meant that these voters have been conflated into the category 'others'.

Sources: Adapted from Gibowski, 1999; Weins, 1999.

demonstrates that, despite an election swing sufficiently big enough to unseat an incumbent coalition for the first time in the history of the Federal Republic, the CDU/CSU retained its advantage among Catholics, the self-employed and agricultural workers. This was mirrored by the SPD's advantage among manual workers and secular voters. But the raw figures do not illustrate the reinforcing effect on social cleavages of membership of auxiliary organisations such as church organisations and trades unions.

Paradoxically, the two cleavages impact on voting preferences in diametrically different ways. On the one hand, the religious cleavage retains a strong degree of leverage over partisan identification and being Catholic is the most powerful predictor of the likelihood of a voter supporting the CDU/CSU. Yet the slow secularisation of German society (and the CDU/CSU's relative success in adapting to this) means that membership of church organisations and/or regular church attendance are no longer crucial indicators of voting preference. On the other hand, while social class remains important it is not as strong a predictor as religious affiliation, especially when uncoupled from trade union membership, which remains a strong indicator of voter preference for the SPD over the CDU/CSU. Thus, both cleavages have become pacified to a certain extent by the processes of secularisation and social and economic modernisation. But at the same time, the atavism of the religious cleavage remains strong despite the decline in importance in auxiliary organisations; whereas the potency of the class cleavage has become increasingly dependent on its organisational expression through the trade union movement.

This latter point is demonstrated by Table 4.5, which sets out voting preferences in the old federal states in the 1990-, 1994- and 1998-Bundestag elections, according to trade union membership and employment status. The data includes white-collar employees and civil servants as well as manual workers and shows that both class and union membership act as independent variables on voting behaviour.

The relationship between social class and union membership is complex, and the two variables interact dynamically with each other. Social class retains some power as an indicator of voter preference. Among manual workers, support for the SPD was generally higher than for the CDU/CSU regardless of trade union membership. But there is an exception to this trend. In the 1990-elections, the CDU/CSU enjoyed a 10 per cent lead over the SPD among non-unionised manual workers, but lagged behind the SPD by 15 per cent among their unionised colleagues. The SPD regained its lead over the SPD in the 1994- and 1998-elections, but the margins remained much closer among non-unionised workers. Thus, in the 1998-elections the SPD enjoyed a 47 per cent advantage over the CDU/CSU among unionised workers, compared with 10 per cent among non-members. Similarly, the SPD's lead among unionised white-collar employees in the 1998-elections was 37 per cent, but only 4 per cent among non-unionised employees.

Table 4.5 Trade union membership and voting preference in the old federal states, 1990–98 Bundestag elections (%)

	Members			Non-members		
	1990	1994	1998	1990	1994	1998
All respondents						
CDU/CSU	33	32	23	51	45	40
SPD	49	52	60	28	31	39
FDP	09	03	03	15	10	08
Green	07	07	07	05	09	08
PDS	–	02	02	–	01	01
Manual workers						
CDU/CSU	37	29	19	49	41	36
SPD	52	58	66	39	42	46
FDP	05	01	02	04	04	04
Green	04	05	03	06	05	04
PDS	–	02	02	–	01	01
White-collar employees/ civil servants						
CDU/CSU	31	30	21	47	45	37
SPD	47	50	58	27	31	41
FDP	11	06	04	19	11	09
Green	08	09	11	04	09	09
PDS	–	02	02	–	01	01

Sources: Adapted from Forschungsgruppe Wahlen, 1990–94; Gibowski, 1999; data unavailable for PDS in 1990-elections.

In short, trade union membership is a crucial variable that acts in two ways. First, it amplifies the SPD's attempts to mobilise around the class cleavage and buttresses it against periods of short-term political disadvantage, such as the 1990-Bundestag elections. Second, it partially offsets the longer-term effects of partisan de-alignment that have taken place since the 1970s.

The second aspect confirmed by the 1998-Bundestag elections was that despite the slow convergence of what had effectively been two party systems in the old and new federal states, voting behaviour in the new federal states remained more volatile with little evidence that voters' preferences were grounded in stable social cleavages. This not only made it hard for political parties to anticipate and respond to the needs of eastern voters, but an additional difficulty in recruiting members meant that the structure and effectiveness of party organisations in the new federal states were less robust than in the west. This was particularly true of the SPD. Because of its previously poor performance in the new federal states, the SPD was painfully aware that its understanding of the eastern German voters' thinking was tenuous at best. SPD membership in the east was very low in both absolute terms and in terms of organisational density. As a result the party lacked the local intelligence that would be taken for granted in the old federal states, leading to concerns that elements of the party's campaigning that worked well in the west might be counter-productive in the east. As a result, the party set up a specialised 'eastern working group' (*Arbeitsgruppe Ost*) in the run-up to the 1998-elections, made up of party members who had grown up and been socialised into the eastern German political culture. The job of *Arbeitsgruppe Ost* was to tailor the party's national campaign to what remained a profoundly different political culture and weed out anything that easterners might consider to be parochial or irrelevant to their needs (Lees, 2000).

The need of all political parties to adapt their campaigns to conditions in the east raises interesting questions about the nature of cleavages in the new federal states and even the ability of cleavage theory to provide an adequate explanatory framework for analysing politics in the east. It has been argued that Lipset and Rokkan's assumption of underlying social cleavages in Western Europe is a normative one that is not always born out in 'young' democracies (see von Winter, 1996 for instance). At the very least, cleavage theory is only partially successful at explaining the formation of voter preferences in the new federal states (Weins, 1999: 49–50). On the other hand, the differences between the two parts of Germany noted above can be interpreted as symptomatic of a new centre/periphery cleavage made manifest by the nature of the GDR's collapse and the rapid assimilation of the new federal states into the Federal Republic. This view is found in the German politics literature. For instance, Hough regards the PDS as the 'visible representative of the cleavage between eastern and western *Länder*' (Hough, 2001: 184), whilst Niedermayer refers to 'the genesis of an intra-German centre/periphery cleavage between East and West Germany, now no longer separated by a wall of stone but by a wall in the mind' (Niedermayer, 1995: 88; see also Jeffery and Lees, 1998). The question remained whether this cleavage was manifest and permanent or would become pacified over time. However, the pragmatism of the CSU and the decline in salience of Bavarian particularism since the disbandment of the Bavarian Party in the 1950s provided a strong precedent for the successful assimilation of the 'eastern' political agenda in due course.

4.6   The 2002-Bundestag elections

The picture that emerged after 10 years of unification was of a cleavage structure that retained the same basic dynamics as that which existed in the old Federal Republic, but with the added complexity of an electorate in the new federal states characterised by lower levels of partisan identification and higher levels of electoral volatility. At the aggregate level, the two dominant social cleavages remained that of social class and religion, augmented by a small but significant centre/periphery cleavage arising from the terms and conditions of unification. With regard to the two main cleavages, religion remained a more reliable indicator of voter preferences than class, which did not fully explain the pattern of voter preferences among manual workers in the new federal states and seemed to be less salient in Germany as a whole when uncoupled from trade union membership (see Falter and Schoen, 1999; Gallagher *et al.*, 2001).

The September 2002-Bundestag elections provided political scientists and political sociologists with the first chance to map the impact of social cleavages on German party politics in the second decade after unification. Would the elections reinforce the patterns noted above, or would we see a return to the stability of the post-war years? At the time of writing not a great deal of academic analysis has yet been published and the picture will become clearer over time. Nevertheless, German polling institutes such as *Forschungsgruppe Wahlen* have produced some useful interim analyses of the trends revealed by the elections. Initial analysis of the 2002-Bundestag elections is enlightening because the SPD and CDU/CSU ended up in a dead heat (38.5 per cent each) in terms of their overall share of the popular vote. This means that the differentials of support for the two main parties across specific social groups are thrown into sharp focus.

Table 4.6 sets out the share of the vote for the main political parties, by employment and union membership. Using this and other data, the picture that emerges from initial analysis of voting behaviour in the 2002-Bundestag elections is fivefold: first, a continuing decline in the importance of social cleavages as a determinant of voting behaviour; second, the relative persistence of the religious cleavage as a factor in voting behaviour compared with the class cleavage; third, the importance of trade union membership in buffering the impact of the class cleavage on voting; fourth, the persistence of different patterns of cleavage-based politics in the new federal states; and finally, that despite these differences the salience of the center–periphery cleavage as a focus for political mobilisation is in decline.

Social cleavages remain an important determinant of voter preferences, but increasingly only within the confines of organised labour and religion (Schmidt, 2003: 154). On the one hand, Table 4.6 demonstrates that the confessional cleavage still patterns voting behaviour at the aggregate level. The CDU/CSU enjoyed a clear lead of 22 per cent over the SPD among Catholic voters and this clear skew towards the Christian Democrats also extended to the other parties (which all polled less than their average share of the vote among Catholics). Moreover, this advantage is extended to those Protestant voters who claim strong religious ties. On the other hand, 15.8 per cent of voters in the old federal states and 66.1 per cent in the new states claimed no religious affiliation. In this increasingly significant segment of the population the CDU/CSU faired relatively badly, polling 13.5 per cent less than the party's average share of the vote. By contrast, all of the CDU/CSU's political competitors polled more than their average share of the vote. The increasing

Table 4.6   2002-Bundestag elections. Vote share by employment and union membership (%)

| | Second vote 2002 | | | | | |
	SPD	CDU/CSU	Green	FDP	PDS	Other
Total	38.5	38.5	8.6	7.4	4.0	3.0
Employment status						
Working	37	38	10	08	04	03
Pensioner	40	44	04	06	05	02
Training	38	28	16	10	05	03
Unemployed	41	27	09	06	10	07
Employment category						
Blue-collar	44	37	04	07	04	04
White-collar	41	35	10	07	04	03
Professional	33	41	14	06	03	03
Self-employed	21	51	11	13	03	02
Agricultural	19	66	03	06	04	03
Trade union status						
Member	51	27	09	05	05	03
Non-member	36	41	09	08	04	03
Manual workers and trade union status						
Member	54	28	04	05	04	05
Non-member	40	41	04	07	05	04
White-collar employees and trade union status						
Member	56	20	11	05	07	02
Non-member	38	38	10	08	04	02
Religious affiliation						
Catholic	30	52	08	07	01	02
Protestant	44	36	08	08	02	03
No affiliation	40	25	11	08	11	05
Strength of religious affiliation						
Strong	18	70	05	05	00	02
Moderate	33	50	07	07	01	02
Weak or none	43	36	10	08	01	02

Source: Forschungsgruppe Wahlen, 2002.

self-placement of voters on the secular side of the religious cleavage is potentially a problem for the CDU/CSU, particularly in the new federal states. However, the main beneficiaries from voting differentials among secular voters in the 2002-elections was not the SPD, which polled just

1.5 per cent more than average, but rather the PDS and the Greens (polling 7 per cent and 2.4 per cent more respectively) (Forschungsgruppe Wahlen, 2003: 63).

In terms of the class cleavage, the reinforcing effect of trade union membership was more pronounced than ever. Among manual workers, the relatively poor showing for the FDP, PDS, and especially the Greens, demonstrates that the competitive pattern of political mobilisation around the class cleavage is primarily one between the SPD and CDU/CSU. Among unionised manual workers, the SPD enjoyed a clear lead of 26 per cent over the CDU/CSU, but lagged 1 per cent behind the CDU/CSU among non-unionised manual workers. In total, the SPD's share of the vote among manual workers dropped by around five per cent compared with the party's performance in 1998. By contrast, the CDU/CSU increased its share of the vote among manual workers by 8 per cent. Interestingly, the scale of SPD losses among manual workers was higher in the old federal states than in the new states. In the east, the SPD managed to increase its share of vote among manual workers, whilst in the west it lost 8 per cent (Forschungsgruppe Wahlen, 2002: 55). On the surface, the greater level of electoral volatility among manual workers in the west is counter-intuitive and flies in the face of the established patterns of electoral behaviour discussed earlier. However, it must be remembered that the SPD's support among manual workers in the new federal states was rising from an unusually low base in the 1990s, as manual workers continued to return to the 'natural political home' described by Padgett (1995: 87).

In contrast to the partisan de-alignment found among manual workers, the effect of trade union membership on voting preferences was one of ongoing concentration in favour of the SPD and the other left parties. As discussed above, the pattern of political competition for votes among manual workers was broadly a straight fight between the SPD and CDU/CSU, in which the SPD enjoyed a clear lead over the CDU/CSU among unionised workers. However, among the new middle class of white-collar employees the SPD's 36 per cent lead over the CDU/CSU was even larger than among unionised manual workers. This was 3 per cent higher than in 1998 and the best result recorded for the SPD since analysis of electoral preferences among this social group began. Similarly the Greens and PDS performed better among the unionised new middle class than their average for the country as a whole. Taken as a whole, the partisan preferences of the new middle class remained more heterogeneous than that of other social groups, despite evidence of a concentration of support among the unionised new middle class, which includes a large proportion of public sector employees and civil servants.

On the 'bourgeois' side of the class cleavage, the Greens also performed well among the non-unionised new middle class. This was consistent with the pattern identified and discussed earlier in the chapter. However, as already noted, the employment sector most obviously locked in a zero-sum game for resources with the organised working class is that of the self-employed (Pappi, 1984: 18–19). Here, the CDU/CSU and, most notably, the FDP performed especially well compared with the national average vote share for these parties. By contrast, the SPD received only a little more than half of the party's share of the vote in the country as a whole.

Finally, the increasing 'normalisation' of the social basis of voting in the new federal states and the poor performance of the PDS in the 2002-elections can be interpreted as evidence that the genuine grievances of the population in the new federal states are slowly being accommodated by the 'western' parties. Whether this means that the centre/periphery cleavage has been pacified is open to debate. Hough (2002) argues that such a cleavage exists but that there are four factors that determine the relative success or failure of attempts to mobilise around it. These are (1) culture, (2) socio-economic factors, (3) the qualities of political leadership and organisation, and (4) party policy. The precipitous collapse of support for the PDS in the run-up to the 2002-elections was more a result of deficiencies in party policy, leadership and organisation than evidence of a change in the political culture or the underlying socio-economic conditions that continue to divide the unified Germany. In other words, it is tempting to interpret the failure of the PDS as part of the ongoing normalisation of the German party system, but one would need to await the results of subsequent *Land*, European, and Bundestag elections to state this with any degree of confidence.

4.7 Summary

Chapter 4 builds on the historical account of social and political cleavages provided in previous chapters and examines the extent to which these cleavages persisted in the Federal Republic of Germany. The chapter gives an account of the re-emergence of political cleavages during the period of Allied occupation, 1945–49 and examines how these cleavages continued to stabilise and structure the party system during the first 20 years of the Federal Republic, 1949–69. This contrasts with the period 1969–90, leading up to the unification of Germany, which was characterised by profound social and economic change, including ongoing secularisation and embourgeoisement. These processes eroded the impact of established social cleavages, most notably the class cleavage, leading to greater electoral instability and partisan de-alignment. The impact of German unification in 1990 led to the 'grafting on' of a second party system, characterised by an electorate in the new federal states with an 'inverted social profile' of partisan identification. Over the 1990s, these differences were seen to moderate to a certain extent, but the 2002-Bundestag elections demonstrated that patterns of partisan identification in the old and new federal states still differed markedly. Nevertheless, at the aggregate level, the religious cleavage still exercised considerable leverage over voter preferences. By contrast, class location was a less reliable indicator of partisan identification, despite the buffering effect of trade union membership.

What is clear is that although cleavage theory is a powerful analytical tool, its heuristic value as a predictor of electoral preferences has reduced over time. Two conclusions can be drawn from this. On the one hand, Pappi's (1984) sophisticated log linear analysis of voter preferences indicates that a more complex relationship between social location and partisan identification has arisen because society itself has become more complex. As such, it is not so much that cleavage theory is over-deterministic and simplistic *per se*, but rather that the impact of economic and social modernisation requires us to develop more sophisticated research designs to get leverage on an increasingly complicated relationship between social location and voting. On the other hand, the 'revisionist school' discussed in Chapter 2 argues that party politics are – and probably always have been – more uncoupled from social location and more contingent on strategic decisions made by political elites (see Loewenberg, 1968; Converse and Valen, 1971; Berglund and Lindstrom, 1979). In 1987 Paterson observed that, despite the 'marked degree of stability due to the persistence of social cleavages ... electoral volatility has increased appreciably'. He went on to assert that in the light of such developments 'the relative weight one attaches to stability and volatility is very much at the centre of current debate' (Paterson, 1987: 160). Nearly two decades later, following the upheaval of unification as well as the ongoing processes of de-alignment described in this chapter, that debate is more relevant than ever. As discussed in the introduction to this book, the underlying position of the study is grounded in the idea of an agency-based political world, in which there is far less emphasis on impersonal social forces and far more on the variety of cognitive cues that influence individuals electoral preferences. It is to these more diverse models of value-orientation, partisan identification, and issue voting that the book now turns.

5
Partisan Identification, Value-Orientation and Economic Voting

5.1 Introduction

Chapter 5 cuts to the core of the idea of the voter as a sophisticated political customer with reasonably clear preferences. It examines three key concepts used widely in the study of voting behaviour (1) partisan identification; (2) value-orientation; and (3) economic voting. These concepts are used widely in studies of voting behaviour in the Federal Republic and were developed through the empirical and theoretical dialogue that took place between the 'political sociology', 'political psychology' and 'political economy' schools of behavioural research (Carmines and Huckfeldt, 1998: 223–4). As discussed in Chapter 2, most accounts of pre-1939 party systems on historical documents lent themselves to the adoption of the Lipset–Rokkan model. Lipset and Rokkan's work provided a heuristic framework that allowed researchers to concentrate on a handful of variables and construct powerful narratives of the development of party-political competition within the constraints of limited and often incomplete data (Clagget *et al.*, 1982: 644). By contrast, researchers of electoral behaviour today can access a far wider range and quantity of data, using some of the most developed technological and methodological tools in political science (Schultze, 1997: 603). As a result in the contemporary literature we find increasingly sophisticated models of voter choice that allow for more complex and potentially less deterministic accounts of the interaction between social structures and party politics. And crucially these models – either implicitly or explicitly – afford significantly more autonomy to the individual voter.

The genesis of all three behaviouralist approaches can be found in the expansion and professionalisation of American political science in the mid-twentieth Century. Taking advantage of the emergence of computing technology, researchers were able to construct large-*n* research designs and complex models of rationality in order to undertake the systematic study of electoral behaviour in a manner that had not been possible before. Moreover, this research began to span the divide between the 'academic' and the 'public', as many of these studies were sponsored by the US government with the aim of both gathering information on electorates and making the political process more responsive to popular preferences. The 'political sociology' school arose out of the ground-breaking study of the 1940-Presidential election (Lazarsfeld *et al.*, 1944) by academics at the Bureau of Applied Social Research at Columbia University. The 'political psychology' school was associated with the slightly later American National Election Study series carried out by Michigan University's Center for Survey Research, as well as the work of Campbell *et al.* (1960). Finally, the 'political economy' or rational choice tradition arose out of inter-disciplinary work carried out, amongst other places, at the University of Chicago and can be traced back to Downs' 'Economic Theory of Democracy' (1957). This latter school represented a significant extension of models associated with Economics into the discipline of Political Science.

The work of both the Columbia and Michigan schools are primarily data-driven and inductive in their reasoning. Thus, theories and models associated with both approaches arise from meticulous and highly calibrated empirical research. By contrast, economic approaches rely more on the hypothetico-deductive method, in which as much of the intellectual 'heavy lifting' is spent on the formulation of abstracted a priori models as on the operationalisation of these concepts. However, in recent years we have seen some degree of convergence between the three schools, around concepts such as the 'reasoning voter' (Pappi, 1998: 255)

The reasoning voter model is the paradigm of the dialogue between the three approaches. This dialogue is centred on the empirical problem recognised by all three schools: how voters make choices under conditions of uncertainty. Sociological explanations tend to stress the 'expressive' nature of voting, in which voters choices reflect value-systems acquired through socialisation into families, social groups and milieus (Miller, 1956; Key and Munger, 1959; Inglehardt, 1990). The subsequent complex mesh of values and social cues provides the individual with a political 'narrative' that enables her to make a choice without the costs of processing and evaluating all of the available political information. Psychological explanations accept the role of networks and groups but also stress the cognitive impact on the individual of the news media, as well as time, place, and circumstance on voter choice (Bobo, 1983; Iyengar, 1991; Glaser, 1994). Finally, traditional Economics-based explanations emphasise the idea of the voter either as a consumer, willing to take the time to weigh-up and evaluate party positions, or as a somewhat paradoxical figure taking part in a relatively costly activity (bothering to vote) with little or no marginal utility (affecting the outcome of the vote) (Downs, 1957; Olson, 1965; Fiorina, 1990; Aldrich, 1993). As a response to these differing accounts, the reasoning voter model combines elements of psychological research with a somewhat relaxed set of assumptions about the rationality of voters, under conditions of 'limited information and processing capacity' (Sniderman *et al.*, 1991: 18). The model rejects the idea of voters as 'cultural dupes', arguing that voters 'actually do reason about parties, candidates, and issues' (Popkin, 1991: 7). Thus it is very much in line with underlying assumptions of this study.

An exposition of the strengths and weaknesses of the three approaches is beyond the scope of the book. Instead, the three concepts examined in the chapter cross-cut one or more of the approaches and provide alternative perspectives on the empirical study of voting behaviour in Germany. The rest of the chapter is divided into four sections: first, an examination of the idea of partisan identification and the account it provides of support for political parties over time; second, an analysis of the concept of value-orientation and value-change as the basic building-blocks of political location and choice; third, an assessment of the economic voting literature both as a critique of the psychological and sociological approaches and also as a framework for empirical research; and finally, a summary of the chapter's findings.

5.2   Partisan identification

The concept of partisan identification was developed through the Michigan School's socio-psychological studies of electoral behaviour in the United States, which took place from the 1950s onwards. As a result, the concept's inductive base is clearly grounded in the specific conditions of US politics. Four aspects of this are of note; first, the existence of a Presidential rather than Parliamentary form of government; second, a two-party system of political competition characterised by relatively loose party organisation, low levels of party discipline and organisational density, and candidate selection through open primary elections; third, a strong territorial dimension of politics mediated through the US's federal system; and finally, the absence of a strong class cleavage and the subsequent under-developed pattern of trade union organisation. The impact of these four factors is such that while ideology certainly does play a part in political competition (Budge *et al.*, 2001: 24–5), its expression through formal party structures is often diffused and cross-cut by personality, local loyalties and single-issue politics. Because of this, the concept of partisan identification as originally conceived in the US context does not map neatly onto actual voting behaviour/intention. This has led to doubts being raised about the applicability of the concept in West European systems. For instance, Thomassen (1976) argues that the role of socio-structural cleavages and ideology in Europe renders partisanship indistinguishable from voting intention. In the case of Germany, there is an additional debate about the appropriateness of measures and instruments that may or may not be functionally equivalent to those used in the Michigan studies (Weisberg, 1999: 725).

The key conceptual device associated with the Michigan studies is that of the 'funnel of causality', describing the interaction between social and

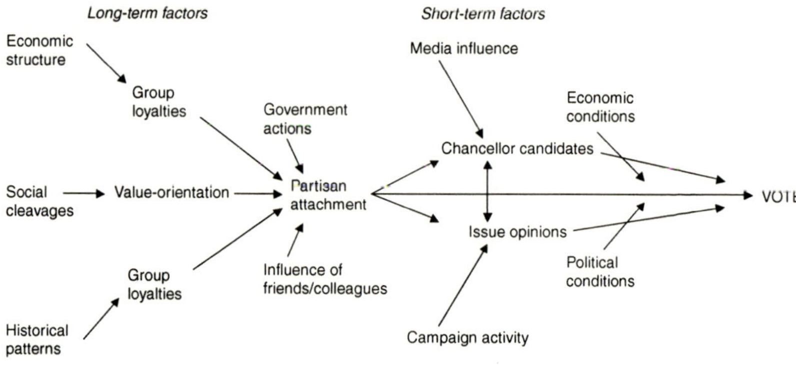

Figure 5.1   The Michigan model 'funnel of causality' of partisan identification applied to Germany

psychological influences on voting (Campbell *et al.*, 1966, 1960). Figure 5.1 demonstrates the funnel of causality applied to political conditions in the Federal Republic. At the wide end of the funnel we find the long-term socio-economic structures and conditions such as economic structure, class and religious cleavages, and other historical alignments. These are the preconditions that generate the basic patterns of political conflict that underpin party competition in advanced democracies and go some way to shape individuals' group loyalties and value-orientations. Group loyalties include class, religious, ethnic, and kinship affiliations, whilst value-orientations might include an individual's position along the left-right, economic-noneconomic, libertarian-authoritarian, and materialist-post-materialist dimensions (Ingelhart, 1981, 1990; Flanagan, 1982, 1987). In turn, group loyalties and value-orientations interact with each other, and with medium-term variables such as government actions and the influence of friends and work colleagues, in such a way as to shape the individual's partisan attachment. This partisan attachment is further mediated through the individual's own assessment of campaign issues and the performance of the various Chancellor candidates. These assessments are arrived at in part through the campaign activity of the political parties as well as the influence of the media. Finally, the impact of the political and economic conditions of the day also plays a part in the individual's ultimate decision of what party to vote for (or whether to vote at all).

As Dalton observes, the funnel of causality 'represented a major conceptual breakthrough for voting research' (1996: 198). Moreover, it covered a range of causal variables spanning from long-term macro-level factors through to the more contingent micro-level influences of an individual's immediate social and work environment. Despite reservations about its applicability in other advanced democracies, the funnel of causality as a model has considerable heuristic value and predictive power. It also problematises the relative impact of the 'private' (family, friends, colleagues and life-cycle events) and 'public' (media effects, chancellor candidates and issue opinions) domains in the formation of an individual's vote choice. Let us consider both domains in turn.

The 'private' domain (family, friends, colleagues and life-cycle events)

Within the private domain, the key institution is the family – in particular the influence of parents and, to a lesser extent, spouses. Parental impact on the individual's belief systems in her early years makes the family the cradle of party attachment. Table 5.1 compares the transmission of parental partisanship in the United States, Great Britain and West Germany, using data from the 'political action survey' carried out by Sam Barnes, Max Kaase and colleagues in the late 1970s (see Barnes *et al.*, 1979; also Dalton, 1996).

The political action survey data found high levels of partisan agreement in German families, in which parents' party preferences were often seen to be recreated in their offspring. It is noticeable that this effect is stronger with FDP-supporting parents (in which parents partisan preference is recreated in 59 per cent of offspring) and those that support the SPD (in which preferences are recreated in 53 per cent of the offspring) than with CDU/CSU-supporting parents (32 per cent). Interestingly, however, CDU-supporting parents still appear to have had a strong negative influence on their offspring's partisan preferences in that the biggest single category for the children of CDU/CSU-supporting parents is that of no partisan preference (53 per cent) rather than support for the rival SPD or FDP.

How does this pattern compare with other advanced democracies? The data demonstrates that Germany is not unusual and parental influence is strong in all three countries, with one or two interesting outliers. For instance, in the same manner that FDP-supporting parents in Germany seemed to have a particularly strong effect on their children's partisan attachments (with 59 per cent supporting the FDP as well), Democrat-supporting parents in the United States appeared to be even more successful in inculcating the same attachments in their children, 70 per cent of whom also reported support for the Democrats. By contrast, the figures for Great Britain show no significant outliers. In all three countries, the data demonstrates that the negative effects of parental attachments on their children are stronger on the centre-left of the political spectrum. Thus, the children of parents who support the Democrats, Labour Party, or SPD are less likely to support the Republicans, Conservatives, or CDU/CSU than children of parents who support the Republicans, Conservatives, or CDU/CSU are likely to support the Democrats, Labour Party, or SPD. However, this pattern was weakest in Germany. Nevertheless, the mean of non-partisan children in Germany (46.5 per cent) is a little higher than in Great Britain (41.3 per cent), and both

Table 5.1   Transmission of parental partisanship (%)

(a) United States

Child's party preference	Parental party preference		
	Democrat	Republican	Independent
Democrat	70	25	40
Republican	10	54	20
Independent	20	21	40
Total	100	100	100
N	28	77	30

(b) Great Britain

Child's party preference	Parental party preference			
	Labour	Liberal	Conservative	None
Labour	51	17	06	29
Liberal	08	39	11	06
Conservative	01	11	50	06
None	40	33	33	59
Total	100	100	100	100
N	83	18	54	17

(c) West Germany

Child's party preference	Parental party preference			
	SPD	FDP	CDU/CSU	None
SPD	53	08	14	19
FDP	04	59	01	03
CDU/CSU	09	–	32	12
None	34	33	53	66
Total	100	100	100	100
N	68	12	78	67

Source: Table adapted from Dalton, 1996: 201.

the German and British means are nearly double that of the United States (27 per cent). So in this run of data it is the United States that is the outlier rather than Germany.

Barnes and Kaase's study demonstrates that basic partisanship is learned relatively early in life and becomes more entrenched over time, through the reaffirming of political beliefs in the course of regular voting and other partisan activities. The exception to this rule is when life-cycle events break up this ongoing intensification of party loyalty. Drawing on the sociological and demographic literature, 'event history analysis' is used to examine the impact of these life-cycle events (Yamaguchi, 1991; Allison, 1992). On the whole, the most important life-cycle events that impact upon voting behaviour are (1) mobility over time in terms of an individual's educational, occupational, or class location, as well as (2) more discrete events or 'episodes' such as marriage, divorce, a change of jobs, or a geographical change of location (Tuma and Mayer, 1990; Diekmann and Weick, 1993). Analyses of such episodes highlight the impact that specific aspects of an individual's private social world have on voting choice. For instance, access to higher education protects an individual's partisan attachment (Schmitt-Beck *et al.*, 2002: 22), whilst the partisan composition of her neighbourhood (MacKuen and Brown, 1987), and the ideology of colleagues (Schmitt-Beck *et al.*, 2002), close friends, partners and spouses (Kenny, 1994) also have a strong impact. Interestingly, when such research was carried out in the 1960s, the effect of a partner or spouses' ideology appeared to be particularly strong on women, who often 'adjusted' their beliefs to those of their partners (Lazarsfeld *et al.*, 1968: 145). It is probably safe to assume that this gendered effect has moderated markedly over the last forty years.

Life-cycle events are generally private affairs, specific to each individual albeit conforming to broader patterns in terms of the nature of their impact on individual vote choice. However there are instances in which a specific life-cycle episode is *so* common within a section of the population as to transcend the private domain and become part of the public. In the context of Germany, two such episodes have shaped mass electoral preferences. The first, and most significant, instance was the impact of National Socialism, the Second World War and the subsequent defeat of Germany on the older generational cohorts. Weak socialisation into democratic values, combined with a retreat into the private world following the Second World War meant that up until the 1980s Germany did not conform to the general pattern by which partisanship increases with age (Baker *et al.*, 1981; Dalton, 1996). This age cleavage no longer exists but appears to have been replaced by a territorial one, in which research indicates that residents in the new Federal states of the former East Germany display lower levels of partisan identification than their counterparts in the old Federal states. Nevertheless, even studies that register high levels of electoral volatility and weak partisan ties in the East do not argue that there are no patterns of partisanship at all (see Rattinger, 1995, 2000). On the contrary there is evidence that a form of 'virtual partisanship' existed in the GDR before 1989, based on citizens' exposure to the West German media (Kaase and Klingemann, 1994).

Kaase and Klingemann's findings point to the role of the other more 'public' set of variables that impact on vote choice, in particular the role of the media in shaping individuals' perceptions of both chancellor candidates and the issues around which candidates and their parties mobilise. It has long been accepted that the mass media are agenda-setters in the widest sense of the word (Iyengar and Reeves, 1997). For instance, part of the explanation for the lower levels of political salience surrounding the issue of European integration in Germany compared with the United Kingdom is the pattern of media ownership in the two countries and the more compliant media approach to the issue that can be seen in Germany (Lees, 2002). However, there is now a growing body of research that indicates that the media does not just set the tone of political debate but actually has a direct effect on voter choice (Bartels, 1993; Curtice and Semetko, 1994; Curtice, 1997). This had been known for some time and will be discussed at greater length in the next segment of the chapter. What is important to note at this point is that, although the original Michigan studies acknowledged the impact of the media on voter choice, this was offset by the 'filter effect' of partisanship, ideology and group identity (Berelson *et al.*, 1954; Campbell *et al.*, 1960). More recent psycho-social studies have confirmed that personal networks serve as a validator of media messages (Merten, 1994). However, this filter effect is undermined by the kind of social change that all advanced democracies have experienced over the last half century. Where individuals' personal networks remain relatively homogeneous they serve as anchors to partisan attachment, block out discordant media messages and re-enforce those that conform to individuals' existing worldview. However, in a more complex world with higher levels of social, occupational, and geographical mobility this anchor function is eroded and the media's influence becomes more potent. This does not just reduce the impact of partisanship on vote choice but has the potential to undermine partisanship itself, by constraining the opportunities by which partisan identification is re-enforced during an individual's lifetime and weakening the socialisation process by which such attachments are passed on to subsequent generations.

Table 5.2 examines the complex relationships between individual's personal networks, partisan identification and vote choice, using Comparative National Elections Project (CNEP) research data generated in Germany, Britain, Spain and the United States (Schmitt-Beck, 2003). The data clearly establishes that there is a relationship between individual voters' partisanship and the political composition of their personal networks.

Looking at the German data, two points are of note. First, individuals with partisan attachments are much less likely to report having politically neutral networks (12.3 per cent) compared with political independents (28.1 per cent). This in itself does not necessarily mean that partisans and independents actually have different types of networks, but does indicate that partisan respondents are more prone to recognise and report partisanship in others. The second point, however, is that these partisans actually do appear to have different types of networks to independents. In particular, partisans are much more likely to have homogeneous networks (44.3 per cent) compared with independents (28.1). However, within this group, the vast majority (38.3 per cent) of partisans have networks made up of fellow 'inparty'

Table 5.2 Political composition of individuals' personal networks by voters' partisanship (%)

	Britain		Spain		United States		West Germany	
	Party ID	**Indep.**	**Party ID**	**Indep.**	**Party ID**	**Indep.**	**Party ID**	**Indep.**
No discussants	32.9	54.2	14.9	24.0	06.3	07.4	22.0	21.7
Neutral networks	02.3	12.5	13.8	23.7	02.1	07.0	12.3	28.1
Homogeneous networks	(44.0)	(23.1)	(59.4)	(44.7)	(45.0)	(45.0)	(44.3)	(28.1)
Inparty	34.3		50.0		37.2		38.3	
Outparty	05.7		09.4		07.8		06.0	
Heterogeneous networks	(24.7)	(10.1)	(11.7)	(07.6)	(46.7)	(40.6)	(21.3)	(22.0)
Inparty included	22.2		10.6		43.6		19.5	
Outparty only	2.5		01.1		03.1		01.8	
Total	99.9	99.9	99.8	100.0	100.1	100.0	99.9	99.9
(*N*)	(2292)	(247)	(434)	(843)	(810)	(500)	(819)	(277)

Note: Total percentage diverges slightly from 100.0 because of rounding up/down.

Source: adapted from Schmitt-Beck, 2003: 246.

partisans (in other words, supporters of the same party). By contrast, only 6 per cent report that they have homogeneous networks dominated by partisans of another party. In a similar vein, roughly the same amount of partisans (21.3 per cent) as independents (22 per cent) reported heterogeneous networks but of these the vast majority (19.5 per cent) reported some degree of inparty inclusion in the network. Taken in the round, the German data reinforces the discussion above about the importance of the relationship between private networks, partisan identification and actual vote choice.

When we compare the German data with data from the other three countries in the study, it is apparent that the patterns found across the four countries are not identical, raising four points worthy of note. First, although in all four countries individuals with partisan attachments are less likely to report politically neutral networks than political independents, this effect is particularly pronounced in West Germany. As already noted, only 12.3 per cent of West German partisans reported neutral networks compared with 28.1 per cent of political independents. This is a difference of 15.8 per cent between the two groups and is relatively large compared with a small difference of 4.8 per cent in the United States and moderate differences of 10.2 per cent in Britain, and 9.9 per cent in Spain.

Second, in West Germany and Britain partisans are more likely than independents to report homogeneous networks than in Spain and, most notably, United States. The difference is largest in Britain (20.9 per cent), slightly smaller in West Germany (18.2 per cent), significantly less in Spain (14.7 per cent) and non-existent in the United States. At first glance, the US findings would appear to contradict the assumption that homogeneous networks tend to buttress strong partisan ties. However, what it actually does is highlight some of problems of applying the partisan ID model to political systems outside the United States, and in particular finding appropriate measures and instruments that allow for functional equivalence across cases (see Weisberg, 1999). In the US case, a combination of pre-election primaries, the weak party system, and the practice of election to explicitly non-partisan public posts (such as District Attorney) means that voters quite often self-report as 'independents' for electoral registration purposes. Thus, the category of independent is arguably 'stronger' or more 'positive' than the equivalent categories in Britain, Spain and West Germany. Because partisan attachment and vote choice is almost identical in European countries, the category of independent tends to be a 'negative' one – made up predominantly (although not exclusively) of voters with relatively weak political, as well as partisan, preferences. By contrast, many US independents have very strong political preferences, albeit ones that do not map neatly on to the US' weak party system. Thus independence is often a positive predisposition with similar dynamics to partisanship and, thus, can be buttressed by homogeneous networks in the same manner.

Third, partisans in all four countries were far more likely to report homogeneous networks made up of 'inparty' partisans (supporters of the same party), but again there were differences between them. Spanish partisans were significantly more likely to report inparty networks, with a difference of 41.6 per cent between inparty and outparty networks. By contrast, this effect was less evident in West Germany (32.3 per cent), the United States (28.6) and Britain (28.6 per cent). Nevertheless, these findings reinforce the assumptions about the buttressing effects of networks of like-minded individuals on respondents' political choice.

Finally, although in West Germany roughly the same amount of partisans (21.3 per cent) as independents (22 per cent) reported heterogeneous networks, this was not the case in the other three countries. Significantly more partisans than independents reported heterogeneous networks in Spain and Britain, with differences of 14.7 per cent and 14.6 per cent respectively. In the United States this difference was much smaller, at just 6.1 per cent. However, this apparently counter-intuitive finding is made more comprehensible by the fact the vast majority of partisans who did report heterogeneous networks also reported some degree of inparty influence within those networks. The differential between reported heterogeneous networks with inparty influence and such networks with only outparty influence is roughly ten-to-one in all four cases. Again, this is consistent with the assumptions discussed above.

All-in-all the data for the four countries confirms the importance of the relationship between private networks, partisan identification and actual vote choice. Moreover, it seems to place West Germany very much inside what we can call the 'normal distribution' within the group of four countries. German partisans are comparatively less likely to report neutral networks, a little more likely to report homogeneous networks, and no more likely to report homogeneous networks dominated by inparty influence. The one exception is the equal numbers of partisans and independents reporting heterogeneous networks but, as discussed, the more significant finding is the clear preponderance of inparty influence within these networks compared with outparty influence.

The 'public' domain (media effects, chancellor candidates and issue opinions)

Despite the buttressing effect of private networks, the private world must compete with that of the public, in particular the mass media. Over the last century, technical progress in the mass media has changed the respective roles of parties and candidates as personalities and the way in which voters are exposed to political information. Broadly speaking, this process has had three stages. Stage one saw the reporting of politics concentrated in the print media. Voters gained access to information and campaign messages directly through party publications, newspaper advertisements and billboards, and indirectly through newspaper coverage of the political process. The 'raw material' of this process was made up of public meetings and whistle-stop tours, and the role of the party in this process (through local party organisations, and canvassers reinforcing the party message) was paramount. Stage two coincided with the advent of television and saw a shift away from the print media as a source of direct party propaganda. Voters were still exposed to indirect messages in the print media, but the direct messages became increasingly concentrated within the television media. With these changes came an emphasis on television debates, press conferences, and other telegenic events, co-ordinated less by local party organisations and far more by centralised party salariats. Finally, stage three is characterised by the rise of the 'new media' – such as mobile telecommunications and the growth of the internet – in which voters are increasingly exposed to party messages directly through mailshots, videomail, and cable television (in addition to direct and indirect messages through the established television channels). Although these developments have led to a decentralisation of operations back to local parties, the co-ordination of party activities across the old and new media is increasingly carried out by the leader's office (Farrell and Webb, 2002: 102–5). These developments are discussed at greater length in Chapter 8.

The concentration of co-ordinating capacity in the leader's office is matched by a similar move towards what has been called 'candidate-centred politics' (Dalton *et al.*, 2002: 49). This process has been most pronounced in the United States but has also taken place in Germany. There are interlinked reasons for this. First, the decline in partisan attachments has led to a loss of purchase of the traditional left-right ideological discourse on the average voter. Second, the process of social pluralisation and growth of individualism (Beck, 1986) has shifted popular discourse away from collective action and endeavour. Third, the subsequent increase in instrumental performance-based voting and, as a result, the increasing focus on competence and perceptions of candidates. Fourth, the decline of the mass party model of politics, which has led to a reduction in the number and density of mediating institutions between political elites and individual voters. Finally, the format of mainstream television and the print media, which tends to discount complex arguments in favour of candidates as personalities.

Table 5.3 demonstrates the relative effects of the media on vote choice. The table shows the results of logit regression analysis of the structural ('political predispositions'), public ('media exposure'), and private ('personal communication') variables – identified in the Michigan model's funnel of causality – against the dependent variable 'vote choice' in Germany. For reasons of clarity and simplicity the latter is restricted to support either the CDU/CSU or SPD. What is clear from the table is that regardless of socio-economic location, ideology or partisanship, 'exposure to the media increased or diminished the inclination of voters to elect particular parties or candidates' (Schmitt-Beck, 2003: 247). Moreover, the data indicates that the impact of the media on vote choice is not primarily restricted to television. The one clear instance in which watching television skews vote choice is with regard to watching the private broadcaster SAT 1, which seemed to have a strong negative impact on voter perceptions of the SPD (−0.18). Elsewhere, the slight positive effect of watching the news on the state broadcaster ARD on support for both *Volksparteien* (0.03) seems to reflect the impact that regular news coverage – and thus familiarity – have on voting intentions. By contrast, the impact of reading certain news magazines and newspapers on vote choice is marked. For instance, reading a rightist or leftist quality newspaper clearly has a positive impact on support for the CDU/CSU or SPD respectively. Similarly, reading a local or regional daily newspaper has a relatively strong positive effect (0.11) on voting CDU/CSU, whilst reading a news magazine seemed to have a negative effect on votes for both parties but particularly the CDU/CSU (−0.43).

The data in Table 5.3 demonstrate that patterns of media consumption has a reasonably strong relationship with vote choice, at least in terms of a postulated binary choice between the two catch-all parties. Nevertheless, the table also shows that the strength and direction of the relationship between media influence and vote choice is nowhere as strong and clear as that between, say, union membership and SPD votes (0.76) or Catholicism and CDU/CSU votes (0.49). Thus, the 'traditional' class and religious cleavages continue to fundamentally pattern political competition in Germany. Moreover the impact of personal discussant networks is without doubt the strongest single independent variable acting on vote choice for both the CDU/CSU (0.87) and

Table 5.3 Effects of political predispositions, media exposure and personal communication on vote choice in West Germany (Logit Estimates)

Choice	CDU/CSU	SPD
Constant	−2.48 (0.84)***	1.10 (0.74)
Political predispositions		
Old middle class	−0.43 (0.61)	−1.06 (0.66)
New middle class	−0.08 (0.46)	−0.36 (0.41)
Working class	−0.75 (0.50)	−0.28 (0.45)
Union membership	−0.35 (0.28)	0.76 (0.26)***
Catholic	0.49 (0.40)	0.04 (0.39)
Protestant	−0.01 (0.40)	0.54 (0.37)
Ideological identification	0.38 (0.09)***	−0.44 (0.09)***
Post-materialism	−0.50 (0.37)	−0.04 (0.34)
Materialism	−0.54 (0.30)*	0.11 (0.32)
Identification with this party	2.32 (0.32)***	1.73 (0.31)***
Identification with any other party	−1.88 (0.34)***	−2.50 (0.38)***
Media exposure		
Reading a rightist quality newspaper	0.11 (0.13)	−0.03 (0.17)
Reading a leftist quality newspaper	0.03 (0.14)	0.19 (0.09)***
Reading *Bild*	0.11 (0.06)*	0.12 (0.07)*
Reading tabloid other than *Bild*	0.10 (0.12)	0.23 (0.12)*
Reading a local or regional daily newspaper	0.11 (0.04)**	0.03 (0.05)
Reading a news magazine	−0.43 (0.10)***	−0.26 (0.10)**
Watching news on ARD	0.03 (0.05)	0.03 (0.05)
Watching news on ZDF	−0.03 (0.05)	0.05 (0.05)
Watching news on RTL+	0.06 (0.09)	0.03 (0.09)
Watching news on SAT1	−0.05 (0.09)	−0.18 (0.10)*
Watching magazines on ARD and ZDF	−0.03 (0.03)	−0.03 (0.03)
Personal communication		
Discussant network	0.87 (0.72)	1.98 (0.38)***
News on ARD* discussant network	0.20 (0.12)*	
Nagelkerke's R2		
Predispositions	0.69	0.69
Increase for media and discussants	0.06	0.05
N	802	802

Notes: Standard errors are in parentheses. Significance levels: * $p < 0.10$; ** $p < 0.05$; *** $p < 0.01$.

Source: Schmitt-Beck, 2003: 250.

SPD (1.98). Again, this supports the assumption discussed above that personal networks act as a filter on political messages in which political predispositions are reinforced and discordant messages are often discarded. In other words, private networks provide a countervailing influence to that of the public domain.

So far we have concentrated on a reasonably direct relationship between socio-economic location, private networks and the public domain on vote choice. However, the funnel of causality posits a more complex relationship that also includes (1) voters' perceptions of the performance and competence of candidates, as well as (2) their own positions on particular political issues, (3) their perceptions of the past and future performance of incumbent and potential governments, and (4) the actual political and economic conditions that prevail at the time of voting. Of these, point (2) is dealt with later in the chapter in the section on value-orientation, whilst (3) and (4) is examined in the section on economic voting. So let us now examine the first point: the impact of voters' perceptions of the performance and competence of candidates.

Table 5.4 examines the changing relationship between partisan identification, issues, and perceptions of candidates and vote choice in Germany, with an emphasis on perceptions of competence and candidate preferences. The table plots the development of these relationships over time in the old Federal states, using data from the 1972-, 1983-, and 1990-Bundestag elections. The data demonstrates that in instances in which partisans registered positive feelings of identification for 'their' party, combined with positive perceptions of party competence and party candidates, the estimated likelihood of these individuals voting for their party was over 90 per cent and in some instances was as high as 99 per cent. However, the table also

Table 5.4 Development of the influence of partisan identification, issues and perceptions of candidates on vote choice in the old Federal states, 1972–90

| | 1972 | | 1983 | | 1990 | |
Choice	CDU/ CSU	SPD	CDU/ CSU	SPD	CSU/ CSU	SPD
Partisan ID+	0.91	0.93	0.94	0.95	0.96	0.95
Perception of competence+	0.98	0.95	0.95	0.99	0.97	0.96
Preference for candidate+	0.98	0.95	0.96	0.99	0.97	0.96
Partisan ID−	0.36	0.50	0.41	0.37	0.30	0.47
Perception of competence+	0.67	0.84	0.77	0.77	0.70	0.77
Preference for candidate+	0.89	0.89	0.90	0.78	0.79	0.81
Partisan ID−	0.36	0.50	0.41	0.37	0.30	0.47
Perception of competence−	0.30	0.44	0.20	0.39	0.21	0.38
Preference for candidate+	*	0.63	0.45	0.58	0.40	0.53
R2	0.79	0.72	0.80	0.78	0.80	0.75

Note: * denotes an *n* smaller than 20.

Source: Table adapted from Gabriel, 1997: 247.

demonstrates that issues and candidates also exercise a strong influence on individual's vote choice in the absence of positive partisan feelings. In particular, positive perceptions of competence have a strong positive relationship with individuals' vote choice, with the estimated likelihood of voting for a particular party rising by anything up to 40 per cent (for the SPD in 1983). By contrast, negative perceptions in no-partisans depress the estimated likelihood of voting by anything up to 21 per cent (the CDU/CSU in 1983). In a similar vein, candidate preferences alone increased the likelihood of voting for a particular party by up to 25 per cent (the CDU in 1983).

So, again, how does the German data compare with that found in other advanced industrial democracies? Table 5.5 presents data on voting behaviour by party and candidate preference in Germany, the United States, France, Canada and Australia. As in the previous table, the data is restricted to votes for the two major parties in each party system at the time of the election. Three points are of note. First, as would be expected, voters with consistent candidate and party preferences are highly likely to vote for their

Table 5.5 Voting behaviour for two major parties by patterns of party and candidate preferences (%)

	USA 1980–96	France 1988	Canada 1974–79	Canada 1988–93	Germany 1972–87	Germany 1990–98	Austria 1993–98
% voting with candidate preference							
Consistent candidate and party preference	97	99	96	89	98	97	98
Prefer a candidate/no party preference	89	83	78	68	59	75	70
Inconsistent candidate and party preference	77	84	32	39	15	37	24
% voting with party preference							
Prefer a party/no candidate preference	79	73	80	79	93	75	93

Source: Adapted from Dalton *et al.*, 2002: 52.

party candidate of preference (within a range of 89 per cent to 99 per cent). Second, if voters are presented with a decisional dilemma in which they either prefer a candidate but have no party preference or vice versa, there are two clear patterns of voter behaviour. On the one hand, voters in the United States and France are more likely to vote for a preferred candidate when indifferent to party (89 per cent and 83 per cent respectively) than they are to vote for a preferred party when indifferent to the candidates (79 per cent and 73 per cent). On the other hand, voters in Germany, Australia and, to a certain extent, Canada are more likely to vote for a preferred party when indifferent to all candidates (within a range of 75 to 93 per cent) than they are to vote for a preferred candidate when indifferent to party (59 to 78 per cent). This pattern makes sense when we consider that the United States and France are Presidential systems that are by definition relatively candidate-centred, whereas Germany, Canada and Australia are parliamentary systems that are relatively party-centred. Third, however, this effect is not as marked in the more recent data for the unified Germany. In the 'old' West Germany, voters indifferent to candidates were clearly more likely to vote for a preferred party (93 per cent) than vice versa (59 per cent). However, in the period after unification (1990–98) this effect has completely disappeared.

The conclusion that parties must draw from the data in Tables 5.4 and 5.5 is that not only must they get the issues right in election campaigns but must field the right candidates as well, as in a close-run election a strong candidate will make the difference between victory and defeat.

This stark electoral logic is even more notable in the new Federal states, where settled patterns of partisanship are much weaker than in the 'old' Federal Republic. Table 5.6 examines the influence of partisan identification, issues and perceptions of candidates on vote choice in the old and new Federal states, using data from the 1994-Bundestag elections. Three points are of note. First, taken in the round the data indicates that the cumulative impact of positive party identification, perceptions of competence and candidate preference has remained relatively stable since the early 1970s. In both eastern and western Germany, when all three variables load positively the likelihood of an individual voting for 'their' party is almost 100 per cent. Second, in 1994 the relative impact of perceptions of competence and candidate preference was greater in the new Federal states. For instance, strong positive perceptions of competence raised the likelihood of voting for a particular party to 74 per cent in the old states compared with up to 86 per cent in the new states (for the CDU/CSU). In addition, when this was complemented by strong preferences for a party's candidate then the likelihood in the east rose to 96 per cent (for the CDU/CSU). Moreover, even on its own a strong candidate preference raised the probability of voting for a particular party to 75 per cent (again, for the CDU/CSU). Finally, these figures demonstrate the third point, that the impact of perceptions of competence and candidate preferences has an asymmetric impact on support for the two parties

Table 5.6 1994-Bundestag elections. Influence of partisan identification, issues and perceptions of candidates on vote choice in the old and new Federal states

Choice	Old Federal states		New Federal states	
	CDU/CSU	SPD	CDU/CSU	SPD
Partisan ID+	0.95	0.92	0.95	0.91
Perception of competence+	0.97	0.95	0.97	0.94
Preference for candidate+	0.98	0.95	0.97	0.95
Partisan ID−	0.32	0.35	0.36	0.40
Perception of competence+	0.74	0.74	0.86	0.83
Preference for candidate+	0.87	0.78	0.96	0.86
Partisan ID−	0.32	0.35	0.36	0.40
Perception of competence−	0.25	0.24	0.28	0.36
Preference for candidate+	0.70	0.43	0.75	0.62
R2	0.80	0.69	0.77	0.63

Source: Table adapted from Gabriel, 1997: 249.

in the new Federal states. In particular, a strong candidate preference loaded disproportionately on to the CDU/CSU vote (75 per cent) compared with that for the SPD (62 per cent). Thus, in 1994 the SPD's electoral campaign in the new Federal states was not only hampered by a lack of partisan ties but also from the fact that the party did not benefit from positive perceptions of competence or candidate preferences to the same extent as the CDU/CSU.

Given the impact of candidate perceptions noted above, it is perhaps not surprising that the major political parties have adapted to the increasing personalisation of party competition, particularly in Bundestag election campaigns. For instance, in the 1994-elections the CDU/CSU devoted almost 10 per cent of the parties' entire election budget to Helmut Kohl's speech-delivering campaign (Boll, 1995: 138). At the same time, the major parties have increasingly turned to television and radio spots on private broadcasters such as SAT1 and RTL+, leading to a further emphasis on personalities over issues. This trend continued in the 1998-elections, although the state-owned ARD and ZDF did try and concentrate more on substantive issues compared with the private broadcasters (Semetko and Schoenbach, 1999: 86). By the 2002-elections even the Greens had overcome their traditional aversion to personalisation and campaigned under the slogan 'the second vote is a Joschka vote' (*Zweitstimme ist Joschkastimme*), hoping to profit from the high visibility and popularity of Joschka Fischer. At the same time, Gerhard Schröder sought to exploit his own popularity by portraying the election as a straight fight between him and the CDU/CSU's chancellor candidate Edmund Stoiber. As Table 5.7 demonstrates, this was a shrewd move on the part of Schröder who – despite the relative unpopularity of the SPD

Table 5.7   2002-Bundestag elections. Public perceptions of candidates and their competences (%)

		Schröder	Stoiber	No difference
Q. Who can best …	(1) Create jobs	18	33	43
	(2) Solve economic problems	24	33	37
Q. Who can best …	(1) Solve future problems	34	26	33
	(2) Represent German interests	52	21	21
	(3) Lead the government	42	22	27
Q. Who is …	(1) More trustworthy	40	20	38
	(2) A more 'sympathetic' character	63	17	18
	(3) A 'winner'	61	13	23

Source: Forschungsgruppe Wahlen, 2002.

compared with the 1998-elections – enjoyed a clear lead over Stoiber in terms of general candidate preferences and most specific evaluations of competence.

Interestingly, the table demonstrates that in the run-up to the 2002 elections, Stoiber was ahead of Schröder on the key issues of unemployment (33 per cent to 18 per cent) and the economy (33 per cent to 24 per cent). However, crucially on both these issues the largest single group of respondents saw no difference between the two candidates. By contrast, Schröder led Stoiber in terms of the public's perceptions of the two candidates abilities to 'solve future problems' (34 per cent to 26 per cent), 'represent German interests' (52 per cent to 21 per cent) and 'lead the government' (40 per cent to 20 per cent). But the most striking figures relate to the public's general perceptions of the candidates as personalities. Here Schröder beat Stoiber convincingly, enjoying massive leads over Stoiber with regards to trustworthiness (40 per cent to 20 per cent), 'sympathetic' qualities (63 per cent to 17 per cent), and being a 'winner' (61 per cent to 13 per cent) (Forschungsgruppe Wahlen, 2002: 35–7).

Schröder's lead over Stoiber contrasted with the SPD's generally poor showing in terms of party competence. Table 5.8 sets out the public's perceptions of the relative competence of the SPD and CDU/CSU in the six issue areas of (1) jobs; (2) the economy; (3) the future; (4) education and training; (5) the family; and (6) foreigners. Although the SPD enjoyed leads over the CDU/CSU in the three areas of the future (35 per cent to 32 per cent), the family (43 per cent to 30 per cent), and foreigners (35 per cent to 34 per cent),

Table 5.8 2002-Bundestag elections. Public perceptions of party competence (%)

Issue area	Party		
	SPD	CDU/CSU	Don't know
Jobs	29	38	29
Economy	31	36	29
The future	35	32	28
Education/Training	30	35	23
The family	43	30	18
Foreigners	35	34	17

Source: Forschungsgruppe Wahlen, 2002.

it lagged behind the CDU/CSU in the key issue areas of jobs (29 per cent to 38 per cent), the economy (31 per cent to 36 per cent), and education and training (30 per cent to 35 per cent) (Forschungsgruppe Wahlen, 2002: 42–4). Given this disparity between popular perceptions of Schröder as a candidate and the competence of his party, the strategy of fighting a highly personalised campaign in the 2002-Bundestag elections was a rational one.

Nevertheless, it would be unwise to over-state the decisiveness of candidate preferences in deciding the outcome of the Bundestag elections. The Michigan model's funnel of causality posits multiple variables that impact on vote choice, some of which have a complex and multi-directional relationship with each other. In particular, it is clear that the relative weighting of value- and performance-based voting needs to be explored in more detail. It is to these two influences on vote choice that the rest of the chapter turns.

5.3   Value-orientation

The concept of value-orientation is one of the cornerstones of social research. Values themselves are a form of cognitive short-hand. They provide a relatively stable and predictable narrative in order to enable individuals to make choices in the moral, social and political spheres. Values are both different from, and more substantial than, preferences and encompass both 'preference for certain personal and social goals, as well as the methods to obtain those goals' (Dalton, 1996: 90). They are less elastic, less contingent on circumstances, and can be conceptualised as being less 'private'. This is because they are at least partially grounded in processes of group socialisation and group identity.

The initial wave of research into values and value-orientation was carried out in the mid-twentieth century (see Weber, 1924, 1962; Durkheim, 1956, 1979; Parsons, 1978). As a result of the rapid social and economic change of the 1950s and 1960s, these and other studies began to detect a shift from ideas of group-solidarity and other-directed values to self-actualising and inner-directed values (Riesman *et al.*, 1950; Inkeles and Smith, 1974; Sennett, 1978). However, the study of value-orientations took on a truly inter-disciplinary aspect with Ingelhart's (1990; 1981; 1977) work on value-shifts and the rise of post-material values in advanced industrial democracies.

Ingelhart's work is based on two premises: (1) the 'scarcity hypothesis' and (2) the 'socialisation hypothesis'. The scarcity hypothesis is summed-up in Inglehart's assertion that individuals assign 'the greatest value to those things that are in relatively short supply' (Inglehart, 1981: 881). This assumption builds on Maslow's (1954) model of a 'hierarchy of needs' in which basic subsistence needs (water, food, shelter) give way to higher order needs (belonging, self-esteem, participation, self-actualisation, fulfilment of intellectual and aesthetic potential) as individuals' material conditions improve. Similarly, the aggregate improvement of individual conditions associated with economic progress prompts a mass shift in individual values and the emergence of a 'new politics' (Miller and Levitin, 1976; Baker *et al.*, 1981) based on these emergent post-material values. Thus we see a shift from a political discourse based on ideas of sustenance (successful economy, growth, stable prices) and safety (strong defence, law and order) to those of self-actualisation (more autonomy and participation in one's job or community, more say in the political process) and aesthetic and intellectual values (beautiful cities, improved environment, the importance of ideas, free speech, etc.).

Ingelhart's scarcity hypothesis deals with the direct impact of material conditions on politics. But how does the new politics transcend the contingency of real-time conditions and become embedded in the social base of politics? In other words, how does it 'stick' within the culture? Inglehart's second socialisation hypothesis addresses these questions by arguing that post-materialist values become embedded within the age cohorts that are socialised as material conditions improve to the point that this value-shift becomes manifest. Thus individuals' values 'to a large extent ... reflect the conditions that prevailed during (individuals') preadult years' (Inglehart, 1981: 881). The socialisation effect of relative affluence in individuals' early years is compounded by other effects of improved material conditions, including higher levels of educational attainment – particularly access to higher education – more diverse cultural experiences and more information, including that of a political nature. The overall impact of this process is a 'cohort effect' in which the younger generational cohorts display a qualitatively different value-orientation to older cohorts. Moreover, the logic of Inglehart's thesis is that as economic progress continues, and the younger cohorts grow older and have children themselves, successive generations will display increasingly high levels of post-materialism. The implications of Inglehart's two hypotheses for the future development of party politics is obvious: a further decline in the traditional left-right dimension, based on materialist issues of economic management and re-distribution, and the continued growth of the new politics.

Other scholars have challenged some aspects of Inglehart's hypotheses. For instance, Flanagan (1982, 1987) argues that there are in fact two dimensions of value-change taking place; the first a shift from economic to non-economic values and the second an emerging dichotomy between traditional authoritarian values and a new libertarian value-orientation. However, these two dimensions can be regarded as being sub-sets of the category of post-materialism (Dalton, 1996: 94). Nevertheless, the fundamentals of Inglehart's thesis on post-materialism and the new politics have been widely accepted and used as explanatory variables within the German politics literature (cf. Müller-Rommel, 1984; Hülsberg, 1988; Padgett, 1993). But three questions can be asked in relation to Germany, just as they can with regard to all advanced democracies. These are: (1) how widespread are post-materialist values in Germany?; (2) how do post-materialist values manifest themselves in the party system?; and (3) how robust are post-materialist values compared with cross-cutting materialist values?

The spread of post-materialist values

The first question is how widespread are post-materialist values in Germany, and elsewhere? Dalton's extensive research in this area has identified a significant shift in German attitudes in favour of the higher-order issues identified by Maslow and Inglehart. If one takes what are in Inglehart's schema the dichotomous values of 'freedom from want' and 'freedom of speech' this shift is made clear. Thus in 1949, 35 per cent of Germans thought freedom from want was the most important political goal, compared with only 26 per cent who valued freedom of speech. However when the same questions were asked again in 1975 only 23 per cent regarded freedom from want as the most important, compared with 54 per cent who valued freedom of speech. This change was indicative of the progressive emergence of post-materialism in Germany, in which the proportion of post-materialists rose from 10 per cent in 1970/71 to 16 per cent in 1982 and 28 per cent in 1990. In addition, as Inglehart predicted, there appeared to be a clear 'cohort effect' in the growth of post-materialism. Longitudinal analysis across eight generational cohorts revealed that the balance between materalist and post-materialist values – what Dalton calls the Materialist/Post-materialist Index – in the oldest cohort (those born between 1886 and 1905) ranged between −40 and −50, compared with up to +10 in the youngest (born between 1966 and 1975). Differentials between cohorts were clear and remained constant over time and there appeared to be a curvilinear relationship between economic progress and the emergence of post-materialism, in which the most impact (represented by the steepest part of the curve) took place in the initial transition from a subsistence economy to consumer capitalism. The cohort effect was enhanced by the impact of increased access to education, especially

Table 5.9 Distribution of post-materialist attitudes among generations for the period 1973–91 (%)

	Generational cohorts born in							
	1901–10	1911–20	1921–30	1931–40	1941–50	1951–60	1961–70	After 1970
Belgium	02	05	07	09	12	14	16	17
Denmark	02	05	08	10	15	21	21	18
France	02	05	08	10	14	17	20	16
Germany	04	07	08	10	14	21	27	24
Greece	03	04	05	06	09	13	16	17
Ireland	03	03	04	05	07	08	12	20
Italy	02	03	04	06	08	13	14	17
Luxembourg	05	04	07	07	10	17	22	17
Netherlands	05	08	10	13	19	24	28	27
Portugal	03	02	03	04	06	06	09	10
Spain	03	03	03	05	10	18	23	24
UK	04	07	08	10	12	14	19	19

Source: Adapted from Scarbrough, 1995: 139.

Higher Education, in which there was a strong relationship between levels of educational attainment and support for post-materialist goals (Dalton, 1996: 90–103).

So how does Germany compare with other advanced democracies? Table 5.9 sets out the distribution of post-materialist attitudes among generations for the period 1973–91 in 12 European Union member states. The table demonstrates two main points. First, that in all 12 states the broad dynamics of the growth of post-materialist values over successive generational cohorts is remarkably similar. Some states, such as Italy, Denmark and France, start from very low baselines (2 per cent) in the oldest generational cohort whilst in other states, such as Luxembourg and the Netherlands, this cohort displays relatively high levels (5 per cent) of post-materialism. In addition, the upward curve in the growth of post-materialist values is flatter in some countries (Luxembourg) than in others (the Netherlands). Nevertheless, the pattern is broadly the same in all countries. The second point, however, is more complex. Whilst all 12 countries display this broad upward trend, there is divergence between countries in the pattern of growth across the two youngest cohorts – with two patterns emerging. First, there is a group of countries (Belgium, Greece, Ireland, Italy, Portugal and Spain) in which this upward trend continues in the generational cohort born after 1970, albeit (in the case of Belgium, Greece, Portugal and Spain) at an incremental rate of growth. Second, in the remainder of the countries (Denmark, France, Germany, Luxembourg, the Netherlands and the UK) the upward curve is either flat or in slight decline (the UK and the Netherlands respectively) or is in decline. The decline in post-materialist values is most evident in France, where the level of post-materialism in the youngest cohort (16 per cent) is only two percentage points higher than the level found in the generation born between 1941 and 1950. The decline in post-materialism in Germany is less marked (falling from 27 per cent to 24 per cent) and it remains the joint second-highest level after that found in the Netherlands (27 per cent). Nevertheless, the unification of Germany had two effects that have served to lower levels of post-materialism within the German public. First, the assimilation of the former of German Democratic Republic meant that a significant segment of the new all-German electorate had never undergone the process of embourgeoisement described above. This has lowered overall levels of post-materialism amongst voters. Second, the economic and social problems associated with unification have shifted the parameters of political discourse away from post-materialist issues and towards traditional 'bread and butter' issues. This has lowered levels of salience of post-materialist issues amongst voters.

In comparative terms, what the pattern of divergence between the two groups of countries noted above demonstrates is that it is not the absolute level of affluence that is associated with the growth of post-materialism but rather the rate of material progress across time and the ability of the economy to accommodate and integrate each new cohort, especially at the elite level associated with high levels of educational attainment. Thus the continuing upward trend in countries such as Ireland and Spain reflect the expansion of educational and economic opportunity associated with the high levels of economic growth these countries have enjoyed in the last 20 years. By contrast, countries displaying relatively sharp drops in levels of post-materialism across the two youngest cohorts, such as France and Germany, remain affluent but no longer enjoy the high rates of economic growth and expansion of opportunity associated with the 1950s and 1960s. Indeed, over the last decade France and to a lesser extent Germany have struggled to create jobs and integrate the youngest cohort into economic life. The shift back towards materialist concerns in the youngest cohort in these countries is thus consistent with Flanagan's assertion that the emergence of post-materialism can be expected to reverse if material progress is not maintained (1982: 420). It also reinforces the idea of voters being reasonably sophisticated and reflexive about values, rather than cultural dupes whose values are fixed by pre-adult socialisation.

The manifestation of post-materialist values
in the party system

The second, related, question posited at the start of this section was how do post-materialist values manifest themselves in the party system? Throughout Western Europe post-materialism has been linked with higher levels of political participation (Inglehart, 1990), particularly in new social movements organising around issues such as environmentalism, minority rights and nuclear energy (Dalton and Kuechler, 1990). However, as Dalton points out, higher levels of political participation does not equate to turnout in the traditional political forum of elections. Whereas post-materialists are twice as likely to take part in political protests, the rejection of established modes of political involvement implicit in such a value-orientation may contribute to lower levels of turnout in recent elections (Dalton, 1996: 107). The one exception to this rule is the tendency of post-materialists to vote for the Greens. As Rönsch (1980) observes, Green voters in Germany in the early 1980s tended to be young, relatively well-educated, upwardly mobile, and employed within the service sector. As such, they appeared to conform to Inglehart's hypotheses. Bürklin echoes this view, asserting that 'a typical voter of the Green (party) is below 35, with a university education' (Bürklin, 1987: 111), whilst Langguth observes that 43 per cent of Green supporters had been educated to the level of *Abitur* (the equivalent of an A2 level in England and Wales), compared with 16 per cent for the population as a whole (Langguth, 1984: 44). Betz, however, problematises the orthodox assumptions noted above. He does not question the underlying logic of Inglehart's hypotheses but does assert that the linkage between educational attainment and high income is misguided. According to Betz, the significant increase in access to higher education that took place in the 1960s was not matched by the integrative capacities of the West German economy. As a result, the 1970s and early 1980s saw the emergence of a 'new academic proletariat' for whom higher education had proved a 'dead-end'. But in keeping with Ingelhart's hypotheses, these young highly educated individuals did prize post-materialist goals such as self-actualisation, as well as doing interesting rather than well-rewarded work (Betz, 1990: 241–50).

This raises the question of whether the attitudes of this cohort were *ex ante* value-orientations or *ex post* rationalisations of straightened circumstances. Whatever the psycho-social logic of responses in the study what is clear is that in the early 1980's there was a strong correlation between high levels of education, 'blocked chances of social mobility' (Alber, 1985: 220), and support for the Greens. Table 5.10 demonstrates the dynamics of this relationship. Throughout the run of data, there is a positive correlation between levels of education and support for the Greens, as well as a cohort effect in which the youngest cohort is generally more likely to vote Green. At the same time, however, there is a broadly negative correlation between levels of income and support for the Greens. So, for instance, the lowest level of support for the Greens (10.3 per cent) is found amongst the segment of the oldest cohort with the lowest level of educational attainment but which enjoys 'good' levels of material prosperity. Similarly, the highest level of support (60.7 per cent) is found amongst that element of the youngest cohort with the highest level of educational attainment but with a 'bad' level of material prosperity. There are one or two outliers in the data (such as the tendency in two out of three

Table 5.10 Green preference by education, age and economic circumstances (%)

Age	Good	Patly	Bad	*n*	Significance
		Material Circumstances			
Education: no qualifications or primary school qualifications (Hauptschulabschluss)					
18–30	16.9	25.2	32.7	59	**
31–38	17.9	23.3	13.5	47	ns
39+	10.3	10.5	11.5	130	ns
Education: middle-level qualifications (Mittlere Reife, Fachschulabschluss)					
18–30	31.7	32.4	42.3	72	*
31–38	14.7	36.4	40.0	26	**
39+	14.2	15.6	15.4	46	ns
Education: secondary-school qualifications (Hochschulreife, Fachhochschulreife)					
18–30	26.3	44.0	60.7	70	**
31–38	44.8	38.5	33.3	49	ns
39+	19.9	31.6	33.3	54	*

Notes: * significant at the .05 level; ** significant at the .01 level; ns = not significant.

Source: Table adapted from Betz, 1990: 246. Data from Kumulierter ALLBUS 1980–82–84 (ZA. No. 1335).

cases for the youngest cohort enjoying good material circumstances to express less support for the Greens than in the intermediate age cohort), but the overall picture is of what appeared at the time to be an emerging 'lumpen intelligentsia' linked to support for the Greens. In the words of Bürklin, voting Green was not so much 'a conflict over different lifestyles of successive generations than the continuing conflict over distributional principles' (Bürklin, 1987: 122). In other words, post-materialist values provided an alternative political discourse in the perennial battle between the generally economically established and relatively affluent older generations and the less integrated younger cohorts.

With the benefit of 20 years' hindsight Bürklin's words seem unduly dismissive of the significance of post-materialist values and their impact on voting behaviour, particularly for the Greens. During the 1990s the Greens moderated their ideological profile to the point that much of the party's economic policy could be placed to the right of the SPD (for instance in the first term of the Red–Green coalition the Greens argued for a lower top rate of income tax than that advocated by the Social Democrats). This was at least partly in response to the increasing prosperity and economic embeddedness of the Greens' original cohort of support (Lees, 1998, 2000). Moreover, evidence from the 2002-Bundestag elections suggests that the Greens' original cohort of support continues to stay remarkably loyal to the party. This tends to undermine the idea that support for the Greens was part of the generational conflict discussed above. Table 5.11 sets out the patterns of voting in

Table 5.11   2002-Bundestag elections. Voting by age, occupation and education (%)

| | Second Vote 2002 | | | | | |
	SPD	CDU/CSU	Green	FDP	PDS	Other
Total %	38.5	38.5	8.6	7.4	4.0	3.0
Age						
18–29	38	33	10	10	04	05
30–44	40	34	11	08	04	04
45–59	38	40	09	07	04	02
60+	38	45	05	06	04	02
Employment category						
Blue-collar	44	37	04	07	04	04
White-collar	41	35	10	07	04	03
Professional	33	41	14	06	03	03
Self-employed	21	51	11	13	03	02
Agricultural	19	66	03	06	04	03
Education						
Elementary school	44	41	04	06	02	03
Ordinary school	37	39	07	08	05	04
Grammar school	38	34	13	09	04	03
University	30	34	18	09	07	02

Source: Forschungsgruppe Wahlen, 2002.

the 2002-elections, by age, occupation, and education. In the table, the Greens original electoral cohorts are now the cohorts 30–44 and 45–59. The data demonstrates that both of these cohorts displayed above-average support for the Greens: with 11 and 9 per cent respectively voting Green, compared with 8.6 per cent for the population as a whole and 10 per cent for the youngest cohort. However, in the oldest cohort (60+) support for the Greens drops to 5 per cent. Not only does this demonstrate the resilience of postmaterialist values in these generational cohorts but also the relative parity of support between all except the oldest cohort is consistent with the curvilinear relationship between economic progress and the emergence of postmaterialism discussed above. In addition, the pattern of support for the Greens according to employment status and education remains consistent with the assumptions made about Green support two decades earlier. In terms of employment status, support for the Greens is lowest among agricultural (3 per cent) and manual workers (4 per cent), but much higher among professionals (14 per cent), the self-employed (11 per cent), and white-collar employees (10 per cent). As for education, support for the Greens steadily rises with levels of educational attainment. It is in this category that we see the biggest differentials, with only 4 per cent of individuals with elementary

(*Hauptschule*) school qualifications voting Green compared with 18 per cent of those who had graduated from university. This indicates that access to higher education remains the most potent indicator of electoral support for the Greens.

Cross-cutting materialist and post-materialist values

'Rational' models of political behaviour assume that political preferences are transitive – in other words if x is preferred to y and y is preferred to z then x is preferred to z. In practice voters are not rational in this sense but rather hold cross-cutting and often logically incompatible values of both a materialist and post-materialist nature. Moreover many post-materialist values are not necessarily expressed as political goals but rather manifest themselves in a more inchoate and personal manner. This raises some tricky methodological questions about how to measure and 'weight' the political impact of these values (cf. van Deth and Scarbrough, 1995).

The reasons for this apparent lack of voter rationality are discussed later in the chapter, particularly in the segment on economic voting. However it raises the question of how robust are post-materialist values compared with cross-cutting materialist values? As discussed earlier Bürklin (1987) and Betz's (1990) research suggested that much of the post-materialist discourse masked an underlying redistributive and therefore materialist conflict arising out of the West German economy's lack of integrative capacity in the 1970s and early 1980s. To some extent this is born out by the evidence. For instance, in 1983 even 90 per cent of Green voters ranked unemployment as the major political issue of the time compared with 81 per cent who argued that environmental protection was the most important. By 1987, when West Germany's immediate economic prospects had improved markedly, 80 per cent of Green voters still expressed concern about unemployment (albeit less than the 90 per cent that regarded environmental protection as the most important issue) (Schultze, 1987: 7).

If the persistence of materialist concerns can still be strongly discerned among Green voters it would be no surprise to find that among amongst the population as a whole materialist values remain dominant and, as a result, post-materalist concerns were relegated to the status of second-order issues within the political discourse. However, the picture appears to be a more complex one.

Table 5.12 ranks what voters considered to be the 12 most important political issues in West Germany, the United States, Britain and France. The data is derived from Dalton's (1996) analysis of the 1990–91 World Values Survey. The table demonstrates that post-materialist issues do have considerable salience amongst the population as a whole, with six out of the 12 issues conforming to the ideal type of higher-order concerns identified by Maslow and Inglehart. Of these, the highest ranked issue (protect free speech) might be considered not to be purely a post-materialist issue, given that the principle

Table 5.12 Prioritisation of political issues in four advanced industrial democracies, 1990–91 (%)

Issue	Type	United States	Great Britain	West Germany	France
Stable economy	M	76	67	66	72
High level of economic growth	M	55	69	65	68
Protect free speech	PM	71	62	61	47
More say in work/community	PM	65	64	59	55
Maintain order in the nation	M	48	45	55	63
More humane society	PM	57	46	55	44
More say in government	PM	55	51	50	38
Fight against crime	M	33	43	49	57
Make cities/country beautiful	PM	44	52	42	50
Fight rising prices	M	23	36	28	38
Ideas count more than money	PM	27	27	25	35
Strong defence	M	38	19	12	12
n		1,839	1,484	2,101	1,002

Notes: M = materialist political issue; PM = post-materialist political issue.

Source: adapted from Dalton, 1996: 95.

of free speech exercised a powerful hold on the political imagination long before the transition to consumer capitalism sparked the emergence of post-materialism. However, it can credibly be argued that free speech used to be an issue held to be important more by political elites and opinion formers rather than the population as a whole and that it is the level of salience that the issue now holds amongst ordinary voters that represents a qualitative change from the past. The same argument can also be made for the seventh highest-ranked issue (more say in government). These two issues apart, the four other post-materialist issues (more say in work/community; more humane society; make cities/country beautiful; ideas count more than money) are without doubt higher-order concerns that cannot be easily placed on the traditional left-right continuum. As such, they signify a break with the materalist/redistributive issues that dominated electoral politics hitherto.

Comparing Germany to the other three countries, two points are worthy of note. First, the range of opinion between the most important and least important issue in each country ranges from 50 per cent in Great Britain to 60 per cent in France. Germany's relative position is broadly in the middle of this spread, with a range of 54 per cent. Taken in the round, the data for all four countries demonstrate that although voters have clear preferences between issues there is no instance of an overwhelming skew towards one particular issue. Thus, although economic issues (stability and growth) are clearly the most important issues for voters, other issues also matter to electorates that display a complex mix of materalist and post-materialist preferences. Second, that although the aggregate of these preferences varies from country to country this variance does not map neatly onto differences in the prevalence of post-materialist values discussed earlier. On the one hand, Table 5.9 demonstrated that France experienced the most significant drop in post-materialist values across the youngest two generational cohorts. Therefore it is no surprise that the World Values data indicates that the French electorate also appear to be the least interested in political issues underpinned by such values, with only 'more say in work/community' and 'make cities/country beautiful' making it into the top six issues prioritised by voters. On the other hand, voters in Great Britain – which displayed relatively modest levels of post-materialism – placed four post-materialist issues ('more say in work/community'; 'protect free speech'; 'make cities/country beautiful'; and 'more say in Government') in the top six. This was one more than Germany, despite the fact that German voters displayed far higher levels of post-materialism amongst the post-war generational cohorts.

The interaction between post-materialism, old cleavages and party choice

The paradox of this apparent lack of fit between latent levels of post-materialism and the actual mix of salient political issues in a given polity raises three points of note. First, the World Values data cited here is very much a snapshot of public opinion at the beginning of the 1990s and is vulnerable to short-term factors that may skew the data. With regard to this data, two such factors are apparent. On the one hand the data was gathered shortly after the collapse of communism in Eastern Europe and end of the Cold War, which led to much debate about 'peace dividends' and may explain the low priority voters in all four countries attributed to the issue of defence. Thus, a similar study carried out today – in the aftermath of the events of 11 September 2001 and the subsequent 'war on terrorism' – might find that voters attributed a higher priority to defence then they did in 1990–91. On the other hand, the German data was collected during the immediate period of Unification, which shifted much of the political debate away from the post-materialist concerns of the 1980s and back towards the materialist and/or authoritarian concerns of economic stability and law and order (Lees, 1998). As a result, more reliable results would have been generated using time series data. The second point to note is that structural explanations alone are not sufficient in themselves to explain voter behaviour. As the study reiterates, voters are not cultural dupes and the act of voting is the product of a complex cognitive process, involving both long-term and short-term factors, and instrumental and expressive preferences. In addition, as will be explored later in the book, this process is also highly dependent on the relative success or failure of political parties' mobilisation strategies. Finally, even if we accept that structural explanations do have explanatory purchase, the relationship between post-materialist values and voting behaviour is made

Table 5.13   Old and new cleavages and party choice in six West European countries, 1970–90

Country	Cleavage	1970–75	1975–80	1976–85	1986–90	1990
Belgium	Religious/secular	0.54	0.51	0.54	0.44	0.44
	Left-right materialism	–	0.23	0.25	0.36	0.36
	Materialism/post-materialism	0.23	0.13	–	0.31	0.24
France	Religious/secular	0.39	0.37	0.34	037	0.37
	Left-right materialism	–	0.40	0.49	0.42	0.42
	Materialism/post-materialism	0.38	0.38	–	0.31	0.28
Germany	Religious/secular	0.35	0.22	0.30	0.34	0.34
	Left-right materialism	–	0.13	0.24	0.30	0.30
	Materialism/post-materialism	0.24	0.22	–	0.45	0.41
Netherlands	Religious/secular	0.65	057	0.58	051	0.51
	Left-right materialism	0.55	0.52	0.52	0.56	0.45
	Materialism/post-materialism	0.36	0.40	–	0.42	0.44
Sweden	Religious/secular	–	–	0.36	0.34	0.28
	Left-right materialism	–	0.66	0.64	0.64	0.47
	Materialism/post-materialism	–	–	–	0.27	0.28
UK	Religious/secular	0.14	0.14	0.09	0.16	0.16
	Left-right materialism	0.53	0.49	0.53	0.54	0.46
	Materialism/post-materialism	0.23	0.17	–	0.45	0.38

Source: Adapted from Knutsen, 1995: 488–9.

more complex because of the interaction such values have with the older, more group-oriented, confessional and class cleavages.

Table 5.13 presents time series data of the relationship between the new cleavage of materialism/post-materialism and the older religious/secular and left-right materialist cleavages. The data covers six West European countries (Belgium, France, Germany, the Netherlands, Sweden and the United Kingdom) over the period 1970–90, and the scores are correlation coefficients (thus, the higher the score the higher the impact of that particular cleavage on party choice). Two points are of note. The first point is that the impact of the three cleavages on vote choice in the six countries is quite heterogeneous. A comparative analysis of each cleavage produces three categories: (1) countries in which the impact of the cleavage is stable over time or displays a pattern of trendless fluctuation; (2) countries in which the impact of the cleavage is in decline; and (3) countries in which the impact of the cleavage is rising. However, although none of these taxonomical categories are empty there does not appear to be a clear pattern across countries that would indicate some sort of 'trade-off' between the three cleavages. The impact of the religious/secular cleavage is stable in France and Germany, in decline in Belgium, the Netherlands and Sweden, and rising slightly in the United Kingdom. By contrast, the left-right cleavage appears stable in France and the United Kingdom, in decline in the Netherlands and Sweden, and rising in Belgium and Germany. However, neither of these patterns seem to present a clear picture of what we might expect in terms of the impact of post-materialism. Thus, in Germany the impact of the materialist/post-materialist cleavage appears to be rising over time, despite the fact that the impact of the left-right cleavage also seems to be rising and the religious/secular cleavage remains stable and significant. By contrast, the impact of the materialist/post-materialist cleavage has not risen in Sweden, despite the apparent decline in the impact of the old cleavages. Conversely, the impact of the materialist/post-materialist cleavage is in decline in France. This is consistent with the data discussed earlier, but does not appear to have been accompanied by an increase in the impact of the older cleavages, which have remained stable over time. This leads us to the second point of note: that none of these correlation scores indicate an overwhelmingly strong relationship between a given cleavage and actual vote choice. Other factors are at work, including the more instrumental and 'rational' judgments associated with economic or issue voting. This is discussed at greater length in the next section.

Looking more specifically at Germany, the persistence of the old cleavages is still marked. Indeed, if anything, political issues associated with these cleavages have a higher level of salience than in the early 1990s. Table 5.14 ranks the five issues considered most important by voters in the run-up to the 2002-Bundestag elections. The wording of the issues differ from those used in the World Values Survey, but what is striking is that all but two of the issues identified by voters are unambiguously materialist and/or authoritarian in nature rather than post-materalist. The clear number one concern, cited by 82 per cent of German voters in 2002, was the issue of unemployment, reflecting the high levels of structural unemployment – especially in the new Federal states – that have dogged Germany since the early 1990s. Similarly, worries about the economy (15 per cent) was the joint second most important issue and concern over foreigners and asylum seekers (9 per cent) the fourth,

Table 5.14   2002-Bundestag elections. Five most important problems facing Germany (%)

Rank	Issue	Type	%
1	Unemployment	M	82
2	Economy	M	15
3	Terrorism/War	M/PM	15
4	Foreigners/Asylum seekers	M	09
5	Education/Training	PM/M	07

Notes: M = materialist political issue; PM = post-materialist political issue.

Source: Forschungsgruppe Wahlen, 2002.

according to respondents. The issues of terrorism and war (15 per cent) and education and training (7 per cent) are more problematic and open to contestation. The salience of terrorism and war with voters was understandable, given the aftermath of the atrocities of 11 September 2001 and the build-up to the 2003-Gulf War. Nevertheless, despite the conflation of the two issues in the data they in fact load differently onto the materialist/post-materialist dimension. Using Flanagan's (1982, 1987) idea of two dimensions of value-change, the two issues can be regarded as being located towards different poles of the authoritarian-libertarian dimension. On the one hand, state action against terrorism is clearly a materialist issue that loads towards the authoritarian pole of the dimension, given the negative implications such measures inevitably have in terms of personal freedom and autonomy. On the other, popular unease about the build-up to war is more of a post-materialist issue that reflects libertarian concerns about the importance of non-violence, co-operation rather than force, and the primacy of international law. Similarly, the concept of post-materalism can be stretched to include the issue of education, whilst training is located more towards the materialist pole, given the tradition of vocational training that has long been part of the 'Rhineland model' of German capitalism.

However, what is clear is that materialist concerns dominated the political agenda in the 2002-Bundestag elections. Given the economic challenges that face post-unification Germany, this is consistent with Flanagan's assertion that the emergence of post-materialism can be expected to reverse in the light of individuals' tendency to 'reorder their priorities in favour of economic issues, should their economic needs increase or their economic security be threatened' (1982: 420). But despite this, the link between these materialist concerns and voters' electoral preferences is not a direct one. As discussed earlier in the chapter, the CDU/CSU was well ahead of the SPD in terms of party competence to tackle unemployment (38 per cent versus 29 per cent) and the problems facing the economy (36 per cent versus 31 per cent). Yet, despite this lead over the SPD the CDU/CSU lost the 2002-Bundestag elections. Obviously, neither values nor perceptions of competence necessarily map directly onto voters electoral preferences. This raises complex questions about the nature of performance-based or economic voting. It is to these issues that the chapter now turns.

5.4   Economic voting

Underlying the 'economic' or 'performance' voting literature is a profoundly different conception of the voter and the motives for voting behaviour than that found in most of the value-orientation literature (arguably with the exception of Flanagan's work). By-and-large, the values literature is focussed on the broad end of the funnel of causality, emphasises long-term structural influences and to a certain extent is posited on an ideal-type of the voter as a cultural dupe in which personal assessments of vote choice are driven by an individual's pre-adult socialisation and community history. By contrast, the economic voting literature is grounded in the ideal-type of the voter as *Homo Economicus*: reflexive, rational, and – crucially – in possession of sufficient information to make an informed vote choice. All three of these assumptions are highly contested, of course. Nevertheless, the economic voting approach sheds a different light on both the motivations behind vote choice and the efficacy of the institutional design of the electoral and party systems within which such choices are made.

As the assumptions noted above imply, the economic voting literature originally arose out of the rational choice school of political science, particularly the work of Downs (1957), Tufte (1978), and Schneider and Frey (1988). As discussed in Chapter 1, Downs' 'Economic Theory of Democracy' has been particularly influential, constructing a formal theory of politics that explicitly portrayed political parties as analogous with firms and voters as customers. Thus for parties, the ultimate goal of political strategy is office-seeking and to that end they 'formulate policies in order to win elections, rather than win elections in order to formulate policies' (Downs, 1957: 28). For their part, voters reward parties for their policies, which are analogous with products. Downs' ideas were developed in the work of Tufte, Schneider and Frey, and others who posited the concept of 'political business cycles'. This built on the idea that individuals voted instrumentally but made it explicit that the core policy area that concerned voters was economics. In other words, the state of the economy was decisive in determining vote choice. As a result, governments endeavoured to synchronise the electoral and business cycle in order to generate booms in election years.

The original political business cycle literature was relatively deterministic in approach and difficult to demonstrate empirically (see Whitely, 1986; Pennings *et al.*, 1999). However, in the 1990's a theoretically and methodologically more sophisticated literature appeared that also raised interesting questions about the institutional design of consensual systems such as Germany's. At the core of much of the economic voting literature are two problems. First is the so-called 'Voting and Popularity (VP) Function'. Literature that assesses the VP function works from the same idea to that found in the partisan identification literature: that support for, or the popularity of, a certain party is not the same as actual vote choice. However, it is also predicated on the 'paradox of voting' found in the rational choice literature: that voting is in itself an irrational act in which individual voters are faced with significant opportunity costs (acquiring the requisite information to assess party performance, physically voting etc.) for little or no marginal utility (as the likelihood that the individual's vote will be decisive in the outcome of the election). However this argument is less strong with regards to Germany, where elections are relatively infrequent, take place on Sundays or public holidays, polling stations are close to people's homes, voters can use both proxy and postal votes and – unlike in the United States – there is no duty of registration. Information costs are also relatively low, with official polling cards and other essential information being sent directly to voters' homes (Becker, 2002: 46; see also Kühnel and Fuchs, 1998). In addition, Germany's strong tradition of public political education further reduces information costs for the individual voter.

Moving along from assessments of the marginal utility, the issue of information acquisition leads us to the second problem, which is summed up in what is called the 'Responsibility Hypothesis': the assumption that voters hold the government responsible for economic events. This seems intuitively plausible but is actually quite hard to demonstrate empirically. According to economic voting models, there are two main links in the causal chain between economic conditions and vote choice: (1) from the economy to voter perceptions; and (2) from voter perceptions to the vote. However, how the two links load into the chain as a whole seems to vary from country to country (Lewis Beck and Palham, 2000).

The problem with the responsibility hypothesis is that it is grounded in the US and British literature and is uniquely fitted to two-party majoritarian political systems, because these systems allow the voters to judge the achievements of a single party of government (Pennings, 2002). In consensual systems with minority or coalition governments it is much harder for the voter to establish responsibility for economic conditions. In turn this makes the system less responsive to voters' preferences. The issues of blurred responsibility and weakened system responsiveness potentially cast doubt on the core idea of performance-based voting: the reflexive, rational and information-rich voter. It also raises three other more empirical questions. First, to what extent do voters reward past performance or future potential? In other words, do governments lose elections because of past economic failures or can opposition parties actually trump an incumbent's respectable economic record with promises of future delivery? Second, do voters have enough information to form balanced judgements about the economy as a whole or do they 'satisfice' (Simon, 1965) and concentrate on the so-called 'big two' issues of inflation and unemployment? Finally, and linked to the previous question, when assessing economic conditions what is the balance that voters strike between their own personal material conditions (egotropic voting) and the general economy (sociotropic voting). Inflation and unemployment load differently onto the balance between egotropic – or pocketbook – and sociotropic voting. Inflation affects everybody, but in different ways. Individuals on fixed incomes or with savings suffer from rising inflation whereas individuals who stand to gain from rising asset prices (such as housing) or who are servicing debt can benefit from it. By contrast, unemployment has a much more selective impact on the polity. The only individuals who are directly affected by unemployment are the unemployed, although other individuals may be affected by fear of unemployment or its knock-on effects (loss of business/consumer confidence or even long-term structural decline). All-in-all this means that macro-studies that explore the link between economic conditions and voting behaviour require finely calibrated and sophisticated research designs if they are to avoid the hazards of ecological fallacy or over-determinism.

Economic conditions and vote choice

The link between economic conditions and vote choice in Germany was explored in a study carried out by Feld and Kirchgässner (2000), in which they examine the impact of official and hidden unemployment on the popularity of the Kohl governments of the 1980s and 1990s. Feld and Kirchgässner follow the logic of previous studies (see Kirchgässner, 1986; Nannestad and Paldam, 1994) and work from the assumption that, as one of the 'big two' economic issues, unemployment has a central impact of the formation of individual vote choice. However acquisition of reliable information on unemployment is not only relatively costly to the individual voter, but its impact on her is difficult to measure. There are three reasons for this. First, the official statistics on unemployment are open to manipulation and are amended over time. For instance, in 1982 the official unemployment count for that year was 7.5 per cent of the workforce, whereas in 2000 the revised official count for 1982 was 6.7 per cent. Second, there is a 'hidden manpower reserve' made up of individuals who have temporarily withdrawn from the labour market on a voluntary basis. Finally, National Service requirements, relatively long spells in higher education, and the plethora of Federal and *Land* government work creation initiatives mask higher levels of 'hidden unemployment' than those found in the official statistics (Feld and Kirchgässner, 2000: 333). In addition, the authors identified two other variables that impacted on measurement of vote choice. First, the phenomenon of 'grievance asymmetry': in which voters punish bad economic performance more than they reward good performance. Second, the practice of 'rational ignorance': in which voters make up for limited economic knowledge through a process of intuition of the facts. As a result, voters' assessments of levels of unemployment merge official statistics and personal perceptions together in a form of fuzzy logic that is hard to unpack empirically. On the plus side, however, Germany's system of fixed parliamentary terms does go some way to negate a third factor that has dogged similar studies in other countries. This is the problem of 'counter-causality': in which elections are called if at all possible during economic good times. Under these conditions, the Responsibility Hypothesis still holds but the underlying logic of reward and punishment is difficult to capture.

Table 5.15 sets out Feld and Kirchgässner's findings on the relative impact of real and perceived unemployment on voting choice in the old Federal states (1984–96), compared to a more limited dataset from the new states (1992–96). The data is sourced from the Allensbach Institut für Demoskopie's

Table 5.15 Estimates of 'Big Two' economic voting for old and new Federal states, 1984–96

| Explanatory variable | Old Federal states (1984–96; quarterly observations) | | | | New Federal states (1992–96; monthly observations) | | | |
| | Dependent variable | | | Wald test | Dependent variable | | | Wald test |
	Government popularity	Opposition popularity	Other parties' popularity	X2	Government popularity	Opposition popularity	Other parties' popularity	X2
Y_t-1		0.777*** (9.01)				0.212* (2.47)		
Y_t-2		−0.170* (2.07)				0.179* (2.23)		
Constant term	84.898***(9.92)	31.687***(4.23)	−16.586** (3.17)		79.921*** (7.07)	21.390* (1.71)	−1.311 (0.23)	
Unemployment 1	−2.516***(3.67)	1.543* (2.54)	0.973* (2.33)	13.882***	−1.893** (2.78)	1.647* (2.20)	0.246 (2.06)	8.096*
Unemployment 2	−8.622** (3.20)	1.644 (0.70)	6.978*** (4.16)	18.919***	−0.839*** (4.10)	0.832*** (3.66)	−0.007 (0.07)	16.824***
Inflation	−2.386***(4.29)	0.608 (1.26)	1.778*** (5.30)	31.690***	−0.516** (2.80)	0.288 (1.49)	0.228* (2.48)	12.156
R2	0.711	0.495	0.858			0.576	0.400	0.554
SER	1.578	1.374	0.980			2.129	2.343	1.078
J.-B.	0.006	0.884	61.132***			2.051	0.353	0.160

Notes: Number in parentheses = absolute values of *t*-stats; asterisks = rejection of null hypotheses at following significance levels * 5 per cent; ** 1 per cent; *** 0.1 per cent.

Source: Adapted from Feld and Kirchgässner (2000).

longitudinal studies, using quarterly observations in the old states and monthly observations in the new states (in order to increase the *n* of the latter). In addition to the official unemployment rate (unemployment 1 in the table), the authors added their own estimator of hidden unemployment (unemployment 2), by adding data relating to individuals in work creation programmes, vocational training and German language courses, as well as those taking early retirement. Both variables are seasonably adjusted. Over the time series the mean rate of hidden unemployment was 1.18 per cent, or roughly 14 per cent of the official rate (Feld and kirchgässner, 2000: 340). Finally, the authors add the other 'big two' economic variable: the rate of inflation.

Two results are made very clear within the data. First, the Wald test results (which check for the impact of the independent variables on the system as a whole) and the scores for the individual variables support the assumption that unemployment and inflation are significant: although this is clearer in the old Federal states than in the new states. Second, it is clear that over the period the impact of the three economic variables on the relative popularity of the government and main opposition party was asymmetric. In the old Federal states, the only coefficient in the equation for the opposition with any degree of significance is official unemployment (Unemployment 1: (2.54)). In the new Federal states, unofficial unemployment (Unemployment 2: (366)) is also significant, but the overall picture that emerges is one in which voters 'punished' the government for poor performance more than they 'rewarded' the main opposition. Thus, although the SPD did benefit from a loss of government popularity the main beneficiaries of any loss of government popularity were the smaller parties, including far-right parties such as the Republicans and the German People's Union (DVU) (Feld and kirchgässner, 2000: 340–6). The tendency for dissatisfaction with government performance to benefit smaller parties rather than the official opposition raises an important issue: the danger that such dissatisfaction can translate into a more general dissatisfaction with the performance of the regime as a whole. As noted in Chapter 1, this is a danger to which German political elites are particularly sensitive. Research by Cusak indicates that the tendency to punish incumbents by voting for small and often anti-system parties exists in both parts of Germany, but that it is particularly pronounced in the new Federal states, where economic hardship and a weaker democratic culture have resulted in comparatively low levels of commitment to the political system itself (Cusak, 1999).

Economic competence and vote choice

The failure of oppositions to garner the full benefits of government failure is indicative that the economic calculus is cross-cut by ideology, albeit primarily a left-right ideological dimension centred on redistributive issues. In other words, the political marketplace is not a frictionless one and although many voters do swing between the two main left- and right-wing parties others may prefer to either vote for a smaller party within the same bloc or, alternatively, abstain. In addition, the dominant left-right dimension means that voters' assessment of what constitutes a good or bad economic 'performance' are affected by their positions along that dimension. As part of the fuzzy logic of 'rational ignorance', a priori partisan positions will affect voters' judgements and the way political parties position themselves on issues of economic management.

Thus what really matters are voters' perceptions of the relative economic problem-solving competence of the political parties. This is demonstrated in Table 5.16. Using data from Maier and Rattinger (2004), the table charts the relationship between (1) economic conditions, perceptions of economic competence, and party identification, and (2) vote choice in the old and new Federal states in the 1998-Bundestag elections. Two points are of note. First, despite the bad economic conditions voter judgements about general (Economy 1) and individual (Economy 2) conditions played a relatively minor role in explaining individual vote choice. Second, however, the data

Table 5.16   2002-Bundestag elections. Intended vote by perceptions of economic conditions, economic competence and party identification

	Intention to vote for							
	CDU/CSU	SPD	FDP	Greens	PDS	Reps	Gov.	Opp.
Old Federal states								
R2 complete model	53.4	49.7	14.3	34.1	29.8	–	51.8	45.8
R2 only party ID	44.7	43.0	11.6	34.1	25.7	–	44.7	39.6
Economy 1	−0.03	0.03	−0.04	0.03	−0.02	–	0.04	−0.07**
Economy 2	0.00	0.02	−0.02	0.00	0.00	–	0.01	−0.03
Economic competence	0.36***	0.29***	0.18***	0.03	0.21***	–	0.29***	0.29***
Party ID	0.46***	0.51***	0.28***	0.58***	0.50***	–	0.52***	0.46***
New Federal states								
R2 complete model	46.1	38.5	22.4	19.0	32.6	–	42.7	28.9
R2 only party ID	38.2	28.5	19.1	13.2	31.1	–	33.1	21.8
Economics 1	0.08	−0.02	−0.02	0.03	−0.07	–	−0.02	−0.04
Economics 2	−0.01	0.02	0.01	0.02	0.01	–	0.03	0.02
Economic competence	0.33***	0.36***	0.21***	0.26***	0.13**	–	0.35***	0.29***
Party ID	0.45***	0.37***	0.35***	0.29***	0.51***	–	0.41***	0.37***

Notes: Significance levels at * 5 per cent; ** 1 per cent; *** 0.1 per cent.

Source: Adapted from Maier and Rattinger, 2004.

on voter perceptions of the parties' economic competence demonstrates a relatively strong effect on vote choice. Thus, even when one allows for partisan identification, the clearly decisive variable acting on vote choice was perceptions of party competence in the economic field. This is broadly consistent with the findings from previous studies examining the 1994- and 1998- Bundestag elections (see Maier and Rattinger, 1999: 41–3). As in these studies, the observed relationship between perceptions of economic management competence and vote choice in the 2002 elections is strongest in the CDU/CSU and SPD equations: which might be expected given that (1) at least one of the two parties was definitely going to be in government after the election; and (2) as catch-all parties with broad appeal, much of the competition between them is based on perceptions of competence rather than clear blue ideological water.

To sum up, the economic or performance-based voting behaviour literature is theoretically well developed, methodologically robust, and empirically rich. In the case of Germany, it provides a powerful account of the importance of economic performance and, more importantly, perceptions of economic competence in the determination of vote choice. In addition it raises interesting questions about the efficacy of institutional design and responsiveness of political systems to voters' preferences. At the same time, however, it is clear that voters are not truly 'rational' but rather use a kind of fuzzy logic in order to obtain and process the economic information required to make an informed choice, based on their preferences. Nevertheless, for political parties the distinction is in many ways academic and in order to avoid punishment incumbent parties in particular must respond to voters' behaviour *as if* they had arrived at their choice in a rational manner.

5.5 Summary

The chapter has examined the three key concepts of (1) partisan identification; (2) value-orientation; and (3) economic voting: emerging from the theoretically quite distinct schools of political sociology, political psychology and political economy. The chapter demonstrates that not only do they all lend themselves to empirical research into voting behaviour in Germany but they complement each other in highlighting different facets of the complex causality of vote choice in the Federal Republic. Recent convergence between the three schools – around concepts such as the 'reasoning voter', for instance, has enhanced this complementarity.

The picture that emerges of the contemporary German voter is one of an individual whose vote choice is shaped by both the internal and external worlds. In terms of the internal world, individuals' vote choice is a product of long-term values interacting with more immediate preferences on issues that affect them. Values are the product of socio-economic location, early years socialisation, and life-cycle events and provide a cognitive frame with which individuals can short-circuit the information costs of coming to a 'position' on complex issues. In as far as they are different, preferences are both more contingent than values and in many ways more private. They arise from the same sources as values and are often complementary to them. However – the assumptions of much of the 'hard' rational choice literature notwithstanding – they are not always transitive, consistent or complete. They are part of the fuzzy logic of 'rational ignorance'. That is why partisan identification is not the same as vote choice.

The main reason for this is human fallibility. *Homo Economicus* is a useful ideal-type but by-and-large individuals lack the intellectual or emotional capabilities to fulfil the role. Thus, individual voters are not cultural dupes but, at the same time, humans are social creatures and individuals are heavily reliant on the external world to provide the cues with which to come to a vote choice. This external world can be divided into the 'private' and the 'public' domains. The private world is one of networks of individuals such as family, friends and work colleagues: each of whom is also a product of socio-economic location, socialisation and life-cycle events and in turn is receiving cognitive cues themselves. For this reason, it is easier to divide the internal and external worlds conceptually than it is to do so empirically. More clearly 'external' is what I refer to in this chapter as the 'public' domain: particularly the impact of the media on vote choice. When private networks are relatively homogeneous they provide a relatively strong filter to media effects; but where they are weak or heterogeneous the media becomes increasingly decisive in determining vote choice.

There is very little purchase available for the *Sonderweg* narrative in this discussion – and all of what has been discussed above are human truths that do not just apply to the German voter. However, what does differ across political systems are the strategies that parties as organisations adopt to mobilise voters and respond to their preferences, as well as the nature of the political arenas in which they compete and co-operate. It is to these institutional contexts that the book now turns.

6
State Structures, Electoral Systems and Party Systems

6.1 Introduction

Chapter 6 moves the focus of the study away from voter behaviour and towards the architecture of the political marketplace in which political parties operate. The chapter examines the impact of three institutional structures on party politics in Germany and in a comparative perspective. The first two are formal institutions. These are, first, the structure of the state and, second, the electoral system or – as in the case of Germany – systems used to aggregate voter choice. The third is the party system or, again in the case of the Federal Republic, party systems that are framed by these formal institutions. The chapter is structured as follows: state and administrative structures are examined in Section 6.2, followed by electoral systems in Section 6.3 and party systems in Section 6.4. Finally, the chapter ends with a brief summary of the data and arguments.

The institutional architecture of the political marketplace provides opportunities and constraints for political parties – it determines the conditions by which parties can gain entry into the market, their chances of survival within it, the extent of direct or indirect access to governmental office, and the number and type of credible strategies available to parties in order to achieve these goals. To help us compare Germany's institutional architecture with that of other advanced industrial democracies, the analysis in this chapter is framed within a generalisable meso-level theoretical literature: that of 'political opportunity structures', or POS (Kitschelt, 1986; Tarrow, 1994). The POS model has been chosen because it is focussed on the opportunities for, and constraints upon, political action presented to political actors by institutions. By and large the POS literature concentrates on social movements, but there is no reason why the ideas underpinning the literature cannot also be applied to political entrepreneurs using the more conventional route of party politics. Tarrow describes political opportunity structures as 'consistent ... dimensions of the political environment' and goes on to say that 'state structures create stable opportunities, but it is changing opportunities within states that provide the openings' (1994, op cit: 18) for political action. These 'changing opportunities' come about through shifts in the configuration of institutional power, and can be grasped by social movements and political parties alike.

Tarrow's focus on institutional power begs the question: what is an institution? There is no consensus around this question in political science. On the one hand, the rational choice literature provides a parsimonial account of institutions (Laver and Schofield, 1990; Tsebelis, 1990; Laver and Shepsle, 1995; Shepsle and Weingast, 1995), in which they are a little more than a set of 'congealed tastes' (Riker, 1980) or, alternatively, 'prescriptions' about the permissibility of actions in a given setting (Ostrom, 1986). On the other hand, scholars such as Hall provide a more developed account of institutions which, he argues, include 'the formal rules, compliance procedures, and standard operating practices that structure the relationship between individuals in various units of the polity and economy' (Hall, 1986: 19). Ikenberry echoes this, arguing that institutions operate on three levels: ranging 'from specific characteristics of government institutions, to the more overarching structures of the state, to the nation's normative social order' (Ikenberry, 1988: 222–3).

Broadly speaking, the conflicting definitions and parameters of institutions found in the literature are embedded in the wider 'structure-agency' debate. It is clear that political parties adapt to the strategic environment in which they operate, but the big question is can they also bring about changes within that environment? Structurally inclined accounts of institutions allow for institutional change, but only of an incremental fashion. Social constructivists and other normative institutionalists argue that institutional change takes place as the result of policy-learning on the part of a given institution, and the changes that take place conform to a 'logic of appropriateness' (March and Olsen, 1984), which serves to limit the range of policy alternatives and render some alternatives 'beyond the pale'. A similar model of institutional change can be found in the historical institutionalist literature (Krasner, 1988; Hall, 1989; Skocpol, 1992; King, 1995). Here, institutions exist within a state of 'punctuated equilibrium' in which 'rapid bursts of change (are) followed by long periods of stasis' (Krasner, 1988: 242). In other words, policy choices made at the time of institutional formation have a persistent and determinate impact over long run patterns of behaviour within these institutions, with standard operating procedures (SOPs) routinising activities and inhibiting anything other than incremental change. Both of these approaches are consistent with the *Sonderweg* narrative of German politics, in that explanations for present political phenomena are framed within a narrative that ascribes high levels of significance to past events.

Although these accounts of institutional change are plausible, they both assume that values are primarily endogenous to institutions. In other words, values are embedded within institutions, and agents bring little or no individual motivations, values, or preferences from the wider environment. This raises two objections in the context of this study. First, it returns us to the idea of 'cultural dupes' – but this time it is the political parties themselves who are the dupes and their scope to 'make the weather' is very limited, because any change that does take place within a given polity is slow and prone to high degrees of path-dependence. This may be true in most instances, but not all. It is true that the *Sonderweg* provides a useful narrative for explaining why certain elements of German politics (for instance, the Federal system, or the broad commitment of political elites to ongoing European integration) are how they are, drawing on the experience of the past. But it is also true that at key historical junctures in that past it was the strategic action of political actors – often individuals – that shaped that history, the weight of which bears down on politicians today. Thus as discussed in Chapter 3 it was Bismarck's deliberate polarising of German society along confessional lines in the *Kulturkampf* that made manifest the confessional cleavage that still underpins party politics. Similarly, it was the decision of conservative elites to try and accommodate and, they assumed, neutralise Hitler in the early 1930s that allowed him to assume the Chancellorship, suspend the constitution, and usher in the tyranny of the Third Reich. And after the Second World War, as Chapter 4 demonstrates, it was Adenauer and Erhardt who did so much to set the geo-political and economic course of the new Federal Republic. This is not to say that theirs was the only influence, but rather to point out that these developments were neither path-dependent nor inevitable. They owed a great deal to strategic political action by political agents. Normative and historical institutionalist accounts have problems explaining abrupt changes of this nature.

These arguments lead us to the second objection, that the assumption that changes in institutional culture and SOPs are path-dependent and site-specific in their parameters, privileges comparison across time and neglects comparison across space. Regarding values as being purely endogenous to institutions makes comparison across polities highly problematic, because the logical – and easiest – way to explain any phenomena is through diachronic study, with reference to the political and normative context in which the phenomena exists, rather than looking outwards to other instances. But if we take this approach we run the risk of generating tautological or self-referential explanations.

That being said, in recent years the new institutionalist literature has seen some blurring of the utility maximiser/cultural dupe divide (see Peters, 1998; Weingast, 1998; Checkel and Moravcsik, 2001), and, even the most entrenched rational choice theorist would accept that institutions do constitute signifi-cant constraints on instrumental action. Thus the chapter echoes these developments, arguing that institutions act as constraints upon political agency that constrain the scope of strategic action available to political parties. Values are both exogenous and endogenous to these institutions.

Nevertheless, it also assumes that institutions can change over time and are often changed by political agents to reflect their strategic needs. Crucially, therefore, the study also assumes that, where the institutional architecture remains unchanged, it is because it gives a particular shape to the warp and weave of party politics that both privileges political 'insiders' and limits the political opportunities available for entry into the political marketplace. To test these assumptions, the data and arguments that follow explore the idea of institutional settings in Germany and elsewhere as potential facilitators or constraints upon the emergence of what I call political outsiders (specifically, new parties) within that institutional environment. Thus, instead of taking institutional continuity and stability as self-evident, the chapter explicitly asks if change has taken place and, if not, why not?

6.2   State and administrative structures

The first set of institutional variables that impact upon party politics in Germany and elsewhere are those of state and administrative structures. In terms of state structures, the key variable is the division between federal and unitary states. All things being equal, we would assume that federations provide a more 'open' political opportunity structure for political agents, because of the importance of sub-national party systems and the complex system of constitutionally codified checks and balances between different tiers of government which characterise such states (see Lees, 2002). At the same time all federations are not the same and can be categorised in different ways. For instance, Riker creates a dichotomy between 'decentralised federalist' and 'centralised federalist' systems (Riker, 1964) whilst Stepan places them along a 'demos constraining-demos enabling' continuum (Stepan, 2001).

Stepan's account of federal systems works from the assumption that 'all democratic federations, *qua* federations, are centre constraining'. There are four reasons for this. First, the constitutional checks and balances described earlier are designed to protect the powers of the constituent units against the centre, in effect placing some policy areas beyond the centre's jurisdiction. Second, constitutionally protected sub-national tiers of government diffuse the demos into multiple demoi, divided into multiple authority structures. As is explored later in the chapter, this also has implications for both the internal organisation and distribution of power within parties and also in terms of the relative distinctiveness of, and weight assigned to, sub-national party systems (and thus the distribution of power between parties). Third, federal constitutions require a certain level of assent from the constituent parts before amendment is possible – thus creating veto players at the sub-national level and constraining the centre's room for manoeuvre. Finally, as a corollary to the previous three factors, federal constitutions are, as a rule, more complex than those of unitary states and the judiciary's status as an arbitrator of boundary disputes enhances its status as a political actor in its own right (Stepan, 2001: 335–6). This means that judicial review becomes a potent tool of political competition, not just for political parties but also for other political actors.

Stepan argues that in Federal systems there are four key variables that determine the degree of constraint, which can be exerted on the centre. These are, first, the degree of overrepresentation in the territorial chamber; second, the 'policy scope' of the territorial chamber; third, the degree to which policy making is constitutionally allocated to super majorities or to subunits of the federation; and, fourth, the degree to which the party system is polity-wide in its orientation and incentive systems. Stepan applies his analysis to a number of modern federations (including Germany, the United States, Brazil, India, Austria, and Belgium) and concludes that there is a high degree of variance between federations in aggregate terms and on a dimension-by-dimension basis. This 'demos constraining–demos enabling' continuum is set out in Table 6.1. Stepan places Germany's system of

Table 6.1   Stepan's four 'demos constraining–demos enabling' variables

Variables	Propositions
1. The degree of overrepresentation in the territorial chamber	The greater the overrepresentation of the less populous states (and thus the underrepresentation of the more populous states) the greater the demos-constraining potential of the territorial chamber
2. The 'policy scope' of the territorial chamber	The greater the 'policy scope' of the chamber that represents the principle of territory, the greater the potential to limit the law-making powers of the chamber that represents the population.
3. The degree to which policy making is constitutionally allocated to supermajorities or to subunits of the federation	The greater the amount of policy making competencies that are constitutionally prescribed as requiring supermajorities or as being beyond the law-making powers of the central government, the greater the demos is constrained
4. The degree to which the party system is polity-wide in its orientation and incentive systems	The more political parties are disciplined parties whose incentive systems, especially concerning nominations, privileges polity-wide interests over provincial and local interests, the more polity-wideparties can mitigate the inherent demos limiting characteristics of federalism

Source: Stepan, 2001: 340–1.

federalism at the middle of his comparative ranking. In terms of the first variable, the degree of overrepresentation of the territorial chamber, the least over represented system is Belgium (with a Gini-coefficient of over representation of 0.015), whilst the most over represented is Brazil (with a coefficient of 0.52). Germany, by contrast has a coefficient of 0.32 (Stepan, 2001: 342). Nevertheless, Germany's middle-ranking status still represents a significant degree of territorial overrepresentation. The 1949 Basic Law (amended after Unification) gives all German states between three and six votes in the second chamber, the Bundesrat. The two most populous states, North Rhine-Westphalia (population: 17.8 million) and Bavaria (11.9 million), have only six votes whilst, at the other end of the scale, the city-states of Hamburg (1.7 million) and Bremen (0.7 million) have three votes. This is quite a high degree of territorial overrepresentation and its demos constraining potential is considerable. However, the extent to which this provides a benign POS for political outsiders depends to some extent on their territorial location and the balance of power in the Bundesrat. For instance, the success of the SPD and Greens in toppling the incumbent CDU–FDP coalition in Lower Saxony in 1990 shifted the majority in the Bundesrat from CDU to SPD-led states (Lees, 1998, 2000). It also served to give the state's Greens considerable leverage and political profile at the national as well as sub-national level.

In terms of the second variable, the degree of 'policy scope' of the second chamber, the Bundesrat's competencies are fairly modest by comparison with some other federal states. In the United States, for instance, the principle of 'symmetry of policy scope' has often led to legislative gridlock, but the German system of federalism accords the Bundesrat comparatively less policy scope – although this has changed to some extent recently. In the early years of the Federal Republic, only 40 per cent of Bundestag legislation required Bundesrat assent, but this rose to around 60 per cent in the 1990s. Much of this increased legislative consent ratio was the result of concessions won by the German states during the Maastricht Treaty ratification process and Bundesrat consent is now required when European legislation impacts on those policy competencies reserved for the constituent states, such as Education and Science (Jeffery, 1994).

The ranking of countries according to the third variable, the degree to which policy making is constitutionally allocated to supermajorities or to subunits of the federation, also places Germany about half-way along the 'demos constraining-demos enabling' continuum. However, analysis of this variable yields an interesting dichotomy. On the one hand, Article 31 of the Basic Law states that 'Federal law shall take precedence over *Land* law', which means that, in terms of law-making power, the central demos is far less constrained in Germany than it is in, for instance, the United States. On the other hand, whereas in the United States federal employees administer many federal programmes directly, the vast majority of German federal programmes are administered by *Länder* officials on behalf of the federation (Stepan, 2001: 352–3).

Stepan's first three variables relate to the degree to which the Bundesrat, as the territorial chamber, is a potential constraint upon the political centre. By definition this will be in inverse proportion to the level of constraint placed on political outsiders. And according to Stepan, compared with four other federations (the inclusion of Spain in this category is debatable, but engaging with the issue here is unnecessary), the Bundesrat is a moderately constraining territorial chamber. Stepan's continuum is set out in Table 6.2.

Stepan's placement of Germany at the median point in the continuum casts an interesting perspective on debates about the capacity for political and administrative gridlock in the Federal Republic. Much has been made of the transaction costs associated with federal systems such as Germany's and the relative preponderance of potential veto players in such systems (see Scharpf (1985, 1988) on the 'joint-decision trap' in both Germany and the EU, for instance). In terms of German party politics, it has long been recognised that control of the Bundesrat allows opposition parties to potentially act as veto players on government legislation. The SPD under the leadership of Oskar Lafontaine, for instance, used their control of the Bundesrat to this effect during the last years of the Kohl government in the mid-1990s. The degree of veto power enjoyed by the Bundesrat depends on the nature of specific legislation being considered. In some instances it can exercise an absolute veto over legislation whilst in others it has the power of suspensary veto. In these later instances an absolute majority or, in some instances, a two-thirds majority, in the Bundestag is required to overturn such a veto. Where agreement between the Bundestag and Bundesrat is impossible, legislation is taken to a conciliation committee made up of representatives from the two chambers.

It is clear that the Bundesrat's powers add a second dimension to party political competition at the national level, beyond the Bundestag itself, which can under certain circumstances be put to formidable use by opposition parties. At the same time political parties that make up the Federal government can try and neutralise this new dimension by making use of the institutional resources at their disposal and engaging in pork-barrel politics. A recent, and controversial, example of this practice took place in 2000 when SPD Chancellor Schröder personally made promises of financial assistance to selected *Land* governments in return for supporting the passage of a raft of tax reforms through the Bundesrat (FAZ.15/07/00). In this instance the interests of the individual *Land* governments trumped the collective political preferences of CDU-led majority in the Bundesrat, demonstrating that the federal structure can constrain opposition parties in the same way that it does for governing parties.

What is clear from this discussion is that the Bundesrat provides a benign institutional arena for potential veto players. But the comparative taxonomy

Table 6.2   Continuum of the upper chamber's constitutional prerogatives to constrain a majority at the centre

Least constraining				Most constraining
India Virtually only a revisionary chamber. Upper chamber has no constitutional powers to protect subunit autonomy against (a 'sixty day') central intervention. Upper chamber has capacity to review or deny President's rule only after 60 days.	*Spain* Major power is Article 155 of the constitution, which precludes intervention by centre unless it has received the absolute majority approval of upper house. Plays no role in constructive vote of no confidence or normal legislation. Largely a revisionary chamber.	*Germany* Upper chamber plays no role in constructive vote of no confidence. This is the exclusive competence of the lower chamber that alone can play the potential veto role in approximately 65% of legislative agenda that directly relates to center–subunit issues. Relatively slight capacity to block potential majority of lower chamber. Even in years when upper chamber was controlled by a different majority than majority of lower chamber, the upper chamber sustained less than 3% of its vetoes. Upper chamber plays almost no role in confirming or denying major administrative appointments.	*United States* Extensive capacity to block democratic majority. The unrepresentative chamber has same voting rights on all legislation as 'one person, one vote' chamber. Senate has exclusive competence to confirm or deny all major judicial and administrative appointments. A chair of a committee can at times be a 'win set' of one. A 'win set' of senators representing only 15% of total electorate can block ordinary legislation.	*Brazil* Excessive for the efficacious and legitimate functioning of democratic government. The extremely disproportional upper chamber must approve of all legislation. The Senate has twelve areas where they have exclusive law making prerogatives. A 'win set' of senators representing 13% of total electorate can block ordinary legislation supported by senators representing 87% of population.

Source: Adapted from Stepan, 2001: 350.

put forward by Stepan demonstrates that although the Bundesrat's powers are significant, comparisons with more notorious examples of gridlock, such as that found in the United States, need to be made carefully. In the United States and, particularly, in Brazil, relatively small minorities can constitute a 'win set' of veto players able to block democratic majorities. Moreover, in the United States, the relative strength of the committee system allows the chair of a committee to constitute a 'win set' of one. This is not the case in Germany where, as Stepan observes, on average only 3 per cent of vetoes threatened by the Bundesrat are sustained. Bundestag–Bundesrat relations are governed by a system of formal decision rules and informal norms that prevent such standoffs from happening. In short, Germany has a federal system of government but the constitutional balance between the Bundestag and Bundesrat is designed to endow the ruling political party or parties at the centre with far more power than is the case in the United States.

As already noted, Bundestag–Bundesrat relations constitute a second dimension of party political competition at the national level. In addition, a third dimension is opened up through the division of administrative competences between the Federation and the constituent *Land* governments. The impact of this dimension on party politics is mainly indirect, but it does have implications for inter- and intra-party relations. Broadly speaking, the Basic Law sets out four different types of policy competence. First, purely federal administration (*Bundeseigene Verwaltung*) deals with 'high politics' policy areas such as foreign policy, federal finance, defence, and so on. *Land* governments have no involvement in these policy areas once the particular shape of legislation in these areas has been agreed by the Bundestag and Bundesrat. A second set of delegated competences (*Bundesauftragsverwaltung*) is administered by the *Länder* under the guidance of the Federation. These include the administration of federal motorways, some major taxes and some strategically important policy areas such as the management of nuclear power. This area does provide some limited scope for party political input by *Land* governments, as demonstrated by the activities of the Energy Advisory Council (*Energiebeirat*) in Berlin between 1989 and 1990 and the Advisory Council for the Phasing Out of Nuclear Power (*Kernenergieausstiegsbeirat*) in Lower Saxony between 1990 and 1994. In both these instances the *Länder* in question were ruled by SPD–Green coalitions that used the limited scope of their delegated competences to modify the impact in their states of energy policies formulated by the CDU/CSU–FDP coalition at the national level (Lees, 1998, 2000). The third and most common category is that of competences simply carried out by the *Länder* (*Landeseigene Verwaltung*). These include federal traffic laws, federal emission control laws, waste disposal and much EU legislation. Even more than with delegated competences, this class of competences allows ruling parties in the *Länder* to modify the impact of legislation in their jurisdictions and institutions. Thus the Lower Saxony Advisory Council for Recycling and Waste Disposal (*Kommission der Niedersächsischen*

Landesregierung zur Vermeidung und Verwertung von Reststoffen und Abfällen),
set up by the state's SPD–Green coalition during the early 1990s, became a
central plank of the policy programme agreed between the two parties (Lees,
1998, 2000). Finally the fourth category of 'own-law' administration, in
which the *Länder* formulate and administer their own legislation, is not dealt
with in the Basic Law. In these instances, *Land* constitutions and legislatures
are 'decisive' (Gunlicks, 2003: 65). Thus, the scope of such legislation provides the core of party political competition at the sub-national level.
Moreover, in the case of high profile *Land* coalitions, such as Red–Green
coalitions in Lower Saxony, Hesse, and Saxony–Anhalt in the 1990s or
Edmund Stoiber's CSU administration in Bavaria in the run-up to the 2002
Bundestag elections, the record of *Land* governments is a potentially powerful tool in the conduct of partisan competition at the national level as well.

The impact of this third dimension of party political competition is threefold. First, parties of Federal government are strategically constrained and, at
the same time, opposition parties as parties of *Land* government enjoy more
access to political power, input into policy making, and leverage over the
discourse of party politics, than is the case in unitary states. It also provides
the means by which political parties attain their primary goal of survival
within the political marketplace. Thus, parties such as the CSU in Bavaria or
the PDS in the new Federal states explicitly mobilise around a 'regional'
agenda (for recent work on this theme see Sutherland 2001; Hough, 2001) in
order to secure their continuing presence in the 'national' party system.
Second, and related to the last point, the internal management of political
parties is made quite complex, with the *Land* tier of government providing
alternative power- and resource-bases that compete with the 'national' party.
Third, the separation of policy formulation and implementation powers sus-
tains the traditional German norm of the 'administrative state' (*Beamtenstaat*),
characterised by the idea of the apolitical specialist bureaucrat. At the same
time, the post-1945 settlement brought political parties into the centre of
the governmental/administrative nexus of the new Federal Republic. The
'party state' (*Parteienstaat*) principle was enshrined in Article 21 of the Basic
Law, which stated that 'the political parties shall participate in the formation
of the political will of the people'. This created a new norm of state power in
which state legitimacy was directly linked to the legitimacy of the political
parties (and vice versa). The development of the party state over the post-war
period is demonstrated by the fact that by 1972 the main political parties
staffed over half the senior posts (state secretaries, heads and departmental
heads of division) at the state and federal level of the civil service.
Nevertheless, despite the politicisation of the civil service through political
appointees, the persistence of the residual *Beamtenstaat* ideal privileges
expert opinion and discourages dramatic shifts in policy content or
style. The overall effect is to encourage consensus, incremental change,
and the adoption of a technocratic political discourse by insider parties.

Clearly political parties operating within this party–state nexus are vulnerable to the kind of institutional capture feared by Brittan (1975) and discussed in Chapter 1. However, the existence of this nexus also sets up an additional barrier to full participation in the political marketplace in that it presents relative newcomers such as the Greens in the early 1990s, which lacked an established administrative cadre, with the problem of how to acquire the administrative expertise necessary to staff key ministries once in power (Lees, 2000).

The 'sectorisation' (Bulmer, 1983) of the German state described earlier not only imposes clear limits on the ability of any political party to manipulate the parameters of state power, but also allows veto players within the system to exercise countervailing power. As a result, it becomes more rational for ruling parties to try and co-opt these veto players rather than try to bulldoze policies past them. As Goetz observes, in Germany 'government at the centre is ... the creative use of institutions and people, political and administrative resources, and formal and informal governing devices' (Goetz, 2003: 23) in order to neutralise potential veto players outside of the ruling coalition.

But sometimes the most important veto-player is a member of one's own government. Coalition government is a common outcome of proportional electoral systems such as Germany's and, perhaps inevitably, they present greater co-ordination and steering costs than single-party governments. But the German practice of political appointees, coupled with the norm of ministerial autonomy (the *Ressortsprinzip*) further constrains the capacity of government as a unitary actor. The *Parteienstaat* ideal makes possible the de facto capture of particular ministries by political parties, whilst the fragmentation caused by the *Ressortsprinzip* adds an explicit party political dimension to the routine inter-departmental rivalries that characterise all governments. This is offset by the 'guidelines' competence (*Richtlinienkompetenz*) enjoyed by the Chancellor, which does much to maintain the steering capacity of the government and buttress the power enjoyed by the largest party.

The arguments above are of relevance to Stepan's final variable, the degree to which the party system is polity-wide in its orientation and incentive systems. According to Stepan, Germany ranks highly along this dimension, at least compared with other federations. Compared with other federations such as Brazil, India, and the United States, Germany's party system displays strong centralising tendencies. Polity-wide parties control almost all of the seats in the two chambers and exert a high degree of party discipline over their members. Having said that, as has been noted, these centralising tendencies are offset to some extent by the presence of alternative power- and resource-bases in the *Länder* parties.

To sum up, the net effect of the factors discussed earlier is that the *Land* tier of government is a powerful player in German party politics and that its administrative structures act as significant constraint on the kind of top-down government normally associated with the United Kingdom, at least until the devolution reforms of the late 1990s. They provide the institutional context for opposition parties to act as veto players at the national level and also provide a break on the internal centralisation of political parties. The result of this is that the model of top-down government, and to some extent party discipline – beyond that exercised by the party *Fraktion* – that is familiar in the United Kingdom is made impossible in Germany. As Bulmer and Paterson point out, Germany's decentralized policy-making apparatus encourages 'a uniform and agreed co-operation of all the participants' (Bulmer and Paterson, 1987: 187), and it is no surprise that the tone of party politics in Germany reflects this.

6.3   Electoral systems

As discussed earlier in this study, many rational choice accounts of party politics draw on Anthony Downs' (1957) analogy of party systems as markets, in which parties are regarded as analogous with firms competing with each other for voters who, in turn, are analogous with consumers. Each party's 'product' was a bundle of policy positions and, in the early Downsian models, the dimension along which one could locate these products was a one-dimensional left/right continuum, based on redistributional issues. Later models have tended to supplement this with an additional dimension, often based on an authoritarian/libertarian or materialist/post-materialist dimension.

It is important to reiterate these points at the start of this section of the chapter because such models assume that the individual voter has an ideal policy position along the left–right continuum and that the aggregate of voters' preferences usually assume a 'normal distribution': in other words, a bell-curve along the left–right axis. In plurality and majoritarian electoral systems, Duverger's Law decrees that the long-term outcome will be a party system dominated by two parties, competing around the ideological centre of the party system for the median voter. As the median voter is located at the point where the aggregate of voters' preferences reaches equilibrium, it follows that the logical outcome under such systems is a broadly consensual form of politics, in which the two main parties compete for the centre-ground. This means that the preferences of voters who do not share the median position are neglected in relative terms, which raises the danger that a 'tyranny of the majority' will emerge (Mueller, 1996: 149).

By contrast, proportional electoral systems tend to generate multiparty systems in which no single party is able to command a majority of votes. There are exceptions to this, however, in which multi-party proportional systems generate a 'dominant' party. The Swedish Social Democratic Party or the Bavarian Christian Social Union are examples of this. Nevertheless, under normal conditions the dynamics of proportional systems mean it is feasible – and some would say rational – for some political parties to seek out 'niche' positions across the normal distribution of voter preferences, representing minority ideological positions or interests. As a result such systems are more likely to sustain viable Farmers' parties, Green parties, Communist parties, Far Right parties and so on. The broad thrust of political discourse may remain centrist, but the existence of smaller parties articulating minority interests means that the tyranny of the majority is avoided.

This is all the more the case if the lack of a dominant party means that larger parties have to rely on smaller ones for support in order to form governments. In short, we would expect proportional systems to present a more benign political opportunity structure for political outsiders (see Kitschelt, 1986, for instance).

Nevertheless the dichotomisation of plurality/majoritarian and proportional electoral systems is over-simplistic. An alternative classification of electoral systems is to divide them into six categories. These are, first, Simple District Level Allocation (no threshold); second, District Level Allocation (threshold); third, Additional Member Systems (AMS); fourth, Complex PR Districting (no compensatory upper tier); fifth, Compensatory Seats (threshold for upper-tier allocation); sixth, Nationwide Allocation (no threshold). Obviously, none of these systems are perfectly proportional, although the nationwide allocation system is closest to the ideal-type of a 'pure' proportional system advocated by some public choice theorists (see Mueller, 1996: 132–40). It has been used once, in the Romanian elections of 1990 (Budge *et al.*, 1997: 237).

Electoral systems can be further differentiated. For instance, simple district level systems can be further divided into plurality and PR categories, whilst more proportional systems can be further divided into Multi-Representative List versus Single Transferable Vote systems. In addition, 'multi-rep' systems themselves can be divided into those that use the Hare quotient, the Droop quota, or the Imperiali to calculate parties' allocation of legislative seats. Given that this study's primary focus is on Germany, the further one develops further sub-classifications the more danger there is in being presented with the classic comparative politics problem of 'too many variables and not enough cases'. Nevertheless, for taxonomical purpose it is helpful to use these sub-categories when locating the national German electoral system within the wider context of Western European democracies. This is set out in Table 6.3 that demonstrates that Germany's electoral system is in many senses an outlier compared with the rest of Western Europe. Sixteen out of the 18 systems covered in the table only have one ballot, but Germany's AMS combines a first vote for constituency-based candidates and second vote for *Land*-based party-list candidates. This puts it in a minority of two along with Italy, where elections to the Senate combines a first-past-the-post ballot for the majority of single-member constituency candidates and a proportional system for party lists in multiple-member constituencies. Nevertheless, Germany is the only country covered that combines a plurality system on the first ballot and a proportional system using the Hare/Niemeyer formula on the second ballot.

Table 6.3 Germany compared with other election systems in Western Europe

	Electoral formula 1990s			District magnitude		Disproportionality	
	Ballot	Tiers	Formulas	1980s	1990s	1980s	1990s
Austria	One	2	PR: Hare + D'Hont	020.3	020.3	002.2	002.8
Belgium	One	2	PR: Hare + D'Hont	007.0	007.5	006.0	008.0
Denmark	One	2	PR: MSL+ Hare	007.3	010.5	003.3	004.5
Finland	One	1	PR: D'Hont	013.2	013.3	005.1	007.0
France	One	1	MAJ+PLUR	001.0	001.0	018.7	040.3
Germany	Two	2	PLUR+ PR: Hare	001.0	001.9	001.4	005.8
Greece	One	4	PR: D'Hont	005.3	005.3	005.9	007.8
Iceland	One	2	PR: D'Hont+ D'Hont	006.1	007.9	004.0	003.9
Ireland	One	1	PR: STV	003.8	004.0	005.2	006.4
Italy	Two	2	PLUR+PR: Hamilton	019.5	001.3	004.7	013.6
Luxembourg	One	1	PR: D'Hont	014.0	015.0	004.8	005.4
Netherlands	One	1	PR: D'Hont	150.0	150.0	003.0	002.9
Norway	One	2	PR: MSL+MSL	008.3	008.7	005.1	006.3
Portugal	One	1	PR: D'Hont	012.4	010.5	006.9	008.0
Spain	One	1	PR: D'Hont	006.7	007.0	015.1	012.7
Sweden	One	2	PR: MSL+MSL	011.1	011.6	002.6	003.3
Switzerland	One	1	PR: D'Hont	008.2	007.7	005.1	007.5
United Kingdom	One	1	PLUR	001.0	001.0	012.9	017.6

Source: Adapted from Lane and Ersson, 1999: 200.

Germany and Italy are part of a larger minority of countries with what are effectively two electoral tiers, in that there is a higher national re-allocation of votes under both systems. In the case of Germany, the Hare/Niemeyer system, or 'largest remainder' system of seat allocation operates at the national level and re-allocates seats according to a quota or threshold of votes that each party must win to gain a seat. The quota is established by dividing the number of votes cast by the number of seats to be included in the next legislature. The vote for each party is then divided by this quota.

Germany is also – along with France, Luxembourg, and the United Kingdom – at the low end of the scale in terms of district magnitude (defined as the number of seats allocated to each electoral district). However, as the electoral system adjusted to absorb the larger all-German electorate following unification, the level of disproportionality within the German system has risen in the last ten years. Thus in the 1980s Germany had the most proportionate system in Western Europe, with a score of 1.4, but its 1990s score of 5.8 means that Germany is now located towards the median position. Austria now has the most proportionate system (2.8), while the most disproportionate system remains that of France (40.3).

Of course, given that they are institutional devices to aggregate the electoral preferences of voters, all electoral systems contain an element of disproportionality within them. But the amount of disproportionality is to a great extent the result of institutional design: in other words, the choice of system or systems, electoral formulae, district magnitude and other decision rules such as thresholds to electoral representation, and so on. Thus, the AMS system that developed in the Federal Republic was designed to produce a particular pattern of electoral outcomes and prevent the re-emergence of the kind of electoral and political instability that dogged the Weimar Republic. Unlike mixed-member systems in Japan, Russia or the Ukraine, for instance, the German system is a compensatory one, in which the design of second ballot is specifically intended to offset the disproportionate effects of the first ballot, which tends to favour the larger parties (Siaroff, 2000: 20). This is re-enforced by the Hare/Niemeyer system, introduced in 1985, which tends to favour smaller parties. At the same time, however, these compensatory effects are offset by the electoral threshold, in force since 1957, which prevents small parties from entering the Bundestag unless they have either secured 5 per cent of the popular vote or won three constituency seats. Once votes for these parties have been excluded, seats are allocated to parties that have scaled the threshold on the basis of constituent seats plus parties' list votes as determined by the Hare/Niemeyer quota.

This form of 'personalised PR' (Johnson, 1983; Smith, 1989; Beyme, 1993) is not replicated exactly at the *Land* level, where four states (Baden-Württemberg, Lower Saxony, Saxony and Schleswig-Holstein) use the alternative D'Hondt, or 'highest average', system of seat allocation. Nevertheless, both Federal and Land levels broadly conform to the same mixed electoral system that was designed to (i) prevent one-party dominance; (ii) shut-out extremist parties and prevent party system fragmentation; (iii) encourage centripetal political competition; and (iv) preserve a strong territorial link between electors and elected. There are elements of Germanys mixed member system, such as the allocation of 'surplus votes' (*Überhangsmandaten*), that have attracted criticism but by-and-large the system has worked in the way it was designed. And that design has had predictable consequences for the shape of the German party system, helping to restrict entry into the political marketplace but at the same time to facilitate the survival of small but established players within it.

6.4   Party systems

Moving on to party systems, for the purposes of the chapter, party systems are classified by the number of 'effective' parties within them. Across Europe, there has been an increase in the degree of fractionalisation of party systems over the period since 1980. As a result, the average West European parliament now contains seven political parties. Nevertheless this is a crude indicator and if we count the number of 'effective' parties only, the average (West) European party system only contains four parties (Lane and Ersson, 1999: 142–3).

The degree of fractionalisation within party systems is an important variable and has potentially profound consequences for the stability of such systems. Let us think of political parties as players in a game that can be both competitive and/or co-operative. Game theorists argue that, all other things being equal, the more players that take part in a particular game, the less likely that any particular strategy or set of alternatives will become dominant. This is because the potential number of winning coalitions rises exponentially as players are added (e.g. Shapsley and Shubik, 1969). This can lead to the phenomenon of cycling, in which any potential alternative can be beaten by another, which can be beaten by another, and so on. The larger the number of potential winning coalitions, the wider the range of issue choices become available, and the more likely cycling is to occur. This is because the further away a proposed solution is to a player's ideal position, the more incentive the player has to vote it down and/or propose an alternative. Thus, in theory, the more fragmented the party system the more likely we are to find gridlock and/or instability. The problem of cycling – and solutions to it – has been a core preoccupation of public choice theorists (see Black, 1948; Arrow, 1951). As Kramer (1973) points out, cycling does not occur where a majority of players have identical preferences. In theory therefore the more polarised the party system, the less likely that such a majority exists, and the more likely that the instability associated with cycling occurs (see Niemi, 1969; Tullock and Campbell, 1970; Koga and Nagatani, 1974).

However, in reality party systems in most advanced democracies do not display the kind of instability or gridlock predicted by many theoretical models. This is because of system attributes such as voting rules (plurality versus proportional systems), barriers to representation (such as the 5 per cent hurdle at the Federal level in Germany), laws regulating internal party democracy, and so on. These institutional variables impose what theorists call a 'structure induced equilibrium' (Shepsle, 1979) on the party political game. This is why party systems can be regarded as regulated rather than laissez-faire free markets.

Some of the most important comparative work on West European – and particularly German – party systems over the last twenty years has been carried out by Gordon Smith. Smith does not overtly use a market analogy but he nevertheless recognised the importance of system attributes, not only in determining the degree of fragmentation within party systems, but also in terms of imposing equilibria upon them and avoiding institutional gridlock. Smith (1979) avoids these terms and uses the phrase 'cohesion' to describe a category of output from a given party system that, if present in sufficient quantities, will under normal circumstances bring stability to the system. Smith argues that there are two types of cohesion, which may or may not be causally linked. The first, 'governing' cohesion, relates to one specific type of system output, namely the relative effectiveness of government (as determined by factors such as longevity, stability, steering capacity, etc.). The second, 'social' cohesion, relates to another specific output associated with one of the key roles of political parties in modern democracies: the ability to effectively integrate and aggregate competing societal interests and, by doing this, enhance social cohesion.

The main thing to bear in mind at this point is, as already noted, there is not necessarily a direct link between governing and social cohesion and the particular patterns of the two forms of cohesion will vary from country-to-country. It is possible for a party system dominated by a single party, or small number of parties, to display high levels of governmental cohesion (in terms of stable, durable government) whilst failing to enhance social integration. Conversely, a diffuse party system may create high levels of social cohesion – in the sense that all shades of political opinion have an effective 'voice' within the system – but not deliver the goods in terms of stable government. Nevertheless, using a typology based on the two types of cohesion, Smith posits four simple classifications of party system designed to encompass this potential for differentiation across party systems. These are set out in Figure 6.1.

Smith considers the kind of majoritarian systems found under first-past-the post systems such as that used in the United Kingdom to be the ideal-type of party system, because it is able to deliver both strong, stable government and an integrated electorate. However majoritarian systems are not restricted to the Westminster model of parliamentary system and can

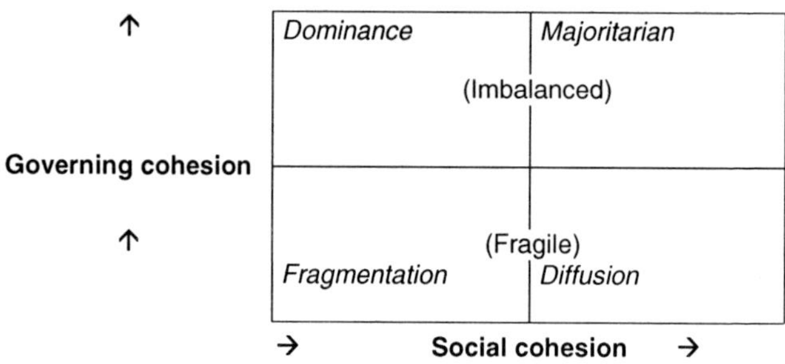

Figure 6.1   The major West European party system types
Source: Smith, 1979: 134.

work under certain circumstances in multi-party systems. Smith regarded the German party system, dominated by what he saw as two 'balanced clusters' of parties (Smith, 1979: 135), as fulfilling the criteria of a majoritarian system. Smith was writing in 1979 and was referring to the cluster of the SPD and FDP in coalition (which lasted from 1969–82), balanced by the CDU/CSU in opposition. As discussed in Chapters 4 and 5, the decline of the total *Volkspartei* vote since then, and the subsequent emergence of smaller parties such as the Greens and PDS have changed this dynamic somewhat. Nevertheless, Smith's assertion is a useful tool within the narrative of both the specific political opportunity structure literature that underpins this chapter and the market analogy used throughout this study. High levels of governmental cohesion increase the opportunity costs of entry into, and exit from, government, whilst high levels of social cohesion raises the opportunity costs for new entrants into the political marketplace itself. This is because the existence of a high level of social cohesion implies a well-integrated electorate, which reduces the amount of unoccupied political space within which a new political outsider can mobilise support.

So has this really happened within the German party system, and is it still the case today? Let us return to Downs' (1957) ideal-type of the median voter. As discussed, the median voter is in a privileged position because, with an equal number of voters on each side, she can vote down alternatives to both the right and the left. Thus the ideal point of the median voter is the equilibrium outcome under majority rule and, in two-party systems, a party can only win an election if its share of the votes includes that of the median voter. In multi-party system such as Germany's the picture is more complex because, as we have noted, it is possible and even rational for smaller parties to seek out niche positions on the left–right continuum and mobilise around more peripheral segments of the bell-curve of electoral preferences. This presents the two big *Volksparteien* with a strategic dilemma. On the one hand, as 'Catch-all' parties they must compete with one another for the median voter, which means they should appeal to the political centre. On the other, the mathematics of coalition formation implies that they may have to rely on flanking parties to the left or right in order to form a government, which means they must also have appeal in that direction. Given that these two options are potentially contradictory it makes sense for the *Volksparteien* to pursue the long-term strategic goal of either preventing the emergence of parties on their political flanks or, failing that, to bring these flanking parties into their political orbit. For their part, it is rational for smaller parties to try and avoid this state of affairs and, where possible, try and achieve a position where they hold the balance of power between the two *Volksparteien*.

So how successful have the parties been in pursuing these goals? Figure 6.2 demonstrates how the German party system at the national level has

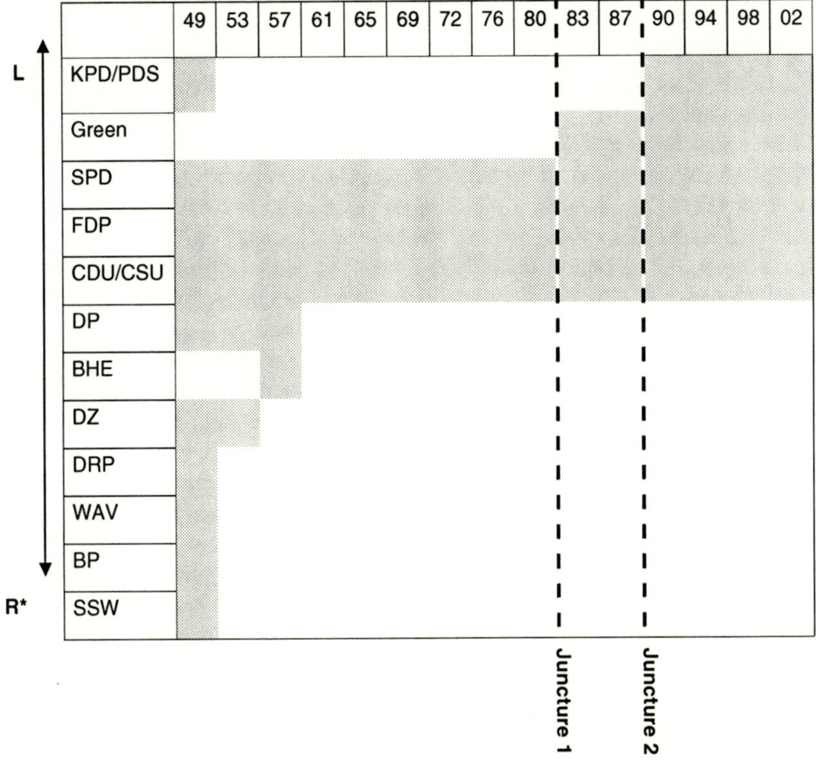

Figure 6.2   The development of the German party system: Federal elections – 1949–2002

Note: * For taxonomical reasons, particularist parties such as the BP and SSW have been placed on the right of the left–right spectrum.

developed over the period 1949–2002. The figure demonstrates, first, a 30-year period of ongoing party-system concentration, in which the party system is dominated by the two big *Volksparteien*, and, second, two systemic junctures which have served to break down this dominance and shift the centre of gravity within the party system towards the political left. The first of these junctures takes place in 1983, with the entry of the Greens, and the second takes place in 1990, following Unification, with the entry of the PDS.

Taken in the round, however, the two *Volksparteien* have been reasonably successful in preventing the emergence of flanking parties. Of the two, the CDU/CSU has been more successful. Since the inception of the Federal Republic the CDU/CSU has pursued a conscious policy of integrating the political right by both absorbing smaller parties and articulating enough of a right wing agenda, including the rights of ethnic Germans expelled from the countries of Central and Eastern Europe, as was sufficient to prevent the emergence of new competitors on the right. Thus by 1961 parties such as the far right German Reich Party (DRP) or the particularist Bavarian Party (BP) had disappeared from the Bundestag. Since then, no party to the right of the CDU/CSU has managed to garner enough votes to scale the 5 per cent hurdle to representation.

By contrast the SPD has been less successful. The party successfully survived the split that followed the *Zwangsvereinigung* and, by 1953, had successfully neutralised the KPD (which failed to be re-elected following the 1949–1953 parliament). However, the two junctures of 1983 and 1990 led to the emergence of two quite different left competitors flanking the SPD. As already noted in Chapter 4, the arrival of the Greens in 1983 presented the SPD with a particular set of problems as to how best to compete with a new party, the support for which was predominantly drawn from younger and/or well-educated voters, and which competed directly against the SPD along the materialist/post-materialist ideological dimension. In addition, the emergence of the PDS after 1990 meant that it also had to compete with a more traditional left wing party that drew most of its support from a different social milieu to that of the Greens and which competed with the SPD along the traditional left–right redistributionist dimension. As it turned out, the SPD has managed successfully to adapt to both these new electoral competitors, not least because the basis of support for the two parties are territorially distinct. The PDS's support is drawn predominantly from the new Federal states, where it remains a significant political force, but the party has failed to make an impact in the old Federal states. By contrast, the initial respectable level of support for the Greens in the new states has faded as the high level of economic distress in the new Federal states has focussed voters' preferences on almost exclusively materialist concerns. Because of this the SPD has rarely been forced to compete with both parties simultaneously but rather has been able to develop different strategies of competition and co-operation depending on the party. The exact nature of these strategies is discussed in detail in Chapter 8, but the degree of success enjoyed by the SPD is evident. In the new Federal states, the PDS remains a force but it lost support to the SPD in the 2002 Bundestag elections and, as a result, failed to scale the 5 per cent hurdle. As a result the PDS's share of seats fell from 36 in the 1998–2002 Bundestag to just two directly elected seats after the 2002 elections. And while it is true that the SPD has not been able to defeat the Greens in electoral terms, it has managed to pull the party into its political orbit. As a result, the SPD and Greens have been in formal coalition at the Federal level since 1998, following over a decade of co-operation at the *Land* level. At the same time, the SPD has been able to co-operate with both the FDP and CDU at the *Land* level and hold out the possibility of similar arrangements at the Federal level should the SPD–Green coalition break down.

And how have the Greens reacted to this? This leads us back to the discussion earlier in this section in which it was posited that it is rational for smaller parties to try and gain a position of leverage between the two big *Volksparteien*: in other words to become the 'kingmaker' within the party system. As already noted, between 1961 and 1983 there were no flanking parties to either the left or right of the two *Volksparteien*. However through-out this period the liberal FDP maintained a pivotal position in what became a 'triangular' party system (Pappi, 1984). This is illustrated in Figure 6.3. In this so-called Pappi model of the triangular party system the left–right dimen-sion of party political competition was still important but a model of co-opera-tion between the parties evolved in which all three parties were able to co-operate with each other along one of three dimensions. Thus, the SPD and CDU/CSU were sufficiently close along the corporatist dimension of the trian-gle to allow the two parties to form a coalition should circumstances demand it. This has happened once at the national level, during the Grand Coalition of 1966–69, which was dominated by the corporatist 'concerted action' agenda

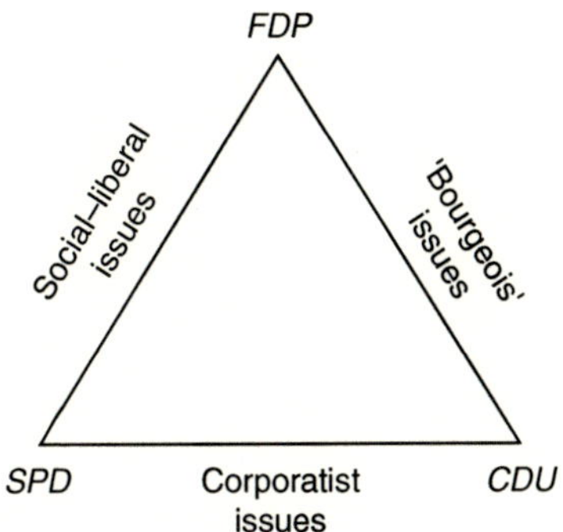

Figure 6.3   The 'Pappi model' of a triangular party system

(see Chapter 8). At the same time, the SPD and FDP could potentially co-operate along the 'social liberal' dimension, emphasising social justice and reform, as the two parties had done as the Federal government between 1969 and 1982. Finally, the CDU/CSU and FDP could co-operate along the dimension of 'bourgeois issues' such as economic growth and prosperity, law and order and the nation, as they did in the 1950s and 1960s and between 1982 and 1998.

The Pappi model explains how the FDP might potentially exert leverage over the two *Volksparteien* but the fact that it did manage to do so comes down to the more fundamental variable of electoral arithmetic. Up until the 1998 Bundestag elections, the distribution of seats between the parties on the left–right dimension meant that the FDP always controlled the median legislator in the Bundestag. In other words, the FDP was always 'Mparty' (Axelrod, 1970), and no 'minimal-connected-winning coalition' (an ideologically connected coalition, big enough to command a majority in the Bundestag, but without an unnecessary surplus majority)[3] could form without the FDP's consent. The reality of this ability to block rival coalitions meant that up until 1998 the FDP had almost continuously been in government since the foundation of the Federal Republic in 1949 and had enjoyed considerable leverage over policy in successive coalitions.

However, as discussed in Chapter 4, since the 1970s there has been a high degree of party system change in Germany. The combined impact of electoral de-alignment, the emergence of the Greens in the late 1970s, and the persistence of the post-communist PDS in the five new states of the former East Germany, broke the cosy triangular dynamic of the Pappi model. Two changes are of particular note. First, the German party system now displays a strong territorial cleavage. In the old Federal states there is now a two-bloc/four party system (consisting of the Greens, SPD, FDP and CDU/CSU), whilst in the 'new states' of the former GDR there is a three-party system (made up of the PDS, SPD and CDU). Taken together, this means that the 'national' political marketplace is occupied by five parties: the PDS, Greens, SPD, FDP and CDU/CSU. Second, this five-party system now has a wider ideological range, within which the ideological centre of gravity has shifted leftwards. These changes have had two main effects. First, the party system is less fluid and shows signs of becoming an entrenched 'two-bloc' system, dominated by the two catch-all parties, although it will need one or two more Bundestag elections to assume that this is a stable phenomenon (see Smith, 2003: 98). Second, the SPD rather than the FDP is increasingly Mparty. These two developments make it much harder for the FDP, far less the Greens, to hold the balance of power between the two *Volksparteien*. As will be discussed in Chapters 7 and 8, the Greens have long pursued a strategy devised by party moderates, led by Joschka Fischer (the SPD–Green coalition's Foreign Minister), to move the party towards the political centre. While it is not clear what the *finalité* of such a shift will be, in the mid-1990s there was talk within the party of trying to become the 'Green FDP'. However it appears that this kingmaker role is now a chimera.

At the *Land* level, however, the party system is more fluid and barriers to entry into the political marketplace easier to surmount. In recent years, in particular, parties such as the populist right PRO in Hamburg, or far right parties such as the Republicans in West Berlin have managed to garner enough votes to enter individual *Land* legislatures. However, up until now this has been an intermittent phenomenon dependent on the specific conditions of particular states at particular times in the national electoral cycle. As such, none of these flanking parties have been able to build a consistent record of success at the *Land* level. The current pattern of party political competition in *Land* parliaments is set out in Figure 6.4 demonstrating the clear territorial divide between the party systems in the old and new Federal states, as well as the failure of the far right parties to mount a consistent political challenge at the sub-national level. There are eight different parties to be found in the various *Land* parliaments, ranging from the PDS on the left of the party system to the DVU on the right. This includes the South Schleswig Voters Union (*Südschleswigsche Wählerverband*, or SSW), which exists to defend the interests of the territorially distinct Danish ethnic minority in the northern state of Schleswig-Holstein. However, of these eight parties only the two *Volksparteien* are present in all 16 *Land* parliaments.

There are two main party system types at the *Land* level. In the old Federal states we find what might be called a 'type 1' party system, made up of the Greens, SPD, FDP and CDU or CSU. At present such systems exist in Baden-Württemberg, Hesse, Lower Saxony, North Rhine-Westphalia, Rhineland Palatinate, and Schleswig-Holstein. There are also variants of the 'type 1' system in Bremen and Bavaria (where the FDP is excluded), Saarland (where the Greens and the FDP are excluded) and Hamburg (which also includes the PRO). In the new Federal states we find a 'type 2' system, made up of the PDS, SPD and CDU. This is a three-party system, but without the triangular dynamic of the old Pappi model, and is currently found in Mecklenburg-West Pomerania, Saxony and Thuringia. There are also two variants, to be found in Brandenburg (which also includes the DVU) and Saxony-Anhalt (which includes the FDP). Finally, we find one hybrid system in the city-state of Berlin, made up of a 'type 1' sub-system in the old West Berlin and a 'type 2' sub-system in the part of the city that used to be part of the German Democratic Republic. At present, the party system in the Berlin state parliament includes the PDS, Greens, SPD, FDP, and CDU and, as such, has the largest ideological range of any of the *Land* party systems.

Although there are two main system types the actual balance of electoral support varies to a considerable extent, depending on the individual *Land*. As a result, patterns of party political competition and co-operation are more flexible than is the case at the Federal level, resulting in more permutations

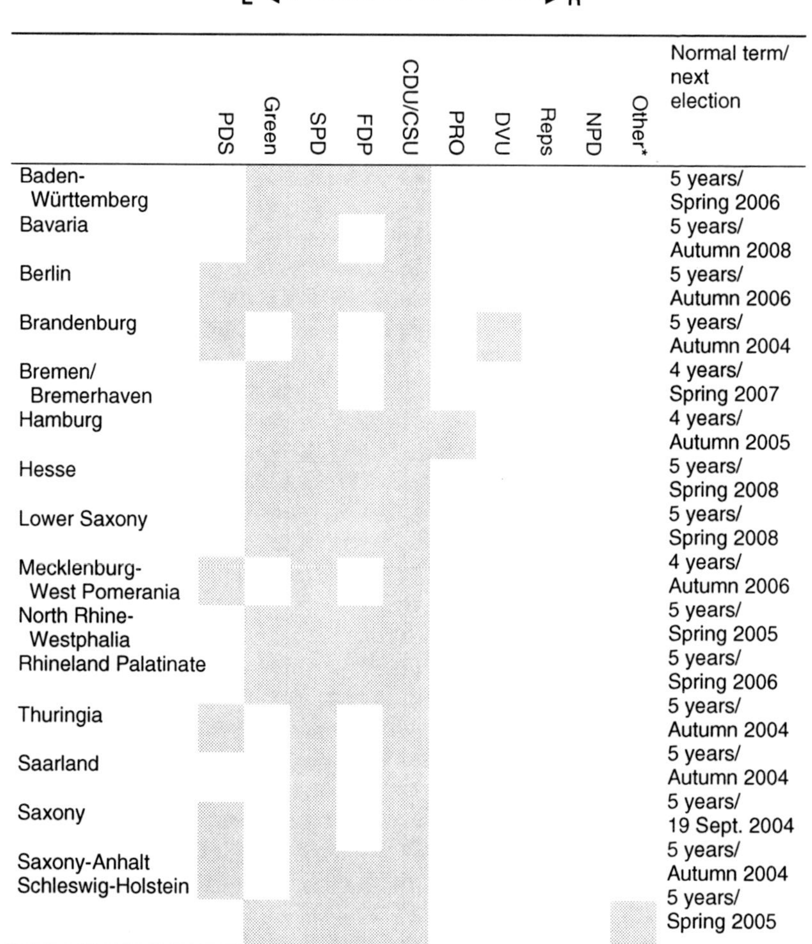

Figure 6.4   Party systems in the German *Länder* Parliaments

Notes: Table refers to party *Fraktionen* only.

* 'Other' refers to local/particularist parties. At present there is one such party in a *Land* legislature: the South Schleswig Voters Union (*Südschleswigsche Wählerverband*, or SSW), which exists to defend the interests of the Danish ethnic minority in the state (placed at right of scale for taxonomical purposes only).

Sources: Deutscher Bundestag (htttp://www.bundestag.de/info/wahlen/152.html); *Land* websites.

of party coalitions than has been the case within the national party system in the Bundestag. This is discussed in more detail in Chapter 8.

6.5 Summary

Chapter 6 examined the impact of three institutional structures on party politics: (i) state structures; (ii) electoral systems; and (iii) party systems. The analysis of these three institutional variables has been framed within POS literature (Kitschelt, 1986; Tarrow, 1994), which was focussed on the opportunities for, and constraints upon, political action presented to political actors by institutions. As a result, the analysis has been framed by the question of the extent to which these institutions facilitate or constrain the emergence of political outsiders, such as new parties? It has been argued in the chapter that certain aspects of the German institutional architecture, such as the existence of constitutionally protected tiers of *Land* government, or the compensatory effects of Hare/Niedermeyer electoral formula of seat allocation do provide opportunities for political outsiders in that they act as a countervailing influence to the disciplinary and electoral power of the two big *Volksparteien*. However, on balance, it is clear that the institutional status quo does throw up significant barriers to entry into the political marketplace for outsiders.

In terms of state structures, the ability of the Bundesrat to constrain the Bundestag is limited and, as Stepan observes, in fact it has only managed to sustain a suspensory veto on Bundestag legislation in 3 per cent of the cases under study (2001: 350). In addition, the 'party state' ethos deliberately privileges political insiders and presents relative outsiders – such as the Greens in the 1980s and early 1990s – with significant problems when it comes to expertise and the staffing of ministries (Lees, 1998, 2000). The Greens have now of course overcome this problem but, at the same time, no serious observer would argue that they are the 'anti-party party' of 20 years ago. Today the Greens are very much political insiders mobilising around a stable niche in the electoral market.

Moving on to electoral systems it is very clear that Germany's AMS or mixed member system was designed to produce a specific set of political outcomes. It has already been noted that the form of 'personalised PR' used at the national level is not replicated exactly at the *Land* level, where four states use the D'Hondt system of seat allocation rather than the Hare/ Niedermeyer formula. But all the systems are designed to prevent one-party dominance, shut out extremist parties and prevent fragmentation of the system, encourage a centrist from of politics, whilst at the same time preserving a strong territorial link between electors and elected. In this, the architects of the system had learned from the mistakes of the Weimar Republic in particular and the terrible consequences that arose from them. However, the 5 per cent hurdle in particular has shut out most political outsiders since its inception in 1957.

Finally, the party system reflects the barriers to political outsiders discussed earlier. Over the half-century since the foundation of the Federal Republic we have seen three main phases of party system development. First, a steady process of concentration by which the number of parties in the Bundestag reduced from ten in the 1949–53 parliament to three in 1961. Second, a period of equilibrium between 1961 and 1983, characterised by the triangular Pappi model of party competition and co-operation. Finally, a period of deconcentration and relative instability associated with the processes of partisan de-alignment and the emergence of post-materialism: punctuated by the two junctures of 1983 (the arrival of the Greens) and 1990 (the emergence of the PDS following Unification).

In terms of the market analogy, therefore, we can see the growth and subsequent modification of oligopolistic market conditions – and at the end of this process the party oligopoly remains in place and only five parties are represented in the Bundestag. So if we take the German party system as being an indicator of the openness of the political opportunity structure more generally, then its relatively high levels of concentration implies that state structures and electoral systems in Germany present significant barriers to political outsiders. It follows, therefore, that the degree of success enjoyed by political parties depends to a great extent on their ability to adapt to or even shape the institutional environment around them. It is to those parties that the book now turns.

7
Political Parties

7.1 Introduction

Chapter 7 examines the key institutional variable in the study of party politics – the political parties themselves. Political parties operate at the heart of the political process and are present in some shape or form in all advanced industrial democracies. In the context of this study, they are the firms operating within the political marketplace. Leaving this assertion to one side for the moment, there is some degree of general agreement as to what parties are for. Most scholars would agree that the core functions of political parties are

- Elite recruitment (putting forward candidates for public office)
- Sustaining public institutions (providing personnel; providing leaders with logistical support/effective opposition)
- Interest representation and aggregation (converting the demands of social interests into manageable packages of public policy choices)
- Mobilisation and integration (integrating citizens into the political system and mobilising civic participation)

It will be noted that the list above relates to party functions only but in this regard goes a little further than the functions described by Ware (1987a) and discussed in the introduction to this book. But as will be discussed shortly, a functional perspective is not necessarily the best way of categorising political parties in a comparative perspective. The systematic study of political parties dates back at least 100 years (see for instance, Michels, 1915). Yet paradoxically the comparative study of political parties remains a remarkably heterogeneous field that lacks the common core of agreed concepts and measures found, for example, in the related sub-discipline of party systems studies (Gunther and Diamond, 2003: 170). This failure has both normative and empirical consequences.

The normative argument relates to how we might redress the perceived failure of party politics in many democracies. The ideal-type of party politics was described half a century ago as that of 'universal mass participation in universal militant parties free to operate in a highly aware population' (Duverger, 1959). However in practice parties have always been oligarchical organisations characterised by 'the domination of the elected over the electors, the mandatories over the mandators, of the delegates over the delegators' (Michels, 1915: 5). This is due to (i) the logistics of organisational size; (ii) the value of specialist information; and (iii) the distance between leaders and the led. But as long as parties performed their key functions, they enjoyed significant levels of legitimacy. However in recent decades there has been a perception in many countries that parties have become less effective in carrying out these key functions, which is manifested in a corresponding loss of legitimacy amongst the general population. Indicators of this loss of legitimacy can be seen at the level of the nation-state across Europe in phenomena as diverse as disillusionment with politics (*Politikverdrossenheit*) in Germany, falling electoral turnout and party membership in the United Kingdom, or even the increase in resistance to membership of the European Union in the new accession states of Central and Eastern Europe – despite the majority of mainstream parties' commitment to this project in these countries. All of these phenomena can be interpreted as indicators of an underlying crisis of party politics in which citizens are increasingly drawn to alternative vehicles for political expression, such as single-issue pressure groups. In the terms of reference used in this study such developments can be regarded as a form of market failure.

At the same time, however, the intensity and mix of indicators of such market failure varies from country to country. This suggests two things. First, that if there is a crisis of party politics it is not necessarily inevitable and, second, that even if it is, the different institutions and modes of governance in European states serve to constrain and shape this process. Thus the method and effectiveness with which parties carry out their key functions vary across countries, depending on political culture and institutional history. For instance, in Austria or Italy all major parties traditionally enjoyed high levels of penetration into civil society: organising social clubs, building links with trades unions and employers' associations, and so on (see for instance, Müller, 1996; Bardi and Morlino, 1994). In Germany, party penetration of the state administrative apparatus remains a key feature (see Lees, 2000). By contrast parties in the United Kingdom have a more limited conception of their social or administrative functions and, arguably, weaker links with the wider society in which they are located. So in this respect the political marketplace in which parties operate varies considerably from state to state and across different levels of governance.

Given the levels of variance noted above, it must be possible to identify key characteristics or elements of best practice with regard to both how parties organise and the functions they perform. Yet even if we set aside this normative argument, the failure of scholars to settle on an agreed set of measures represents a failure of the sub-discipline and presents an empirical puzzle for the political scientist. This chapter addresses some of these issues, albeit with a focus on the empirical rather than normative side of the problem. The chapter is divided into eight sections. First, a review of the strands of the literature and the problems of establishing a single classificatory scheme that functions effectively in a comparative perspective but is also appropriate to the German context. Second, the establishment of a single classificatory scheme, primarily based on degrees of variance in the extent or 'thickness' of party organisation. Then five sections in which the classificatory scheme is used to frame a discussion of the main parties in the German party system in a comparative perspective. Finally, the chapter ends with a summary and discussion of the chapter's findings.

7.2   Problems of establishing a single classificatory scheme

Any comparative scheme for the classification of political parties must focus on a common set of criteria that can be applied across time and space. This is not as simple as it first appears. We have already touched upon the functions of political parties, but the most common and innately intuitive method of classifying political parties has been to focus on different ideological types. These types can be quite coarse grained, such as 'left wing' versus 'right wing', or clustered into a more differentiated set of party 'families' – such as Communist, Social Democratic, Liberal, Christian Democratic, Conservative, Fascist and so on. These classifications work up to a point as a method of conceptual shorthand but do not survive sustained analysis, especially comparative analysis. One problem is that these classifications are both self-reported and path-dependent. Take for instance the family of Social Democratic parties. On one level we know that these political parties are Social Democratic because they understand themselves to be Social Democratic and profile themselves externally as being Social Democratic. Moreover they have institutional ties with other nominally Social Democratic parties, thus re-enforcing the impression that they are all part of a family of Social Democratic parties. But as political scientists we should not rely on such self-categorisation, not least because these institutional ties – for instance through the Second International or the Party of European Socialists – are artefacts of the organisational developments of the past rather than indicators of ideological affinity in the here and now. In other words, the category 'Social Democratic' is less an ideological classification than it is an organisational one. The second problem is related to this, namely the problem of reconciling these party families with a common ideological classificatory scheme based on a universal policy space. Without labouring the point, one only has to ask oneself if the nominally

'Social Democratic' British Labour Party is really ideologically to the left of the German Christian Democrats to see the problem. As a result of this problem most formal classificatory schemes are based on one of the following three criteria: (i) function; (ii) social antecedents and location; or (iii) organisation.

Functional accounts are quite robust because they reject self-classification and concentrate on identifying 'functional equivalents' across time and space. As such they have been popular since the emergence of a distinct structural-functionalist approach in the early 1950s. A seminal example of the functional approach was developed by Sigmund Neumann, who created a triptych of 'parties of individual representation', 'parties of social integration' and 'parties of total integration' (Neumann, 1956). Parties of total integration were in effect totalitarian parties, espousing ambitious goals to radically transform society and demanding high levels of commitment from their members. These would include orthodox Communist parties, Trotskyist groups and Fascist or neo-Nazi parties. Putting these parties to one side, most advanced democracies are characterised by the dichotomy between parties of individual representation and parties of social integration. The former are designed to articulate the demands of specific social groups but eschew any claim to a wider social function, whilst the latter are organisationally developed and provide members with a wide range of services, as well as the sense of being part of a more fundamental partisan community or movement. In the German context, the SSW or even the FDP might be seen as parties of individual representation whereas the SPD or CDU are quite clearly parties of social integration.

On a slightly different tack, yet working within the same tradition, Key also developed a tripartite framework, but rather than differentiating between different types of parties Key's schema is designed to differentiate between the different functions that parties qua parties carry out. Thus Key identifies: (i) 'parties in the electorate'; (ii) 'parties as organisations'; and (iii) 'parties in government' (Key, 1964). The role of parties in the electorate is to simplify complex choices for voters, educate the citizenry, generate symbols of identification and loyalty, and the mobilisation of individuals to participate in the political process. Parties as organisations recruit and train future elites, seek government office, and articulate and aggregate political interests. And parties in government create majorities in government, organise government, implement policy objectives, organise dissent and opposition, ensure responsibility for government actions, control government administration, and foster and sustain government stability. Key's classificatory scheme is underpinned by a strong normative message about the ideal function of political parties, which is echoed in the German constitutional convention of the *Parteienstaat*. However this is also its weakness, not least because not all parties can or want to aspire to the roles ascribed to them. Empirically it also a little suspect, not least because it is much easier to apply this schematic to majoritarian systems dominated by two parties that alternate in government. It is less suited to proportional, multi-party systems in which some parties may assume a far more limited role, or set of roles (for instance, eschewing the parties in government role). Nevertheless it remains the case that the fact that the wider function of political parties is held to be important by both participants in – and analysts of – German party politics mean that an ideal classificatory scheme should include this dimension.

More recent functional schema includes work by Kitschelt, Katz and Maier, and Wolinetz. Kitschelt develops a dichotomy between parties that work through the 'logic of electoral competition', such as the German *Volksparteien*, and those that observe a 'logic of constituency representation', such as left-libertarian and/or ecology parties (Kitschelt, 1989). Katz and Maier's 'cartel party' model is also functionalist in that the changes in the rules relating to the public financing of parties – as well as the settled role of the welfare state – in many European democracies provide incentives for political parties to shift their focus away from direct partisan competition towards a more oligopolistic arrangement, in which the raison d'etre of parties is primarily to maintain their position within the party system and avail themselves of the resources (Katz and Maier, 1995). This is consistent with the 'survival assumption' that underpins this study. Finally, Wolinetz (2002) draws on the language of coalition theory, and distinguishes between 'vote seeking', 'policy-seeking', and 'office seeking' parties. The coalition theory literature is discussed at greater length in Chapter 8.

A second classificatory scheme is based on political parties' social antecedents or location. Examples of such schema can be found in the work of Michels (1915), Eldersfeld (1964) and Kirchheimer (1966). Kirchheimer's classificatory scheme is worthy of note at this point because it underpins one of the key theoretical orthodoxies in the study of German politics, namely the idea of the Catch-all party. According to Kirchheimer the Catch-all party is one of four main party types found in advanced democracies, the others being 'bourgeois parties of mass representation', 'class-mass parties', and 'denominational mass parties'. We shall return to Kirchheimer's typologies later in this discussion but the fact that his model informs the discussion of party politics in Germany illustrates the attractiveness of social or behavioural models in the social sciences. It is not necessary at this point to re-visit the epistemological arguments rehearsed in Chapter 1 but it is worth remembering that such approaches have been superceded (or at least complemented) in recent years by psycho-social studies. Nevertheless the persistence of the confessional and, to a lesser extent, class cleavages as predictors of voting behaviour in Germany and elsewhere means that any ideal classificatory scheme should include some kind of sociological dimension.

A final set of classificatory schema is based on the organisational attributes of political parties. By-and-large these are posited on a dichotomisation between parties with underdeveloped or 'thin' structures and those with more extensive or 'thick' structures. An early example of this is Duverger's 'two-and-a-half' categorisation, which involves a distinction between 'mass parties', 'cadre parties' and 'devotee parties' (Duverger, 1954). Mass parties mobilise large swathes of the electorate, often but not always grounded in underlying class structures, and crucially develop large and organisationally complex structures as part of this mobilisation process. Such structures are organised along geographical lines, through branch, constituency, and/or state parties, and according to functional criteria, through auxiliary organisations, such as trade union, youth, or women's groups. Cadre parties, by contrast, have somewhat less extensive organisational structures and are less committed to nurturing an inner-party democratic culture. Political processes tend to be more top-down in nature, with a powerful and relatively autonomous leadership dominated by individuals of reasonably high socio-economic status. Finally, Duverger developed the idea of the 'devotee party', characterised by a relatively weak organisational structure and dominated by a small charismatic leadership (often effectively just one leader). However, even Duverger admitted that this category was difficult to isolate in empirical terms (Duverger, 1954).

More recent organisational work includes that of Panebianco (1988), who dichotomised 'mass-bureaucratic' and 'electoral-professional' parties, and Kitschelt (1994), who proposed four categories of 'centralist clubs', 'decentralised clubs', decentralised mass parties', and 'Leninist cadre' parties. These organisational approaches have their strengths and weaknesses when looking at parties in a comparative perspective. In terms of this book, two aspects are worth noting at this point. On a positive note, the emphasis on organisation is consistent with the book's emphasis on institutions and their role as constraints upon and facilitators of political action by agents. On the minus side, however, an overemphasis on the internal organisation of German political parties is problematic in a comparative context because of the specificities of the German case. In particular, the Federal Republic's norm of 'militant democracy' limits the autonomy of German political parties in determining the scope of their internal structures. For instance Article 21 paragraph 3 of the Basic Law sets out clear parameters for party organisation, with a strong emphasis on the internal political processes by which parties formulate their 'political line'. These parameters were firmed up in the German Party Law of 1967 and cover such areas as:

- Regulating the grass roots level of organisation
- Admission to and resignation from political parties
- Elections and votes within political parties
- Ballots in the case of the dissolution of political parties or their consolidation
- Ex officio members in party institutions
- Arbitration and internal party discipline
- Protection of minorities with party organisations

A detailed discussion of these constitutional and legal provisions are beyond the scope of the book,[4] but what is important to remember is that such constraints on the internal structure of political parties might be expected to limit the variance in organisational attributes amongst German political parties compared with some other advanced industrial democracies. Thus the persistence of trade union 'block votes' in the internal democracy of the British Labour Party, for example, might quite conceivably be ruled unconstitutional in the German context. This presents problems when examining German party politics in a comparative context and any common classificatory scheme cannot rely on organisational attributes alone.

7.3   Fifteen 'species' of political parties: German parties in comparative context

For the reasons outlined above, this section of the chapter uses a contemporary classificatory scheme developed by Gunther and Diamond (2003). The scheme is used to categorise German parties in relation to each other and in a comparative perspective. The Gunther and Diamond framework is based on three criteria: (i) formal organisation; (ii) programmatic commitments; and (iii) strategy and behavioural norms. In terms of formal organisation, Gunther and Diamond posit a continuum between 'thick' and 'thin' organisational structures. The appeal of the 'thick-thin' categorisation is that, unlike 'developed–underdeveloped' for instance, no other judgements are made about the organisational sophistication of a given political party. At the same time the continuum can encompass parties with large mass memberships, those with particularistic networks, or those that are more reliant on modern techniques of political communication without introducing a normative dimension to the analysis. In terms of programmatic commitments, the framework makes further distinctions between (i) those with coherent ideologies drawn from political philosophies, religious beliefs or nationalist sentiment; (ii) those that are pragmatic or have incoherent or weak ideologies; and (iii) those committed to mobilise and promote the interests of a particular ethnic, religious or socio-economic group, compared with those that are more heterogeneous in approach. In terms of strategy and norms of behaviour the framework makes the distinction between parties that are tolerant, pluralistic and accept the norms of democratic order, with those that are proto-hegemonic in intent and aim to replace the existing order with a new regime more in tune with their programmatic objectives. Finally, these three categories are cross-cut by two other variables: (i) the sociological nature of the milieu parties' appeal to and claim to represent; and (ii) the internal dynamics of party decision making, particularly the role and relative autonomy of the leadership (2003: 171–2). Taken together the Gunther–Diamond framework generates 15 ideal-types of party species, divided into 5 genuses: (i) Elite-based; (ii) Mass-based; (iii) Ethnicity-based; (iv) Electoralist; and (v) Movement parties. The framework is designed to encompass the widest pallet of party types, including parties from non-Western and/or non-democratic systems. These species, and the historical context in which they emerged, are summarised in Table 7.1

Table 7.1 Fifteen species of political parties

Genus	Species	Period	Characteristics (general and specific)
Elite-based	Traditional local notable	Early- to mid-nineteenth century	Little or no organisation Mobilised restricted electorate Relied on personal relationships
	Clientilistic	Late nineteenth/early twentieth century	Weak organisation Mobilised extended electorate Relied on patronage/favours
Mass-based I and II		Late nineteenth/early twentieth century	Mass membership/auxiliary organisations Mobilised mass electorate Strong ideology
(i) *Pluralist*	Class-mass		Socialist; open membership; acceptance of democracy
	Nationalist		Demand for some degree of territorial autonomy; open membership; acceptance of democracy
	Denominational		Incremental religious-based ideology cross-cut by influence of clerics etc; relatively open membership; acceptance of democracy
(ii) *Proto-hegemonic*	Leninist		Socialist; selective membership; aspiration to overthrow democracy
	Ultranationalist		Exaltation of 'nation' above the individual; selective membership; aspiration to overthrow democracy
	Fundamentalist		Absolutist religious-based ideology; selective membership; aspiration to overthrow democracy
Ethnicity-based	Ethnic	Early twentieth century onwards	One party/weak organisation Mobilises own ethnic group Idea of ethnic 'friends' and 'foes' Accepts democratic order
	Congress	Early twentieth century onwards	One or multi-party/weak organisation Mobilises multiple ethnic groups Accepts multi-ethnicity Accepts democratic order
Electoralist	Catch-all	Mid-to-late twentieth century onwards	Shallow organisation/prominent leadership Strong electoral focus Vague ideology
	Programmatic		Thin organisation Strong electoral/candidate focus Clear ideology
	Personalistic		Shallow organisation/prominent leader Strong electoral/leader focus Little or no ideology
Movement	Left-libertarian		Fluid organisational characteristics No barriers to membership Relatively weak electoral focus Post-materialist ideology
	Post-industrial extreme right		Fluid organisational characteristics/strong leadership focus Relatively weak electoral focus Authoritarian/xenophobic ideology

Source: Gunther and Diamond, 2003.

There are two possible problems with using the Gunther–Diamond framework in the context of this book. The first problem is an empirical one: that there is a danger of a framework containing 15 ideal types creating the problem of 'too many variables and not enough cases'. As discussed elsewhere in the book, this problem is aggravated by the fact that the book's primary focus is on just one case, that of Germany. Nevertheless, this is a problem that goes with the territory of examining a single case using the comparative politics literature. The second problem is theoretical: that the fine-grained classification used in the framework sacrifices parsimony for applicability. Again, this is a valid point and one that can be made about many comparative schemas and must therefore be left to the judgement of the reader and her position on the theoretical trade-off between parsimony and descriptive and/or explanatory power. Balanced against these two points are three factors in the framework's favour. First, the framework is designed to transcend what the authors regard as the 'Euro-centricism' of many other schemas and thus avoid that other common pitfall of comparative politics, 'concept stretching'. Second, the framework encompasses the three criteria of ideology (through programmatic commitments), function (strategy and behavioural norms), and organisation identified as being essential in the previous section. Third, on a more pragmatic note, although the framework is designed to avoid Euro-centricism many of the party species identified are found in older, more established classificatory schemas. So, for instance, in the Gunther–Diamond framework we still find 'class-mass', 'catch-all', 'programmatic', and 'left-libertarian' parties. Thus the reader is not forced to ditch all prior classificatory notions but rather can work with familiar concepts, albeit in a modified and somewhat more extensive classificatory framework.

7.4   Genus 1: Elite-based parties

So how do German parties map onto this framework? As already noted, Table 7.1 presents the schema in a historical context. The first of the 5 party genii is that of the 'elite-based' party, which emerged in the nineteenth century. This genus generates two species, the 'local-notable' and 'clientilistic' party, which although strongly related to one another reflect the development of the electoral and party systems found in the emerging popular democracies during this period.

Local-notable parties

The local-notable party emerged in the early- to mid-nineteenth century and is barely recognisable as a political party in the sense that we understand it today. Local-notable parties were characterised by little or no formal organisation and, in an era of a small number of enfranchised voters, mobilised a restricted electorate through the use of personal relationships and reputations. Such parties were found in the British House of Commons before the Great Reform Act, in late-nineteenth-century France, and can even be found today amongst conservative parties in Latin American countries such as Brazil. However, economic and social development, including the expansion of the popular franchise, in many countries in the second half of the nineteenth century meant that local-notable parties were replaced by, or transformed themselves into, clientelistic parties.

Clientilistic parties

Clientelistic parties were closer in structure to the modern political party, in that they were more a confederation of notables, either of the traditional land owning kind, or drawn from the newly emergent commercial classes. They were still characterised by a relatively weak organisation, but nevertheless this was more developed than had been the case during the local-notable phase because of the need to mobilise an extended electorate. The increased scale of the electorate, along with the steady decline of traditional networks and deference associated with socio-economic development, meant that the old reliance on personal ties and reputations no longer sufficed. Parties reacted to this by a more systematic strategy of political mobilisation, based on the granting of patronage and favours in return for electoral support. Clientilistic parties were found in many countries, including the countries of Southern Europe, Latin America, and in the 'Tamany Hall' politics of the cities and Deep South in the United States in the nineteenth century. In Germany it manifested itself in what Lipset and Rokkan (1967) refer to as the 'bourgeois alliance' between nation builders, a substantial segment of the fragmented liberal middle-classes, landowners and industrialists that determined the distribution of public goods in the mid-to late-nineteenth century. The alliance of 'Iron and Rye' in particular is a clear example of this kind of political mobilisation.

7.5   Genus 2: Mass-based parties

By the end of the nineteenth century the genus of elite-based parties made up two out the three elements of the Second German Reich's *Dreilagersystem*. By-and-large the Catholic and nationalist blocs still conformed to the Clientilistic party ideal-type, whilst the flanking Anti-Semites and particularist parties (Bavarian Farmers' Union, the Peasants' Union, and so on) conformed broadly to that of the original local-notable party. But the third Socialist block was dominated by the SPD, a party that is part of Gunther and Diamond's second genus of parties, the 'mass-based' party. Mass-based parties first emerged in the second half of the nineteenth century as a reaction to the gradual extension of the suffrage to the industrial working class. Such parties were characterised by a mass membership and the growth of auxiliary organisations, designed to mobilise and integrate the new mass electorate.

Moreover, in programmatic terms they were notable for a strong ideological base, grounded in either political philosophy (such as Marxism), religious belief, or nationalist sentiment. Thus we see for the first time the need for parties to differentiate themselves from other 'firms' in the political marketplace by offering a distinct 'product' to their 'customers'.

As already discussed, mass-based parties are sub-divided into two sub-genuses, based on parties' overall strategy and organisational norms. Sub-genus 1 refers to those mass-based parties that were broadly pluralist in approach. Pluralist mass-based parties sought to win elections in order to implement their programmatic objectives but accepted that any tenure in office was limited by the democratic rules-of-the-game. As a result these parties were particularly reliant on developing and maintaining a mass-membership as the central core of their electoral mobilisation strategy. Party activists performed many different tasks, be it on a salaried or voluntary basis, such as promoting the party with friends and work colleagues, devising and disseminating campaign literature and propaganda, and escorting voters to the polls. In addition secondary organisations, such as trade unions, religious, and fraternal associations, developed along with party organs such as newspapers, radio stations, and even – in the abnormal conditions of the Weimar Republic, for instance – paramilitary organisations such as the SPD's *Reichsbanner* fighters.

'Class-mass' parties: the SPD 1

At least up until its suppression by Hitler, and probably up until around the late 1950s, the SPD conforms to the first species within sub-genus 1, namely that of the 'class-mass' party. The term class-mass party was coined by Kirchheimer to denote democratic mass parties of the left, in which formal authority is invested in the party congress but where the executive committee of the party secretariat exercises real day-to-day power (Kirchheimer, 1966). The limited but real degree of inner party democracy, combined with a relatively open membership, meant that class-mass parties were often prone to intra-party conflict, either between the left and right wings of the party or between dissident groups within the party and those with a more authoritarian approach to party discipline. Both of these types of conflict affected the SPD. The party's origins date back to the failed 'bourgeois revolutions' of 1848 and, like the Labour Party, half a century later, the party arose out of the labour movement – in the case of the SPD the broad network of workers' clubs that spread throughout the more industrialised north and east of Germany in the latter half of the nineteenth century. The political culture of the SPD remains deeply patterned by this early history. In particular, the struggle between two competing groups, the Lassalleans and the Eisenachers, in those early years has 'left a strange dual heritage to the later party, which helps to explain some of its paradoxes' (Hunt, 1964: 2).

The rivalry between the Lassaleans and Eisenachers was not just one of ideology, for it also inevitably had implications for the party's formal organisation. The eventual ascendancy of the 'German General Workers Association' (*Allgemeiner Deutscher Arbeitervereien* or ADA), led by Lassalle, left the SPD with a strong authoritarian streak and tendency towards autocratic political leadership that was later to inspire Michels to coin the phrase 'Iron Law of Oligarchy' (Michels, 1915). Nevertheless, the Lassalean victory within the party was not by any means a comprehensive one and it retained other modes and norms of organisation. As Hunt observes, 'from its outset the German labour movement has a dual heritage in organisational as well as in political matters. ... two sharply contrasting models of organisation: the one authoritarian, rigidly centralised, efficient, and disciplined, the other ultra-democratic, loosely federalist in structure, and lax in discipline. In the subsequent history of the Social Democratic Party – and even after it moved away from the class-mass model in the 1950s – one can follow the interplay of these two clashing concepts of organisation' (Hunt, 1964: 6–7). The most recent example of where these two norms clashed irreconcilably was the SPD's failed attempts to either effectively integrate or suppress the New Left during the 1970s. It was this failure that was in many ways the catalyst for the eventual formation of the Greens.

'Pluralist-nationalist' parties

The second species of sub-genus 1 is the 'pluralist-nationalist' party, such as the Basque Partido Nacionalista Vasco, the Northern Irish Social Democratic and Labour Party or even – although this is a moot point and perhaps too early to tell – the post-Good Friday Agreement Sinn Fein. Again, the ideal type envisages a party with a mass and open membership, with a relatively democratic internal political culture and a broad acceptance of democracy. Political programmes are specific and centre on demands for at least some degree of territorial autonomy, framed within a notion of national identity based on an objective characteristic such as language or culture. By-and-large no significant German political party has conformed to this ideal-type (the SSW notwithstanding). The main reason for this was the failure, discussed in Chapter 3, of the 'national' block in the Second Reich to adapt to the transition to mass politics (Ritter, 1990: 40–1). As a result, no mass-based nationalist party committed to democracy emerged during this period.

'Mass-based denominational' parties: Zentrum, the CDU/CSU 1

The third party species of sub-genus 1 is the 'mass-based denominational party', a classification that is once again drawn from the work of Kirchheimer (1966). Mass-based denominational parties can be traced back to the late nineteenth century but are particularly notable from the mid-twentieth century onwards. They are characterised by an incremental religious-based ideology, cross-cut by the influence of clerics and other religious and social thinkers, a relatively open membership, and an acceptance of democracy. The dominant late-twentieth century variant of the mass-based denominational party was the family of Christian Democratic parties found in countries such as Italy, Belgium, Austria, the Netherlands and of course Germany. Christian Democracy cannot simply be likened to Conservatism and has distinct characteristics arising from the particular conditions prevalent in Europe in the immediate post-war years. Moreover, Christian Democratic parties across Europe cannot be seen as part of a monolithic whole but rather display nation-specific characters. For instance, the German and Austrian parties are more explicitly right wing than their Belgian or Italian equivalents. Nevertheless, all Christian Democratic parties are grounded in the specific conditions of post-1945 Europe and the imperative to provide an effective bulwark for bourgeois democracy against what they regarded as the threat of leftist parties at home and the Soviet Union internationally.

Strictly speaking there have only ever been two examples of a mass-based denominational party in Germany. Moreover, and in contradiction to Gunther and Diamond's classification of the CDU/CSU as still being a mass-based denominational party, I would argue that there are no examples to be found in the Federal Republic today. The first example was the pre-war *Zentrum* party, which mobilised Catholic voters across class and social strata and drew its membership from a heterogeneous social base of workers, farmers, artisans, shop owners and so on – albeit dominated by farmers, agricultural workers and the old middle-class (Ritter, 1990: 34–6). In programmatic terms, *Zentrum* based its ideology on Catholic social theory, which included a commitment to social justice. As a result, it competed with the SPD along the economic cleavage. The failure of *Zentrum* to re-establish itself within the post-war party system opened the door for the second example of a mass-based denominational party, that of the CDU/ CSU from 1945 until its period of opposition and programmatic renewal in the 1970s.

The character of the CDU/CSU was forged in the particular circumstances of occupied Germany in the period 1945–49. Besides rejecting narrow bourgeois conservatism, there was a recognition that confessional parties such as *Zentrum* had conspicuously failed to hold the middle ground in the Weimar Republic. Moreover, as the only major organised parties at the time were the SPD and KPD, there was both political space and a political need for a right-of-centre, cross-class, cross-confessional party, albeit drawn from 'a complex variety of groups with extremely varied backgrounds in terms of their pre-Hitler party affiliation' (Heidenheimer, 1960: 30). But at this time the party was still some way from the model of a catch-all party as we understand it today. The party had little central core, but rather was built around the *Land* parties that were often run as minor fiefdoms by local notables who controlled membership and, after 1949, party funds and communications with Bonn. Before 1949, hostility between these regions was often intense and it was through this conflict that the organisational division between the CDU and CSU, as well as Adenauer's hegemonic position within the party(ies), was forged.

This division in German Christian Democracy was expressed in programmatic terms, with the emphasis more on the 'Christian' in the Catholic west and south and on 'Democracy' elsewhere. This divide was personified in the power struggle between Adenauer, working out of the Cologne-based British Zonal Secretariat and Jakob-Kaiser, based in West Berlin. Following the currency reform in the western zones of occupation and the CDU's subsequent adoption of Erhard's free-market approach to economic policy, Adenauer slowly gained the ascendancy within the party. This struggle was replicated in Bavaria, where *Land* parliament leader Alois Hundhammer's particularist/capitalist approach won out over the more cross-confessional/Kaiser-esque policies of Josef Muller.

Thus, the CDU/CSU formed the first government of the new Federal Republic with a socially conservative, free-market profile and, despite cross-confessional aspirations, a pronounced Catholic bias. The Cold War, the 'Economic Miracle' of the 1950s and early 1960s, as well as Adenauer's political acumen and charisma enabled the Union parties to widen their support and consolidate their hold on power. But the priorities of power masked organisational weaknesses that became more apparent in the 1960s as the rejuvenated SPD began effectively to compete with the CDU/CSU for the political centre. At this time the CVDU/CSU remained little more than an 'association for electing the Chancellor' (*Kanzlerwahlverein*). When the CDU/CSU went into opposition in 1969 the logic of the *Kanzlerwahlverein* was no longer sustainable. Although the CDU/CSU's self-image was one of a catch-all *Volkspartei* it was clear that it needed appropriate internal structures to match its aspirations.

Geoffrey Pridham defines the primary function of a *Volkspartei* as the aggregation and integration of different groups into the polity. Thus for the CDU/CSU the 'principle importance was in mobilising under one political banner different forces of the centre/right, which had traditionally been divided or even antagonistic' (Pridham, 1977: 14–15). But the long period in power meant that the CDU in particular had never consolidated this mobilisation function. By the time the CDU/CSU went into opposition in 1969, the CDU's original membership of over 400,000 had more than halved. As a result there were fears that the CDU had become a narrow 'solid citizens' party (*Burgerpartei*) or even an 'entrepreneurs' party (*Unternehmerpartei*). The need to widen the participatory base of the party was sharpened by the perceived loss of political initiative to the SPD, which had moved away from its previous structure as a class-mass party to embrace the catch-all model. In response the CDU underwent a process of programmatic and organisational renewal that was to transform it into a true catch-all party.

Leninist parties: the KPD, SED

Moving on from sub-genus 1, the Gunther–Diamond model identifies three party-types that are differentiated from the democratic parties described above by their proto-hegemonic orientation. The first party species of this sub-genus is the proto-hegemonic equivalent of the class-mass party, namely the Leninist party. Like class-mass parties, Leninist parties are informed by a socialist or class-based ideology but there the similarity ends. In particular, Leninist parties are not committed to the democratic order but rather to the overthrow of parliamentary democracy and its replacement with a revolu-tionary society in which the Leninist party assumes the leading role within the new political order. Leninist parties aspire to a mass membership but because of their revolutionary/vanguardist posture they operate a closed structure in which prospective members are vigorously vetted. If accepted party members are subject to the dictums of 'democratic centralism', a form of top-down political culture that does not necessarily preclude debate prior to decisions or positions being taken but does expect a rigid adherence to the party 'line' once a position has been reached. Leninist parties aim to achieve ideological penetration of key sectors of society, such as the intelligentsia and trade unions in the West and the peasantry in Asia.

In Germany the key Leninist party was the KPD and its successor in the former GDR, the SED. The KPD emerged out of the chaos following Germany's defeat in the Great War and encompassed a number of revolu-tionary strands. These included the USPD, which split from the mainstream SPD over the decision of Ebert to allow Groener, the Chief of Staff of the Armed Forces, to use the Army to suppress the revolutionary left, and the Sparticists, whose leaders Rosa Luxemburg and Karl Liebknecht were mur-dered by the Free Corps in 1919. As already noted in Chapter 3, the KPD con-solidated its position during the period of the Weimar Republic but was suppressed when Hitler became Chancellor. Over the course of the next 12 years Stalin sheltered most of the key leadership, including Walter Ulbricht the future leader of the GDR. This period of exile allowed Ulbricht in particular to deal with rivals within the leadership, many of who were liq-uidated or sent to the Gulag as part of Stalin's periodic purges of the Comintern.

Ulbricht and the rest of the KPD's surviving 'Moscow Communists' returned to Germany with the victorious Red Army and, in June 1945, the Russians allowed the KPD amongst others to organise in their zone. In 1946 the Soviet Union was behind the forced merger of the KPD and the SPD in their zone, to form the SED. The new merged SED very quickly assumed the organisational features of the classic Leninist Party, including the organisational/normative features of democratic centralism and an ideological commitment to assume the leading role within society. Thus after the foundation of the GDR in 1949 the SED steadily penetrated and subordinated all aspects of society, including the co-ordination of functional organisations such as trade unions and professional associations, and the establishment of party cells in all workplaces and the armed forces. Other so-called block parties, including the CDU, were allowed to organise in the GDR as part of a notional 'National Front' in defence of the republic, but they remained subservient to the SED's leading role. Finally, in addition to the Red Army which continued to station over 4 million troops in the GDR, the SED relied on the 'Ministry for State Security' (*Ministerium für Staatssicherheit*, or MfS) to maintain it in power and suppress dissent.

The SED never successfully acquired the popular legitimacy to ensure its long-time survival and when Gorbachev removed the guarantee of Red Army support in 1989 the regime fell. The SED's absolute penetration of, and thus association with, GDR society, the vast networks of patronage associated with it, and the hatred for it felt by vast swathes of East German society made the SED's long-term survival highly unlikely in the new unified Germany. However, it became clear that the more thoughtful and/or pragmatic SED members, such as Gregor Gysi, had also reached this conclusion and sought to distance themselves from the old regime. As a result, over the winter of 1989–90 the SED dissolved and reconstituted itself as the PDS, a party that still retains a strong left-wing programmatic orientation but does not conform to the Leninist ideal-type.

Ultranationalist parties: the NSDAP

Ultranationalist parties are proto-hegemonic in intent, and are steeped in an exclusive ideology of nationhood that places the nation or race before the individual, and idealises the use of force in order to pursue their objectives. They are therefore antithetical to the norms of liberal democracy. The quid pro quo of such an exclusive national ideology is the identification of 'the other', normally minorities within the real or claimed territory of the nation, that constitute a threat to the welfare or purity of the national or racial family. Ultranationalist parties share many characteristics with Leninist parties, in terms of a rejection of liberal democratic values and more notably in terms of organisational characteristics such as a highly selective recruitment process, the strong emphasis on the indoctrination of members and strict internal discipline. However the ideological goals of ultranationalist parties are quite unlike those of Leninist parties, not just in terms of specific objectives but also in terms of overall levels of coherence, and are more vulnerable to amendment and redefinition by the leader(s) (Gunther and Diamond, 2003: 181).

Key examples of the ultranationalist party are the Italian Fascists of the early twentieth century, the Croatian Democratic Union, and, of course, the

German NSDAP. As discussed in Chapter 2, the NSDAP did not start off as a mass-based party and would probably have remained a small and relatively insignificant party on the ultranationalist fringe of Weimar Republic politics had it not been for the leadership of Hitler and his ability to shift the ideological and tactical focus of the party to meet the needs of circumstances. Thus, the failed 'Beer hall' Putsch of 1923 led to a move away from a revolutionary strategy and a shift to the right in terms of economic policy. This was part of Hitler's aim to not only reassure the more traditional nationalist right but also to gain the support of all members of the public with a powerful but quite incoherent message built around the leitmotif of anti-Semitism. Thus by the beginning of the 1930s the NSDAP was a genuinely mass-based party with broad social appeal (Falter, 1990). Once in power, the NSDAP's proto-hegemonic tendencies became all too apparent and the party set about subordinating all areas of national life to the dictates of the 'National Socialist Bulldozer' (Mintzel, 1983: 245).

Fundamentalist parties

The third species of proto-hegemonic parties in this genus is that of religious fundamentalist parties. These are characterised by an absolutist religious-based ideology, a highly selective membership and an aspiration to overthrow democracy. The most notable examples of such parties are the various Islamic fundamentalist parties found across the globe, such as the Algerian Islamic Salvation Front and possibly the Turkish Welfare party, as well as the Hindu BJP in India and various Buddhist groupings in countries such as Sri Lanka. In Germany, however, the combination of strict regulation of parties' democratic credentials and the 5 per cent barrier to representation has prevented such parties from emerging. Moreover, as is discussed at greater length below in the segment on ethnicity-based parties, any strands of religious belief amongst naturalised citizens in Germany have by-and-large mapped onto the existing religious/secular and class cleavages and reinforced the existing party system.

7.6   Genus 3: Ethnicity-based parties

Ethnicity-based parties differ from mass-based parties in two fundamental ways. First, they generally do not possess the scale and development of internal organisation found in the mass-based parties discussed earlier. Second, they do not promote a programme designed for all of the societies in which they operate, but rather to promote the interests of a single ethnic group, or coalition of groups within them. At the same time, however, they differ from nationalist parties in that they do not aspire to secession or territorial autonomy from the states in which they organise. For ethnicity-based parties, the goal is to secure the optimum distribution of resources and power within existing state structures (Gunther and Diamond, 2003: 183).

The genus of ethnicity-based parties contains two species. These are, first, simple ethnic parties and, second, congress parties. The simple ethnic party aims purely to mobilise votes from within its own ethnic group. It is characterised by a relatively weak organisation and bases its electoral message on the idea of society being made up of ethnic 'friends' and 'foes'. However, despite this de facto division of society such parties accept the established democratic order in which they find themselves. Classic examples would include the Zulu-based Inkatha Freedom Party in South Africa, as well as the Turkish-based DPS in Bulgaria and the Democratic Union of Hungarians in Romania. By contrast, congress-style parties are made up of an alliance, coalition or federation of ethnic parties, which may even take the form of a single unified party for campaign purposes. Like ethnic parties, congress parties are characterised by a somewhat weak organisation, although this is often more advanced than those of ethnic parties because of the need to manage the transaction costs of the coalitions from which they emerge. In terms of electoral logic they differ from ethnic parties in that they mobilise multiple ethnic groups and, as a result, accept the principle of multi-ethnicity rather than set up a narrative of friends and foes. Moreover, they accept the established democratic order. The most successful examples of such parties are the South African ANC and the Indian Congress Party. Other notable, but less democratic, examples of such parties include the Kenyan African National Union, the National Front coalition in Malaysia (Gunther and Diamond, 2003: 185) and, in Europe, the short-lived Rainbow party in Sweden (Odmalm and Lees, 2005).

In Germany there has been no example of the congress party species, but it could be argued that the Polish party of the Second Reich period corresponded to the ethnic party model in that it mobilised a specific ethnic group, accepted the established democratic order (such as it was) and at least back-pedalled on the issue of secession from the state. However no such party has emerged in the Federal Republic and, as research by Wüst indicates, the electoral preferences of naturalised citizens have by-and-large mapped onto existing class and confessional cleavages and therefore the existing party system. Thus, where strong ethnic, linguistic or religious identities exist amongst naturalised citizens they play a strong influence in individuals' choice between the established parties and have not to date provided a resource for the emergence of new political parties (Wüst, 2004). Recent research into the political behaviour of immigrant groups in other European democracies, such as Sweden and the Netherlands, have generated similar findings (see Odmalm and Lees, 2005).

7.7 Genus 4: Electoralist parties

The fourth genus of electoralist parties comes closest to the metaphor used throughout this study of the political party as a highly professionalised firm operating within the political marketplace. In more specific terms, electoralist parties can be compared to large companies or corporations who aspire to a major share of the market and construct a 'product mix' in order to achieve this. The genus contains three species: (i) catch-all; (ii) programmatic; and (iii) personalistic parties. In descriptive terms, the genus is close to Panebianco's category of 'electoral-professional' party. The electoral-professional party is categorised by (i) the central role of professionals in possession of the expertise necessary to practice electoral mobilisation under modern conditions, (ii) weak vertical ties to social groups and the subsequent emphasis on broad appeals to the so-called 'issue electorate'; (iii) the privileging of public representatives and a highly personalised leadership; (iv) a reliance on party financing through interest groups and state funding (as opposed to members' dues); and (iv) campaign strategies that place a strong emphasis on issues and leadership (Panebianco, 1988: 264). Gunther and Diamond's electoralist party shares these characteristics and reflects the decline in the power of social location as a predictor of voting intention (see Chapter 5), as well as technological changes in the ways political parties can and must compete with one another (Chapters 5 and 8).

Electoralist parties are organisationally thinner than mass-based parties and do not (or do not any longer) sustain the scale and intensity of links with members and the wider society that were sustained by mass-based parties in the past. Thus instead of relying upon the financial resources, enthusiasm and sheer weight of numbers of members and supporters to mobilise the electorate, the electoralist party utilises modern campaign techniques that stress the use of the mass media (in particular television) (see Farrell and Webb, 2002) to get the party's message over to an increasingly atomised, volatile and non-partisan electorate. Given this new emphasis the role of personalities and perceptions of competence is more important in the campaign process and, as a result, the criteria for nomination of candidates has shifted from factors such as length of service or loyalty to the party towards those of personal attractiveness and other media-friendly attributes.

The major changes that have taken place in the campaign strategies of political parties are discussed at greater length in Chapter 8. However, it is necessary at this point to explore further the notion that electoralist parties are organisationally thinner than mass-based parties, not least because this chapter posits the notion that the two main mass-based parties in Germany, the SPD and CDU/CSU, are now better understood as being electoralist parties. So does this assumption stand up to scrutiny in the German context?

Table 7.2 plots the decline of total party membership and party membership as a percentage of the electorate in Germany, over the period 1980–99. The table demonstrates that over the period the absolute number of citizens who were members of political parties in Germany declined from 1,955,140 in 1980 to 1,780,173. On the face of it, this does not seem like a huge fall but

Table 7.2 The decline of total party membership and membership as a percentage of the electorate in Germany, 1980–99

Year	Electorate	Total membership	Party membership as % of electorate (M/E ratio)
1980 (West)	43,231,741	1,955,140	4.52
1989 (West)	48,099,251	1,873,053	3.89
1999	60,762,751	1,780,173	2.93

Source: Data from Mair and van Biezen, 2001: 15.

what must be taken into account is the sizeable increase in the total electorate (from 43,231,741 to 60,762,751) over the period as a result of German unification. Thus the more important run of data in Table 7.2 relates to membership as a percentage of the total electorate, known as the M/E ratio (Katz and Mair, 1992). And the decline in the M/E ratio in Germany is quite dramatic, having almost halved over the period from 4.52 per cent of the electorate in 1980 to 2.93 in 1999. This puts the rate of membership of political parties in Germany at the lower end of the scale compared with other European countries. Across a basket of 20 European democracies in the late 1990s the mean M/E ratio is almost 5 per cent, with a high of 17.7 per cent in neighbouring Austria. By contrast, only the Netherlands (2.51.), Hungary (2.15), the United Kingdom (1.92), France (1.57) and Poland (1.15) have lower M/E ratios (Mair and van Biezen, 2001: 8).

Table 7.3 looks more specifically at the levels of membership of the main political parties in Germany over the period 1980–99. Interestingly it does not paint a picture of decline in membership across all political parties. Let us leave the PDS to one side, as the only available data for the party in the table is for 1999. Of the other parties, the clear success story is that of the Greens, which increased its membership from 18,320 in 1980 to 50,897 in 1999, although it remains the smallest political party in membership terms. In addition, the CSU also increased its level of membership from 172,420 in 1980 to 184,765 in 1999, which given that the party only organises in Bavaria is an impressive performance. Elsewhere, however, the picture is one of decline in the absolute numbers of party members and, by definition, the M/E ratio as well. Both the SPD and FDP suffered a 23.5 per cent drop in party membership over the period, with the SPD's membership dropping from 986,872 members in 1980 to 755,244 and the FDP's falling from 84,208 to 64,407. By contrast the CDU faired a little better, suffering a drop of 9.1 per cent from 693,320 in 1980 to 630,413 in 1999. And if we take the CDU/CSU as effectively a single unit the drop is a more modest 5.9 per cent from a combined membership of 865,740 members in 1980 to 815,178 in

Table 7.3   Membership levels and M/E ratios of the main political parties in Germany, 1980–99

Year	SPD	CDU	CSU	FDP	Greens	PDS
1980 (West)	986,872	693,320	172,420	084,208	18,320	–
1989 (West)	921,430	662,598	185,853	065,216	37,956	–
1999	755,244	630,413	184,765	064,407	50,897	94,447
% M/E ratio 1980*	2.3		2.0	0.2	0.0 (.04)	–
% M/E ratio 1999*	1.2		1.3	0.1	0.1 (.08)	0.2
% change**	−47.8		−35.0	−47.8	+100	–

Notes: * M/E ratios my calculations; ** for simplicity's sake M/E ratios are rounded up/down to nearest point ten of a percentage, hence what looks like a 50 per cent drop in the FDP's M/E ratio is in fact only 47.8 per cent when working from the original membership figures.

Source: Data adapted from Mair and van Biezen, 2001: 18.

1999. As a result, the combined membership of the CDU/CSU is now greater than that of the previously class-mass SPD.

Taken in the round we see M/E ratios of 1.2 per cent (down from 2.3 per cent) for the SPD, 1.3 per cent (down from 2.0 per cent) for the CDU/CSU, 0.1 per cent (down from 0.2 per cent) for the FDP, 0.08 per cent (up from 0.04 per cent) for the Greens, and 1.6 per cent for the PDS. So how does this help us assign these parties to the electoralist party genus, and does it apply to all of the parties? Let us start with the two *Volksparteien*. On one level the absolute numbers of party members for these two parties remains high compared with those of the FDP, Greens and PDS. But if we take into account the increase in the size of the German electorate following unification, the drop in those numbers as M/E ratios is striking. Thus the SPD's M/E ratio has declined by 47.8 per cent over the period and, while performing better than the SPD, the CDU/CSU's combined M/E ratio has fallen by 35 per cent. Much of these falls can be attributed to the different political culture found in the new Federal states, which is characterised by much weaker patterns of partisanship. Recent research by Karsten Grabow, albeit using a different classificatory scheme than that used in this chapter, demonstrates that the organisational structures of *Land*-level SPD and CDU parties in the new Federal states are much thinner than those found in the old Federal states. This leads Grabow to conclude that whilst *Land* parties in the old Federal states still recognisably conform to the *Volkspartei* model, those in the new Federal states are closer to the ideal-type of the cadre party (Grabow, 2001). It will be recalled that cadre parties are characterised by thin organisational structures, weak inner-party democratic culture, top-down political processes and a powerful and relatively autonomous leadership. These are features that also conform to the electoralist party genus and, whilst this pattern may be more pronounced in the new Federal states, it is clear that in organisational terms the SPD and CDU/CSU as national parties are moving away from the mass-based party model and towards that of the electoralist party. This process of organisational hollowing-out, combined with the two parties' commitment to a broad cross-class, cross confessional appeal means that the old mass-based party categories of class-mass and denominational mass-based parties is no longer appropriate to decribe the modern SPD and CDU/CSU. So for taxonomical purposes the two present-day *Volksparteien* are included in the genus of electoralist parties.

This also applies to the FDP, which also suffered a near 50 per cent reduction of its M/E ratio to just 0.1 per cent, and the PDS, which although it has a larger M/E ratio of 0.2 per cent is still far away from the variant of the mass-based party that characterised its predecessor the SED. However, the chapter does not include the Greens in the genus of electoralist parties. This is because the Greens' historical antecedents as part of the broader peace and anti-nuclear movements, and its resulting different organisational characteristics, mean that it conforms more closely to the genus of movement parties. The reasons for this are discussed at greater length later in the chapter.

Catch-all parties: the SPD 2, CDU/CSU 2

The first species within the genus of electoralist parties is that of the catch-all party. This 'pluralist and tolerant ideal type' (Gunther and Diamond, 2003: 185) is characterised by a shallow organisation dominated by a prominent leadership class, a strong electoral focus and hence a vague ideology designed to appeal across narrow milieus and encompass the preferences of the median voter. Because of this, party programmes are often eclectic and shift with the preferences of the 'issue electorate'. Contemporary examples of catch-all parties include, of course, the British Labour Party under Tony Blair, the US Democratic Party, and the Spanish PSOE.

But does this apply to the SPD and CDU? Gunther and Diamond's model of the catch-all party is a refinement of Kirchheimer's original model. Kirchheimer's catch-all party was an inductive model, based on the changes that Kirchheimer observed taking place within mass-based parties in Western European democracies, including Germany. Thus, Kirchheimer did not regard the catch-all party as necessarily being a distinct or new type of party and acknowledged that many of the artefacts of the mass-based party, such as a large membership base and a substantial amount of 'ideological baggage', remained. However, Kirchheimer argued that they steadily became less important to the catch-all party as time went on and changes took place in party organisational structures and campaign methods (Kirchheimer, 1966). Gunther and Diamond's catch-all party differs from that of Kirchheimer in that they do not presuppose that the ideological and organisational legacy of mass-based parties remains but neither do they deny that they do in many cases remain (Gunther and Diamond, 2003: 186).

The SPD 2

Thus we can see similar features emerge in the evolution of the SPD and CDU over the post-war period, as the two *Volksparteien* moved away from the mass-based party model. This move away has been most pronounced in the SPD, not least because it was previously the paradigmatic example of the class-mass species of the mass-based party. As already noted in Chapter 4, in the Spring of 1946 the faction of the SPD in the Russian zone of occupation, led by Otto Grotewohl, merged with the communist KPD to form the SED. Ever since, SPD lore has referred to this event as a 'forced merger' (*Zwangsvereinigung*). However, although there was significant coercion involved in the process, many on the left of the SPD at the time had considerable sympathy for the thesis that it was the failure of the SPD and KPD to form a united 'people's front' in the early 1930s that was responsible for the ease with which Hitler was able to establish a dictatorship on becoming Chancellor. So the logic of the formation of the SED was very much one of building a unified mass-based party of the left, albeit one that evolved quickly into the proto-hegemonic Leninist variant of the species.

It would be a mistake, however, to misinterpret the SPD's rejection of merger with the Communists and as a result regard the post-split SPD as being the moderate *Völkspartei* it is today. In the late 1940s the SPD remained very much a Marxist-inspired class-mass party of the non-Communist Left. And it took a long time for the party to come to terms with the post-war settlement, the division of Germany and the 'social market economy' model being developed by Adenauer and Erhard, with the encouragement of the Americans. Thus the post-war SPD's early policy pronouncements continued to promise to 'socialise' the production of coal, iron and steel, energy, chemicals, basic building materials, large banks and insurance companies. Such a stance set the SPD against the political tide in the western zones.[5]

By this time, of course, the Federal Republic had come into being and, following election defeats in 1949, 1953 and 1957, the SPD began to modify its electoral stance. The process of adapting to the new political realities of the Federal Republic culminated in the Bad Godesberg conference of 1959, where the party adopted a new raft of policies. As already noted, the Bad Godesberg Programme disavowed Marxism and attempted to embed the SPD's core principles of democratic socialism within the wider context of Christian ethics, classical philosophy and the tradition of humanism. The programme endorsed the liberal pluralist settlement in the Federal Republic and the centrality of the social market economy to it. In symbolic terms it meant that the SPD had accepted a political settlement made in the

CDU/CSU's image. And in practical terms it meant a re-configuration of the political product that the SPD could credibly offer to the electorate.

The underlying logic of this re-configuration was that the SPD had recognised that it needed to appeal across class-loyalties in order to enhance the party's support. In other words it began consciously to develop the fuzzy ideological profile that characterises the catch-all party. This process coincided with a generational change of leadership. Now led by the charismatic Willy Brandt, the party was rewarded for its new moderate stance by sustaining a 10 per cent rise in popular support over the period 1957–69. In turn the combination of ideological moderation and rising electoral support inevitably led to participation in national government, first as junior partner to the Christian Democratic CDU in the Grand Coalition of 1966–69, and then as senior partner to the liberal FDP in the Social–Liberal Coalition of 1969–82. But after the collapse of the Social–Liberal coalition in 1982 the party would have to endure another 16 years in opposition before being returned to power following the 1998 Bundestag elections.

The immediate years of opposition after 1982 were difficult ones for the SPD in which it had to respond to four fundamental threats to its position. Three of these were structural in nature, whereas the fourth was arguably more a problem of political personnel. First, as discussed in Chapter 4, the decline in the overall vote for the two 'catch-all' parties had affected the SPD in particular and prompted some observers to forecast growing instability within the Federal Republic's party system. Second, the growth of the Greens served to put pressure on the SPD along the post-materialist dimension of politics. Third, after 1990 the persistence of the PDS in the new Federal states contributed to the SPD's weakness in the east and (with the additional weakness of the Greens and FDP) severely restricted the party's coalition options. Finally, the extraordinary personal appeal and political acumen of Helmut Kohl managed to keep the SPD on the back foot in the fight for the political centre-ground. Indeed, as discussed later, it was only when the SPD adopted Gerhard Schröder as Chancellor-candidate in 1998 that the party finally found a political personality with sufficient charisma and popular appeal to unseat Kohl.

As already noted in Chapter 6, the SPD did eventually respond effectively to the three structural challenges. At the *Land* level the SPD has continued to thrive as a party of government and, from the early 1980s onwards, the party began to cooperate with the Greens. This process of cooperation led to coalitions with the Greens in, for example, the states of Hesse (1985–87, 1991–95 and 1995–99), West Berlin (1989–90), Lower Saxony (1990–94) and North Rhine-Westphalia (1995–). In addition there were so-called Traffic-Light coalitions in Brandenburg between 1990 and 1994 (with Alliance '90 and the FDP) and in Bremen between 1991 and 1995 (with the Greens and the FDP). Finally, the SPD also managed to develop cooperative ties with the PDS in the new Federal states. This process started with the PDS's 'toleration' of a minority SPD–Green coalition in Saxony-Anhalt between 1994 and 1998, but soon developed into a new 'Red–Red' model of formal coalition between the parties in states such as Berlin (since 2001) and Mecklenburg-West Pomerania (after 2002). Taken in the round, the SPD's ability to form coalitions with every other mainstream political party at the *Land* level is indicative of the party's now entrenched pragmaticism as well as the vagueness of its ideology.

The mid- to late-1990s also demonstrated the extent to which personality politics amongst the leadership, and the reduced importance of the mass membership, now dominated within the SPD. Up until the mid 1990s the SPD continued to struggle to field a serious challenger to Helmut Kohl on the national stage. During the period 1982–94 the SPD fielded four different candidates for Chancellor and lost four Bundestag elections in a row. However in the run-up to the 1998 Bundestag elections the party was presented with a choice between two potential Chancellor-candidates that finally encapsulated and clarified the strategic dilemma they faced. Should the SPD choose someone who appealed to grass roots activists but left the general population unmoved or alternatively someone who was viewed with suspicion within the party but had broad electoral appeal?

The candidate with grass roots appeal was Oskar Lafontaine, who had been leader of the party since ousting the hapless Rudolf Scharping at the SPD's annual conference in November 1985. In the following two and a half years Lafontaine instilled the party with a new self-confidence and used the SPD's majority in the Bundesrat to ruthlessly undermine the legislative capacity of the incumbent Kohl government. However, Lafontaine's political strategy was not one of ideological moderation. On the contrary, his aim was to sharpen the political debate and offer a more confrontational and explicitly left-wing stance to the electorate. In addition to his control of the Bundesrat, Lafontaine's position as Minister President of Saarland gave him a real power-base with which to take on the Federal Government, which he used to great effect. His speech to the SPD's national conference in Hannover at the beginning of December 1997 summed up this approach, advocating state intervention to secure social justice, more regulation, 'green' taxes and greater European integration as a bulwark against the forces of globalisation.

The other significant speech at the 1997 party conference was made by Gerhard Schröder, Lafontaine's rival for the nomination as Chancellor-candidate. But whereas Lafontaine advocated state intervention and regulation, taxes and European integration, Schröder advocated flexibility and de-regulation, trimming social costs and a more cautious approach to Europe. Such sentiments allowed Schröder to be cast in the role of a Blair-type 'moderniser' and like Blair he had a deeply ambivalent attitude towards the traditions and values of his own party. Moreover, Schröder was obviously popular with the general public, especially compared with Lafontaine. For despite Lafontaine's obvious political strengths and high regard within the party, all of the opinion poll data at the turn of the year indicated that he would fail once more to unseat Kohl, or his possible successor Wolfgang Schäuble. Schröder by contrast enjoyed an opinion poll lead over Kohl of 57 per cent to 33 per cent and over Schäuble of 49 per cent to 44 per cent (*Der Spiegel.* 20/12/97). Finally, following the Schröder's resounding win in the March 1 elections in his home state of Lower Saxony, Lafontaine conceded defeat and announced that he would give Schröder a clear run at Kohl. In the 1998 Bundestag elections, Schröder campaigned on the idea of the 'New Centre' (*Neue Mitte*), a variation on the New Democrat/New Labour strategy of 'big tent' politics. The 'New Centre' strategy was designed to build an electoral coalition that would occupy the centre ground whilst leaving open the possibility of coalition with the Greens after the elections. The SPD's prize for this strategy was a return to Federal government and a re-affirmation that it remained a serious *Volkspartei* with cross-class appeal (see Lees, 2000). In short, Schröder's success in both winning the nomination as Chancellor-candidate and the subsequent Bundestag elections was confirmation that the modern SPD has moved away from the class-mass model and now conforms more closely to Gunther and Diamond's typology of the electoralist catch-all party.

The CDU/CSU 2

The process of evolution is less marked in the CDU/CSU, not because it is less of a catch-all party than the SPD, but rather because it conformed less closely to the mass-based party type to begin with. As already noted, Gunther and Diamond do place the CDU/CSU in the category of mass-based denominational party but I would argue that if this was the case in the early years of the Federal Republic it is not so now.

Ever since the foundation of the Federal Republic, CDU/CSU has mobilised the centre/right majority in the Federal Republic by reaching across class/confessional cleavages to a broad electoral base, and commanding the largest share of the electorate for most of that period. The CDU/CSU shares common policy principles with other Christian Democratic parties that can be identified as being part of a specific Christian-Democratic ideological 'mix' such as (i) a broad commitment to 'Christian' values as basic human rights, the rights of the individual and the defence of the family; (ii) a liberal conception of democracy; (iii) an explicitly integrative function, both nationally (through the *Volkspartei* principle) and internationally (especially European integration); and (iv) an emphasis on reconciling the principles of social justice (in the tradition of Catholic teaching) with support for the market. Over half a century after its foundation, the CDU/CSU's policy mix retains considerable electoral appeal, despite the increasing secularisation of German society. However, it has done this precisely because of the vagueness of its ideology and thus its ability to attract voters on the secular side of the confessional cleavage.

The CDU in particular has managed to recast its programmatic profile when confronted with evidence that it is losing electoral appeal. The first instance in which this took place started in the late 1960s, when the party moved into opposition. This process involved a move towards a broader, more contemporary programme that encompassed the 'social-market' and, after the disaster of the 1972 Bundestag elections, *Ostpolitik*. This process began with formulation of the 'Berlin Programme' of 1967/8 and continued through the 1973 Hamburg conference to the adoption of the 1978 'Basic Programme'. The new moderate, pragmatic approach continued when the CDU returned to government, despite the accompanying political rhetoric about a 'sea change' (*Wende*) after 13 years of the Social–Liberal coalition, and pressures from the CSU as well as the CDU's own right-wing. As a result the 1980s Kohl administration was qualitatively quite different from the more explicit conservatism of the contemporaneous Reagan and Thatcher governments – it lacked the ideological certainty and sharp edges.

In terms of organisational renewal, the CDU moved away from the previously loose union described earlier in this chapter towards a more professional and centralised structure. The existing Federal Executive and Federal Committee were given enhanced powers and the General Secretary was provided with a well-resourced central apparatus which not only had a co-ordinational capacity but also a policy-making function. Leading on from this, the method of party financing was restructured and membership drives were launched. As a result, when the CDU returned to government it had an efficient party machine and had boosted its membership to over 750,000 (Padgett and Burkett, 1986: 107). Nevertheless, residual traces of the *Kanzlerwahlverein* remained and once in power Helmut Kohl and his ministers retained their dominance over the party machine. Moreover, Kohl's own political influence grew over time and by the 1990s he enjoyed similar levels of personal power to that enjoyed by Adenauer.

The period since the defeat of the Kohl administration has seen a further evolution away from the denominational mass-party model and towards the catch-all party model. This process has taken place along the lines of leadership, ideology and organisation. In terms of leadership, Kohl resigned from the party leadership following the Bundestag election defeat of 1998 and was replaced by Wolfgang Schäuble. However, Schäuble's brief leadership was ended by the financial scandals that rocked the party in the period 1999–2000, and he was replaced by Angela Merkel. Merkel epitomises the CDU's evolution away from the denominational mass-party type, being the first female and Protestant CDU leader. Under her leadership, the CDU has undergone another re-evaluation of the party's ideological position. In particular, Merkel has displayed a willingness to 'think outside the box' of Christian social theory and prescribe policy solutions to Germany's ailing economic performance that owe more to the neo-liberal orthodoxies of the Anglo-Saxon countries than to the denominational politics of traditional Christian

Democracy. Finally, in terms of organisation, although the absolute numbers of the party members has held up reasonably well over the last twenty years it is marked by the same asymmetry between the old and new Federal states that has affected the SPD (see Grabow, 2001).

However, when one includes the CSU as well, the picture becomes a little less clear. If we leave the CSU's role as a 'state grouping' (*Landesgruppe*) in the CDU/CSU parliamentary faction, the CSU as an organisation remains completely autonomous and is run from its state leadership office (*Landesleitung*) in Munich. The legacy of early internecine power struggles, as well as the need to outmanoeuvre the Bavarian Party, meant that the CSU has never explicitly aspired to develop a cross-confessional appeal. On the face of it, this – combined with the strong conservative strand in the CSU's ideology – might preclude the CSU's categorisation as a catch-all party. But in fact the conditions of Bavarian particularism dictate that, as long as the CSU remains a regional party and retains its substantial electoral share, it can be seen as a catch-all party within its own terms of reference. For despite its ideological conservatism, the CSU consistently commands around 60 per cent of the Bavarian electorate and, despite a long history of charismatic/authoritarian leadership under Franz-Josef Strauss in the 1970s and 1980s, it has a highly efficient party organisation that attracts young, urban and Protestant members as well as its more traditional Catholic milieu. Under its current leader Edmund Stoiber the CSU has further broadened its appeal and, whilst Stoiber's personal appeal nationally was insufficient to unseat Schröder in the 2002 Bundestag elections, he has fashioned a strong cross-class, cross-confessional support base in his home state. Thus, in many ways the CSU is the paradigmatic catch-all party, albeit one that only mobilises within the singular political environment of Bavaria – and in which the product mix that it offers dominates the political marketplace to an extent unknown elsewhere in Germany.

Programmatic parties: the PDS and FDP

Gunther and Diamond's second species of electoralist party is the programmatic party. This species differs from the catch-all party in three ways. First, it has a more distinct, sustained and coherent ideological profile than that of the catch-all party. Second, unlike the catch-all party it does not seek to blur its ideological profile but rather uses it for mobilisation purposes. Third, its social base is somewhat dependent on the type of electoral system in which it operates. Thus, in majoritarian systems it may sustain a broad social base, but in proportional systems it tends to fall back on a clearly defined social base with which it may maintain relatively strong links. Nevertheless, in organisational terms it is much thinner than the traditional mass-based party and has a stronger leadership or candidate focus. Examples of the programmatic party species include the Civic Democratic Party and Social Democratic Party in the Czech Republic, the Hungarian Socialist Party and the Civic Democratic Party-Young Democrats in Hungary, and the Democratic Progressive Party in Taiwan (Gunther and Diamond, 2003: 187). To return to the metaphor of parties as firms, programmatic parties are the equivalent of small-to-medium size companies operating from niche positions within the mainstream political market. In such circumstances, the first objective of such parties is clearly survival in a marketplace dominated by the bigger parties. However, as we shall see, this does not preclude participation in or exercising control over government as well.

In Germany there are two clear examples of the programmatic party – the PDS and the FDP. That is not to say that the two parties conform to the type in the same way. Let us return to Gunther and Diamond's three dimensions used to define programmatic parties against catch-all parties.

First, in terms of ideological profile, both parties have a relatively clear ideological message. In programmatic terms, the PDS remains opportunistic and oriented towards the east. The PDS sees itself as part of the *reform* (as opposed to opposition) movement in the former GDR and has not explicitly rejected the aims of the former regime. It opposes what it regards as Westernisation and the material and cultural dominance of capital, as represented by the BRD political settlement, and is for decisive social change through both strong parliamentary representation and extra-parliamentary means. Perhaps inevitably, given the territorial nature of the PDS's support and political strategy, much of the party's programme is embedded within a domestic – and primarily 'eastern German' – political discourse. By contrast some observers have, on the strength of content analysis of party documents, assigned the FDP a position to the right of the CDU/CSU (see Budge and Keman, 1990). This is an artefact of the history of the FDP which was the first liberal party to achieve a *modus operandi* between the two conflicting wings – social – and economic/national – of German liberalism. The tension between the two wings of the FDP has a territorial dimension, with the progressives better represented in the south-western *Länder* and the Hansa city-states, and the national-liberal wing strongest in the *Länder* of Hesse, Lower Saxony and North Rhine-Westphalia (the party is still weak in the former East Germany).

Second, rather than blur the edges of the product they offer voters, both parties tend to use their ideological profiles as assets in the political mobilisation process. Thus, in election campaigns the PDS deliberately stresses its left credentials and concentrates its political attacks on the SPD (see Chapter 8), whilst the FDP, notwithstanding the decision in the run-up to the 2002 Bundestag elections to profile itself as a 'fun party', has tended to campaign as the 'liberal corrective' to the catch-all parties. The 2002 Bundestag elections was notable for a very strong ideological message from the leader of the North Rhine-Westphalian FDP, Jürgen Möllemann, who raised the temperature of the campaign with a number of pro-Arab and, some argued, anti-Semitic pronouncements.

Third, both parties have a clearly defined social base and maintain strong links with it. Thus, the PDS sees itself as representing the new Federal states and, in particular, the losers of the unification process, whereas the FDP is a party of the better-off, the middle classes and small employers. But interestingly, the scope and organisation of these links differs between the parties. Thus the PDS, as the successor to the proto-hegemonic SED, still enjoys broad social links in the new Federal states and still has a relatively large membership. By contrast, the FDP has evolved within a proportional system and has narrower social links and a much smaller membership, despite winning a higher share of the vote. In addition, the FDP is relatively leadership-centered whereas the PDS, at least since the exit of Gregor Gysi and Lothar Byski from the national stage, lacks a leadership presence. Thus the 'company culture', so to speak, differs in many key respects between the two parties.

Personalistic parties

Personalistic parties differ from the other two species of electoralist parties in that their sole raison d'etre is to act as the organisational vehicle for the party leader to win elections and exercise power. In terms of the market metaphor used in this study we might classify them as 'shell-companies'. Thus, in addition to a prominent leader, they are characterised by a shallow organisation, with little or no internal party life, a strong electoral focus (centred on the leader), and little or no ideology. The key driver of such parties is the charismatic leadership and appeal of the individual who heads the party and as a result the party's existence is more contingent in more socially – and organisationally – grounded parties. Examples include the Thai Rak Thai Party of Thai businessman Thaksin Shinawatra, the Congress-I party of Indira Gandhi, the Pakistan People's Party of the Bhutto clan, and, in Italy, Silvio Berlusconi's Forza Italia.

There are no real examples of such a party in Germany. The nearest a German party has come in recent years to this model is the 'Rule of Law State Offensive Party' (*Partei Rechtsstaatlicher Offensive*, or PRO). The PRO is also known as the 'Schill Party', because it emerged as a vehicle for the populist lawyer Ronald Schill. Schill came to national prominence in the late 1990s as a result of a hard-hitting campaign, based around the themes of law and order and zero tolerance of crime, in his native city-state of Hamburg. From 2000 onwards the PRO made tentative moves to become a political force at the national level but failed to make any impact during the 2002 Bundestag elections. In 2003 Schill lost his post as Interior Minister in Hamburg and was expelled from his own party following a series of political scandals. Two reasons can be put forward as to why the PRO does not fall into the category of personalistic party. First, the fact that Schill was expelled from his own party and that the party continues as part of the ruling coalition in Hamburg means that the party's existence is not contingent on the charismatic authority of the leader. Second, that the party does have a reasonably coherent ideology – albeit a populist one based almost exclusively on a narrow law and order agenda.

7.8 Genus 5: Movement parties

Gunther and Diamond's fifth genus of political party is slightly different from the other four because it is used to describe a form of political organisation that covers both a political party and a wider movement within which the party is embedded. However, for taxonomical purposes the category is only used to describe those organisations that field candidates at elections. Thus in terms of our market metaphor we could draw a parallel with the 'trading arms' of certain co-operative or mutual societies. The two most common species of movement party are, first, the left-libertarian party and, second, the post industrial extreme right parties. The paradigmatic examples of the two species are, respectively, the German Greens and the Austrian Freedom Party (Gunther and Diamond, 2003: 188).

Gunther and Diamond's conception of the left-libertarian party is drawn from the work of Kitschelt, who uses the term to draw a distinction between them and the 'conventional parties' of Western Europe. For Kitschelt, conventional parties of right or left are primarily orientated towards winning government power through elected office, have a professional salariat of party functionaries, a well-developed party organisation, represent specific economic interests and campaign on materialist/redistributionalist issues. By contrast, left-libertarian parties campaign primarily on post-materialist issues, reject the predominance of economic issues, and argue that markets and bureaucracies must be replaced with more solidaristic and participatory institutions. In its purest from, the left-libertarian party does not erect barriers to participation and has a diverse social and attitudinal profile. In addition its focus on direct participation means it rejects formal bureaucratic norms and structures leading to disorganised and often chaotic decision-making processes and a lack of clear leadership and line-management. In organisational terms, the left-libertarian movement party is heavily reliant on a loosely knit grass roots organisation with little formal structure, hierarchy or central steering capacity (Kitschelt, 1989: 62–6). Finally, the left-libertarian party works to the logic of constituency representation rather than electoral competition, which has the potential to make it an unpredictable and over-idealistic coalition partner (Gunther and Diamond, 2003: 189).

This rejection of the rational-bureaucratic model of party organisation is also shared by the other species of movement party, namely, the post-industrial extreme right party. Like left-libertarian parties, post-industrial extreme right parties are also deeply hostile to what they regard as the political 'establishment' and are often embedded in a wider, often shifting and inchoate network of like-minded militants and fellow-travellers. But unlike left-libertarian parties, post-industrial extreme right wing parties campaign primarily on a deeply authoritarian agenda based on ideas of order, tradition, identity and security. Moreover, like their predecessors the Fascists, such parties follow a leadership principle in which the leader's directives are generally obeyed without question or debate. Unlike the Fascists, however, post-industrial right wing parties are less in favour of the kind of strong providing state that characterised Mussolini's Italy or Hitler's Germany, and are inclined to use anti-state rhetoric (Ignazi, 1996; quoted in Gunther and Diamond, 2003: 189).

Left-libertarian parties: the Greens

As discussed above, the Greens are considered the paradigmatic example of the left-libertarian party. However, as will become apparent in this and the following chapter, a quarter of a century later it is harder to assign the present-day Greens to this species, at least not without a strong caveat about the trajectory of the party's organisational and ideological development.

The genesis of the Greens is very much in keeping with the left-libertarian model, and they emerged out of the 'citizens initiative' groups of the mid- to late 1970s, in response to the perceived failure of the Social–Liberal coalition's socio-economic policies and the SPD's refusal to adapt to the 'New Politics' agenda. Party development in the early years was hampered by the ongoing struggle between the movement's 'New Left' and 'value conservative' wings. The New Left regarded environmental protest as just one aspect of a wider critique of the capitalist system, whilst the latter favoured co-operation with the established economic and political order. As a result, the two wings initially fielded rival lists at local and *Land* elections. However activists on both sides of the divide understood that factional infighting was preventing either of the ecological groupings from surmounting the Federal Republic's 5 per cent electoral barrier. So in October 1978 the two wings in the state of Bavaria joined forces and fielded a joint list in the state's elections, in what became known as the 'Bavarian cooperation model'. The model was to become the template for future co-operation in other states. But once inside the same organisation the superior caucusing skills of the New Left, many of whom were veterans of the student movement and other left-wing groupings, served to marginalize the value conservatives. In a relatively short period of time the Greens began to assume the now familiar left-libertarian and/or post-materialist characteristics we associate with it (Markovits and Gorski, 1993: 192–7).

As noted in Chapter 6 party systems at the *Land* level are more fluid than at the Federal level and provide more opportunities for political outsiders. Thus it is no surprise that the Greens used the sub-national level to consolidate its status within the political marketplace. The party also campaigned in the 1979 elections to the European Parliament and, although failing to win seats, did win 3.2 per cent of the vote. During this period the progress of party development remained uneven across the Federal Republic. In some areas local Green parties formed relatively early, whilst in others the Greens did not contest local elections until after the formation of the national party in 1980. Indeed, with the exception of a local party in Trier, in Rhineland-Palatinate no local parties contested elections until 1984 (Scharf, 1994: 64–6), a year after the national party had secured its first seats in the Bundestag. This pattern of heterogeneous local political cultures and little central steering capacity persisted into the 1990s and, along with a strong norm of constituency representation, proved a significant barrier to the development of a routinised model of political co-operation between the Greens and the SPD (Lees, 1998, 2000).

The Greens fought the March 1983 Bundestag elections for the fist time as a unified party and polled 5.6 per cent of the vote (Padgett, 1993: 28). At the time this was hailed as a historic juncture, which 'transformed the Federal Republic from the last refuge of party system immobility into an El Dorado of success for alternative politics' (Beyme, 1991: 161). As it turned out this was jumping the gun somewhat and, after the initial burst of success, the party became mired for some years in an ongoing factional struggle between the so-called *Realos*, a pragmatic grouping that favoured co-operation with the SPD, and the *Fundis*, who were opposed to this strategy. Other issues that divided the two factions included the principles of 'rotation', a form of delegational democracy in which elected list members were expected to step down after one term, and 'basis democracy' (*Basisdemokratie*), which endowed the party membership with relatively high levels of influence over the parliamentary faction. Both of these principles were consistent with Petra Kelly's description of the Greens as an 'anti-party party', in that they were designed to impair the professionalisation of the party and the emergence of the kind of career politicians found in the other parties. Over time both of these issues were resolved in the *Realos'* favour. However, in doing this the Greens began to move away from the left-libertarian model and more towards that of a programmatic electoralist party.

Thus, the *Realos'* victory was symptomatic of the gradual institutionalisation of the Greens as a mainstream political party. Six factors were at work to bring this about. First, German unification eventually led to the Greens in the old Federal states merging with the more moderate Alliance '90 and 'eastern' Greens in the new states. This resulted in an overall moderation of both the Green voters' and membership's ideological profile. Second, the '68ers' – the original generational cohort from which the movement in the old Federal states originally arose – had inevitably become older, more established and economically integrated. As a result some of the Greens' more overtly anti-capitalist policies began to lose their appeal to many of the party's voters and membership. Third, over time the Greens organisational structure became more institutionalised and hierarchical, with a net transfer of resources and power from the 'party in the country' to the parliamentary party. This made the now predominantly *Realo* parliamentary party more autonomous vis-à-vis the membership. Fourth, the most attractive aspects of the agenda around which the Greens originally mobilised were co-opted by the other parties – especially the SPD – in a process that became known as 'issue theft' (*Themenklau*). Fifth, the weakness of the FDP and its increasing reliance at both the local and national level upon the second-votes of CDU supporters increased the viability of the Greens as a potential coalition partner. Finally, the emergence of the PDS after unification meant that much of the stigma that had previously attached itself to the Greens was now transferred to them. As a result there was less political risk in other parties co-operating with the Greens.

By the time the Greens entered government as junior coalition partner to the SPD, following the 1998 Bundestag elections, the 'national' party had moved quite a way from Kitschelt's model of the left-libertarian party. For instance, although its organisational structures and norms remained significantly looser than the other mainstream parties the principle of 'grass-roots democracy' had been severely weakened over the intervening years. In particular, the practice of rotation had ended in the 1980s and, with the emergence of Joschka Fischer as de facto leader of the party, the capacity of the membership to exercise control over the leadership was much reduced. This was demonstrated by the furore within the party that surrounded the decision of the Red–Green coalition to contribute forces to Nato's Kosovo campaign in 1999. It is true that Fischer was subjected to far more direct, vigorous and, occasionally violent modes of internal party resistance than would have been the case in a more rational-bureaucratic organisation. But nevertheless, in the end the decision to commit German forces to out-of-area operations for the first time in the history of Federal Republic stood (Lees, 2000). As will be discussed in Chapter 8, this and other decisions taken as a member of the Federal government, as well as the Greens' increasing personalisation of its campaign message around the strengths of Fischer as leader, cast doubt on the future trajectory of the Greens as a left-libertarian party. Nevertheless, on the basis of past history and standard operating procedures it remains the correct categorisation at the time of writing. Moreover, if the Greens were to return to opposition it is not beyond the realms of possibility that this strand of the party's culture and organisational norms might reassert itself.

Post-industrial extreme right wing parties:
the Republicans, DVU, and NPD

In Germany the closest examples to the ideal-type of the post-industrial extreme right party are the Republicans (*Republikaner*), German People's Union (*Deutsche Volksunion*, or DVU) and German National Democratic Party (*Nationaldemokratische Partei Deutschlands*, or NPD). And as will become apparent the best 'fit' between reality and ideal-type is the NPD. At the same time, if we use the idea of the post-industrial extreme right party as a heuristic typology rather than an ideal-type then it can apply to all three parties, albeit with certain caveats.

Historically, far right parties have never really made much of an impact within the Federal Republic's party system. In the 1960s, the NPD enjoyed a brief period of support, coinciding with the combined political opportunities presented by a brief recession and the incumbency of a Grand Coalition in Bonn. The next period of relative success was the 1980s, culminating in the shock result for the Republicans of over 8 per cent of the vote in West Berlin in 1989. The initial period after unification was characterised by much concern about the Republicans and its rival on the far-right, the DVU. The two parties successfully mobilised around the so-called Asylum issue of the early 1990s, but soon saw their fortunes fade. This was as a result of the tightening-up of the Federal Republic's asylum laws and also because of the endemic internal feuding that has characterised the post-war far right in the Federal Republic.

At the level of national politics in Germany, there are no 'relevant' parties to the right of the CDU/CSU. This is the result of what was, and remains, a key strategic aim of the Christian Democrats who, from the Adenauer era onwards, have tried to absorb competitor parties on the political right (Klingemann and Volkens, 1992: 190). As a result, although the CDU/CSU is flanked by right wing parties these have not posed a serious electoral threat to it at the national level of politics. Thus any success enjoyed by far right parties has been confined to party systems at the *Land* level.

The Republicans were founded in Munich in 1983 by ex members of the CSU, who had left the party in protest at the decision of the then leader of the CSU, Franz Josef Strauß, to agree to substantial loans to the East German government. The leadership of the new party was shared between three individuals, Franz Handlos, Ekkehard Voigt and Franz Schönhuber. The party's original programme was broadly conservative in tone and, although it argued for Germany to act more in its national interest, remained essentially pro-EU integration. However during the 1980s Schönhuber gradually became ascendant within the party, the Republican's ideological profile shifted further to the right, and in turn its position on Europe became more hostile. The party enjoyed a spate of relatively good electoral performances in the late 1980s but went into decline in the 1990s. At the 2002 Bundestag elections the Republicans published a relatively detailed election manifesto that pursued the party's now established themes of national sovereignty, German cultural values, law and order and hostility to the European Union (Republikaner, 2002; Lees, 2005a). Where the Republicans do differ from the post-industrial extreme right party model is in its relatively weak leadership principle – at least compared with the DVU and NPD. This is in part the result of the Republicans' genesis in the right wing of the CSU, and the subsequent importation of orthodox rational-bureaucratic values and practices into the new party. These relatively 'party-like' characteristics, coupled with the party's reasonably coherent ideological profile means that the Republicans could also arguably be categorised as a programmatic electoralist party. However, the fluid links enjoyed by many party members and key leadership personnel with the other extreme right parties, as well as the wider extreme right and/or neo-Fascist milieu, mean that the Republicans remain better confined to the category of post-industrial extreme right party.

In contrast with the Republicans, the DVU fits quite well into the typology. The party was founded in 1971 – again in Munich – by Gerhard Frey. He did not originally intend to form an orthodox party, but rather wanted the DVU to be a cross-party alliance of right wing conservatives stretching from the right wing of the CDU/CSU to the more extreme right wing NPD. Over time, however, Frey transformed the DVU into a party in its own right and moved it to a position clearly to the right of the CDU/CSU. The DVU's ideology is at the very least ultra-conservative, with a tendency to blame what it would consider to be 'unGerman' groups (such as foreigners, Jews or left-wingers) for social problems such as unemployment. The general ideological direction of the DVU's campaign literature is similar to that of the Republicans, but it is framed within a more uncompromising discourse and as a result lacks the same degree of programmatic detail (DVU, 2003; Lees, 2005a).

Finally, at the far right of the party spectrum is the oldest of the extant far right parties, and the one that conforms most closely to the typology of post-industrial extreme right party. The NPD was founded in Hannover in 1964 as a result of the collapse of the ultra conservative German Reich Party. It enjoyed some prominence during the economic downturn of the mid-1960s but even then failed to scale the 5 per cent electoral hurdle in the 1965 Bundestag elections. During the 1970s and 1980s, the NPD operated on the fringe of the German party system(s), often in alliance with the DVU. However, in the 1990s the party underwent a process of radicalisation and adopted a new strategy that included extra-parliamentary action and developing close links with the Skinhead scene and other neo-Nazi milieus – thus becoming a true movement party. As a result, the SPD–Green Federal government tried unsuccessfully to ban the party. In ideological terms the NPD combines a settled extreme right wing ideology with more opportunistic attempts to mobilise around more transient political issues, such as opposition to the United States' campaign in Iraq (NPD, 1999, 2002; Lees, 2005a).

7.9   Summary

This chapter started with a review of the strands of the literature and a discussion of the problems associated with trying to establish a single classificatory scheme that functions effectively in a comparative perspective but is also appropriate to the German context. Having done this we established such a scheme, drawn from the work of Gunther and Diamond (2003), that was primarily based on variance in the extent or 'thickness' of party organisation. In addition to these organisational characteristics, the scheme also placed parties according to ideology, strategy and norms of behaviour, sociological grounding, and the internal dynamics of party decision-making, particularly the role and relative autonomy of the leadership. Taken together the schema generated 15 party species, divided into 5 genuses: (i) Elite based; (ii) Mass based; (iii) Ethnicity based; (iv) Electoralist; and (v) Movement parties. These five genuses were then used to frame a discussion of the main parties in the German party system in a comparative perspective.

The Gunther and Diamond schema provides a robust framework with which to examine both individual political parties and, in broader terms, families of political parties. Nevertheless, when applying a generalisable scheme to a specific subfield there is rarely a perfect fit, and it remains up to the individual researcher to ascribe particular parties to particular families, based on their understanding and judgement of how best the schema applies to their field of interest. Thus, most of the classifications found in the chapter are the author's alone – either because specific parties were not included in Gunther and Diamond's categorisation or, as in the case of the CDU/CSU, because it was judged that the categorisation was inappropriate.

Figure 7.1 provides an overview of the categorisation of extant German political parties in an historical context. Taking a time line from the 1850s until the present day, the table demonstrates the balance between continuity and change in party types, as well as the placement of individual political parties, over the period. Four observations are worth noting at this point. First, some of the parties dealt with in this chapter, such as Zentrum, the KPD, SED and NSDAP, obviously no longer exist and are therefore not included in the data. Second, one party – the PRO – does not fit easily into any of the categories and, given that it is primarily confined to Hamburg and has no national presence, it has not been included in the data at this point in time. Nevertheless, if the PRO does manage to both break out of its territorial laager and consolidate its internal party life after the fall of Schill, any future taxonomical exercise of this type would have to include it (most likely as a programmatic electoralist party, along with the FDP and PDS). Third, throughout the entire timeline from the mid-nineteenth century onwards the SPD is a constant presence in the German party system(s). Given the momentous changes that took place in that time this is a remarkable feat of persistence and illustrates the strengths of the model of a political party that is socially grounded and organised in a rational-legal fashion. But fourth, and somewhat in contradiction to the last point, the SPD – like all of the mainstream parties – is moving towards a position nearer the organisation- ally thin end of the continuum. In terms of our broad market metaphor we can still discern differences between types of firms operating within the political marketplace – with the SPD and CDU resembling large companies or corporations, the FDP and PDS small to medium size companies and the

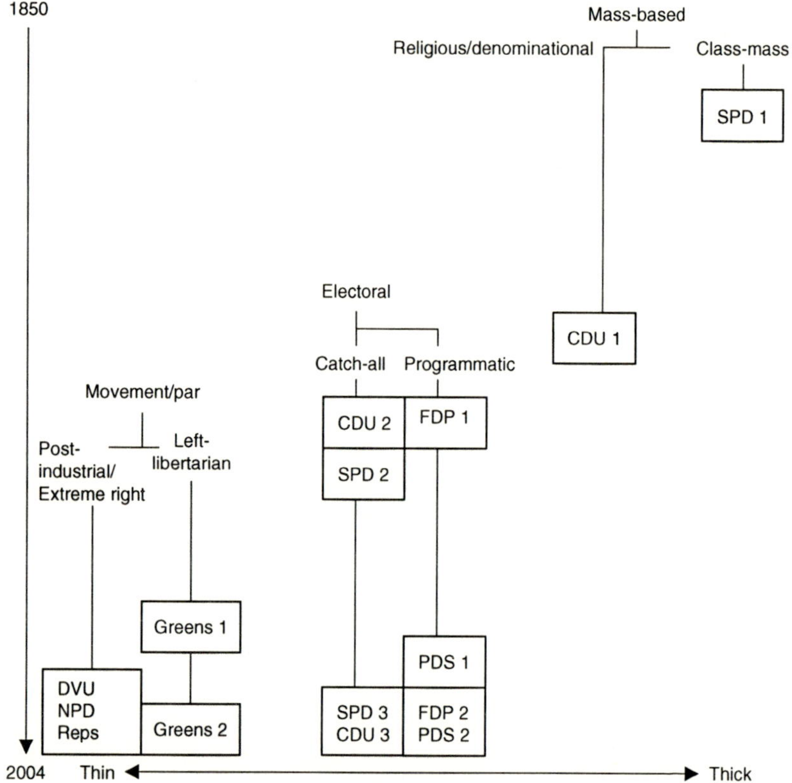

Figure 7.1   Continuity and change of species of political parties in the German party system(s), after Gunther and Diamond (2003)

Greens remain to some extent consistent with the model of the trading arm of a co-operative or mutual society. However, these differences are in decline and, using Gunther and Diamond's specific classificatory schema, all of the mainstream parties, including the Greens, seem to be converging on the electoralist party model.

The fact that all of the mainstream parties appear to be converging on one category indicates that there may be some potential problems with using Gunther and Diamond's schema over time. However, let us leave that to one side for now and take the emerging dominance of the electoralist party type at face value. As already discussed the electoral party is the product of social and technical change. And as social location becomes a weaker predictor of voting intention and the mass media dominates the public discourse about party politics, electoralist parties become organisationally thinner, scale down the scope and intensity of links with both members and society, and utilise modern campaign techniques to reach an atomised, volatile, and non-partisan electorate. This happens regardless of ideological or historical baggage and, as a result, we have seen a significant change in methods and discourse – mostly in the way in which parties compete with one another but also, if elected, in how they co-operate with one another. It is to these dynamics of competition and co-operation that the book now turns.

8
Competition and Co-operation

8.1 Introduction

Chapter 8 is divided into two main sections. In the first section, the chapter looks at competition between political parties, in Germany and in a comparative perspective. This section is focussed on parties' programmes, in other words the political firm's 'product', and the campaign strategies used to promote the product, namely the 'message'. The section also discusses some of the empirical and theoretical literature that suggests that the product/message divide is no longer appropriate and that the decline of ideology, combined with today's sophisticated political marketing, has led to a situation in which the message increasingly *is* the product as well. In the second section, the chapter looks at the flip-side of party political competition, that of co-operation, with an emphasis on coalition politics at the national and sub-national levels, in Germany and in a comparative perspective. Both sections of the chapter, and the second section in particular, include new data on the most significant model of coalition politics in recent years in Germany, that of 'Red–Green' coalitions between the SPD and Greens, both in the *Länder* and at the Federal level. Finally, the chapter concludes with a summary of the main points raised within it.

8.2 Political competition

Specific patterns of competition between political parties vary from country-to-country, depending on the nation-specific variables that frame the political marketplace in any given context. As already discussed in Chapter 2 in particular, these variables include underlying cleavage structures, the degree to which these cleavages have been made manifest, the nature of alliances forged between key societal groups, the shape of the national political economy, and so on. Yet, on another level, the elemental nature of political competition within the marketplace is remarkably similar across politics. As Holzhacker puts it, '(all) political parties in parliamentary democracies compete for support by communicating appeals to the electorate during periodic election campaigns' (Holzhacker, 1999: 439). But on what basis do parties make such appeals?

At the most basic level all parties try to convince potential voters that their product is superior to that of their competitors and that as a result a vote for party x will bring the voter higher levels of utility than a vote for rival party y. Of course, the actual nature of that utility flow is different across time and space. As discussed in Chapter 5, voters' preferences are a product of many variables, including socio-economic location, peer pressure and cues, the degree of information available through the mass media, perceptions of personal competence and leadership amongst candidates in particular, ex post assessments of real performance in government, and of course future expectations in that regard, as well as a mix of instrumental and socio-tropic judgements on economic circumstances. Ultimately we have seen that the individual's decision of whether, and for whom, to vote is arrived at through a form of fuzzy logic-based judgement of the political products on offer. For their part, political parties must devise programmes that appeal to an aggregate of individual preference orderings – although the size of this aggregate is partly determined by the role parties play within the market, whether they are pursuing a mass- or niche-market and so on.

The most tangible codified evidence of the political product that parties offer up to potential customers are party programmes, be they basic programmes, action programmes, election programmes or government programmes. Of course, the norms and customs that help determine the shape of these programmes vary between national markets. In the Federal Republic, for instance, it is customary for political parties to place great emphasis on the formulation of their basic programme and such programmes are designed to frame the party's fundamental ideological underpinnings in a coherent and communicable manner. This contrasts somewhat with action programmes and election programmes that are more contingent on the conditions of time and place. But what binds all of these programmes together is an assumption that such documents should have a degree of ideological and intellectual ballast to them. In normative terms they are still considered to be one of main conduits by which voters can obtain the information necessary to make an informed electoral choice – despite the fact that a minority of the electorate in most countries bother to obtain and/or read them. At the same time, however, we also accept that parties will devote much of their time to what appears at first glance to be an associated but distinct form of activity – the more ephemeral and manipulative art of political campaigning.

But can we make such a distinction between programmes and campaigns, between the product and the promotional message through which the product is marketed? Here it is possible to take equally valid but mutually exclusive positions.

On the one hand, much of the political marketing literature does blur the divide between product and promotion (see for instance, Niffenegger, 1989; Sackman, 1996; Scammel, 1999). This reflects the reality of political competition in which political parties have become increasingly reactive to the prejudices of what they regard as a febrile and incoherent climate of public opinion. The push factors in this process have been the phenomena already discussed in this book, namely the decline of ideology, increasing social fragmentation, falling levels of partisan identity, higher levels of electoral volatility and the role of the mass media in framing issues; whereas the pull factors include advances in applied social science research and the subsequent ability on the part of political parties to discern and react to public preferences as well as to attempt to prime the electorate to those issues which parties feel play to their strengths. In a recent example from the political marketing literature Lees-Marshment posits a three-stage developmental model of political marketing in which political parties may or may not move from the status of 'product-oriented party', through that of 'sales-oriented party', to that of 'market-oriented party'. Crucially, in what the author calls the 'CPM model', the first two categories of product and sales oriented party implicitly preserve the divide between the product and its promotion. Thus, the product-oriented party is focussed almost exclusively on its programme (the product), and very little thought is given to whether the content of that programme, or the means by which it is communicated beyond the party, is in itself amenable to voters' preferences. Lees-Marshment suggests that the British Labour Party at the time of the 1983 General Election is a good example of this form of party. On a slightly different tack, a sales-oriented party differs from the product-oriented party in that, although the basic programme as product remains central, a relatively high level of strategic importance is given to selling the product beyond the party by means of a slick campaign at election time. Thus the Labour Party fought the 1987 elections on a broadly similar election manifesto as that of 1983, but with a much different campaign – that was judged by many observers to have been superior to that of the Conservative party. By contrast, the market-oriented political party – as typified by New Labour in 1987 – does not just adjust its message to reflect the preferences of the electorate but actually transforms all aspects of its behaviour, including institutional structures and party programmes, in pursuit of market share/electoral success (Lees-Marshment, 2001). Thus, product and promotion are blurred and the party 'brand' becomes increasingly decoupled from any underlying content. It is useful to note at this point that the increasingly free-floating nature of what is called 'brand meaning' over the period since the early 1990s is a phenomenon much commented on in the mainstream marketing literature (see Doyle, 2003: 79–80). Although there are clearly differences between marketing training shoes or coffee and performing an analogous function for political parties, there would appear to be no empirical reason why political parties and the political marketplace should be wholly immune to the process noted above.

Having said that, however, there is also a respectable intellectual case against this blurring of product and promotion. The argument is as much epistemological as it is empirical, and it has two strands. First, although much of the political marketing literature, especially that drawing on psycho-social models of cognitive mobilisation, is highly sophisticated it also suffers from a number of drawbacks. Scammell (1999) identifies five such problems: (i) problems with agreed definitions; (ii) inadequacies of marketing explanations of electoral success; (iii) difficulties of testing marketing models; (iv) ambiguity of evidence of deliberate marketing consciousness in campaigns; and (v) normative concerns at marketing's consequences for democratic practice (Scammell, 1999: 735). To these I would add two other concerns. First, much of the literature is quite ahistorical and neglects the impact of SOPs, ideology and internal politics on the development of political parties' programmatic and institutional development. Second, and tangential to the last point, by making a party's marketing profile the main causal variable of these developments, as Lees-Marshment does for instance, there is a tendency not only to neglect SOPs and so on, but also to ascribe too much of a central 'will' to the political party as an institution. As Kenneth Arrow pointed out half a century ago, it is irrational to assume that complex organisations *qua* organisations behave as unitary actors with a single set of preferences (Arrow, 1951). We do make this assumption in many circumstances when it is heuristic to do so and it has been made in many instances during the course of this book. But in this particular case – when one is trying to strike a culturally sensitive balance between specific historical context and generalisable trends across cases, it causes more problems than it solves. The second strand of the argument against the blurring of product and promotion is more pragmatic: namely that the vast majority of studies within the party politics literature – including much of the political marketing literature itself – does work from at least an implicit assumption that such a divide exists and accords high levels of importance to political ideology and party programmes. Whether it is through general election surveys (Sani and Sartori, 1983), expert judgements (Castles and Mair, 1984; Laver and Hunt, 1992), or through the now highly developed analysis of manifestos (Budge, *et al.*, 1987; Laver and Budge, 1992), these approaches afford an importance to parties' ideological and programmatic positions that is more than just an adjunct to the need to secure or expand political market share. Thus, given that this book is reliant on drawing on secondary sources in order to cast a comparative light upon electoral and party politics in Germany, we will go with the grain of the majority of scholarly work and assume that the divide between programmes and campaigns can still be talked about in a meaningful way.[6]

Party programmes

Given the extent and sophistication of the information on voters' preferences that is now available to political parties it would be a surprise if the process

Table 8.1 Types of party programme and their core functions

Functions	Basic programme	Action programme	Election programme	Government programme
Internal				
PR	X	XX	XXX	XX
Profile	XX	XXX	XXX	XXX
Agitation	X	XX	XXX	XX
Operational basis	X	XX	XX	XXX
External				
Integration	XXX	XX	XX	X
Identification	XXX	X	X	X
Stimulation	X	XXX	XXX	X
Control	XX	XX	XXX	XX
Legitimation	XXX	XX	X	X

Notes: X (low salience); XX (medium salience); XXX (high salience).

Source: Adapted from Kaack, 1995: 318.

by which party programmes are devised and disseminated had not changed over the last century of party politics. Nevertheless it still remains the case that all types of programmes have a number of core functions.

The four types of party programme (Basic, Action, Election and Governmental) and their core functions are set out in Table 8.1. The degree of salience of each programme type in fulfilling these core functions is denoted by an X score (see table notes). Broadly speaking the functions in Table 8.1 can be divided into two categories: that of (a) 'external' and (b) 'internal' functions. There are four external functions: namely (i) PR within the populace, recruiting new members and winning political support; (ii) profiling the party against competitors; (iii) agitation and preparing the ground for confrontation with competitors; and (iv) establishing the operational parameters within which political parties can frame their political demands both vis-à-vis other political parties and in the context of public opinion. Similarly, there are five internal functions: (i) a core integration function, which binds all members to a common set of principles; (ii) to foster identification on the behalf of members, so that support becomes instinctive and routinised; (iii) to stimulate political activism on the basis of that identification; (iv) to allow the leadership to exert control over the political organisation and the membership; and (v) to legitimate political action in the eyes of agents and observers alike (Kaack, 1995: 318–19). The four different types of party programme have different levels of impact on these various functions, with basic programmes for instance being more salient to the fulfilment of internal functions whereas election and governmental programmes are more salient to the external environment.

The model described above is very much an ideal type and empirical research into the fulfilment of programmatic commitments in 19 democracies indicates that although political parties claim to take their programmes seriously as a way of connecting with voters, there are strong cross-national differences in the degree to which one can predict future policy performance on the basis of their programmatic commitments (see for instance, Hofferbert and Klingemann, 1990; Budge and Hofferbert, 1990). In a sense, however, this is not surprising if we adopt a 'positional' approach to the data. Political parties' programmes can be interpreted in two ways – as either 'positional' or 'directional' data. The more common positional approach works from the assumption that political parties compete with one another by assuming and communicating specific positions on a range of policy issues. Thus, given the needs of practical politics and especially the needs of coalition bargaining, initial positions at *T1* will quite feasibly be given up in order to secure inter-party agreement at *T2*. By contrast the directional approach argues that political parties' programmatic positions are actually quite fungible and in practice parties send cues to both the electorate and other parties about the direction and intensity of their preferences (Holzhacker, 1999). If one adopts this approach the mismatch between programmatic position and policy outputs is of less relevance.

This chapter works from the assumption that in practice political parties and electorates all work with a form of fuzzy logic in which programmatic positioning does matter, at least as a form of opening gambit in any future bargaining game, but that it is the salience and direction of a party's preferences that provide the cues for voters when assessing a party's product and also indicate to other parties where fruitful co-operation might take place (as well as those areas that are effectively 'red-lined' and not for negotiation). The importance of salience and direction of preference means that although parties might be quite far apart in a positional sense on some issues, the underlying strategic position could well be more fluid and promising than might appear from a purely positional analysis. Conversely, although certain political parties might be quite close in programmatic terms, the tone and discourse used to give out cues might preclude the possibility of co-operation between them.

To demonstrate this, let us consider the position, direction and salience of the Greens vis-à-vis other mainstream parties, based on an analysis of national election programmes from the 1998 and 2002 Bundestag elections. These are set out in Tables 8.2. and 8.3.

Tables 8.2 and 8.3 demonstrate that the Greens are now a mainstream party. Building on Budge's analysis of election programmes, the tables set out seven general 'domains' of policy (1987: 230), to which I have added an eighth, that of 'discursive form'. All data is of a judgemental/qualitative nature rather than the result of quantitative content analysis, but it should be noted that in reality it is through such judgements that parties and voters

184

Table 8.2 Typology of Greens, SPD and CDU party programmes for 1998-Bundestag elections

Domain	Greens	SPD	CDU
1. Foreign affairs	(i) Ambivalence towards Nato (ii) Ambivalence towards 'Western values' (iii) Ambivalence towards out-of-area operations	(i) *Pro-Nato* (ii) *Moderate emphasis on 'Western Values'* (iii) *Limited acceptance of out-of-area operations*	(i) *Pro-Nato* (ii) *Strong Emphasis on 'Western Values'* (iii) *Pro-out-of-area operations*
2. Freedom and democracy	(i) *Some ambivalence towards 'Bourgeois Democracy'* (ii) *Emphasis on autonomy of individual*	(i) *Acceptance of 'Bourgeois democracy'* (ii) *Moderate emphasis on autonomy of individual*	(i) *Acceptance Of 'Bourgeois Democracy'* (ii) *State as guardian of individual freedoms*
3. Government	Ambivalent	*State-oriented*	*State-oriented*
4. Economy	*Ambivalence towards social-market economy (some emphasis on role of private enterprise)*	*Pro social-market economy (but emphasis on role of the state)*	*Pro social-market economy (but emphasis on role of Private enterprise)*
5. Welfare	(i) *Expansion of state provision and increased self-help* (ii) *Increased role for the market*	(i) *Expansion of state provision* (ii) *Limited role for the market*	(i) *Limited expansion of state provision* (ii) *Increased role for the market*
6. Fabric of society	(i) *Radical/libertarian* (ii) *Emphasis on alternatives to nuclear family*	(i) *Traditional/ moderate libertarian* (ii) *Implicit orientation towards nuclear family*	(i) Traditional/ authoritarian (ii) Strong emphasis on nuclear family and gender roles
7. Social groups	(i) *Affirmative action (Quotas)* (ii) *Single-issue campaigning*	(i) *Affirmative action (Targets)* (ii) *Emphasis on broad civic rights*	(i) Ambivalence (ii) Emphasis on broad civic rights
8. Discursive form	(i) Administrative (ii) Some policy detail	(i) *Administrative/ technocratic* (ii) *Detailed policy*	(i) *Administrative/ technocratic* (ii) *Detailed policy*

Sources: '*Programme zur Bundestagswahl 98*', B.90/Greens 1998; *Arbeit. Innovation und Gerechtigkeit: SPD-Wahlprogramme für die Bundestagswahl 1998,* SPD, 1998; *1998–2002 Wahl-platform,* CDU/CSU, 1998; *Zukunftsprogramme der Christlich Demokratischen Union Deutschlands,* CDU, 1998.

Table 8.3 Typology of Greens, SPD, FDP and CDU party programmes for 2002-Bundestag elections

Domain	Greens	SPD	FDP	CDU
1. Foreign affairs	(i) *Little explicit hostility towards Nato* (ii) *Little ambivalence towards 'Western values'* (iii) *Acceptance of some out-of-area operations*	(i) *Pro-Nato* (ii) *Moderate emphasis on 'Western Values'* (iii) *Limited acceptance of out-of-area operations*	(i) *Pro-Nato* (ii) *Moderate emphasis on 'Western Values'* (iii) *acceptance of out-of-area operations*	(i) *Pro-Nato* (ii) *Strong Emphasis on 'Western Values'* (iii) *Pro-out-of-area operations*
2. Freedom and democracy	(i) *Acceptance of 'Bourgeois Democracy'* (ii) *Emphasis on autonomy of individual*	(i) *Acceptance Of 'Bourgeois democracy'* (ii) *Moderate emphasis on autonomy of individual*	(i) *Acceptance Of 'Bourgeois democracy'* (ii) *Strong emphasis on autonomy of individual*	(i) *Acceptance Of 'Bourgeois Democracy'* (ii) *State as guardian of individual freedoms*
3. Government	*State-oriented*	*State-oriented*	*State-oriented*	*State-oriented*
4. Economy	*Pro social-market economy (Some emphasis on role of private enterprise)*	*Pro social-market economy (but emphasis on role of the state)*	*Pro social-market economy (strong emphasis on role of private enterprise)*	*Pro social-market economy (but emphasis on role of private enterprise)*
5. Welfare	(i) *Expansion of state provision and increased self-help* (ii) *Increased role for the market*	(i) *Expansion of state provision* (ii) *Limited role for the market*	(i) *Restriction of state provision* (ii) *Increased role for the market*	(i) *Limited expansion of state provision* (ii) *Increased role for the market*
6. Fabric of society	(i) *Radical/ libertarian* (ii) *Emphasis on alternatives to nuclear family.*	(i) *Traditional/ moderate libertarian* (ii) *Implicit orientation towards nuclear family*	(i) *Traditional/ moderate libertarian* (ii) *Implicit orientation towards nuclear family*	(i) *Traditional/ authoritarian* (ii) *Strong emphasis on nuclear family and gender roles*
7. Social groups	(i) *Affirmative action (quotas)* (ii) *Single-issue campaigning*	(i) *Affirmative action (Targets)* (ii) *Emphasis on broad civic rights*	(i) *Ambivalence* (ii) *Emphasis on broad civic rights*	(i) *Ambivalence* (ii) *Emphasis on broad civic rights*
8. Discursive Form	(i) *Administrative/ technocratic* (ii) *Detailed policy*	(i) *Administrative/ technocratic* (ii) *Detailed policy*	(i) *Administrative/ technocratic* (ii) *Detailed policy*	(i) *Administrative/ technocratic* (ii) *Detailed policy.*

Sources: Grün Wirkt!. Unser Wahlprogramm 2002–2006, Bündnis 90/Die Grünen, 2002; *Erneuerung und Zummenhalt -Wir in Deutschland. Regierungsprogramm 2002–2006*, SPD, 2002; *Bürgerprogramme 2002*, FDP, 2002; *Leistung und Sicherheit. Zeit für Taten. Regierungsprogramm 2002/6*, CDU/CSU, 2002.

in real life assess parties' stance on such issues. The cells in italics denote the potential policy domains within which the SPD and other parties are able to selectively emphasise the 'common ground', rather than specific positions, between them (the liberal FDP is excluded from Table 8.2 because the party emphatically ruled out a coalition with any party other than the CDU/CSU before the 1998 elections).

An analysis of domain one (foreign affairs) indicates that the Greens were still excluded from the cross-party consensus on this issue in 1998. This was because, with the exception of the 1989–1990 Berlin coalition (which had to work with the special status of Allied Forces in the city at that time), sub-national Red–Green coalitions had little direct input into this policy domain. The one exception to this rule was relations with the European Union, over which the *Länder* enjoy significant powers and in which the Greens have long been part of the pro-European consensus (see Lees, 2002, 2005a). However, at the time of the 1998 Bundestag elections the Greens still retained a long-standing hostility to NATO and rejected any moves towards enabling Bundeswehr troops taking part in out-of-area operations. This was demonstrated by the first version of the Greens' draft 1998 election programme, which advocated the disbandment of NATO. Only after protests from the SPD and from within the party itself (for instance, Joschka Fischer decried his own party for making 'unrealistic demands') was the document redrafted and the NATO passage downgraded to that of a long-term goal. Nevertheless, the Greens' position on this issue was still a long way from that of the SPD or CDU, as demonstrated by the vote at the party's national conference, in March 1998, against German participation in 'S-FOR' in Bosnia (Lees, 2000: 122). However, within a year of becoming part of the Federal coalition, circumstances forced the Greens to consent to deploying German forces in the Kosovan conflict. At the time, the decision caused an uproar within the Greens' rank-and-file, but Fischer ultimately won the argument. This paved the way for the more orthodox position on defence adopted by the Greens during the 2002 elections (see Table 8.2). In addition, Schröder's unequivocal rejection of German involvement in military action in Iraq served to re-enforce the common ground between the two parties.

Foreign affairs might have been the big sticking point between the two parties, but the legacy of the Greens' 'anti-party party' past was also evident in 1998 within the domains of 'Government' and 'Discursive form'. With regard to government, the Greens' tradition of grass roots democracy (*Basisdemokratie*) and its rejection of what it regarded as authoritarian and hierarchical structures meant that it displayed a residual ambivalence to Germany's culture of the 'party state'. This was also reflected in terms of the discursive form, which eschewed the more technocratic discourse of the two big catch-all parties. However, by 2002, even these artefacts of the Greens' past had all but disappeared. Almost inevitably, the need to defend existing government policy and spell out its future direction has meant that the party has lost any remaining distance from the 'party state' ethos that permeated the other mainstream parties. Thus, it had acquired much of the technocratic discourse of the other parties as well (see SPD, 1998, 2002; Bündnis 90/Die Grünen, 1998, 2002; CDU, 1998, 2002; FDP, 2002).

These three domains aside, in both 1998 and 2002 the Greens were clearly able to find common ground with the SPD across the other policy areas. But the SPD also had other choices. For instance, in 1998, the Greens were not as close to the SPD across the eight domains as the CDU. Thus, in theory, if positioning was the only driver of coalition bargaining, the SPD might have found the CDU an equally, if not more, attractive coalition partner. Furthermore, although it is true that in both elections the CDU appears to be at odds with the SPD across domains six and seven (fabric of society; social groups), it would be foolish to underestimate the strong authoritarian tendency that has been an aspect of the SPD's ideological profile since the time of Lassalle in the late nineteenth century. However, the key thing to remember is that the direction and salience of the SPD's and Greens' positions trumped any purely positional alternative. The discursive devices through which direction and salience are conveyed are not just to be found in political parties' official documentation. It can be found in the public utterances and controlled leaks of party elites, for example in Joschka Fischer's re-awakening of the prospect of co-operation with the CDU at the *Land* level, which involved the selective emphasis of those areas where there is common ground between the two parties (Der Spiegel, 19/01/04). But it is also found in the subtleties of party campaigning, and it is to this that the chapter now turns.

Campaigns

Work on political parties' campaigns has been one of the growth areas of the comparative politics literature in recent years (see for instance Bowler and Farrell, 1992; Butler and Ranney, 1992; Swanson and Mancini, 1996; Farrell and Webb, 2002). By-and-large the literature presents political parties in one of two ways. On the one hand there is the idea of political parties as institutions that have been hollowed out in some way – in a process by which the old mass party, with its ideological certainties and army of enthused party members, is replaced by an increasingly non-ideological and professionalised campaign machine. On the other hand, developments can be seen in a more positive light – that political parties are adaptive institutions that have learnt to both adjust to socio-economic change and harness technical developments in order better to satisfy voters' preferences. At the core of both narratives, however, is the acceptance that the professionalisation of parties' campaign function has undoubtedly taken place. Once again, this is consistent with the broad market metaphor used throughout this study.

Farrell sees the process of professionalisation as having taken place in three stages, although the actual chronology of these stages obviously varied from country-to-country, depending on local circumstances. Stage 1 was the era of early mass politics, characterised by personal appearances, mass meetings and relatively little reliance on what was still an underdeveloped mass media. Stage 2 was the era of 'classic' post-war party politics, embedded in the development of the mass media, with an emphasis on opinion polls and television appearances rather than mass meetings. Finally, stage 3 is the present era – which arguably began in the United States in the late 1980s and spread to Western Europe during the 1990s – characterised by more differentiated marketing strategies and the use of new communication technologies such as email, the internet (Farrell, 1996) and – since Farrell originally devised the model of course – SMS text messaging. These stages of professionalisation and development have impacted on political parties along three dimensions: (i) technical; (ii) resources; and (iii) thematics. A summary of the three stages and three dimensions is set out in Table 8.4.

Table 8.4 demonstrates that the different stages of development of campaign professionalisation are characterised by quite different 'styles' of campaign, in terms of themes, organisation and also the temporal frame within which these activities take place. During stage one campaigning tended to be ad hoc in nature, in which parties communicated through the party press, posters, mass rallies and advertising, and the main resource base was the cadre of party officials and the membership, working on a voluntary basis. In terms of themes, parties relied on mass rallies and whistlestop tours to put over a propaganda-based party message to a passive audience (in communication terms) that was identified through their social location. In stage two, parties adapted their campaign strategies to the seismic shift that the advent of television made on the scale and degree of compression of the message. Great emphasis was put on 'indirect' forms of communication, through press conferences and PR methods and, as a result, resources shifted towards a professional salariat with specialist skills. As in stage one, the public is largely a passive recipient of the message but the message itself is of a more catch-all nature, designed to appeal across social locii. Finally, in stage three political parties have further adapted to the growth of the internet and other technologies by moving towards what has been called the 'permanent campaign', working through established campaign departments and characterised by 'direct' forms of communication. Campaigns are heavily reliant on outside consultants and agencies, which often answer directly to a relatively dominant leader's office rather than to the mainstream party organisation. Unlike in stages one and two, the message is increasingly an interactive one, given that it is voters' preferences rather than parties' ideological baggage that is central. Moreover, it is at last clear to everyone that voters are not just part of an undifferentiated electorate, but rather are customers in a highly segmented political marketplace to which the message must be tailored in a far subtler manner than had hitherto been the case (see Farrell and Webb, 2002).

Farrell and Webb's account is intuitively plausible and chimes perfectly with the market metaphor used in this study. But does it apply to Germany

Table 8.4 Three stages and three dimensions of development of election campaigning

Dimension	Stage 1	Stage 2	Stage 3
Technical			
Campaign preparations	Short term, ad hoc	Long term: specialist committee established 1–2 years in advance of election	'Permanent campaign': establishment of specialist campaign departments
Use of media	'Direct' (party press, newspaper ads, billboards) and 'indirect' (newspaper converage)	Emphasis on 'indirect' (public relations, media training, press conferences) rather than direct (ad campaigns)	Emphasis on 'direct' (targeted ads, direct mail, videomail, cable TV, internet, SMS) rather than 'indirect' (as in stage 2)
Resource			
Campaign Organisation	Decentralised; local party organisation; little standardisation; staffing is party/candidate-based and voluntary	Nationalisation, centralisation; staffing is party-based, salaried and professional	Decentralised but with central scrutiny; staffing is party/candidate-based, professional, contract-based; growth of leaders' office
Agencies and Consultants	Minimal use; 'generalist' role; politicians in charge	Growing role of 'specialist' consultants; politicians still in charge	Consultants as campaign personalities; International links; 'who is in charge?'
Sources of feedback	Impressionistic; canvassers; group leaders	Large-N polling; more scientific	Greater range of polling techniques; interactive (cable, internet, SMS)
Thematic			
Campaign events	Public meetings; whistle-stop tours	TV debates; press-conferences; pseudo events	As before, but events targeted more locally
Targeting of voters	Specific social loci	Catch-all; across social loci	Segmentation; targeting specific Social loci
Campaign communication	Propaganda	Selling	Marketing

Source: Adapted from Farrell and Webb, 2002: 104.

(and elsewhere) and at what stage in the process of development is campaigning activity in the Federal Republic today? Table 8.5 provides data on the campaign 'environment' in Germany and 17 other advanced democracies. The data demonstrates that in comparative terms there are relatively few restrictions on party campaigning in Germany and nothing that would in prima facie terms be seen as a clear constraint upon the development of campaign financing along the lines described above. Like the majority of countries in the analysis, including Australia, Canada, Japan and of course the United States, political parties in Germany are allowed to buy TV spots. Again, like a majority of countries, parties' campaigns are highly reliant on leaders' 'debates'. Parties' rights to TV access are slightly restricted, in that access is apportioned on a proportional basis, but other than that there are no real restrictions and, in addition, parties have access to public campaign finance. So, taken in the round, the Federal Republic provides a benign political opportunity structure for the professionalisation of political campaigning.

Perhaps inevitably, however, the reality of campaigning in Germany – as in other countries – is one in which parties have reacted to technical change whilst still retaining many of the SOPs established in a less sophisticated age. Up until the 1990s campaign techniques were essentially sales-oriented, relying on the kind of structures and themes associated with stage two of Farrell's model. Marketing techniques were fairly unsophisticated, relying on TV spots, leadership debates, and at the local level providing citizens with free beer from the ubiquitous campaign stalls that sprung up in German town-and city-centres just before election day. However the success of the sophisticated political marketing techniques associated with the Clinton Presidential campaign of 1992 had a huge influence on left-of-centre parties in Western Europe and similar techniques were used in a number of campaigns, including that of New Labour in the period 1994–97, and that of the SPD in the period 1995–98. That both instances noted above took place over three-year periods is no accident: in the era of the 'permanent campaign' political campaigning is no longer an episodic phenomenon primarily associated with election year alone.

In retrospect the transition from stage two to stage three of the campaign professionalisation process can be traced back to November 1995, when Rudolf Scharping, the SPD leader at the time, was ousted by Oskar Lafontaine at the party's annual conference. Scharping's leadership had never been noted for its charisma and drive but his failure to unseat Kohl in the 1994 elections, combined with a run of disappointing *Land* elections in Hesse, North Rhine-Westphalia, Bremen and Berlin, made his position untenable. The Berlin Land election of October 1995 in particular was to prove the catalyst for Lafontaine's move against Scharping. In what had traditionally been an SPD heartland, the SPD lost 6.6 per cent of the vote across the city, with their vote share dropping by 4 per cent in the western half and 12.1 per cent in the east. As a result, the SPD was no longer the strongest

Table 8.5 The campaign 'Environment' in 18 advanced industrial democracies

Country	TV spots	Leaders' 'debates'	Restrictions on TV access	Other campaign restrictions	Campaign finance
Australia	Yes	Yes	Proportionate		Yes
Austria	Yes	Yes	Proportionate		Yes
Belgium	No	Yes	n/a		No
Canada	Yes	Yes	n/a	Limits on expenditure; 24-hour ban on polls	Yes
Denmark	No	Yes	Equal		No
Finland	No	Yes	Equal		No
France	No	Yes	Equal	Limits on expenditure; 7-day ban on polls	Yes (for President)
Germany	Yes	Yes	Proportionate		Yes
Ireland	No	Yes	Proportionate	Limits on expenditure (since 1988)	Yes (since 1988)
Italy	Yes	No	No	7-day ban on polls	Yes
Japan	Yes	Yes	Proportionate	Limits on expenditure; candidate restrictions	Yes (since 1995)
Netherlands	Yes	Yes	No		No
New Zealand	Yes	Yes	Proportionate	Limits on candidates' expenditure	No
Norway	No	Yes	No		Yes
Sweden	Yes	Yes	Equal		No
Switzerland	No	No	n/a		No
United Kingdom	No	No	Proportionate	Limits on local expenditure	No
United States	Yes	Yes	No	Limits on local expenditure	Yes (for President)

Source: Adapted from Farrell and Webb, 2002: 107.

party in any district of Berlin and, in the eastern half of the city, it lagged behind both the PDS and the CDU (cf. Lees, 1996: 63–72).

Although on a smaller scale, the Berlin result was analogous with the Labour Party's disastrous 1983 General Election defeat and prompted a similar degree of soul-searching. In 1996 Lafontaine gave permission for the commissioning of a study into how the SPD was perceived by ordinary voters. It did not make for comfortable reading, and the core of the problem was reduced to three points. First, the SPD was seen as fundamentally an opposition party rather than a potential party of government. Second, the party did not project a clear image to the electorate and in those areas in which it did the image was not attractive to voters. Finally, voters did associate the SPD with the idea of 'social justice', but by-and-large the electorate had more confidence in the CDU/CSU when it came to policy areas that were of relevance to the future prosperity of the Federal Republic. In other words, the SPD was seen as old fashioned and increasingly irrelevant to the needs of modern Germany (Machnig, 1999).

Although easier said than done, the SPD's report did point the way forward for the party. It will be recalled that Farrell's three-stage model stresses developments along three dimensions: (i) technical; (ii) resources; and (iii) thematics. Let us examine each of these three dimensions in turn.

In technical terms, both the use of the media and preparations for the campaign were different compared with previous SPD campaigns. With regard to the use of the media there was a shift towards a more 'direct' form of marketing, with a strong emphasis on a powerful poster campaign aimed at key groups, backed up by the use of so-called below-the-line marketing, such as direct mail and, to a lesser extent, the Internet. These methods were designed to appeal to the young voters to whom the SPD had in recent years ceased to appeal. Moreover, as was to be demonstrated by the so-called two heads campaign (discussed below), the marketing campaign was designed to swing into action much earlier in the pre-election period than would have been the case under the old stage two model. In terms of the preparations for the campaign, the move towards the permanent campaign model was made explicit by the establishment of a new and permanent campaign apparatus in what became known as the 'Kampa', which was not only organisationally autonomous from the mainstream party organisation but also physically housed in a separate building in the centre of Bonn.[7] An 'organigram' of the Kampa organisation is provided in Figure 8.1.

Although not identical, the Kampa's organisational structure drew heavily on that established by the United Kingdom's Labour Party's operation, which was at the time located at Millbank in central London. Campaign organisation stressed the idea of co-ordination and lines of command between project teams, the most important of which were, first, agency polling, second, opposition monitoring and rebuttal (*Gegner Beobachtung*), and finally, a special working group for the eastern states (*Arbeitsgruppe Ost*). The agency

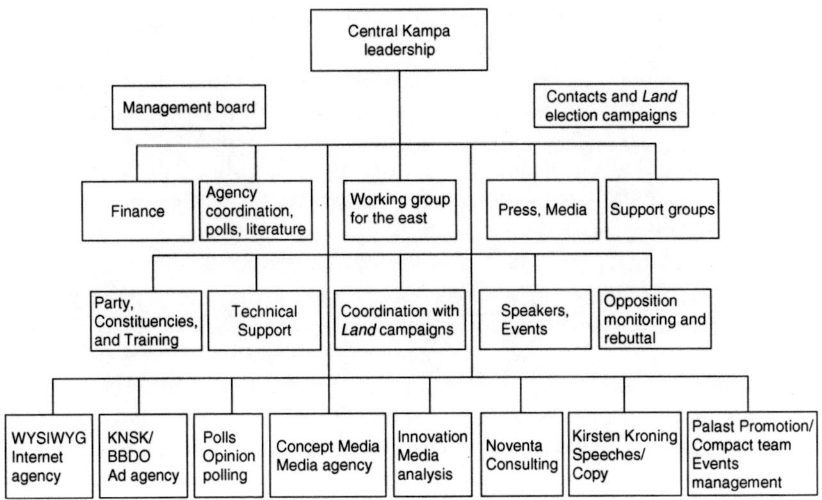

Figure 8.1   Organisational structure of the SPD's 'Kampa' election headquarters, 1998
Source: Briefing at Kampa by Matthias Machnig, September 1998.

polling team concentrated upon monitoring the work of the SPD's partner agencies with focus groups and reported back to party headquarters. It was their job to make sure that the campaign used only 'positives' and that the SPD did not use anything in the campaign that offended voters. In the parlance of the Clinton campaign, they 'watched the numbers'. The rapid rebuttal unit complemented this by making sure that any 'negatives' about the SPD did not become entrenched within the news cycle. Although this normally entailed countering stories put forward by the other parties, it also occasionally meant spinning against members of their own campaign if they went 'off-message'.[8] Finally, the eastern working group was tasked with tailoring the SPD's overall message to voters in the new Federal states. The SPD's previously dismal performance in the new Federal states meant that the party was painfully aware that its understanding of the eastern German voters' thinking was tenuous at best. Party membership in the new states was very low in both absolute terms and in terms of organisational density. As a result they lacked local intelligence and were worried that elements of the campaign that worked well in the west might be counter-productive in the east. So the eastern working group consisted of members who had grown up and been socialised into the eastern German political culture. Their job, in effect, was to weed out anything that easterners might consider irrelevant to the needs and perceptions of voters in the new Federal states.

All three teams worked with the SPD's partner agencies, dealing with marketing and advertising. There were eight of these in all, looking after different elements of the campaign. There were two 'creative' agencies, which were responsible for the broad ideas that underpinned the campaign, and a third agency was responsible for the dissemination of the campaign to the media. As the permanent campaign moved into the 'hot stage' during election year, the SPD employed another agency to poll target voters and assess its impact upon them. The results of these private polls were then given to a team of media analysts, who monitored and refined the campaign in the light of this data. The SPD also employed a number of consultancies to ensure that the party machine operated smoothly at both the national and *Land* levels. One company was responsible for training of party personnel, another had overall control of the organisation and marketing of party events, and all speeches were prepared and disseminated by yet another agency. Finally, the entire operation was co-ordinated through a secure 'intranet' network of over two thousand users by another specialist agency.

Moving on to the dimension of resources, the type of campaign operation noted above indicates that the SPD's Kampa was clearly an example of the move to stage three of the Farrell model. In terms of campaign organisation, the spatially separated Kampa building was very much a decentralised operation, whilst at the same time the central Kampa leadership remained under close scrutiny from the party leadership (in the case of the 1998 campaign Kampa operations chief Matthias Machnig reported directly to senior SPD politician Franz Münterfering). In terms of staffing, there was a significant move towards the use of consultancies and outside expertise and these consultancies had a much higher profile than was the case in the past. In addition the campaign had strong international links, including personnel who had also taken part in the previous Clinton and Blair campaigns. And as noted earlier, the Kampa operation relied heavily on a wide range of polling techniques, including focus groups, to monitor the success of the campaign and fine-tune it if necessary.

Finally, in terms of thematics, the SPD and its outside consultants devised a campaign with two distinct but inter-related goals. On the one hand, the campaign was designed to reconfigure the image of the party itself whilst, on the other, the campaign would have a strong focus on promoting voters' perceptions of competence and leadership in the Chancellor-candidate as and when this choice was made. In terms of the first goal, the SPD had to project a message that would serve to restore its credibility as a party of government and stake a claim to competence in new policy areas, whilst retaining its comparative advantage over the CDU/CSU within the field of social justice. This was similar to the objectives the New Labour leadership had set themselves in the United Kingdom a couple of years earlier. The campaign strategy was based upon four 'positives' associated with the SPD that had become apparent in the party's private research. These were: (i) the idea of 'political change'; (ii) 'leadership'; (iii) 'innovation'; and (iv) 'justice'. Bundled together, these four positives were meant to add up to what the marketing experts called an aura of 'future competence'. In practice, it meant concentrating upon policy areas where the SPD was perceived to be strong, such as labour market regulation, social and health provision, family life and youth. It also meant winning back a reputation for economic competence that was lost in the late 1970s and early 1980s. The SPD managed to do this and pulled ahead of the CDU/CSU on economic competence for most of the period running up to the elections.

The most interesting theme in the SPD's campaign was the use of the phrase 'innovation' and the thinking that underpinned it. The phrase dates back to 1996, when the party first embarked on its re-think, and was a response to the popular perception of the SPD as an old-fashioned party in thrall to vested producer interests. The problem for the party was that its research also indicated that simply stressing the SPD's reformist credentials would not overcome this problem. This was because the word 'reform' also carried considerable negative resonance with voters, being associated with cuts in social provision (and thus undermining the SPD's association with social justice). How voters reacted to the phrase reform depended upon how they were questioned. When asked a generalised question about the need for change in the Federal Republic the voters answered in a socio-tropic manner, claiming that Germany needed to make big changes and that they were willing to vote for a party that would make such changes. But when questioned more closely about their own personal circumstances, the voters' declared willingness to change became more ambivalent and self-interested responses came to the fore. In short, the researchers had uncovered a classic free-rider problem, in which voters recognised that the future prosperity of the country depended on reform but were at the same time unwilling on a personal level to make the necessary sacrifices. Therefore, the trick for campaign experts was to pick up the positives associated with the idea of reform and change without the negatives. Polling indicated that 'innovation' was the phrase that fitted, and it was to play a central role in the party-oriented strand of the campaign for the two years prior to polling day.

By contrast, the candidate-oriented strand of the campaign was initially hampered by the failure of the SPD to nominate a Chancellor-candidate until March 1998, when Lafontaine finally conceded the role to Schröder following the latter's triumph in the Lower Saxony *Land* elections. Up until this point, the party promoted the two politicians as a leadership duo in the so-called two-heads campaign. On the one hand the 'two-heads' campaign re-awakened unhappy memories of the 1994 Bundestag elections, when the lacklustre performance of Chancellor-candidate Scharping led to the promotion of the so-called Troika, in which Scharping's public profile was increasingly augmented (or blurred, depending on one's outlook) by images of Lafontaine and Schröder. On the other, however, the 'two-heads' campaign appeared to turn necessity into a virtue and the image of Lafontaine served to re-assure the SPD's members and electoral core as the SPD underwent a process in which the old Social Democratic certainties were re-configured as the political campaign developed.

In contrast to Lafontaine, Schröder made a point of being directly associated with this process of re-configuration and, in particular, the development of the SPD's doctrine of the New Centre. As already noted, the New Centre was a variation on the strategy of 'big tent' politics and served a dual purpose in that it provided the means to build an electoral coalition that would occupy the centre ground whilst allowing the SPD to leave open the possibility of coalition with the Greens. However, just like Blair's Third Way, the New Centre was easier to define by what it wasn't rather than what it was and it was therefore ironic that the publication, in June 1999, of the British–German joint policy document on the Third Way/New Centre – designed to flesh out the idea of a new progressive politics – was greeted with some derision and, in Germany at least, a significant degree of hostility (Lees, 2000). The idea of the New Centre was a useful discursive tool, both in the SPD's electoral struggle with the CDU/CSU and also in Schröder's more personal political struggle with the more traditional Lafontaine. But it became clear that any attempt to clarify and develop the concept was inimical to the SPD's enduring – and still electorally popular – image as the party of social justice. It also undermined the political-economic vision that went with that reputation (see Wendle, 1999).

In retrospect, the 1998 SPD campaign was a watershed in political campaigning in the Federal Republic and the Kampa model in particular was adopted by the CDU/CSU in the 2002 campaign where it was called 'Arena'.[9] As it turned out, the Arena organisation produced a forceful CDU/CSU campaign that, although ultimately unsuccessful, demonstrated that political campaigning had moved on permanently from the old stage two model, in line with developments in other advanced democracies. Nevertheless, older electoral devices associated with the stage two model remained in place. For instance, political parties were still reliant on the old indirect form of marketing through press and television coverage and, in this respect, research indicates that the SPD and Greens as political incumbents won that particular battle (Eilders *et al.*, 2004). In addition, the traditional format of television debates between the Chancellor-candidates also played a high profile role, at least in re-enforcing the overall message and mobilising those voters already well-disposed towards a particular candidate (Faas and Maier, 2004). It remains to be seen how much resonance these SOPs will have in the next Bundestag elections, scheduled for 2006, and the academic research associated with it.

8.3   Political co-operation

Let us now move on to an examination of the main form of co-operation between players within the political marketplace, that which takes place as a result of political coalitions. A coalition is any combination of separate players – such as political parties – that cooperate in order to win a voting game, or to secure some other strategic goal. Thus, they include formal government coalitions but can also include more informal modes of political co-operation. Coalitions are found in some shape or form within just about all social and political settings. However, in the context of the book, the most notable form of political coalition is that of formal coalition government, which is common in political systems where no one political party is strong enough to win a given legislative game. This state of affairs is most common in those states with some form of proportional system of representation, such as the Federal Republic of Germany and Israel. As a rule, the more proportional the system, the less likely that any party is decisive and the more complex the coalition arrangements needed to win the coalition game. A large and heterogeneous literature exists relating to coalition behaviour, with game theoretical models dominating the field. Theorists emphasise different types of 'structural attribute' and, as a result, a clear divide between 'office-seeking' and 'policy-seeking' models has emerged. In recent years attempts have been made to develop so-called unified theories that bridge this gap and are more applicable to empirical research.

Establishing a comparative framework

One way of looking at the coalition process is to see it in terms of multiple stages, such as those of positioning and/or directional cues, bargaining, portfolio allocation, coalition maintenance, coalition termination, and so on. However as Müller and Strøm observe, despite the often highly developed game-theoretical nature of many coalition models, there has been a tendency in the literature to concentrate on the initial formation stages (positioning, bargaining, allocation of portfolios) rather than those relating to maintenance and termination. As they point out, 'the cabinet coalitions literature resembles the romantic Hollywood films of the 1950s. Much is made of the courtship process and 'who gets whom', whereas relatively little light is shed on how such alliances actually work or their prospects for long-term success' (Müller and Strøm, 2003: 13). But why has this been the case?

Early models of coalition behaviour tended to stress office-seeking as the primary goal of party strategy. Thus they were almost totally uninterested in anything other than the formation stage of the coalition process. The paradigmatic example of this approach is the work of William Riker, who focussed on the strategies adopted by parties (assumed to be rational actors) as they attempt to gain admission to any coalition that may form. This process takes place within a game-theoretical environment that is both 'constant sum', in that it is limited in size and scope, and 'zero-sum', in that one player's gain diminishes the potential utility of all other players. Riker predicts that players will try to create coalitions that are only as large as they believe will ensure winning, in order to maximise the payoffs to each coalition member.

In its pure theoretical form, this will result in a 'minimum winning' coalition of 50 percent plus one vote. In reality, however, exogenous constraints such as formal party structures mean that slightly larger 'minimal winning' coalitions are more likely (Riker, 1962). Riker's 'size principle' became the leitmotif of office-seeking models, although similar modelling had already been carried out by scholars such as Gamson, who argues that parties are intent on entering the 'cheapest winning' coalition. Gamson assumes that parties would rather be a relatively large party in a small coalition than a junior partner in a bigger coalition, even when the benefits of doing so are broadly comparable (Gamson, 1961). Despite their theoretical importance, Riker and Gamson's models have been challenged on espistemological grounds, but it is also worth noting that their heavy emphasis on office-seeking means that they have only a modest record in predicting real outcomes to processes of coalition bargaining.

Later models moved away from the purely office-seeking literature and examined policy as an important structural attribute. An early example of this was the work of Robert Axelrod, who introduces a policy dimension, albeit as a secondary formation criterion. Axelrod's model assumes that office-seeking remains the central strategic goal of all players, but members of the successful coalition will ideally be adjacent to one another along a single Downsian left–right ideological continuum. According to Axelrod this 'ideological adjacency' will serve to minimise conflicts of interest between political parties (Axelrod, 1970). Thus Axelrod does introduce the idea of coalition maintenance, albeit as part of the constellation of future expectations that impacts on the bargaining process, but it is very much a secondary consideration to the primary focus on coalition formation. Axelrod's 'minimal connected winning' model performs better than pure minimal winning models in predicting actual outcomes of cabinet formation, but the underlying assumption that minimal connected winning coalitions have lower levels of conflicts of interest has been empirically challenged. Moreover, although Axelrod's model assumes ideological adjacency, it has no conception of the ideological distance between parties and cannot pick up the nuances of ideological conflict. By contrast, the related work of de Swaan does encapsulate the idea of ideological distance, by constructing what de Swaan calls the 'closed minimum range' of cabinet formation. De Swaan's theory predicts that the winning set will comprise the minimal connected winning coalition with the smallest ideological range. The policy dimension remains a single Downsian left-right axis, running from progressivism to conservatism, and all parties are assumed to have preference orderings of all potential coalitions, based upon their relative proximity to the median or 'Mparty'. De Swaan's theory is often referred to as the 'median legislator' or 'median party' model because it is based on the assumption that the party that controls the median legislator in any legislature is decisive because it blocks the axis along which any connected winning coalition must form (De Swaan, 1973). The median legislator model is intuitively more satisfying than pure office-seeking accounts and has more predictive power. However the size principle is retained and the model does not effectively account for how the trade-off between coalition size and ideological range is resolved. In addition, expectations of coalition maintenance remain little more than a bargaining chip during the formation process.

Another strand of the coalition formation literature dispenses with the size principle altogether and concentrates on policy as the prime structural attribute. In theory, therefore, these models do implicitly look beyond the formation process and focus on the potential programmatic profile of coalitions but, again, this is not developed. Formal policy-seeking models of coalition behaviour tend to be spatial in their conceptualisation and posit the idea of a multi-dimensional policy space. Given the potential for disequilibrium in such a space, such models have focussed upon conceptualising the processes that impose order upon voting games. This often involves some variation upon the game-theoretical concept of the 'core' or 'barycenter'. Core theory is generally highly mathematical in nature and has been more popular with political theorists than empiricists. Nevertheless, Krehbield (1988) does provide a good introduction to its application to practical politics. On a similar note, Browne suggests that core theory could be used to augment De Swaan's median legislator model. Browne considers the process of calculating the mean of points in multi-dimensional space to be analogous to De Swaan's measurement of the distance of potential coalition partners from the median of that potential coalition. The predicted coalition will be that which is winning and minimises the policy distance of members from the core. The core is bound to exist in one-dimensional space, and finds an analogue in de Swaan's median legislator (Browne, 1973).

The problem with purely policy-driven models is that it is now accepted that ideological space cannot be captured by a single left-right dimension and that other dimensions, such as materialism–postmaterialism or authoritarianism–libertarianism, play a significant role. Yet if we accept this it raises significant theoretical and empirical questions about how to impose an equilibrium on policy space, because it follows that in multi-dimensional space the potential for disequelibrium increases because alternative coalition packages can block any potential winning coalition. The problem is that empirically this is obviously not the case. It is true that the phenomenon of constantly shifting coalitions and allegiances is not unknown in practical politics, but most European democracies are characterised by coalitions that manage to maintain themselves over time. So how does one explain the persistence of such stable institutions? Shepsle addresses this problem by factoring in the institutional context while retaining a formal deductive approach. Using the US Congress as an empirical example, Shepsle concentrates upon the role of committees and their ability to deliver what he calls a 'structure imposed equilibrium', maintained by control of the legislative agenda and a tendency towards specialisation. This effectively re-imposes a one-dimensional policy environment upon the legislative game. Key decisions are taken on one dimension at a time and dimensions cannot be linked to one another through trade-offs. The overall package of policies agreed by the legislature will be the aggregate of the policy position of the median legislator on each separate dimension (Shepsle, 1979). This idea of a 'dimension by dimension median' (DDM) has been developed more recently by Laver and Shepsle (1990, 1995). Although more useful empirically than earlier coalition models[10] (see Lees, 1999; Saalfeld, 1999), it remains theoretically elegant. Nevertheless, it does not cast light on the stages of coalition maintenance and termination.

Recently, however, scholars have begun to readjust the balance somewhat and give a new weight to maintenance and termination. A notable recent example of this is to be found in the work of Müller and Strøm (2003) and associated authors, which stresses five bundles of key variables that determine the effectiveness of coalition governments. These are: (i) constraints on coalition formation; (ii) the process of coalition formation; (iii) coalition governance; (iv) coalition stability and termination; and (v) the electoral costs and benefits of coalition participation (Müller and Strøm, 2003: 559–92). Let us use each element of Müller and Strøm's fivefold model in turn as a heuristic framework to examine the coalition process in Germany and in a comparative perspective.

Constraints upon coalition formation

The Müller and Strøm model divides constraints on coalition formation into two main factors: (i) institutional and (ii) party system constraints. Given the approach of this book, it will be argued that this division between institution and party system is a false one and that party systems are themselves institutions, albeit of a more informal and contingent nature. That being said, what we will lump together in the category of institutional variables ranges from formal constitutional rules and norms – particularly those relating specifically to cabinet formation – to the more fungible but still significant constraints imposed by party system competition and norms, including the existence of pariah parties, 'no coalition' pledges by major parties, and constraints imposed by the political agenda at any given time.

As discussed in Chapter 6, Germany's institutional configuration facilitates coalition formation, albeit within a number of quite clearly defined parameters. This point is echoed by Saalfeld, who focussed in on a number of formal and informal institutional constraints upon coalition formation in the Federal Republic (Saalfeld, 2003).

In terms of formal constraints, Saalfeld highlights five factors. First, the way in which the lessons of the Weimar Republic led the drafters of the Basic Law to clearly limit the discretionary powers of the Federal President to appoint governments. As a result, the *Deus ex machina* of Presidential intervention in the bargaining process is no longer available and the Head of State only becomes formally involved in the process after agreement has been reached between the political parties. Second, the subsequent relatively strong position of the Federal Chancellor under the Basic Law and in particular the manner in which individual cabinet ministers are responsible to the Chancellor rather than to the Bundestag, as well as the principle of 'guidelines competence'. Third, the failure of the Basic Law to stipulate the manner in which the process of coalition bargaining takes place – thus bestowing considerable discretion and flexibility on the political parties involved. Fourth, the 5 per cent barrier to electoral representation, which reduces the total number and ideological range of parties in the coalition game. Fifth, the Federal Republic's system of 'co-operative federalism' and the power of the Bundesrat in the legislative process, which serves to restrict the strategic options available to the political parties during the give-and-take of coalition bargaining.

In terms of informal constraints upon coalition formation, Saalfeld concentrates on three key factors. First, the norm of concluding informal pre-election pacts between political parties that developed over the period since the 1960s. This practice is especially common amongst incumbent coalition parties for whom, as Saalfeld points out, it is perfectly rational to reduce the uncertainties of electoral competition. Moreover, if we recall the parameters of the bargaining environment following the 1998 Bundestag elections – when any possibility of a potential SPD–FDP coalition was precluded by pre-election commitments (Lees, 1999, 2000) – it is clear that this practice of pre-agreements further privileges incumbent parties because it serves to constrain the strategic options open to potential challengers. Second, the related practice of self-imposed refusals on the part of individual parties to enter into coalition with some or all of the other political parties in the bargaining game, such as was the case in 1949 when representatives of the BP pledged to play the role of 'constructive opposition', or in the 1990 1994 and 1998 Bundestag elections when all other parties in the Bundestag rejected the PDS as a potential coalition partner (see Lees, 1995b). Finally, Saalfeld notes that the increasingly common practice of 'split-ticket' voting has served to stabilise coalitions because such voters have the effect of shoring-up support for both the 'senior' party (which normally receives the first constituency vote) and the 'junior' party or parties (which get the second party list vote) (Saalfeld, 2003: 35–40).

All of these factors have been discussed at length in Chapter 7 and do not need further reiteration. So let us go on to examine the empirical consequences of this configuration of formal and informal constraints on the pattern of coalition formation in the Federal Republic. Coalition government is the norm at the national level of party politics in the Federal Republic. Table 8.6 sets out the duration and composition of all of the German Federal cabinets since 1949. What is striking from the data is that out of 27 cabinets that have formed over the period, only four were not coalitions.[11] Of these

Table 8.6   German Federal cabinets since 1949

Cabinet number	Chancellor	Date in	Duration (in days)	Composition
1	Adenauer I	15/09/49	1,452	CDU/CSU–FDP–DP
2	Adenauer II	09/10/53	1,457	CDU/CSU–FDP–DP–GB/BHE
3	Adenauer III	23/07/55	805	CDU/CSU–FDP–DP
4	Adenauer IV	25/02/56	588	CDU/CSU–DP–DA/FVP
5	Adenauer V	22/10/57	984	CDU/CSU–DP
6	Adenauer VI	02/07/60	442	CDU/CSU
7	Adenauer VII	07/11/61	377	CDU/CSU–FDP
8	Adenauer VIII	19/11/62	24	CDU/CSU
9	Adenauer IX	13/12/62	307	CDU/CSU–FDP
10	Erhard I	16/10/63	704	CDU/CSU–FDP
11	Erhard II	20/10/65	373	CDU/CSU–FDP
12	Erhard III	28/10/66	34	CDU/CSU
13	Kiesinger	01/12/66	1,032	CDU/CSU–SPD
14	Brandt I	21/10/69	1,125	SPD–FDP
15	Brandt II	14/12/72	518	SPD–FDP
16	Schmidt I	16/05/74	898	SPD–FDP
17	Schmidt II	15/12/76	1,390	SPD–FDP
18	Schmidt III	05/11/80	681	SPD–FDP
19	Schmidt IV	17/09/82	14	SPD
20	Kohl I	01/10/82	156	CDU/CSU–FDP
21	Kohl II	29/03/83	1,398	CDU/CSU–FDP
22	Kohl III	11/03/87	1,329	CDU/CSU–FDP
23	Kohl IV	30/10/90	33	CDU/CSU–FDP–DSU
24	Kohl V	17/01/91	1,368	CDU/CSU–FDP
25	Kohl VI	15/11/94	1,412	CDU/CSU–FDP
26	Schröder I	27/10/98	XXX	SPD–Greens
27	Schröder II	XXX	n/a	SPD–Greens

Source: Saalfeld, 2003: 52; http://www.wahlrecht.de

four, only one – Adenauer IV, which lasted over year – has been a stable arrangement, whereas the others have been interim or 'nightwatchman' arrangements. Thus, for example, Schmidt IV only lasted the two weeks between the FDP leaving the SPD–FDP coalition on the 17 September 1982 and the removal of Schmidt by means of a constructive vote of no confidence in the Bundestag on the 1 October 1982.

Interestingly, however, this tendency to coalition government was not always the case for party systems at the *Land* level. Table 8.7 uses data from 82 *Land* elections over the period from 1979 to 2001. If one aggregates all of the coalitions over the twenty-three years, single party governments are the most common outcome – with CDU governments (25.6 per cent of the total) the most common, followed by SPD governments (23.2 per cent). Given that coalitions are assumed to be the norm within the German party system, this

Table 8.7   Rankings of government cabinets in the German *Länder*, 1979–2001

	1979–83	1984–88	1989–93	1994–98	1999–2003	Total	Ranking
Total Cases	17	14	18	20	13	82	–
CDU	08 (47.0%)	05 (35.7%)	02 (11.1%)	03 (15.0%)	03 (23.0%)	21 (25.6%)	1
CDU/SPD	00 (0.0%)	00 (0.0)	01 (5.5%)	04 (20.0%)	01 (7.6%)	06 (7.3%)	5
CDU/FDP	02 (11.7%)	04 (28.5%)	04 (22.2%)	01 (5.5%)	02 (15.3%)	13 (15.8%)	3
CDU/FDP/ Schill	00 (0.0)	00 (0.0)	00 (0.0)	00 (0.0)	01 (7.6%)	03 (3.6%)	7
SPD	06 (35.2%)	04 (28.5%)	04 (22.2%)	05 (25.0%)	00 (0.0%)	19 (23.2%)	2
SPD/FDP	01 (5.8%)	01 (7.1%)	01 (5.5%)	01 (5.0%)	01 (7.6%)	05 (6.1%)	6
SPD/Statt	00 (0.0%)	00 (0.0)	01 (5.5%)	00 (0.0)	00 (0.0)	01 (1.2%)	10
SPD/Green	01 (5.8%)	00 (0.0%)	03 (16.6%)	05 (25.0%)	03 (23%)	12 (14.6%)	4
SPD/FDP/ Green	00 (0.0%)	00 (0.0%)	02 (11.1%)	00 (0.0%)	01 (7.6%)	03 (3.6%)	7
SPD/PDS	00 (0.0)	00 (0.0)	00 (0.0)	01 (5.0%)	01 (7.6%)	02 (2.4%)	9

Source: Data from http://www.wahlrecht.de

is a very interesting finding. However, the table also demonstrates that the ability of either of the two big catch-all parties to form governments alone has been eroded over the period. This is particularly the case with the SPD's numbers, which drop off precipitously during the 1990s: from 25 per cent in the period 1994 to 1998 to zero per cent after 1999. This coincides with the Chancellorship of Gerhard Schröder and is probably due to voter protest at the incumbent Federal government. By contrast, the CDU's numbers recover from 15 per cent in the last few years of the Kohl government to 23 per cent after 1999. Nevertheless, if one strips out what appear to be the short-term effects of incumbency, the ability of both parties to form governments alone appears to be in decline. By the same token, therefore, coalition governments have become more common over the period.

What is also striking from the data is the asymmetry of coalition options open to the mainstream parties within the various *Land*-level party systems. This is not just the result of electoral mathematics but also reflects the impact of the kind of pre-election agreements between parties and unilateral self-denying ordinances that Saalfeld considers of such importance. The least coalitionable party is the PDS, which has taken part in just one type of coalition (SPD–PDS), followed by the Greens, which has taken part in two types (SPD–Greens; SPD–FDP–Greens). Significantly neither of these parties has managed to forge a coalition without the involvement of the SPD. By contrast, the SPD is the most voracious party in terms of its ability to forge coalitions with other parties, and has taken part in six different types of coalition (SPD–CDU; SPD–FDP; SPD–Greens, SPD–Greens–FDP; SPD–PDS; SPD–Statt) over the period. The second most flexible party is the FDP, which has taken part in four different types of coalition (CDU–FDP; CDU–FDP–PRO; SPD–FDP; SPD–FDP–Greens), and then the CDU, which has taken part in three

Table 8.8 *Land* governments in Germany (as of 03/02/03)[a]

Land	Minister-President	Government	Opposition
Baden-Württemberg	Erwin Teufel (CDU, since 1991)	CDU/FDP (since 1996)	SPD/Greens
Bavaria	Edmund Stoiber (CSU, since 1993)	CSU (since 1962)	SPD/Greens
Berlin	Klaus Wowereit (SPD, since 2001)	SPD/PDS (since 2002)	CDU/FDP/ Greens
Brandenburg	Matthias Platzeck (SPD, since 2002)	SPD/CDU (since 1999)	PDS/DVU
Bremen	Henning Scherf (SPD, since 1995)	SPD/CDU (since 1995)	Greens/DVU
Hamburg	Ole van Beust (CDU, since 2001)	CDU/PRO/FDP (since 2001)	SPD/Greens
Hesse	Roland Koch (CDU, since 1999)	CDU (since 2003)	SPD/Greens/ FDP
Mecklenburg-Western Pomerania	Harald Ringstorff (SPD, since 1998)	SPD/PDS (since 1998)	CDU
Lower Saxony	Christian Wulff (CDU, since 2003)	CDU/FDP (since 2003)	SPD/Greens
North Rhine-Westphalia	Peer Steinbrück (SPD, since 2002)	SPD/Greens (since 1995)	CDU/FDP
Rhineland Palatinate	Kurt Beck (SPD, since 1994)	SPD/FDP (since 1991)	CDU/Green
Saarland	Peter Müller (CDU, since 1999)	CDU (since 1999)	SPD
Saxony	Georg Milbradt (CDU, since 2002)	CDU (since 1990)	SPD/PDS
Saxony-Anhalt	Wolfgang Böhmer (CDU, since 2002)	CDU/FDP (since 2002)	SPD/PDS
Schleswig-Holstein	Heide Simonis (SPD, since 1993)	SPD/Greens (since 1996)	CDU/FDP/ SSW
Thuringia	Bernhard Vogel (CDU, since 1992)	CDU (since 1999)	PDS/SPD

Note: [a] The author wishes to thank Dr Simon Green, who compiled this table.

Source: Data from http://www.wahlrecht.de

(CDU–SPD; CDU–FDP; CDU–FDP–PRO). At the same time, however, the CDU's position is a strong one. Table 8.8 sets out the composition of the 16 *Land* governments, as of February 2003, and demonstrates that the CDU/ CSU is the only party grouping that has in recent years still been able to form single-party governments at the *Land* level. Thus the CDU rules alone in Hesse, Saarland, Saxony and Thuringia, whilst the CSU continues its remarkable period of uninterrupted government in Bavaria.

Coalition formation

The second bundle of variables relates to coalition formation and is focussed on (i) the number of formation attempts before a successful coalition emerges and (ii) the length of the coalition formation process (measured in the number of days required to form a cabinet). The number of formation attempts is often a function of the degree of information available to the players and thus the amount of uncertainty that characterises interaction between them.

Table 8.9 sets out data on these variables for 13 Western European party systems that have been characterised by coalition government during the post-war period. Starting with the number of formation attempts needed before a successful coalition is formed, the table demonstrates three different types of countries. The first type is made up of those countries in which elections generally determine cabinet composition and where such inconclusive formation attempts are rare (with a mean score ranging from 0.1 to 0.2). This group of countries includes Germany, Portugal, Sweden, Ireland, Norway, France and Austria. In these countries elections often produce working majorities or, as is the case in Germany, are contested on the basis of pre-existing pacts between parties. The second type (with a mean score of 0.4–0.5) is made up of those countries in which the actual coalition decisions are made after general elections, albeit within clearly defined parameters of established coalition 'formulas'. This group includes Italy, Luxembourg and Denmark. Finally, the third type (with a mean score ranging from 1.3 to 2.0) is made up of those countries in which coalition outcomes really are dependent on post-election bargaining and where uncertainty is

Table 8.9   Cabinet formation in 13 Western European countries, 1945–2000

Country	Number of parties in Parliament		Number of inconclusive bargaining rounds		Number of days required for cabinet formation	
	Range	Mean	Range	Mean	Range	Mean
Austria	03–05	03.5	00–02	00.2	000–129	037.0
Belgium	04–14	08.5	00–07	01.3	000–148	037.8
Denmark	05–11	07.7	00–03	00.5	000–035	008.3
Finland	06–10	07.7	00–06	01.3	000–080	026.9
France	04–06	05.0	00–01	00.1	000–011	002.2
Germany	03–09	04.0	00–02	00.1	000–073	020.2
Ireland	03–07	04.8	00–01	00.1	000–048	015.7
Italy	08–16	10.5	00–03	00.5	001–126	029.5*
Luxembourg	04–07	04.8	00–03	00.4	000–052	024.1
Netherlands	07–14	09.9	00–06	02.0	010–208	070.6
Norway	05–08	06.4	00–01	00.1	000–016	004.2
Portugal	04–06	05.4	00–01	00.1	000–045	022.5
Sweden	05–07	05.3	00–02	00.2	000–025	005.4

Note: *No data on five Italian cabinets as to the number of days required in cabinet formation, and thus they are excluded from the calculation.

Source: Adapted from Müller and Strøm, 2003: 570.

often high. This group includes Belgium, Finland, and – most notably – the Netherlands.

Moving on to the number of days required for cabinet formation, the table demonstrates four types of country. First, there are those countries in which the process of cabinet formation is relatively short and generally takes less than ten days. This type includes France, Norway, Sweden and Denmark. Second, what Müller and Strøm call an 'intermediate' type, made up solely of the Republic of Ireland, in which the formation process ranges from 10 to 20 days. Third, a type of country in which the bargaining process takes up to a month, including Germany, Finland, Portugal and Denmark. Finally there is a group of countries, made up of Italy, Belgium, Austria and the Netherlands, in which the bargaining process generally takes more than a month before successful cabinet formation is achieved (Müller and Strøm, 2003: 570–2).

It is clear from the data that there is a positive relationship between the number of inconclusive bargaining attempts needed and the duration of the bargaining process. However, what is also clear is that there is no correlation between the number of parties within the party system and the duration of bargaining – as the case of Austria demonstrates. Thus it is not necessarily the case that the number of formation attempts inevitably increases with the number of players in the bargaining process. Moreover it must also not be assumed that an inconclusive formation attempt is necessarily a failure *per se*. As I have discussed elsewhere (Lees, 1999, 2000), the often shaky and acrimonious early years of political co-operation between the SPD and Greens at the sub-national level was necessary in order to overcome conditions of incomplete information and to establish SOPs that would pay dividends when the chance eventually came to form a coalition at the national level. Moreover, the fact that it only involved two political parties did not in any way make the building of this 'Red–Green model' an easy one.

The key player in the development of the Red–Green model of political co-operation was the SPD, which turned increasingly to the Greens in response to strategic dilemmas arising from party system change over the last twenty years. As discussed in Chapter 4, party system deconcentration became pronounced in the 1970s and 1980s, first at the margins then, increasingly, at the core of the electorate. Both big catch-all parties lost out in this process, but the SPD suffered disproportionate losses amongst its electoral core of Protestants and/or manual workers, falling by 19 per cent by the end of the 1980s (Padgett, 1993: 38) before recovering slightly in 1994 and 1998 (Forschungsgruppe Wahlen, 1990, 1994, 1998). At the same time, the rise of the Greens opened up a second 'post-materialist' dimension of political competition along which the SPD had to compete (Müller-Rommel and Poguntke, 1992; Müller-Rommel, 1993). Finally, the SPD's powers of adaptation were further stretched in the 1990s with the addition of a 'second' party system in the states of the former East Germany, and the persistence of the post-communist PDS, which competes with the SPD along the left-right dimension (Lees, 1995b; Hough, 2001).

The presence of two left competitors, mobilising along different ideological dimensions, presented the SPD with an acute strategic problem. Germany's AMS system of electoral representation generates broadly proportional outcomes that provide a generally benign political opportunity structure for its two left competitors, particularly at the sub-national level. Thus it became clear very quickly that these two parties were not going to go away in the short term. At the same time, Federal-level elections are fought and won from the political centre, where the SPD must compete with the CDU. As a result, the SPD is torn between two conflicting strategic imperatives: the need for ideological moderation at the campaign stage on the one hand, and on the other, the imperatives of coalition formation after the election. The party list system does not enhance the influence of moderate swing voters in the same way that purely constituency-based systems do but it remains rational for the SPD to adopt a Downsian 'median voter' strategy in the run-up to elections. Having maximised the SPD vote on election day, however, the rules of the game change considerably. Unless it has done exceptionally well and achieved an overall majority within a given legislature, the SPD has to form a coalition with one or more of the other parties if it is to get past the minimal winning post of 50 per cent plus one seat. Given that potential coalition partners are located both to the left and right of the SPD, the party must leave its ideological options open. This is why directional cues are at least as important as the actual ideological positioning of political parties.

As was discussed above, at the sub-national level the SPD is able to form governments alone, but has found this harder to achieve in recent years. As a result, the SPD's coalition preferences at the *Land* level have been very flexible, forming coalitions with all of the other parties, with the exception of the Bavarian CSU. Over time, however, Red–Green coalitions have become increasingly the coalition arrangement of choice for the SPD when the party is the decisive player in the coalition game. This decisiveness occurs when the SPD controls the median legislator along the Downsian left–right axis in a given legislature. Thus, when the SPD is Mparty and, in particular, Mparty(k), that is controlling the median legislator within a potential coalition, it must be included in any ideologically connected winning coalition (see de Swaan, 1973). Moreover, in the same way that there has been an increase in the frequency of cases of SPD/Mparty there has also been an increase in the frequency of Red–Green coalitions. In addition, the frequency of SPD/Green coalitions, as a proportion of all cases of SPD/Mparty, has risen over time. Table 8.10 and Figures 8.2 and 8.3 demonstrate this. The purely descriptive data in the table and figures demonstrate that the Red–Green coalition option has become the dominant sub-set of SPD/Mparty at the *Land* level. But what is the position at the Federal level? The period from the late 1970s until 1998 was one of electoral decline for the SPD at the

Table 8.10 Numerical/temporal distribution of (i) the SPD as Mparty and (ii) Red–Green coalition dominated legislatures, as percentage of total seats, 1979–2001

Year	Total seats	SPD = Mparty / Red–Green	%
1979	1367	665	48.6
		000	00.0
1980	1373	666	48.5
		00	00.0
1981	1371	531	38.7
		000	00.0
1982	1387	531	38.3
		000	00.0
1983	1388	531	38.2
		000	00.0
1984	1390	531	38.2
		000	00.0.
1985	1427	557	39.0
		110	07.7
1986	1411	608	43.1
		110	07.8
1987	1411	498	35.3
		000	00.0
1988	1410	572	40.6
		00	00.0
1989	1404	709	50.5
		138	09.8
1990	2027	1133	55.9
		243	12.0
1991	2028	1344	66.3
		453	22.3
1992	2065	1360	65.9
		453	21.9
1993	2066	1361	65.9
		453	21.9
1994	2029	1471	72.5
		309	15.2
1995	1976	1418	71.8
		430	21.8
1996	1969	1301	66.1
		503	25.5
1997	1969	1301	66.1
		624	31.7
1998	1982	1314	66.3
		525	26.5
1999	1946	1117	57.4
		515	26.5
2000	1962	1143	58.3
		541	27.6
2001	1917	1089	56.9
		561	29.3

Source: Data from www.Wahlrecht.de

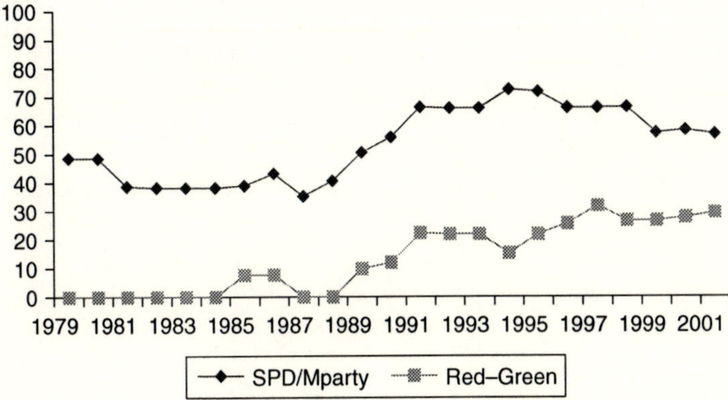

Figure 8.2 Time series of distribution of SPD/Mparty and Red–Green coalition dominated legislatures, as percentage of all seats, 1979–2001

Note: Calculated as a year-on-year proportion of total legislative seats.

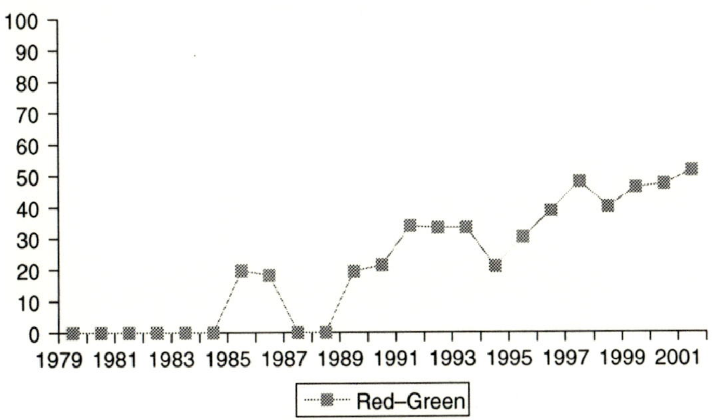

Figure 8.3 Frequency of SPD/Green coalitions, as a percentage of all cases of SPD/Mparty, 1979–2001

Federal level: demonstrated by an uninterrupted sequence of CDU/CSU–FDP coalitions over the period 1982–2002. But as Table 8.11 indicates, in 1998 the SPD managed to (i) muster enough seats in the Bundestag to unseat the incumbent centre-right parties, (ii) usurp the FDP as Mparty, and (iii) become Mparty(k) – making its inclusion in any ideologically connected minimal winning coalition 'inevitable' in theoretical terms.

Table 8.11   Seats secured in Bundestag elections 1983–2002. Coalition outcomes

	Dates of Bundestag Election					
	06/03/83	25/01/87	02/12/90	16/10/94	27/09/98	22/09/02
CDU/CSU	244	223	319	294	245	248
FDP	34	46	79	47	44	47
SPD	193	186	239	252	298	251
Greens	27	42	8	49	47	55
PDS	–	–	17	30	35	02
Total Seats	498	497	662	672	669	603
Minimum Winner	250	249	332	337	335	302
Mparty	FDP	FDP	FDP	FDP	SPD	SPD
Mparty(k)?	No	No	No	No	Yes	Yes
Coalition	CDU/CSU–FDP	CDU/CSU–FDP	CDU/CSU–FDP	CDU/CSU–FDP	SPD–Greens	SPD–Greens
Degree of Change	None	None	None	None	Total	None

Source: Forschungsgruppe Wahlen, 1983, 1987, 1990, 1994, 1998, 2002.

Coalition governance

The third bundle of variables impacts on the question of coalition governance. Here, the first variable relates to the nature of the coalition agreement drawn up between different political parties in a given coalition and the degree to which such agreements are formalised, as well as their size and degree of detail and their policy content. Other variables, some of which may be spelt out in the coalition agreement itself or may be more a product of constitutional rules, norms or precedent, include the degree of 'tightness' or 'looseness' of the commitments made between the parties, as well as the nature of mechanisms employed to maintain coalition discipline, the nature of appointment powers within the coalition and the kind of conflict management mechanisms that are available to it.

Table 8.12 sets out the mechanisms of coalition governance most often used by cabinets in the 13 Western European countries characterised by coalition governments, drawing on the judgement of country experts. Taken in the round, a number of cross-national trends are apparent. First it is apparent that the use of coalition agreements is relatively common and that it was intended to make most of these public during the lifetime of the coalition. Second that, despite the use of formal agreements, in only three countries (Austria, France and the Netherlands) are coalitions governed by an 'election rule' – in other words that an election would be called in the advent of a collapse in the coalition. In all other cases, it was envisaged that an alternative coalition would form for the remainder of the lifetime of the parliament. Third that, across the cases coalitions rely on a broad palette of conflict management mechanisms, such as cabinet committees (CaC), coalition committees (CoC), meetings of parliamentary leaders (Parl), a combination

Table 8.12   Coalition governance mechanisms in 13 Western European countries, 1945–2000

Country	Number of coalition cabinets	Coalition agreement	Agreement public	Election rule	Conflict management mechanism	Coalition discipline in legislation	Coalition discipline in other parliamentary behaviour	Freedom of appointment	Policy agreement	Junior ministers	Non-cabinet positions
Austria	17	14	12	14	CoC, Cac, IC	1, 2	1, 2	17	0, 1, 2,	Y	9Y, 8N
Belgium	28	20	18	0	CaC, PS, IC	1, 2	4	28	0, 1, 2, 3	22Y, 6N	Y
Denmark	17	08	06	0	IC, CaC, Pca, O	1	1	17	3	N/A	Y
Finland	33	33	33	0	IC, CaC, Pca	2, 3	2, 3	28	1, 2, 3	N/A	Y
France	17	08	08	17	CaC, O, PS, CoC	2, 4	2, 4	02	0, 2	N	N
Germany	22	10	07	0	Pca, Parl, PS, IC, CoC, Cac	1, 2	1, 2	00	1, 2, 3	Y	Y
Ireland	10	08	08	0	Parl, PS	1, 2	1	10	0, 1, 2	Y	Y
Italy	34	01	00	0	CoC, PS	2	3	34	1, 2	33Y, 1N	33Y, 1N
Luxembourg	16	16	00	0	O, CoC, PS	2	4	16	3	9Y, 7N	Y
Netherlands	23	11	10	12	Parl, IC, CoC	2	4	23	0, 1, 2, 3	20Y, 3N	N
Norway	08	08	08	0	IC, CaC, Pca	1	2	05	1, 2, 3	5Y, 2N	4Y, 3N
Portugal	06	06	06	0	CoC, Cac, PS	1, 2	3	06	3	1Y, 5N	N
Sweden	07	07	07	0	IC, Cac	2	2	07	2, 3	Y	Y

Source: Adapted from Müller and Strøm, 2003: 574.

of cabinet committees and parliamentarians (PCa), party summits (PS) or other means (O). Fourth, in terms of the extent of coalition discipline we see no real pattern emerging across all 13 cases.[12] Fifth that, in terms of freedom of appointment, we find three categories of country: (i) a majority of countries (Austria, Belgium, Denmark, Ireland, Italy, Luxembourg, the Netherlands, Portugal and Sweden) in which individual coalition parties enjoy autonomy of appointments to 'their' posts; (ii) those countries (Finland, France and Norway) in which this is sometimes the case; and (iii) one case (Germany) in which coalition parties have never enjoyed this degree of autonomy but rather in which all appointments have to be agreed by the coalition as a whole. Sixth, that there is no real pattern across the 13 cases in terms of the amount of policy agreement within coalitions, although nearly all countries (with the exception of France and Ireland) have had coalitions rely at some point on the agreement of a comprehensive policy platform.[13] Finally that there is also no clear pattern across cases in the extent to which the distribution of appointments of either junior ministers or non-cabinet positions is agreed by the coalition parties (Müller and Strøm, 2003: 20–1 and 574).

Moving specifically to Germany, the table demonstrates that in many ways the Federal Republic is a fairly typical example of coalition governance. As in other countries (such as France or the Netherlands), in Germany coalition agreements have been signed in about half of cabinets formed (10 out of 22) and that in all but three instances where this was the case such agreements were intended for public consumption. Like in many other countries, no German coalition has yet been governed by an election rule that stipulates that an election must be called in the circumstances of a coalition not lasting a full term. In common with Austria, for instance, coalition discipline has generally extended to all aspects of parliamentary life, although there have been instances when certain matters have been specifically exempted from this. And again, quite typically, the level of codification of policy agreement has varied over time. Finally, like in many countries, the distribution of junior ministerial and non-cabinet appointments is agreed between coalition parties as part of the division of payoffs. However, there are two areas in which the German case is atypical compared with the other 12 countries. The first is in the number of different conflict management mechanisms that have been used by coalition parties in Germany, whilst the second is the total lack of freedom of appointment enjoyed by individual coalition parties in successive coalitions over the post-war period. Let us further examine both of these issues in turn.

In terms of conflict resolution mechanisms, Saalfeld (2003) makes a convincing case in arguing that the changing dynamics of conflict resolution mechanisms over the post-war period is in part a function of structural attributes of each coalition and also the result of institutional adaptation to a changing strategic environment. With reference back to Table 8.6, the first Adenauer cabinet (Adenauer I) of 1949–53 was a minimal winning coalition made up of the CDU/CSU, FDP and DP. Thus it was important to keep all parties 'in the loop' of cabinet governance although, at that point, a formal coalition committee did not exist. Instead Adenauer relied on extensive informal links with all parties, as well as encouraging the attendance of leading parliamentarians at important cabinet meetings. By contrast, the cabinets Adenauer II–VIII (1953–61) were surplus majority coalitions dominated by the CDU/CSU and characterised by the part collapse of the smaller coalition parties. Under these circumstances it was not so necessary for Adenauer to keep all players in the loop as any individual defections were of less potential danger to the survival of the coalition as a whole. As a result the original informal consultation procedures were ignored and a CDU/CSU-dominated inner circle of ministers and leading parliamentarians emerged. The negative experience of one of the smaller parties in the coalition, the FDP, led to the emergence of two new institutional devices – the coalition agreement and the formal coalition committee – during the 1961–65 Bundestag. At around the same time, the failure to successfully impose coalition discipline on parliamentary business led to a coalition crisis in 1962 and the development of regular 'coalition rounds' between cabinet ministers and the coalition parties' leading parliamentarians. It was decided that the coalition committee would co-ordinate the government's legislative programme but that more important, or contentious, issues would be dealt with by the coalition round. This reliance on the coalition round intensified during the 1965–66 coalition, which did not have a coalition committee. Subsequent coalitions developed their own hybrid devices including the so-called 'Kreßbronn Circle' (*Kreßbronner Kreis*) during the 1966–69 Grand Coalition, the 'inner cabinet' in the latter stages of the Schmidt government, and the mix of coalition rounds and bilateral links used during the Kohl years. Finally, despite the establishment of a formal coalition committee, the post-1998 Schröder administrations have tended to rely on the same kind of informal and flexible instruments used by Kohl (Saalfeld, 2003: 60–3). Indeed more recent research indicates that, like his predecessor, Schröder has deliberately used the Chancellor's Office to coordinate the various fora of conflict management available to him and therefore buttress his own power both within his own party and in relation to the Greens (Patzeldt, 2004).

In terms of the lack of freedom of appointment enjoyed by individual coalition parties in successive coalitions over the post-war period, this is because (i) such appointments are constitutionally within the fiat of the Federal Chancellor and (ii) all such issues are also considered part of the bargaining game. Indeed, as is discussed later, the bargaining game even goes beyond non-cabinet posts and extends to the staffing of the civil service and other issues of expertise (Lees, 1998, 2000). By-and-large specific portfolios are allocated relatively late in the bargaining process and the numerical distribution of portfolios in Germany has been close to that of the proportional-allocation norm (Saalfeld, 2003: 65). However, this numerical criterion is in practice modified by both the issues of non-cabinet and civil service posts noted above and by the fact that political parties have developed strong preferences for particular portfolios, either because of sunk costs and SOPs from previous coalitions or because some policy areas have higher levels of salience for parties' ideological identities (Kropp and Sturm, 1998: 34). The Greens' strong preference for the Environment portfolio is a clear example of this phenomenon (Lees, 1998, 2000).

To demonstrate how the dynamics behind the allocation of junior ministerial and non-cabinet portfolios, as well as the importance of civil service staffing and expertise works in practice let us look in more detail at the division of coalition payoffs within the Red–Green coalition following the 1998 and 2002 Bundestag elections. When the Red–Green coalition was returned to power after the 2002 Bundestag elections the SPD remained Mparty and Mparty(k). However, the SPD's position as Mparty is dependent on the Greens remaining – or at least being perceived to remain by other parties – to the left of the SPD on the left-right dimension. For its part, and as already discussed, the Greens made significant gains in the 2002 elections, but the benefits of electoral success are nullified by the fact that the SPD blocks the axis along which any alternative ideologically connected winning coalition can form. Thus, as was noted earlier in the chapter, the Greens remain very much within the orbit of the SPD.

The composition and division of portfolios in the 1998–2002 and 2002 Red–Green coalitions are codified in two formal coalition agreements (SPD–Bündnis 90/DieGrünen, 1998, 2002). Such agreements were developed during the run of *Land*-level coalitions between the SPD and Greens and have proved themselves invaluable in stabilising and routinising the channels of political co-operation between the two parties. Over the course of successive agreements the SPD has proved itself to be determined to retain certain 'core' portfolios such as the Finance Ministry and the Economics and Industry Ministry. This not only reflected the SPD's strong welfarist instincts but was also regarded – at least in the early years when the Greens were still widely viewed with some suspicion and hostility – as a means of reassuring the business community that there would be no experimentation with what had become a cross-party consensus about the shape of Germany's political economy. For their part, the experience of the 1990–94 coalition in Lower Saxony – in which the Greens failed to secure the Environment portfolio – reinforced the Greens' own perceptions of the need to secure the Environment portfolio.

Nevertheless the numerical distribution of ministerial portfolios following the 2002 Bundestag elections is worth looking at in more detail. It will be recalled from Chapter 4 that Chancellor Schröder did not enjoy an unalloyed victory in these elections. The election resulted in losses for the SPD across all sections of the electorate, with disproportionate losses amongst male and its core working class voters. At the same time, however, the Greens did exceptionally well and as a result could credibly claim responsibility for the return of the Red–Green coalition, albeit with a reduced majority. Given the Greens' relative success, it might have been expected that the party would drive a hard bargain during coalition negotiations and demand another ministerial post. This did not happen. In fact, as Tables 8.13 and 8.14 demonstrate, the Greens' share of office-seeking payoffs (calculated here as the number of legislative seats required to generate each ministerial portfolio) was worse in 2002 (when it needed 18 Green legislative seats to generate each ministerial portfolio allocated to the party) than it was in 1998 (when the ratio was 16:1). So it would appear at first glance that the party that was apparently decisive in ensuring the Red–Green coalition's survival was effectively 'punished' in the coalition negotiations that followed the 2002 Bundestag elections. Moreover, an analysis of Table 8.15 indicates that the established 'Red–Green model' of portfolio allocation that was used in 1998 was also repeated in 2002. In both 1998 and 2002 the SPD was allocated the key ministerial portfolios of Finance and Economics/Economics and Industry, giving it strategic control over the government's political economy. In addition, the party controlled sensitive portfolios such as Interior, Justice and Defence, as well as Employment and Social Policy. With the exception of the Foreign Ministry, the Greens appear to have once more

Table 8.13   The 1998 Bundestag elections (%) and ratio of seats to portfolios for coalition partners

Party	(Second) vote	Total seats (669)	Portfolios	Ratio of seat to portfolios	Surplus majority: 10
SPD	41.0	298	11*	28: 1**	–
Greens	6.7	47	3	16: 1**	–

Note: * Excluding Federal Chancellor; ** rounded up/down to nearest whole number.

Sources: Statistisches Bundesamt; *Aufbruch und Erneuerung – Deutschlands Weg in 21. Jahrhundert.* SPD. Bündnis 90/Die Grünen, 1998.

Table 8.14   The 2002 Bundestag elections (%) and ratio of seats to portfolios for coalition partners

Party	(Second) vote	Total seats 603	Portfolios	Ratio of seat to portfolios	Surplus majority: 4
SPD	38.5	251	10*	25:1**	–
Greens	8.6	55	3	18:1**	–

Note: * Excluding Federal Chancellor; ** rounded up/down to nearest whole number.

Sources: Statistisches Bundesamt; *Erneuerung – Gerechtigkeit – Nachhaltigkeit: Koalitionsvertrag 2002–2006.* SPD. Bündnis 90/Die Grünen, 2002.

Table 8.15 Composition of SPD–Green cabinets (functional equivalents) 1998 and 2002

Ministry (1998)	Minister	SS/SM	Ministry (2002)	Minister	SM/SS
Interior	SPD	SPD	Interior	SPD	SPD
Justice	SPD	SPD	Justice	SPD	SPD
Finance	SPD	SPD	Finance	SPD	SPD
Economics	N/P	SPD	Work and Economics	SPD	Greens
Nutrition, Agriculture and Forestry	SPD	SPD			
Employment and Social Policy	SPD	SPD	Health and Social Policy	SPD	SPD
Defence	SPD	SPD	Defence	SPD	SPD
Families, Pensioners, Women and Youth	SPD	SPD	Families, Pensioners, Women and Youth	SPD	Greens
Development, Construction etc	SPD	SPD	Development, Construction etc	SPD	SPD
Education, Science, Research and Technology	SPD	SPD	Education, Research and Technology	SPD	SPD
Economic Co-operation and Development	SPD	Greens	Economic Co-operation and Development	SPD	Greens
Foreign	Greens	SPD	Foreign	Greens	SPD
Environment, Nature Protection and Reactor Safety	Greens	Greens	Environment, Nature Protection and Reactor Safety	Greens	Greens
Health	Greens	Greens			
			Consumer Protection, Nutrition, and Agriculture	Greens	SPD

Note: Excludes Chancellor's Office. Net SM/SS gain to Greens: +1. Total Greens' SM/SS in SPD ministries: 3.

Sources: Aufbruch und Erneuerung – Deutschlands Weg in 21. Jahrhundert. SPD/Die Grünen, 1998; Erneuerung – Gerechtigkeit – Nachhaltigkeit: Koalitionsvertrag 2002–2006. SPD. Bündnis 90/Die Grünen, 2002.

been restricted to its core Environmental portfolio and second-order ministries such as Health (1998) and Consumer Protection, Nutrition and Agriculture (2002).[14] But a closer analysis of the coalition agreement between the two parties indicates that the Greens negotiated considerable enhancements of the policy scope of 'their' ministries. For instance, oversight competence for the development of renewable energy was transferred from the (SPD-run) Economics Ministry to the Environment Ministry, whilst the Consumer Protection, Nutrition and Agriculture Ministry was given the sole 'right of initiative' (*Initiativrecht*) for consumer protection issues and also a wider responsibility for the regulation of genetic technology (SPD–Bündnis

90/Die Grünen, 2002). Moreover, the Greens briefed the press aggressively during the negotiations to make sure that these gains were seen as clear strategic victories for the junior coalition partners (FT Deutschland, 16/10/2002).

The one first-order portfolio which the Greens have consistently been able to pick up is the Foreign Ministry, which on both occasions was allocated to the Greens' Joschka Fischer. However, four factors need to be taken into account here. First, since 1966 it has been the norm to allocate the Foreign Ministry to the junior partner in Federal level coalitions (Andersen and Woyke, 1997: 61), so precedent made it very difficult to deny the Greens the portfolio. Second, Joschka Fischer's candidature as Foreign Minister was not perceived to be a threat, given his political moderation, closeness to Schröder, and commitment to the established direction of German foreign policy (although a question remains as to whom else the Greens could appoint to the post, should Fischer retire). Third, it is traditional for German foreign policy to be steered in part by the Federal Chancellor under the constitutional doctrine of guidelines competence. Finally, although the ministerial post itself is allocated to the Greens, the crucial political post of State minister (*Staatsminister*)[15] was allocated to the SPD. Moreover after the 2002 elections, this post was allocated to Hans Martin Bury, a former State Minister in the Chancellor's Office and close confidante of Schröder.

'Splitting' the top echelons of a Ministry – with one party nominating the Minister and the other the State Secretary – is a common practice in German coalition negotiations (Saalfeld, 2003: 71). It is also a useful method of making the division of ministerial portfolios a finer-grained process; avoiding all-or-nothing decisions and allowing for side-payments between the parties. However, it also allows the 'other' party to gain purchase on the political activities of the Ministry – thus, limiting the benefit of possessing the ministerial portfolio. In other words, the State Secretary position is a significant side-payment in the coalition game.

Thus Table 8.15 demonstrates that if we include the distribution of State Secretary posts across the Cabinet, the Greens' overall payoffs in 2002 do constitute an improvement on 1998. In the table, the enclosed cells indicate those ministerial portfolios that were split in the manner described above. In 1998 only two out of the 14 posts were split. These were the Foreign Ministry, as already discussed, and Economic Co-operation and Development, which had an SPD Minister and Green State Secretary. This represented a rough parity between the two parties. However, in 2002 the splitting of portfolios was extended to five out of 13 ministries. Of these, three (Work and Economics; Families, Pensioners, Women, and Youth; and Economic Co-operation and Development) have an SPD Minister and Green State Secretary, whilst two (Foreign Affairs; Consumer Protection, Nutrition, and Agriculture) have the reverse arrangement. This represents a clear gain for the Greens, not only in terms of numbers, but also because – crucially – the party has gained a foothold in the SPD-'owned' Economics Ministry. This allows the Greens to develop and profile this aspect of the party's programmatic stance.

The Greens' portfiolio gains in the 2002 coalition bargaining process also have implications for the question of the staffing and structure of the civil service, a theme that has often been a politically sensitive factor in the successful management of Red–Green coalitions. Until very recently there was a distinct asymmetry in expertise between the two parties. On the one hand, the SPD were 'expertise rich', and when the party took over a Ministry, existing staff could be replaced from in-house if so desired. In turn, this created a virtuous circle, in which start-up costs when taking office were relatively low, leading to continuity of policy making, the retention of institutional knowledge, and the easier training of future cadre. On the other hand, the Greens have tended to be 'expertise poor', with less in-house resources to call upon when taking over a Ministry, and little experience within the party networks. Over time, however, the Greens have been able to open up existing policy networks to their client groups. This has meant that the Greens have been able to acquire the necessary administrative expertise, albeit slowly (Lees, 1998, 2000, 2005b).

This asymmetry of expertise is both a symptom, and a cause, of the Greens' inability until now to break out of the SPD's orbit and make itself coalitionable to parties to the right of the SPD. In terms of the former, given that the Red–Green model has generally limited the Greens to a core of second-order ministerial posts, it is not surprising that it has been unable to place personnel across the broad sweep of ministries. Moreover, Germany has a specialist administrative culture, with relatively little movement of personnel across ministries and an emphasis on expert knowledge (see Katzenstein, 1987). As discussed in Chapter 6, when staffed by one party for a long time, ministries can become colonised by a cohort of entrenched and partisan bureaucrats. Again, this makes it an even harder and longer process to break into new ministries and acquire expertise than would be the case in a more generalist bureaucratic culture. In turn, the failure to break out of their ministerial niche has meant that the Greens have failed to fully develop those aspects of the Greens policy portfolio which are, if anything, closer to the CDU and FDP than the equivalent policy positions held by the SPD. A good example of this is in fiscal policy, where the Greens are more committed to reducing non-wage labour costs (through the use of eco-taxes, for instance) and advocate a lower top rate of income tax (see SPD, 2002; Bündnis 90/Die Grünen, 2002). In this context, the placing of Green State Secretaries in the Work and Economics and Economic Co-operation Development ministries serves not just to widen the Greens ministerial portfolio per se, but also serves to both advertise the party's increasingly broad and moderate policy profile to parties other than the SPD and help nurture a political presence at the meso-level of the administrative apparatus. Thus even the apparently dry issue of civil service staffing and expertise is part of the coalition bargaining game.

Cabinet stability and termination

The fourth bundle of variables relates to the issues of cabinet stability and termination. According to the Müller and Strøm model, a cabinet is defined as 'an administration under the same prime minister, representing the same parties and uninterrupted by general elections' (Müller and Strøm, 2003: 584). Thus, the degree of stability is not just measured by the amount of days such cabinets last but also by their duration in relation to the maximum possible length of a given cabinet, in light of nation-specific rules about the amount of time allowed between general elections. Although not mutually exclusive the model distinguishes between (i) technical and (ii) discretionary cabinet terminations, with the former being those that are beyond the control of the coalition parties. By contrast, discretionary arrangements include dissolutions before the end of parliamentary terms, voluntary enlargements of coalitions, terminal inter- and intra-party conflict, and parliamentary defeat at the hands of opposition (Müller and Strøm, 2003: 585).

Table 8.16 sets out data on cabinet duration and mechanisms of termination in 13 Western European countries over the period 1945–2000. What is clear from the data is that although there are clear cross-national patterns in terms of the stability of cabinets, this is not the case in terms of mechanisms by which such cabinets are terminated.

In terms of cabinet duration the data reveals three types of country. The first type is made up of those countries which display high levels of cabinet stability. This includes Luxembourg (with a mean duration of 1,171 days), Ireland (891), Austria (854) and the Netherlands (808). A second intermediate type is made up of Sweden (771), Norway (755), Germany (700), Denmark (626), France (625), Portugal (597) and Belgium (520). Finally, there is a third type of country which is characterised by relatively low levels of cabinet stability, made up of Finland (453) and Italy (355). In terms of cabinet termination mechanisms, the data reveals a significant level of variance across all 13 countries. In total, cabinet termination in the 13 countries was a technical issue in 39 per cent of the cases. However, it is in the 61 per cent of terminations brought about by discretionary mechanisms that clear national differences emerge. In cases such as Ireland, Italy, Belgium and Denmark, discretionary arrangements account for between 75 and 80 per cent of all terminations. At the other end of the scale less than half of cabinet terminations in countries such as Sweden, Norway and Luxembourg take place due to discretionary mechanisms (Müller and Strøm, 2003: 585–7).

Looking at Germany specifically, its inclusion in the intermediate group of countries in terms of cabinet duration is interesting to note given the assumption within the Anglophone German politics literature that German cabinet government is characterised by high levels of stability and is therefore part of – or perhaps an outcome of – the Federal Republic's 'efficient secret' (see for instance, Smith, 1989, 1986). German cabinet government is stable, but perhaps not *as* stable in relative terms as we might assume. At the

Table 8.16 Cabinet duration and mechanisms of termination in 13 Western European countries, 1945–2000

	Duration				Technical termination mechanisms				Discretionary termination mechanisms		Inter-party conflict		
Country	Number of cabinets	Mean duration (days)	Minimum duration	Maximum duration	Regular election	Other constitutional reason	Death of prime minister	Early election	Voluntary enlargement of coalition	Defeat by opposition in parliament	Policy	Personnel	Intra-party conflict
Austria	21	0854.3	0160	1,431	07	02	00	09	00	00	06	01	03
Belgium	32	0520.2	0007	1,502	05	01	00	08	02	01	17	02	03
Denmark	30	0626.4	0040	1,337	01	03	03	18	01	10	02	00	01
Finland	36	0452.6	0036	1,409	09	07	00	01	04	02	14	00	01
France	22	0625.1	0031	1,191	04	05	00	04	00	01	02	00	06
Germany	25	0699.5	0014	1,452	11	00	00	02	03	02	05	02	08
Ireland	21	0891.1	0228	1,532	00	02	00	160	00	03	03	03	07
Italy	47	0355.1	0011	1,628	04	00	00	6	05	12	15	12	17
Luxembourg	15	1,170.5	0153	1,936	09	01	01	02	00	00	03	01	01
Netherlands	22	808.1	0080	1,638	10	01	00	04	00	01	06	00	02
Norway	25	755.3	0024	1,435	13	05	00	00	01	03	02	00	02
Portugal	10	596.8	0096	1,506	03	00	01	03	00	02	02	03	00
Sweden	25	771.0	0167	1,468	16	02	02	01	01	00	03	00	00
Total	331	–	–	–	92	29	07	74	17	37	80	24	51
Mean	25.5%	0702	0080.5	1,497	27.8%	08.8%	02.1%	22.4%	5.1%	11.2%	24.2%	7.3%	15.4%

Note: Table excludes non-partisan cabinets.

Source: Data adapted from Müller and Strøm, 2003: 585–6.

same time, however, nearly half of cabinet terminations (44 per cent) take place through the technical mechanism of a regular Bundestag election. But in a sense this is evidence of Germany's efficient secret in that the German electorate has only voted an incumbent coalition out of office once in the period since 1945 – and that was in 1998 with the fall of the CDU/CSU–FDP coalition. Thus although these coalitions have terminated in a technical sense, the majority of them have been reconstituted immediately after the election. Interestingly, where cabinets have been terminated through discretionary means the vast majority (68 per cent) have been as a result of inter-or intra-party conflict rather than parliamentary defeats and so on. Moreover, more than half of such conflicts have been of an intra-party nature rather than as one might expect inter-party conflict. Thus, the moral to be found in the data is that if an incumbent coalition can effectively manage its internal affairs then, based on past performance, it stands a very good statistical chance of remaining in office.

It is not surprising, therefore, that when the Red–Green coalition assumed power at the national level in 1998 observers agreed that the key to the new government's stability would be its ability to manage inter-and intra-party conflict within the coalition. Underlying this issue were two questions. First, how much common ground could be forged between Europe's oldest Social Democratic party – with its relatively hierarchical and authoritarian traditions – and a party that arose out of the Peace and Environmentalist movements of the 1970s, with a culture predicated on the idea of grass roots democracy and dissent? Second, how long before the cumulative impact of inevitable election reverses in *Länder* elections aggravated inherent tensions between two distinct political philosophies and undermined co-operation between the two parties? On the surface the answers to these questions might be 'not much', and 'not long'. But the picture is far more complex and nuanced than that.

Take the events of the 16 November 2001, for instance, when German deputies to the Bundestag voted on a government motion calling on parliament's support for the deployment of Bundeswehr troops in support of the United States' 'war on terror'. Faced with heavy criticism from elements within his Green coalition partner about German involvement in the Afghan crisis, SPD Chancellor Gerhard Schröder tied a vote of confidence to the motion, in what appeared to be a high-stakes gamble on the very existence of his government. In the event, the motion was passed with a majority of three and Germany's first Red–Green coalition survived – despite unease within the Greens' grass roots membership. Nevertheless, academics and media commentators alike questioned Schröder's political judgement in provoking a vote of confidence, and wondered how long this apparently unstable and ideologically charged coalition could last (De-News@listserv.gmd.de. 17/11/01, 12/11/01).

In fact the Red–Green coalition was not as unstable as it appeared at the time, and although Schröder's deliberate confrontation with the Greens was an act of political brinkmanship, it was also one of cool calculation: that the Greens – notwithstanding the protests of the party's more militant activists – had nowhere else to go. He appeared to be right: on 22 September 2002 the Red–Green coalition was returned to government in the Bundestag elections and Schröder embarked upon another four-year term as Federal Chancellor.

Schröder's success came despite what could best be described as a very mixed record during the Red–Green coalition's first term of office. On coming to office, the new Red–Green coalition faced four interrelated political dilemmas. These were, first, the need to tackle unemployment, second, to enhance Germany's attractiveness as a place of investment (the so-called *Standort* problem), third, to tackle the 'reform blockage' (*Reformstau*) within the Federal Republic's political and policy-making apparatus and, fourth, to counter an increasing mood of disenchantment with the political process (*Politikverdrossenheit*) – especially in the eastern states of the former German Democratic Republic. To this end, the coalition identified three main themes that would provide the core of their programme. First, the reduction of unemployment by a million over the four-year term. Second, withdrawal from the use of nuclear power, as well as a parallel programme of ecological tax reform. Third, the reform of Germany's outdated citizenship laws, in order better to reflect the multicultural reality of contemporary life in the Federal Republic. Of these the first priority of tackling unemployment was flagged by the new Federal Chancellor Gerhard Schröder as the key issue on which his term in office would be judged. But at the end of Schröder's first term as Chancellor, unemployment was still around the four million mark inherited from the outgoing CDU/CSU–FDP coalition, damaging the government's reputation for economic competence.

As for the other two priority areas – environmental reform and reform of Germany's citizenship laws – the record is one of a partial success. In line with most Western European countries, ecological tax reform was introduced (Luckin and Lightfoot, 1999: 243). This represented a move away from Germany's traditional reliance on regulatory approaches to public policy (Lees, 2000). However such taxes are socially regressive (because they fall disproportionately on lower income families) and, as a result, the 'eco-tax' has therefore proved unpopular with both the electorate and SPD traditionalists and made the management of inter- and intra-party conflict more difficult. In addition, there has not yet been evidence that the tax reforms have produced the promised 'double dividend' of an improved environment and lower unemployment, by shifting the burden of taxation from labour to emissions and resource use. As for the phasing out of nuclear power, by the time an agreement was reached with the nuclear industry in June 2000, the original plan to phase out reactors over a ten-year period had been extended to 32 years – thus making it relatively easy for successor governments to reverse the process if they so wished. Finally reform of Germany's citizenship laws did represent a substantial step forward, but again the original plan to ditch the idea of an ethnic or blood-related concept of citizenship ('Ius Sanguinis') was watered down in order to ensure the passage of legislation through the second chamber, the Bundesrat.

Despite this mixed record, the SPD and Greens went into the 2002 Bundestag elections pledged to renew the coalition if given a majority in the legislature. The Red–Green coalition was, of course, returned to power in 2002 and, at the time of writing, Germany's tradition of stable coalition government remains intact.

Electoral costs and benefits of coalition participation

One might think that the electoral costs and benefits of participation in government are self-evident. Being in government brings with it payoffs, whether of a purely office-seeking kind (salary, car, patronage, connections, etc.) or in terms of the opportunity to use the power of office to bring about policy changes and further a party's or individual politicians' ideological goals. At the same time, however, governing parties and – to a lesser extent – the individual politicians in office – must look beyond the here-and-now and anticipate the impact of being in office at $T1$ on the party's electoral prospects at $T2$. Sometimes this impact might appear to be relatively easy to anticipate. For instance it has been suggested that the British Conservative Party was not overly anxious about not winning the 1945 General Election given that it was clear to most members of the political elite at that time that whoever did win the election would inherit an exhausted and bankrupt nation and an extraordinarily difficult international situation. Notwithstanding the preferences of older individual politicians such as Churchill, it is not hard to imagine that many Conservatives were quite happy not to have to take up the poison chalice of government at that time. Sometimes, the impact of being in office is harder to anticipate and only becomes apparent in retrospect. Thus, it could be argued that the CDU/CSU benefited from being out of office in the 1970s because it allowed the CDU in particular to execute a generational change in leadership and modernise the party's organisation and management structures. Similarly, it might be argued that it was not in the long-term interests of the Conservative party to win the 1992 general election. In this last example, being in office during the early and mid-1990s and, specifically, overseeing sterling's spectacular expulsion from the Exchange Rate Mechanism of the European Monetary System was to eventually lead to the Conservatives being out of power for what could be a generation. However, what all of the instances discussed earlier have in common is that they are speculative judgements based on imperfect or counter-factual information. So what effect does being in government have on a political party's electoral prospects?

Table 8.17 sets out the gains and losses of government parties, in terms of the percentage of the popular vote, in 13 Western European countries over the period 1945–2000. Two points are of note. First, taken in the round there

Table 8.17 Electoral gains and losses of government parties (percentage of the popular vote) in 13 Western European countries, 1945–2000

Country	Party			Government		
	Number of gains/ losses	Range of gains/ losses (in %)	Losses of cases (in %)	Number of gains/ losses	Range of gains/ losses (in %)	Losses of cases (in %)
Austria	12/14	04.8/–09.2	54	09/06	05.7/–12.3	38
Belgium	20/35	06.4/–08.4	60	06/20	03.5/–15.4	74
Denmark	19/30	11.0/–11.7	61	12/14	11.0/–11.7	54
Finland	16/44	02.9/–05.0	72	08/27	03.5/–13.9	75
France	09/15	27.0/–16.2	63	07/08	26.7/–22.4	53
Germany	12/18	14.2/–06.4	60	11/12	11.1/–8.3	52
Ireland	07/20	06.0/–12.1	71	02/13	03.9/–15.1	76
Italy	22/22	13.3/–18.6	47	16/20	14.3/–35.6	54
Luxembourg	06/18	13.1/–08.1	75	02/10	05.8/–11.3	83
Netherlands	19/31	06.5/–13.1	62	05/15	04.8/–21.0	75
Norway	14/18	10.3/–11.2	56	07/13	07.0/–11.2	65
Portugal	04/04	20.4/–26.4	50	03/04	20.4/–26.4	57
Sweden	07/19	04.7/–08.9	70	04/16	04.9/–08.9	76
Total	167/288			092/179		
Mean		10.8/–11.9	61.6		09.4/–16.4	64

Source: Adapted from Müller and Strøm, 2003: 589.

is a clear electoral trend against incumbent parties and governments over time. Thus, only 33 per cent of governments have managed to improve their electoral performance in the election after their term in office, whereas 65 per cent suffered losses. Moreover, in 11 out of 13 countries the size of the largest recorded loss is bigger than the largest recorded gain. Thus political incumbency appears to be a liability in the medium-term (Müller and Strøm, 2003: 588–90). Second, that in the Federal Republic this aggregate trend is not as evident as in the other Western European countries. Indeed, the largest recorded electoral gain (11.1 per cent) is much bigger than the largest recorded electoral loss (–8.3 per cent). The data on the electro costs and benefits to government parties in Germany is set out in full in Table 8.18. It re-enforces the assumption in the German politics literature that voters in the Federal Republic are relatively risk-averse and tend to avoid punishing incumbent coalitions.

8.4   Summary

Chapter 8 examines the patterns of competition and co-operation between political parties with an emphasis on party programmes and political campaigns, on the one hand, and coalition bargaining and cabinet governance and stability on the other. Throughout the chapter, theoretical discussion

Table 8.18 Electoral costs and benefits of government parties in Germany, 1945–2002 (%)

Government	In office?	Election year	CDU/ CSU	SPD	Greens	FDP	GB/ BHE	DP	Government
CDU/CSU-FDP-DP 1949–53	Yes	1953	+14.2	–	–	−02.4	–	−00.7	+11.1
CDU/CSU-FDP-DP-GB/ BHE 1953–5	No	1957	+05.0	–	–	−01.8	−01.3	+00.1	+02.0
CDU/CSU-FDP-DP 1955–6	No	1957	+05.0	–	–	−01.8	–	+00.1	+03.3
CDU/CSU-DP-DA/ FVP 1956–7	Yes	1957	+05.0	–	–	–	–	+00.1	[+05.1]
CDU/CSU-DP 1957–60	No	1961	−04.9	–	–	–	–	–	[−04.9]
CDU/CSU 1960–1	Yes	1961	−04.9	–	–	–	–	–	−04.9
CDU/CSU-FDP 1961–2	No	1965	+02.3	–	–	−03.3	–	–	−01.0
CDU/CSU 1962	No	1965	+02.3	–	–	–	–	–	+02.3
CDU/CSU-FDP 1962–5	Yes	1965	+02.3	–	–	−03.3	–	–	−01.0
CDU/CSU-FDP 1965–6	No	1969	−01.5	–	–	−03.7	–	–	−05.2
CDU/CSU 1966	No	1969	−01.5	–	–	–	–	–	−01.5
CDU/CSU-SPD 1966–9	Yes	1969	−01.5	+03.4	–	–	–	–	+01.9
SPD-FDP 1969–72	Yes	1972	–	+03.1	–	+02.6	–	–	+05.7
SPD-FDP 1972–6	Yes	1976	–	−03.2	–	−00.5	–	–	−03.7
SPD-FDP 1976–80	Yes	1980	–	+00.3	–	+02.7	–	–	+03.0
SPD-FDP 1980–2	No	1983	–	−04.7	–	−03.6	–	–	−08.3
SPD 1982	No	1983	–	−04.7	–	–	–	–	−04.7
CDU/CSU-FDP 1982–3	Yes	1983	+04.3	–	–	−03.6	–	–	+00.7
CDU/CSU-FDP 1983–7	Yes	1987	−04.5	–	–	+02.1	–	–	−02.4
CDU/CSU-FDP 1987–90	No	1990	−00.5	–	–	+01.9	–	–	+01.4
CDU/CSU-FDP-DSU 1990	Yes	1990	−00.5	–	–	+01.9	–	–	[+01.4]
CDU/CSU-FDP 1991–4	Yes	1994	−02.3	–	–	−04.1	–	–	−06.4
CDU/CSU-FDP 1994–8	Yes	1998	−06.4	–	–	−00.7	–	–	−07.1
SPD-Greens 1998–2002	Yes	2002	–	−02.4	+01.9	–	–	–	−00.5
Mean			+0.7	−01.1	+01.9	−0.7	−1.3	−0.3	

Note: Bracketed figures where one government party did not fight subsequent elections.

Sources: Saalfeld, 2003: 79; Infas, 2002.

and long-run comparative data is augmented by up-to-date data on the ruling Red–Green coalition in Germany. As in other chapters, the epistemological position is one that is consistent with literature that works from the idea of the universal goals of political agency (in this case maximising vote share, office-seeking and/or policy making) constrained by nation–specific institutional settings. It is therefore in line with the broad market metaphor used in this study.

In the case of Germany, the key nation-specific institutional settings include a multi-party system with a dominant pattern of coalition government at the national and, increasingly, sub-national level, as well as strong norms of co-operation and consensus and an electorate that has historically been risk-averse and favoured incumbent parties of government. Thus general trends found in most if not all advanced democracies have impacted on the Federal Republic in a way specific to the political conditions found in Germany. Let us examine the two sections of the chapter in turn.

In terms of political programmes there has, as in other countries, been an increasing emphasis on the external impact of election programmes and/or government programmes. At the same time, however, there remains a tendency for German political parties to afford significance to the basic programme. Similarly, it is clear that political campaigning in Germany has moved towards the 'stage 3' ideal type described by Farrell but, at the same time, SOPs from stage two – such as a continuing reliance on indirect marketing and the tradition of televised debates – remain in place, albeit with less impact than had previously been the case. At the same time, in retaining televised debates Germany is in part of the rule rather than the exception amongst advanced democracies. As Table 8.2 demonstrates, it is Italy, Switzerland and the United Kingdom – the countries with no tradition of leaders' debates – that are the odd ones out.

In terms of coalition behaviour, we again see a mix of universal trends and nation-specific patterns that are the meat and drink of comparative political analysis. The literature on coalition behaviour is some of the most theoretically advanced within the comparative politics canon, not least because much of it draws directly upon a highly developed game theoretical literature. In addition, the relatively discrete nature of coalitions and cabinets make comparison across cases quite a fruitful exercise. At the same time, as Müller and Strøm make clear, such cross-country analyses must take into account the particular configuration of institutional rules and norms found in each case. Thus when we look at the Federal Republic, in comparison with other Western European democracies with coalition governments, we find that in most respects the pattern of German coalition behaviour is not unusual in terms of size, stability, ideological range and so on. Having said that, however, to understand the present Red–Green coalition it is necessary to delve deeper into the specific context of German politics and the distinct process of political learning and trust-building that took place between the SPD and Greens that took place at the *Land* level from the early 1980s onwards. This raises some key questions about how far we can take the comparative approach and at what point we must fall back on the expertise of country specialists. It is to this final discussion that the book now turns.

9
Conclusion

9.1 Introduction

Chapter 1 of this book set out two sets of aims and objectives that it was hoped would be achieved by the study. They were:

- First, to draw on a wider literature than is generally found in single-country studies in order to shed new light on political phenomena and suggest new nuances or even explanations to students of German politics and country specialists more generally.
- Second, to allow students of the comparative method to apply some of the key concepts, models and approaches in comparative politics to the rich context of a single country study.

It was also hoped that in pursuing these two goals the study would also serve to problematise the trade-off in such a study between depth and breadth, micro- and macro-level explanation, rich description and abstraction, inductive and deductive reasoning, and so on.

The reader will also recall – and hopefully will have been aware of throughout the book – the intention to weave together two strands of debate:

- First, an empirical strand that examines the balance between the singularities of the German *Sonderweg* and the commonality of characteristics shared by Germany and other nations. It was argued that the balance between the two strands goes to the core of the purpose of the study and that it works from the assumption that the *Sonderweg* narrative is a necessary but not sufficient condition for the analysis of party politics in Germany. From this came the expressed intention to use more comparative data, more often than has been the norm in single-country studies of this type.
- Second, a theoretical strand that problematises the need for the comparative method to be framed within as consistent a theoretical framework as

possible, given the restraints of the book's reliance on secondary data from such a diverse set of sources as can be found within these pages. In order to do this, therefore, the study is driven forward by a loose market metaphor that is intended to encompass and be consistent with the more specific comparative models and approaches used in individual chapters.

It was acknowledged that these were ambitious aspirations and that the reader herself would be the ultimate judge as to how successful the book was in fulfilling them. Nevertheless, let us now return to each of these issues in turn before concluding with some final remarks on what our discussion tells us about the dynamics of party politics in Germany today.

9.2   Combining the German politics and comparative politics literature

It is not necessary to provide an exact breakdown of primary and secondary sources used in this study but suffice to say that just under 10 per cent of all entries in the bibliography to this book are primary sources and the remainder are secondary sources. Of those secondary sources, almost two-thirds are what could be called comparative politics sources, broadly defined, and the rest are German politics sources. For the purposes of this study, the term primary sources refers to party literature, coalition agreements, official documents, newspapers, websites, datasets in German or English. Of the secondary sources, the classification of a source as 'comparative' refers to any journal article, research note or paper, academic monograph, textbook or conference paper with a comparative or non-German focus in German or English. It follows, therefore, that 'German politics' sources includes any journal article, research note or paper, academic monograph, textbook or conference paper with a predominantly German focus in German or English. The reader may agree or disagree with the stated balance between primary and secondary sources, but one hopes that it has been apparent when reading this book that – compared with similar studies with a primarily German focus – this study represents a clear and decisive shift in the balance of sources towards the comparative politics literature.

9.3   Applying key comparative politics concepts, models and approaches

The main reason for the apparent dominance of the comparative politics literature within the book lies in the structure and rationale of the study. And the key driver of the study is the organisation of the seven core empirical chapters, each of which began with an overview of a number of key concepts and models before settling on a comparative framework within which to ground the analysis.

Thus Chapters 2, 3 and 4 drew upon the social cleavage literature and examined the development of political cleavages in Germany using the Lipset–Rokkan (1967) model as its primary framework. But in order to do so it first defined the epistemological and methodological divide between the macro-historical approach of the Lipset–Rokkan model – as well as associated work by Rokkan *et al.* (1970), Rose and Urwin (1969, 1970), Allardt and Rokkan (1970) and Rose (1974) – and the more micro-level focus of scholars such as Loewenberg (1968), Converse and Valen (1971) and Berglund and Lindstrom (1979). The two approaches are distinct, but it was made clear in the discussion that the decision to adopt one or the other has often been driven by practical considerations concerning the availability of data. In particular, the clear shift towards micro-level approaches over the post-war period was made possible by methodological refinements and in particular the availability of sophisticated survey data examining individual vote choices and value-orientations (Clagget *et al.*, 1982: 644). The shift from macro-to micro-level data was tracked through the narrative of Chapter 4, with its account of the erosion of social and political cleavages in post-war Germany and an assessment of the impact of this process on party politics in the modern Federal Republic. But the shift to micro-level data was made most explicit in Chapter 5, which explored in depth three related but distinct models of vote choice – namely (i) partisan identification; (ii) value-orientation and value-change; and (iii) economic or instrumental voting. Again, setting this framework up involved an account of the empirical and theoretical dialogue between the 'political sociology', 'political psychology' and 'political economy' schools of behavioural research (Carmines and Huckfeldt, 1998: 223–4) and the methodological advances that took place within all three as a result of the expansion and professionalisation of American political science in the mid-twentieth century. It was noted that, despite the fact that the sociological and psychological approaches are inductively based whilst the economic approach relies more on the hypothetico-deductive method, there has been some convergence between the three schools around concepts such as the 'reasoning voter' (Pappi, 1998: 255) and the use of micro-level analysis. But this focus on micro-level analysis was modified somewhat in Chapters 6, 7 and 8, which examined the institutional settings in which political agency takes place. Again, this involved a substantial discussion of competing models and approaches before the appropriate comparative frameworks were settled upon – be it political opportunity structures (Kitschelt, 1986; Tarrow, 1994), Gunther and Diamond's (2003) or Farrell's (1996) classificatory schema of political parties, or de Swaan's (1973) 'median legislator' model and other associated models of coalition formation and maintenance (see Müller and Strøm, 2003, for instance).

So how useful are these concepts and models? And what do they tell us about party politics in Germany that has not been covered in established single-country studies? It will be recalled that Landman (2000) suggests that there are four advantages to the comparative method – namely (i) better contextual description; (ii) better classification; (iii) more reliable hypothesis-testing; and (iv) the generation of predictions. It will be argued that the book does provide all of these advantages and, in doing so, provides a different analytical and empirical slant on the phenomenon of party politics – primarily in Germany but also more broadly.

Contextual description

Contextual description allows us to deepen and widen our understanding of the political world by opening up our conceptual and empirical lens in order to bring a new perspective to our analysis. In terms of our understanding of party politics in Germany, the book critically engages the narrative of the *Sonderweg* that underpins much of the German politics literature. In doing so, it allows us to be more reflexive about the temptation in single-country and area studies to assume a certain national exceptionalism when explaining complex phenemona and to construct tautological explanations or partial theories in order to do so. This is not just a problem for the German politics literature and scholars in many fields with a strong specific focus are aware of this problem (see Rosamond, 2000; Wiener and Diez, 2004 on the EU Integration literature for instance).

Having said that, the reader cannot fail to have noticed that we are still left with an analytical narrative that must acknowledge that in many instances the *Sonderweg* still holds true. The broad causal variables that underpin the development of cleavage structures in Germany are to be identified in other national 'stories'. But it is the specific configuration of geo-politics, economic and political development and the strategic decisions of political elites in Germany that created the economically potent, politically stunted, diplomatically aggressive and territorially ambitious state that destabilised Europe from the late nineteenth century onwards and led Germany to total political and military defeat in 1945. Similarly, the roots of contemporary political phenomena can still be traced at least in part to the German 'problem'. For instance, the institutional setting for party politics in Germany – such as the system of co-operative federalism, the proactive nature of the Basic Law, and the existence of an AMS electoral system with a 5 per cent barrier to electoral representation – is the creation of institution builders whose work was carried out with one eye on Germany's unhappy past and driven by the desire to prevent anything of its kind happening again. And even the unusually high levels of political disengagement in the new Federal states can be partially attributed to the legacy of over half a century of National Socialist and Communist dictatorship that are part of the German *Sonderweg*.

Better classification

By its very nature, the use of the comparative method will be more likely to expose any logical or empirical weaknesses in our models and concepts than single-country or area studies. And the more comparative the study, and thus the more observations we make, the more likely that this exposure will take place. One particular weakness of single-country and area studies is the misuse or at least hybridisation of comparative concepts. For example, in the British politics literature it is common to use the term 'corporatism' to describe attempts to co-ordinate economic planning and industrial policy in the 1960s and 1970s (see Flynn, 1983; King, 1983; Rhodes, 1988). Yet most comparative studies of corporatism in Europe and Latin America would argue that the United Kingdom lacks the formal institutional structures at the national or sectoral level that make corporatism sustainable (Schmitter and Lehmbruch, 1979; Lembruch and Schmitter, 1982). Thus, the use of the phrase makes sense within the British politics context but what it is describing is something different to its accepted use in the broader field of comparative politics.

Bearing this in mind, the book deliberately selected classifications that are designed to hold true across as many observations as possible. Some of these, such as those found in the Lipset–Rokkan model, will have been familiar to students of comparative politics and German politics alike. Some, however, will have struck the reader as being unfamiliar or even counter-intuitive in their rationale. The clearest example of this in the book was the use of the Gunther and Diamond (2003) classificatory schema for political parties in Chapter 7. The schema is admittedly more complex than more established equivalents based on either party 'families' or party functions and some of the types within the schema do not apply to party politics in Germany. But its strength lies in its ability to classify political parties across all polities and thus ground our understanding of German political parties within a wider context. Moreover, by applying a different classificatory 'cut' to German political parties the schema highlights some interesting observations, including the convergence of German political parties towards an organisationally 'thin' mode and the strikingly similar organisational antecedents to be found when comparing the Greens and post-industrial far right parties such as the Republicans, DVU and NPD. This last observation may be an unusual or even a disturbing comparison to make, especially to students of Green and environmental politics, but it is an empirically sustainable one that is worthy of further research.

More reliable hypothesis-testing

By and large the book relies on secondary data and this means that the analytical narrative is largely based on inductive rather than hypothetico-deductive reasoning. This emphasis on induction is further emphasised by its primary focus on Germany. However, there are three exceptions to this rule. First, the broad market metaphor that drives this study forward has a clear deductive strand to it that was outlined in the introduction to this study and will be returned to later in this chapter. Second, within the secondary sources used in the study there is a robust strand of literature that does use the hypothetico-deductive method. For instance the economic voting literature that is drawn on in Chapter 5 is strongly hypothetico-deductive in nature. It is grounded in complex formal models of rationality (Downs, 1957; Tufte, 1978; Schneider and Frey, 1988) and relies on large *n* research designs and tests hypotheses about the actual act of voting/non-voting (see Feld and Kirchgässner, 2000; Lewis Beck and Palham, 2000; Pennings, 2002; for instance). Similarly, the literature on coalition theory and maintenance is dominated by game-theoretical models and abstracted accounts of individual rationality (Müller and Strøm, 2003; also Gamson, 1961; Riker, 1962; Axelrod, 1970). Third, although not conforming to a strict reading of the hypothetico-deductive method, the book does explore the implications of a number of loose hypotheses (defined as a postulation about a causal relationship between at least two variables), including the impact of the German institutional setting on the political opportunity structures available to political agents (Chapter 6) and the strategy informing the SPD and Greens' negotiating stances during the coalition formation process following the 1998 and 2002 Bundestag elections. Although not testable in the strictest sense, the book does identify the conditions in which these hypotheses might be more formally tested in a systematic manner through future research.

The generation of predictions

Even more so than was the case with hypotheses-testing, the book does not set out to generate predictions *per se*. But throughout the book predictions are made, not just about the future development of party politics in Germany but also about party politics more generally. Thus, without reiterating the arguments made in specific chapters, it is predicted that if the process of partisan dealignment and growing volatility amongst the electorate continues, then parties in Germany and elsewhere will find it harder to respond to voters' preferences either at elections or when in government. Similarly, it is assumed that in the absence of fundamental institutional change in Germany, the political opportunity structure available to political agents and the incentive systems within which they operate will remain broadly the same – thus presenting significant barriers to entry for new political competitors within the party system. And it is assumed that as long as the established 'Red–Green model' of portfolio allocation remains the template for coalition building between the SPD and the Greens, then the Greens will (i) attempt to widen their policy competences through the appointment of state secretaries, and so on, below the ministerial level, and (ii) explore options to break out of the SPD's orbit, including, in time perhaps, the formation of one or more 'Black–Green' coalitions (with the CDU as senior partner) at the *Land* level.

Of course making predictions is a risky business. Those that prove correct appear self-evident in retrospect and those that do not often look foolhardy at the very least. Nevertheless, it is an article of faith in comparative politics that the more observations or cases inform such predictions, the more likely they are to prove to be correct. Ultimately the modest predictions made in this book will be tested by time and by further research.

9.4   Problematising the trade-off between depth and breadth, micro- and macro-level explanation

In pursuing its two main objectives, it will be recalled that the study also aimed to problematise the trade-off between depth and breadth, micro- and macro-level explanation, rich description and abstraction, inductive and deductive reasoning, and so on. Again, it is the reader who will be the judge as to how successful the book has been in this respect but it is the opinion of the author that it has, not least in those areas of the book in which the application of the underlying rationale is less successful than might otherwise be desired.

It was noted in the introduction to this study that Lijphart identified five different techniques of comparison: (i) global statistical analysis; (ii) case studies; (iii) focussed comparisons; (iv) diachronic studies; and (v) pooled comparative research (Lijphart, 1971). These five categories can be further divided into large n and small n studies (see also Sartori, 1970). It was also pointed out that much comparative research does not fall neatly into such categories but combines methods in order to create a 'triangulated perspective' (Denzin, 1970). Having read the book it will be clear to the reader that this study falls into the category of a triangulated study. Thus, the book draws upon primary data from recent Bundestag elections, recent party publications and other official documents – including election manifestos and coalition agreements – as well as secondary data including statistical analyses of voter choice, value orientation, and other socio-economic data, in addition to the rich narrative of much of the German politics literature. In doing so it uses the case study design, as well as drawing on techniques of global statistical analysis, focussed comparisons and pooled comparative research, and adopts both diachronic and synchronic perspectives as appropriate. The analytical narrative generated by this mixture of methods and approaches is in many respects interpretative in nature, but it also serves to inform and confirm the theoretical frameworks used in the empirical chapters.

However, as discussed in the introduction to this study, the triangulation of data in this manner makes it imperative that care is taken both to avoid individualist and/or ecological fallacies, and to make explicit the underlying ontological and epistemological position of the book. In terms of avoiding fallacies the book uses the 'principle of direct measurement' (Scheuch, 1969) and makes sure that conclusions about individual-level phenomena are only drawn from individual-level data and those about ecological-level phenomena only use ecological-level data. And in order to resolve and clarify the underlying ontological and epistemological position a significant amount of the book is spent setting up the theoretical frameworks that inform the empirical chapters and justifying them in epistemological terms.

Nevertheless, the use of data in the manner described above highlight two issues that problematise the trade-off between depth and breadth, micro- and macro-level explanation, rich description and abstraction, inductive and deductive reasoning, and so on. The first is that, because of the need to make one's ontological and epistemological position explicit, this book might strike some readers as being quite long compared with other studies of party politics in Germany and to contain expositions on matters of theory and methodology that they may consider unnecessary or irrelevant to their interests. If this is the case one must apologise but once more argue that such diversions are unavoidable in a study of this nature. The second, which relates to the stated desire to avoid fallacies, is that the study's ambitions are self-consciously limited. As discussed in the previous section of this chapter, the book is more successful in generating contextual description and refining our classificatory schema than it is in terms of hypothesis-testing and the generation of predictions. It is true that these weaknesses can be rectified through a stronger hypothetico-deductive logic and a greater reliance on large *n* studies. But in doing so it would of necessity eschew the insight and rich description that informs many single-country and area studies and remains essential to our understanding of real world politics in the Federal Republic and elsewhere.

9.5   The balance between the singularities of the German *Sonderweg* and the commonality of characteristics shared by Germany and other nations

Now let us move on to the dominant empirical strand of debate within the book, dealing with the balance between (i) the singularities of the German *Sonderweg*; (ii) the commonality of characteristics shared by Germany and other nations. The picture that emerges from the data presented in the book is that of a highly complex and nuanced political marketplace that defies over-deterministic or mono-causal explanations. This is reflected in the wide range of theoretical and empirical approaches touched upon in the book. Having said that, we can identify the impact of both (i) macro-level, and (ii) meso- and micro-level factors. Taken together, these two sets of factors shape the warp and weft of contemporary party politics in the Federal Republic. Of these, it is the macro-level that defines the 'otherness' of German party politics in as far as the parameters of political competition in the Federal Republic have been defined over time by the specific pattern of historical development that characterises the German *Sonderweg*. In as far as the German *Sonderweg* exists, its explanation can be found at the macro-level.

Macro-level analysis and the German '*Sonderweg*'

If one wishes to articulate and expand upon the *Sonderweg* narrative, the Thirty Years War is as good a starting point as any. The Peace of Westphalia in 1648 imposed a Franco-Swedish settlement on the German states that contributed to their lapse back into feudalism and particularism, even as other Western European states were beginning to take on the trappings of modernity. The reining-in of Hapsburg power left a vacuum that, as Taylor (1982) points out, provided the necessary conditions for the emergence of Prussia. Prussia slowly became the dominant German state and its defining features – a strong administrative structure, robust Protestantism (and anti-Catholicism), militarism and authoritarianism – would become the template for the Second Reich after 1871. These features, paradoxically combined with a world-class economy, were to prove disastrous for Germany and Europe once the Second Reich set about catching up with its Great Power rivals. Domestically, this process of catching-up was driven by the dominant alliance of 'Iron and Rye', made up of landowners and industrialists and supported by elements of the middle classes.

Politically, the pattern of historical development described here was both a cause and a symptom of the failure of German liberalism and what amounted to the stillbirth of German democracy in the late nineteenth century. From the perspective of a century and a half later, the longer-term impact can be seen in both the development of social and political cleavages in Germany and in the German party system that these cleavages underpin. In terms of social and political cleavages, we can see the manifestation of the class and confessional cleavages that continue to shape the pattern of electoral competition in the modern Federal Republic. But the more profound consequences were for the party system itself. The Second Reich's party system was characterised by the isolation of the SPD along the left-right dimension as well as the failure of *Zentrum* to forge a stable electoral base beyond its core Catholic vote. This three-bloc *Dreilagersystem* system (Rohe, 1997: 49) set a pattern that would outlive the Reich itself. Thus, despite the presence of a party that explicitly referred to itself as 'the Centre', the political centre in Germany failed to hold and the party system saw an ongoing polarisation between right and left that persisted well into the twentieth century. For the conservative right, both inside and outside parliament, the Social Democrats would remain political outsiders and conservative support for the Republic with which the SPD so strongly identified was contingent upon the circumstances of the time. After 1919, the right's contempt for the constitutional left was fuelled by the *Dolchstosslegende*, which although clothed in the language of nationalism – by casting the SPD as unpatriotic and un-German – was effectively used as a tool for political mobilisation around the class cleavage. In 1933, when the conservative right were finally forced to choose between buttressing the Republic and the alternative course of allowing Hitler to assume the Chancellorship, the *Sonderweg* narrative depicts a grim inevitability in the way in which they made the wrong choice.

The consequences of that choice require no repetition and continued to shape German politics beyond the third 'year zero' of May 1945. It will be recalled that in many ways it was the Third Reich that created the conditions necessary for democracy to finally take root on German soil. The impact of totalitarianism, combined with the dislocation caused by the war, eroded the sectional and regional loyalties that had hampered the creation of a democratic identity during the Weimar years. Thus, under what I call the benign authoritarianism of Allied occupation, we see the remarkably swift emergence of the parties that are familiar to us today – the CDU and CSU, and FDP. Together with the re-constituted SPD, these parties continue to form the spine of the German party system.

Despite these encouraging developments, however, the past continued to manifest itself in the present. The Nazis' principle legacy to the nation – the *de facto* division of Germany – very quickly became a *de jure* division and this was reflected in the *Zwangsvereinigung* of 1946 and the subsequent western orientation of the party system in Bizonia. For its part, Schumacher's SPD failed to grasp this new dynamic in time to prevent the political initiative passing to Adenauer and the CDU. And it was the CDU that defined the new trajectory of West German democracy, with its emphasis on the social market economy at home and a commitment to European integration and loyalty to American leadership abroad. Within a decade the SPD had adapted to the new settlement, but it must be remembered that the political settlement in the Federal Republic of Germany was – and arguably remains – a Christian Democratic construct.

The first Bundestag elections of 1949 generated a party system that still displayed the artefacts of particularism and authoritarianism. But within a decade parties such as the NLP/DP, WAV or BP had either failed to consolidate an electoral base or been absorbed into the CDU. Thus, by the early 1960s, the German party system had assumed the shape of the triangular 'Pappi model' (Pappi, 1984), made up of the CDU/CSU, FDP and SPD. In time, these three parties were joined by the Greens and the PDS, but the party system remains dominated by the two centrist *Volksparteien*.

The consolidation of both the party system and democracy itself was underpinned by the unprecedented growth of prosperity associated with the *Wirtschaftswunder* of the 1950s and 1960s. Yet if a growth in per capita income from DM 1588 to DM 8725 between 1950 and 1970 was exceptional to Germany, the manner in which such prosperity impacted upon the value-orientations and preferences of German voters served to underline the steady normalisation of German politics. As in other countries, economic and social development led to the emergence of a more numerous, urbanised, educated and secular electorate. Thus, the population increased from just over 46 million to a little under 62 million, the number of Germans living in villages of less than five thousand people fell from around 30 per cent to under 10 per cent, and the number who had attended *Gymnasien* rose from 10 per cent in the 1940s to 30 per cent in the late 1980s (Statistisches Bundesamt). These changes impacted upon electoral politics through the effective disappearance of any urban/rural or centre/periphery cleavages, the weakening of the class cleavage and to a certain extent the confessional cleavage (Dogan, 2000). In addition, researchers began to detect a 'cohort effect' within the electorate, with younger voters displaying a significantly different value-orientation to older voters. Similarly, technical change had its impact upon the internal life of political parties and in particular on the social profile of party memberships. Thus, party membership for all of the parties became more middle class in its makeup, and even the SPD saw a shift away from its working class base and towards the public sector white-collar salariat (see Chandler, 1988).

But this process of modernisation did not serve to simplify the patterns of political competition in the Federal Republic. If anything it made it more complicated, especially in terms of the parties' ability to anticipate and respond to electoral preferences. By-and-large, the CDU was more successful in adapting to these changes and data indicates that it still retains its cross-confessional support amongst practicing Christians, whilst at the same time sustaining its core Catholic electorate and competing with the SPD amongst the secularised electorate (Forschungsgruppe Wahlen, 1994: 639–48). For the SPD, although the class cleavage is less potent than it was, trade unions remain the key auxiliary organisation of the 'worker' side of the class cleavage and continue to exercise an independent impact (Forschungsgruppe Wahlen, 1976–87). By contrast, the behaviour of the new middle class (Conradt and Dalton, 1988) was less predictable and neither of the two *Volksparteien* established a decisive electoral advantage amongst this social group. In addition, although the FDP did reasonably well amongst the new middle class up until the early 1980s, the party came under increasing electoral pressure from the newly emergent Greens after that (Gluchowski and Wilamowitz-Moellendorff, 1997: 190).

The overall effect of social and economic change in the post-war years was an erosion of the power of social and economic location as a predictor of vote choice. The cohort effect noted above led to a generation gap within the electorate, in which the cognitive links of loyalty and identification between younger voters and political parties progressively weakened. This manifested itself in higher levels of electoral volatility, the growth of split ticket voting and the emergence of a postmaterialist value orientation (Inglehart, 1990). German Unification in 1990 aggravated this process of partisan de-alignment (Dalton, 1992: 55).

The accession of the new Federal states served to graft onto the Federal Republic a population and social structure that had undergone a profoundly different historical development over the post-war years. Not only had the population of the new states inherited the legacy of National Socialism, but they had also undergone 40 years of Communist rule. As a result party politics in the new Federal states was grounded in different social dynamics than in the old states. The electorate was characterised by an inverted social profile, in which the accepted logic of the class cleavage was turned on its head and the confessional cleavage had nothing like the power that it still exercised in the old Federal states. In the early 1990s, in particular, this presented a significant strategic problem for the SPD – in which it (i) trailed behind the CDU in what should have been its core working class constituency; (ii) was not able to consolidate support amongst Protestant voters; and (iii) was forced to compete with the post-Communist PDS. The PDS was not just significant to the SPD as a competitor along the Downsian left-right dimension but also represented the emergence of what might be described as a new centre/periphery cleavage mapped onto the 40-year division of Germany (Niedermayer, 1995; Jeffery and Lees, 1998; Hough, 2001). As such they were not just a problem of the SPD, but also for the entire German political class – torn as it was between a desire to isolate the party and its recognition that the interests and preferences of voters in the new Federal states had to be integrated into the polity (Lees, 1995b).

Although the inverted social profile of the electorate in the new Federal states has modified somewhat over the decade following unification, the presence of two German electorates can still be seen in analyses of the 2002 Bundestag elections. At the aggregate level, the two dominant social cleavages remained that of social class and religion, augmented by a declining centre/periphery cleavage arising from the terms and conditions of unification. Religion remained a more reliable indicator of voter preferences than class, and the latter failed to explain the preferences of manual workers in the new Federal states or of workers more generally, once uncoupled from trade union membership (Falter and Schoen, 1999; Gallagher *et al.*, 2001).

For the political parties, the dynamics of the political marketplace remain complicated and present them with formidable strategic problems in terms of political mobilisation and the content of political campaigns. Thus, the CDU continues to enjoy a clear lead over the SPD among Catholic voters and Protestant voters who claim strong religious ties. By contrast, the CDU did badly amongst voters who claimed no religious affiliation. But the main beneficiaries of this religious/secular divide at present appear to be the Greens and PDS, rather than the SPD. At present support for the SPD remains relatively strong amongst unionised manual workers but, in the 2002 elections at least it appears that it has ground to make up amongst non-unionised manual workers. On the 'bourgeois' side of the class cleavage, the Greens also performed well among the non-unionised new middle class but less well amongst the self-employed, who voted for the CDU and, more significantly, the FDP.

To sum up this section, a macro-level analysis such as the one described in this section does provide an intuitive account of the 'big events' of German politics and why the broad parameters of party politics in the contemporary Federal Republic are as they are. We can trace a pattern from the first year zero of the signing of the Peace of Westphalia, through the second of 1918, and on past the third year zero of 1945. Thus, unlike the orthodox narrative of British political history, with its emphasis upon the notion of continuity and stability, the equivalent German national story is one of disjuncture and upheaval. In such a narrative, the complex strategic environment of German party politics can be at least partially explained with reference to the past and the almost uniquely tragic consequences of German history over the last 300 years. In particular, the disasters of the last century of war, genocide, division and – ultimately – unification have undoubtedly played a part. But there are two objections to relying on such an account alone. First, it implies a kind of inevitability about the shape of party politics today of which one should be suspicious. More importantly, given the complexity of electoral preferences and the strategic challenges to the political parties noted above, it does not allow us to 'get inside the heads' of voters or political elites. For this we need to shift our analytical focus to the micro- and meso-levels – with an emphasis upon the actions and motives of electors and elected. In doing so, it will become clear that we can also construct a powerful narrative about the commonalities that Germany shares with other advanced industrial democracies.

Micro- and meso-level analysis: the commonalities between Germany and other advanced democracies

Starting with the micro-level of analysis, this study evaluates the underlying dynamics of voter behaviour through the lens of three concepts: (i) partisan identification; (ii) value orientation; and (iii) economic voting. The increasing sophistication of the methodologies associated with research into these phenomena and the relative availability of comparative data allow us to paint a somewhat different picture to that of the macro-level account discussed in the previous section.

There are two ways in which this has an impact on our account of party politics in Germany. First, the fine-grained micro-level data gleaned from such research undermines the idea of individuals as cultural dupes, whose actions are to a large extent determined by impersonal macro-level forces. Second, and more importantly in the context of this study, the standardisation of techniques and explicitly comparative focus serves as a powerful counter-weight to the *Sonderweg* narrative. So although a nation's historical legacy may have shaped the institutional settings in which political action takes place, it is at least implicit in all three approaches that individuals in any given setting have scope for individual agency, autonomy and the ability to make complex calculations based on the information available to them. And looking through the lenses that these approaches provide, the picture that emerges from Germany is one of a political marketplace that displays significant commonalities with comparable political systems, rather than one defined by the idea of German exceptionalism.

For example, in the study it was established that Germans are socialised into political beliefs in a similar manner to that found elsewhere. As in the United States and in the United Kingdom, for instance, parental influence plays an important role – and it is clear that the negative effects of parental influence are especially strong on the centre-left of the political spectrum (Schmidt-Beck, 2003). Similarly, as Germans go through life, they are influenced by the same lifecycle events associated with mobility, marriage, and in much the same way as voters in other advanced democracies (Tuma and Mayer, 1990; Diekmann and Weick, 1993). Moreover they are similarly affected by the impact of the partisan composition of neighbourhoods (MacKuen and Brown, 1987), the ideology of colleagues (Schmitt-Beck *et al.*, 2002), close friends, partners and spouses (Kenny, 1994), as well as the impact of the mass media (Kaase and Klingemann, 1994). However it is also true that, up until the 1980s, the specific trauma of National Socialism and subsequent retreat from the political sphere by an entire generation meant that Germany did not conform to the general pattern found in other advanced industrial democracies by which partisanship increases with age (Baker *et al.*, 1981; Norpoth, 1983; Dalton, 1996).

In terms of the spread of postmaterialist values, the broad dynamics are remarkably similar to those found in many other countries in Western Europe, although there is some divergence in terms of the orientation of the youngest generational cohorts – with Germany in a group of countries (along with Denmark and France) in which postmaterialist value-orientations now appear to be in decline. Finally, after we take into account the specificities of the German institutional setting, the models and assumptions associated with 'economic voting' literature apply almost as well in the Federal Republic as they do in the United States, where they originated (Kirchgässner, 1986; Nannestad and Paldam, 1994; Feld and Kirchgässner, 2000; Maier and Rattinger, 2004).

This narrative of similarity also applies to the German political parties themselves, when compared with their counterparts in other countries. In the simplest mode of comparison, it is taken as given that German political parties – like those elsewhere – carry out the functions of (i) elite recruitment; (ii) sustaining public institutions; (iii) interest representation and aggregation; and (iv) mobilisation and integration. In Germany, as elsewhere, it has become apparent that political parties are failing to carry out some of these functions, especially that of mobilisation and integration. In Germany the phenomenon of popular disillusionment with mainstream politics and politicians, known as *Politikverdrossenheit*, has been interpreted as a potential challenge to the post-war settlement and has been the subject of much

self-critical and occasionally anguished debate amongst establishment commentators. Yet the evidence indicates that this is not a phenomenon specific
to Germany but can be seen in other countries such as the United Kingdom
and the new EU accession states of Central and Eastern Europe. With the
possible exception of the United States – where it sometimes appears that
elements within the political elite actively conspire to keep potential voters
away from the polls – elites in almost all of the advanced democracies where
this phenomenon is to be found have taken positive measures (such as the
experimentation with all-postal ballots in the United Kingdom) to counter-
act some of its more obvious effects, such as the decline in levels of electoral
participation.

Nevertheless, as was discussed in the introduction to this study, in
Germany the effects of popular disillusionment are potentially more damaging to the political settlement because of the central role parties play within
the state. It will be recalled from Chapter 6 that after 1945 political parties
moved into the centre of the governmental/administrative nexus of the new
Federal Republic. The *Parteienstaat* principle, as codified in Article 21 of the
Basic Law, made parties responsible for overseeing 'the formation of the
political will of the people'. In doing so the maintenance of state legitimacy
and the legitimacy of the political parties became one and the same task.
Paradoxically, in the early years of the Federal Republic the existence of a
somewhat deferential, disciplined and apolitical populace, whose preferences had been shaped by, or in reaction to, Germany's anti-democratic past,
allowed political elites to exploit the subsequent permissive consensus and
consolidate the legitimacy of both the democratic state and the political parties that buttressed it. By contrast the more individualistic and instrumental
preferences of modern Germans – the majority of whom have been accul-
turated in the far more pluralistic and democratic culture of contemporary
Germany – denies the current political class the room for manoeuvre
enjoyed by its predecessors. Thus the Federal Republic now finds itself
trapped by the logic of the *Parteienstaat* in as far as any rejection of the legitimacy of the established political parties can also be interpreted as being a
rejection of the legitimacy of the state itself. It is therefore not surprising that
Politikverdrossenheit is uniquely troubling to German political elites and to
academic observers.

Moving away from functional definitions and on to a more sophisticated
mode of comparison between political parties, the book demonstrates that
German parties share more complex common characteristics with parties in
other polities. Moreover the pattern of commonality is not just to be seen
within the advanced industrial democracies, but also around the globe and
at different levels of socio-economic and democratic development. Focussed
at the meso-level, Gunther and Diamond's (2003) classificatory schema uses
the three dimensions of formal organisation, programmatic commitments,
and strategy/behavioural norms to allow us to 're-arrange' the German party

system in a manner that draws explicit and sometimes counterintuitive comparisons with unexpected equivalents. Thus there is nothing particularly new in the notion of the SPD historically conforming to Kirchheimer's (1966) 'class-mass' party model, or the CDU/CSU emerging in the 1940s as a 'mass-based denominational party'. But Gunther and Diamond's modification of the mass-party model not only allows us to compare and contrast the SPD and CDU/CSU with other German mass-based parties such as the KPD, SED and NSDAP, but also with 'pluralist-nationalist' parties – such as the Basque PNV, the SDLP and Sinn Fein – and religious fundamentalist parties such as the Algerian Islamic Salvation Front, the Turkish Welfare party and the Hindu BJP in India. Similarly the present-day SPD and CDU/CSU can be compared with other 'electoralist' parties, including the FDP and PDS, but also with the Civic Democratic Party and Social Democratic Party in the Czech Republic, and the Democratic Progressive Party in Taiwan (Gunther and Diamond, 2003: 187). And of course, Gunther and Diamond's conception of 'movement parties', describing a form of political organisation that covers both a political party and a wider movement within which the party is embedded, brings together the unlikely bedfellows of the German Greens and the Austrian Freedom Party (Gunther and Diamond, 2003: 188). Moreover, the book demonstrates that the same links can be drawn between the Greens and Republicans, DVU or NPD.

The search for common characteristics can also be extended to party behaviour, and in particular the manner and means by which elites compete and cooperate with one another. In terms of the dynamics of competition within the political marketplace, it is clear that German parties are no different than those in other democracies in that they must convince potential voters that their product mix is superior to that of their competitors. And a key means through which all parties advertise their product is through their programmes – although German parties may place more emphasis upon the formulation of their basic programmes than is the case in Britain, for instance. In a similar vein, it is clear that the growing professionalisation of party campaigning in Germany is part of a common trend that can be detected in all advanced industrial democracies (Bowler and Farrell, 1992; Butler and Ranney, 1992; Swanson and Mancini, 1996; Farrell and Webb, 2002). This was demonstrated in the book with reference to Farrell's (1996) three-stage model of campaign professionalisation, which traces the development of party campaigning from the initial period of mass rallies and whistlestop tours, through the advent of television, and on to the advent of the internet and the emergence of the 'permanent campaign', with its heavy emphasis on the use of outside consultants and agencies. Indeed, when we compare Germany to other democracies we see that German parties are faced with a similar pattern of facilitators and constraints in this regard. Thus, as in Australia, Canada, Japan and the United States, political parties in Germany are allowed to buy TV spots and are highly reliant on leaders' debates but, unlike in some countries, German parties also have access to public campaign finance. In this context the SPD's recalibration of its campaigning machinery in the mid 1990s – and the CDU/CSU's sophisticated campaign in 2002 – can be seen as part of a broader developmental trend that has parallels in the Clinton Presidential campaign of 1992 and that of New Labour in the period running up to the 1997 elections.

Moving on to the flip side of political competition, this study examines the process of political co-operation through the lens of coalition theory – a literature that makes a number of universal claims about the motivations and strategies of political elites that are held to be true across time and space. For instance, it is assumed that coalition games in all settings are subject to different types of structural attribute and that we can analyse such games and predict future outcomes through recourse to formal models. These models emphasise either 'office-seeking' or 'policy-seeking' behaviour, or a mixture of both. Models such as De Swaan's (1973) 'median legislator' or 'median party' model, or Shepsle's (1979) and Laver and Shepsle's (1990, 1995) idea of the DDM provide a relatively parsimonious theoretical framework for the analysis of coalition formation in Germany and elsewhere. However, in order to make sense of the more complex questions relating to coalition maintenance and stability we need to resort to less parsimonious approaches such as that of Müller and Strøm (2003) and associated authors. Using this approach we find that in terms of relative cabinet duration, Germany finds itself around the median position along with Sweden, Norway, Denmark, France, Portugal and Belgium. We know that the mean duration of German cabinets is 700 days and it remains to be seen whether the current Red–Green coalition will surpass this total. But surely any eventual assessment of the successes and failures of the 'Red–Green model' (Lees, 1999) will have to take into account its longevity – not just in relation to previous German coalitions but also in comparison to their equivalents in other countries that share a tradition of coalition government?

9.6 Finding a consistent theoretical framework: assessing the 'political marketplace' metaphor

In the introduction to this book it was made clear that the use of such a diverse set of secondary sources, and the comparative frameworks associated with them, made it imperative that the study be driven forward by some kind of theoretical heuristic or metaphor that would provide an overall narrative and knit its heterogeneous elements together. It will be recalled that the starting point was Ware's analysis of the role of political parties in the democratic process more generally. Ware's discussion was built around three questions. First, what are the different elements of democracy? Second, what are political parties? And third, how have theorists seen the role of parties in facilitating or constraining democracy in society? (1987: 7).

Building on Ware's discussion, it was made clear that the study is primarily focussed on the 'input' side of the democratic process and examines the role by which political parties, operating within a multi-party system, articulate and aggregate citizens' preferences within complex modern industrial democracies like that of the Federal Republic. It was assumed that voters are not cultural dupes and individual preferences matter, although there are powerful intervening variables associated with socio-economic location that shape those preferences. In responding to these preferences, the role of political parties was seen as analogous with that of firms that compete with one another to sell their product (party programmes and, where appropriate, records in government) in the marketplace (the party system) to potential customers (the voters). It was made clear that the market metaphor to be used was similar in epistemological terms to the work of Downs (1957) and others, but that it was not so rigidly deductive and worked from a set of modified assumptions that differed from Downs' original work. Two modifications are worth re-iterating at this point. First, it is assumed in this study that political parties' prime objective is survival rather than office-seeking and that many parties are content to take up and consolidate 'niche' positions in the market, especially in proportional electoral systems that tend to generate multi-party systems. Second, and leading on from the previous point, it is assumed that many political parties as political firms are content to 'satisfice' (Simon, 1976) rather than maximise market share, given the constraints imposed upon them by the institutional and normative environment within which they operate.

The study also examines two aspects of the 'output' side of the political process. First, and somewhat tangentially, the issue of civic orientation is touched as an externality of political competition. Second, that of policy outcomes is considered to be part of the product offered to voters by parties of government and therefore important if political parties as firms are to maintain credibility with their customers.

It must be stressed that, on its own, the political marketplace metaphor does not generate any new or unique insights into party politics in Germany or elsewhere. However, it is hoped that the reader will have found it a useful heuristic that serves to impose a degree of analytical order on what is a wide-ranging and diverse narrative. It is not necessary to reiterate substantive points made elsewhere in this chapter but let us look briefly at the use of the market metaphor in this study.

Starting with the input side of the political process, it is clear that the problematisation of the idea of voters as customers provides a useful narrative frame for both the macro-historical accounts found in the earlier chapters of this study as well as the more nuanced micro-perspectives associated with the psycho-social and economic accounts of contemporary voting behaviour. Similarly, the idea of parties as firms provides a platform for both our analysis of party classification and also patterns of interaction between them. And in terms of the constraints that shape these patterns of interaction, it is clear that party systems as political marketplaces display various degrees of differentiation such as the degree of concentration or deconcentration, partisan alignment or de-alignment, dominant or cross-cutting cleavages, and so forth. Therefore the opportunity costs of entry into the party system differ across time and space, not only because of the differing appeal of parties' 'product mix' but also due to voting rules, barriers to representation, laws regulating internal party democracy, and so on. Using this metaphor we can reject the assumption of perfect competition within the political marketplace and work with the analogy of an oligopolistic market, which in Germany became increasingly dominated by a limited number of parties before opening up again to a certain extent over the course of the last two decades.

Moving on to the output side of the political process, the market metaphor provides both a pessimistic and a relatively optimistic perspective on the role of political parties within the wider democratic process. On the one hand, if we assume that there should be a reasonable fit between voters' preferences and the product mix on offered to them by political parties, the decline in partisan identification, increasing levels of electoral volatility and non-voting described in this study should be a cause for concern – for it would appear that parties are failing to respond to voters' preferences (and certainly not shaping them and/or fostering civic orientation). On the other, if we assume in normative terms that there should be some kind of link between the aggregate of voters' preferences and policy outcomes then the long process of coalition negotiations – based on directional cues rather than pure positioning – and subsequent coalition management that characterises the Federal Republic and other systems must further skew policy outcomes away from the social choice. Moreover, the increasingly common response of political parties to market uncertainty – the advent of the permanent campaign – appears to if anything increase public scepticism about the political process over the medium-to long term (Whitely, 2005). Taken at face value, these apparent market failures would appear to explain the existence of *Politkverdrossenheit* and similar phenomena elsewhere.

At the same time, it could be argued that the market clearing mechanism – however imperfect – still works, albeit in a sub-optimal manner. Thus, as the decline in traditional partisanship and the rise in electoral volatility and non-voting became apparent in the 1970s and 1980s, we also saw the emergence of a new firm within the political marketplace. This new firm was the Greens and, as we have seen, the growth of the party was driven by the need to address voter preferences and issues on the left of the political spectrum that were being otherwise neglected or ignored by the SPD. In a similar vein, rather than regarding the persistence of the PDS in the post-unification Germany as a symptom of the failure of democracy in the new Federal states, I would argue that we might also regard it as a healthy market response to the failure of established political firms to respond effectively to the different preferences of eastern voters. And if the responsiveness of the established parties improves in this regard, then the appeal of the PDS will inevitably decline. Finally, in terms of policy outputs, the entry of newcomers into the political marketplace has over time led to new coalition arrangements at both the *Land* and federal levels. In turn these new coalitions – such as Red–Green coalitions in the 1980s, Red–Red (SPD–PDS) coalitions in the 1990s and, possibly, Black–Red coalitions in years to come – will pursue different policy mixes that may be closer to the aggregate social choice under given circumstances. In short, it could be argued that the system remains responsive to changing preferences but, perhaps inevitably in complex modern societies and with intervening institutions, the process of market clearing is a little 'clunky' and subject to time lag.

To sum up, the use of the market metaphor leads us to a clear position that rejects many long-established empirical and normative arguments about how party systems do and should work. Broadly speaking it rejects the Rousseauesque idea of political parties forming the 'general will' or shaping civic orientation in any consistent manner and takes the fundamentally liberal position that they exist to reflect and respond to popular preferences. Moreover, it provides an analytical narrative that stresses the universality of political agency and the ability of the political marketplace to respond, albeit somewhat clumsily and belatedly, to the changing preferences of an increasingly sophisticated electorate. Crucially, in doing this it also privileges the comparative dimension over the narrative of the *Sonderweg* – and is therefore consistent with the prime empirical assumption that underpins this book.

9.7   Final remarks

It is hoped that the discussion in this chapter reveals some of the complexity of party politics in Germany today. For want of a better term, what we might refer to as the German 'national legend' imposes a unique set of constraints on both rulers and ruled. These constraints span a continuum, ranging from relatively inchoate normative expectations about how Germans and their politicians should behave, through to the more concrete institutional incentive structures and sanctions set out in the Basic Law and elsewhere. In particular, the persistence of the national legend makes German political elites uniquely sensitive to any sign of under-performance within the political marketplace. As Paterson observes, '(Germany's) traumatic past has ensured that changes, whether in the form of different voting patterns, the creation of a new party ..., and dissent within parties are perceived as challenges to the system and threats to stability' (Paterson, 1987: 159). It is hoped, however, that the underlying message of this study is that such changes are in fact evidence of the *normalisation* of German politics. Thus, rather than being seen as potential challenges to a political system made vulnerable by both the reality and the rhetoric of German exceptionalism, they are part of a pattern to be found in most democracies and are probably no more or less of a threat than they might be elsewhere.

Such a conclusion is the logical outcome of both the assumptions that underpin this study and the data and arguments within it that stress that the *Sonderweg* narrative is not – or is no longer, given the increasing sophistication of data collection and analysis – a sufficient vehicle for meaningful discussion of party politics in Germany today. It is true that institutional constraints are very important and many of these may be nation-specific. But this book has tried to demonstrate that, once we take these constraints into account, the dynamics of the political marketplace are remarkably similar across the democratic world. In particular, in any given political market, political elites are entrepreneurial and behave in a broadly rational manner in pursuit of public office, political power and influence. In this there is no evidence – and no reason to expect – that German political parties would or should differ from their counterparts elsewhere. It is for the purpose of drawing this conclusion, if for no other, that the tools of comparative politics have been used in this study to confirm that voters' enduring suspicion – that 'politicians are all the same' – is in the most fundamental sense true.

Notes

3 Social and Political Cleavages in the
Second Reich and Weimar Republic

1. The Cartell period was characterised by a strategy of close co-operation between the Conservatives, German Empire Party and National Liberals, in support of Bismarck's policies.

4 · Social and Political Cleavages in the Federal
Republic, 1945–2002

2. Another more explicitly separatist party, the Bavarian Party (BP), was active in the early years of the Federal Republic but disbanded in the 1950s.

6 State Structures, Electoral Systems and Party Systems

3. Robert Axelrod developed the idea of ideological connectedness as a response to the predictive weaknesses of 'pure' office-seeking models of coalition formation. Axelrod's work was subsequently refined by, amongst many others, Abram de Swaan, who is associated with initial work on the median legislator/Mparty model (see Axelrod, R., 1970; de Swaan, A. 1973).

7 Political Parties

4. For more on this subject see for instance, Mintzel, 1984.
5. On top of this another significant tactical problem faced the party, namely the lack of an effective champion amongst the occupying powers. Clearly the SED had the full support of the Soviet Union and, as discussed later in this chapter, the USA provided significant support to the CDU/CSU. By contrast, the SPD was relatively isolated. It had the support of the British Labour Government, but the United Kingdom's powers were clearly in decline at this time. Moreover the SPD's nationalism, neutrality, and resistance to the division of Germany created a certain degree of tension with the direction of British Foreign policy as pursued by Foreign Minister Ernest Bevin. Finally, the return of a Conservative Government in 1951 meant that the fraternal ties that the SPD enjoyed with the Labour Party were of less importance than they had been in the 1940s.

8 Competition and Co-operation

6. For the discussion and use of the CPM approach to examine parties in the Federal Republic, see Lees (2005c).
7. I wish to thank Matthias Machnig and staff at the 1998 Kampa in Bonn for the briefing that informs this passage.

8. The most notable victim of this aspect of their work was Jost Stollmann (Schröder's economics advisor at the time, but not an SPD member) when he began to talk too explicitly about the need for supply-side reforms of the labour market in the last week of the 'hot stage' of the campaign.
9. The author wishes to thank the staff at CDU/CSU headquarters in Berlin for their briefing on campaign strategy and techniques in September 2002.
10. Other recent empirically useful models of coalition formation include those developed by Laver and Schofield (1990), and Budge and Keman (1990). Laver and Schofield build upon Grofman's (1982) 'protocoalition' model and argue that, when forming a coalition, parties initially attempt to form a protocoalition with the party nearest them ideologically. Protocoalitions are assumed to then try and grow sufficiently to ensure a winning position within the legislature. This 'bargaining approach' can be hierarchical (as Grofman originally suggested), or take place in a more rapacious and non-hierarchical manner. Stability is imposed by three structural attributes, relating to (i) the nature of the regime; (ii) the coalition itself; and (iii) the bargaining environment. Budge and Keman assume a more formal deductive approach, but also take into account institutional contexts. They develop a small set of empirically testable assumptions that are assumed to sustain successful coalition formation and maintenance.
11. This is the case if we treat the CDU/CSU as a single party at the national (Bundestag) level, which – as discussed in earlier chapters – the two parties effectively are.
12. Country respondents were asked two questions: the first relating to extent to which coalition discipline extends to parliamentary votes on legislation and the second to the extent to which coalition discipline also extends to other aspects of parliamentary life, such as the questioning of Ministers, the activities of investigative committees, appointments, and so on. Respondents were able to answer on a 4 point scale: 1 ('Yes always'), 2 ('Yes, on all matters except those explicitly exempted'), 3 ('No, except those matters explicitly specified'), and 4 ('No').
13. To the question 'Is the coalition based on a substantial and explicit policy agreement', respondents could answer 0 ('No explicit agreement'), 1 ('On a few selected policies'), 2 ('On a variety of issues but not comprehensive'), or 3 ('Comprehensive policy platform').
14. It might be argued that ministries that oversee such key policy areas and large budgets as health or agriculture are not second order ministries at all. However, it is generally agreed that first order ministries are those of finance, foreign affairs, environment, defence, transport and the interior. See Müller and Strøm, 2003, for a useful generic ranking of specific ministries in a comparative context.
15. The position of State Minister (as the position is called in the Chancellor's Office and Foreign Ministry) and State Secretary (*Staatssekretär*) is vitally important politically. State Secretaries and State Ministers must be members of the Bundestag (MdB's) and their job is threefold: first, to co-ordinate and support the political leadership function of the Minister; second, to serve as a conduit between the Ministry and the Bundestag; and, finally, to represent the Minister publicly, where appropriate. Of these three, the key activity is as a conduit to parliament – not only to parliamentary factions and working groups, but also to the powerful committees that shadow each ministry. The position of State Secretary has increasingly become a tool of patronage for the Chancellor in particular: hence the appointment of Bury. As a result of this patronage function the number of State Secretaries has increased over the years (Ismayr, 1997: 402).

Bibliography

Alber, J. (1985) 'Modernisierung, neue Spannungslinien und die politischen Chancen der Grünen', *Politische Vierteljahresschrift*, 26, 3: 211–26.

Aldrich, J. H. (1993) Rational choice and Turnout, *American Journal of Political Science*, 37(1): 246–78.

Allardt, E. and Rokkan, S. (1970) *Mass Politics*. New York: Free Press.

Allison, P. (1992) *Event History Analysis*, 8th Edn. Beverly Hills: Sage.

Almond, G. (1956) 'Comparative political systems', *Journal of Politics*, 18: 391–409.

Anderson, M. (1981) *Windhorst: A Political Biography*. Oxford: Oxford University Press.

Andersen, V. and Woyke, W. (1997) *Handwörterbuch des politischen Systems der Bundesrepublik Deutschland*. Bonn: Bundeszentrale für politische Bildung.

Aron, R. (1957) *The Opium of the Intellectual*. London: Secker and Warburg.

Arrow, K. J. (1951) *Social Choice and Individual Values*. New York: John Wiley and Sons.

Axelrod, R. (1970) *Conflict of Interest*. Chicago: Markham.

Baker, K., Dalton, R. and Hildebrandt, K. (1981) *Germany Transformed: Political Culture and the New Politics*. Cambridge, MA: Harvard University Press.

Bardi, L. and Molino, L. (1994) 'Italy: tracing the roots of the Great Transformation', in Katz, R. and Maier, P. (eds) *How Parties Organise*. London: Sage.

Bark, D. and Gress, D. (1993) *A History of West Germany 1: from Shadow to Substance*, 2nd Edn. Oxford: Blackwell.

Barnes, S. and Kaase, M. (eds) (1979) *Political Action*. Beverly Hills: Sage.

Barry, B. (1979) 'Is democracy special?', in Laslett, P. and Fishkin, J. (eds) *Philosophy, Politics and Society*. Oxford: Blackwell.

Bartels, L. M. (1993) 'Messages received: the political impact of media exposure', *American Political Science Review*, 87: 267–85.

Bartolini, S. (2000) *The Political Mobilisation of the European Left: 1860–1980. The Class Cleavage*. Cambridge: Cambridge University Press.

Beck, U. (1986) *Risikogesellschaft. Auf dem Weg in eine andere Moderne*. Frankfurt a.M: Suhrkamp.

Becker, R. (2002) 'Voter participation in the 1998 Bundestag elections: a theoretical modification and empirical application of Downs' theory of voter participation', *German Politics*, 11, 2: 39–87.

Berelson, B., Lazarsfeld, P. and McPhee, W. (1954) *Voting: A Study of Opinion Formation in a Presidential Campaign*. Chicago: University of Chicago Press.

Berglund, S. and Lindstrom, U. (1979) 'The Scandinavian party system(s) in transition(?): a macro-level analysis', *European Journal of Political Research*, 7: 187–204.

Berglund, S. (1994) 'The breakdown of the German Democratic Republic', in Berglund, S. and Dellenbrant, J-Å. (eds), *The New Democracies in Eastern Europe: Party Systems and Political Cleavages*, 2nd Edn. Aldershot: Edward Elgar.

Betz, G. (1999) 'The evolution and transformation of the German party system', in Allen, C. (ed.) *Tranformation of the German Political Party System: Institutional Crisis or Democratic Renewal?* Oxford: Berghan.

Betz, H-G. (1990) 'Value change and postmaterialist politics: the case of West Germany', *Comparative Political Studies*, 23, 2: 239–56.

Beyme, K. von (1993) *Das politische System der Bundesrepublik Deutschland nach der Vereinigung*. Munich: Piper.

Black, D. (1948) 'On the rationale of group decision making', *Journal of Political Economy*, 56: 23–34.

Bobo, L. (1983) 'Whites' opposition to busing: symbolic racism or realistic group conflict?', *Journal of Personality and Social Psychology*, 45: 1196–210.

Boll, B. (1995) 'Media communication and personality marketing: the 1994 German national election campaign', in Roberts, G. (ed.) *Superwahljahr: the German Elections in 1994*. London: Frank Cass.

Bowler, S. and Farrell, D. (1992) *Electoral Strategies and Political Marketing*. Basingstoke: Macmillan.

Breuilly, J. (1985) 'Liberalism or Social Democracy. A comparison of British and German Labour politics *c*. 1850–1875', *European History Quarterly*, 15: 3–42.

Brittan, S. (1975) 'The economic contradictions of democracy', *British Journal of Political Science*, 5: 129–59.

Browne, E. (1973) *Coalition Theories: A Logical And Empirical Critique*. Beverly Hills, London: Sage.

Brozcat, M. (1981) *The Hitler State*. Harlow: Longman.

Budge, I., Robertson, D. And Hearl, D. (eds) (1987) *Ideology, Strategy and Party Change: Spatial Analyses of Post-War Election Programmes in 19 Democracies*. Cambridge: Cambridge University Press.

Budge, I. and Hofferbert, R. (1990) 'Mandates and policy outputs: US party platforms and federal expenditures 1950–1985', *American Political Science Review*, 84: 111–31.

Budge, I. and Keman, H. (1990) *Parties and Democracy: Coalition Formation and Government Functioning in Twenty States*. New York, Oxford: Oxford University Press.

Budge, I., Newton, K., McKinley, R. D., Kirchner, E., Urwin, D., Armingeon, K. *et al.* (1997) *The Politics of the New Europe: Atlantic to Urals*. London: Longman.

Budge, I., Klingemann, H-D., Volkens, A., Bara, J. and Tanenbaum, E. (2001) *Mapping Policy Preferences: Estimates for Parties, Electors, and Governments 1945–1998*. Oxford: Oxford University Press.

Bulmer, S. (1983) 'Domestic politics and European Community policy making', *Journal of Common Market Studies*, XXI, 4: 349–63.

Bulmer, S. and Paterson, W. (1987) *The Federal Republic of Germany and The European Community*. London: Allen and Unwin.

Bündnis'90/Die Grünen (1998) *Programme zur Bundestagswahl 98*. Bonn: Bündnis 90/Die Grünen.

Bündnis 90/Die Grünen (2002) *Grün Wirkt!. Unser Wahlprogramm 2002–2006*. Berlin: Bündnis 90/Die Grünen.

Bürklin, W. (1987) 'Governing left parties: frustrating the radical non-established left: the rise and inevitable decline of the Greens', *European Sociological Review*, 3: 109–26.

Butler, D. and Ranney, A. (eds) (1992) *Electioneering: a Comparative Study of Continuity and Change*. Oxford: Oxford University Press.

Butler, D. and Stokes, D. (1969) *Political Change in Britain: Forces Shaping Electoral Choice*. New York: St. Martin's.

Campbell, A., Converse, P., Miller, W. and Stokes, D. (1960) *The American Voter*. New York: Wiley.

Campbell A., Converse, P., Miller, W. and Stokes, D. (1966) *Elections and the Political Order*. New York: Wiley.

Carmines, E. and Huckfeldt, R. (1998) 'Political behaviour: an overview', in Goodin, R. and Klingemann, H.-D. (eds) *A New Handook of Political Science*. Oxford: Oxford University Press.

Carr, W. (1991) *A History of Germany: 1815–1990*. London and New York: Edward Arnold.

Castles, F. and Mair, P. (1984) 'Left-right political scales: some "expert" judgments', *European Journal of Political Research*, 12: 73–88.

CDU (1998) '*Zukunftsprogramme der Christlich Demokratischen Union Deutschlands*'. Bonn.

CDU/CSU (1998) '*1998–2002 Wahl-platform*'. Bonn.

CDU/CSU (2002) *Leistung und Sicherheit. Zeit für Taten. Regierungsprogramm 2002/6*. Berlin.

Chandler, W. (1988) 'Party system transformation in the Federal Republic of Germany', in Wolinetz, S. (ed.) *Parties and Party Systems in Liberal Democracies*. London: Routledge.

Checkel, J. T. and Moravcsik, A. (2001) 'A Constructivist Research Programme in EU Studies?', *European Union Politics*, 2, 2: 219–49.

Claggett, W., Loesch, J., Phillips Shivley, W. and Snell, R. (1982) 'Political leadership and the development of political cleavages: Imperial Germany, 1871–1912', *American Journal of Political Science*, 26, 4: 643–63.

Conradt, D. (1990) 'The electorate 1980–83' in Corny, K. H. (ed.) *Germany at the Polls*. Durham, NC: Duke University Press.

Conradt, D. and Dalton, R. (1988) 'The West German electorate and the party system', *Review of Politics*, 50: 3–29.

Converse, P. and Valen, H. (1971) 'Dimensions of cleavage and perceived party distance in Norwegian voting'. *Scandinavian Political Studies*, 6: 107–52

Crewe, I. (1985) 'Introduction. Electoral change in western democracies: a framework for analysis', in Crewe, I. and Denver, D. (eds) *Electoral Change in Western Democracies: Patterns and Sources of Electoral Volatility*. London: Croom Helm.

Curtice, J. (1997) 'Is "The Sun" shining on Tony Blair? The electoral influence of British newspapers', *Press/Politics*, 2: 9–26.

Curtice, J. and Semetko, H. (1994) 'Does it matter what the papers say?', in Heath, A. F., Jowell, R. and Curtice, J. (eds) *Labour's Last Chance? The 1992 Election and Beyond*. Aldershot: Dartmouth.

Cusak, T. (1999) 'The shaping of popular satisfaction with government and regime performance in Germany', *British Journal of Political Science*, 22: 641–72.

Cutright, P. (1967) 'Inequality: a cross-national analysis', *American Sociological Review*, 32: 562–78.

Daalder, H. (1966) 'Parties, elites, and political developments in Western Europe', in LaPolambara, J. and Weiner, M. (eds) *Political Parties and Political Development*. Princeton: Princeton University Press.

Dahl, R. (1956) *A Preface to Democratic Theory*. Chicago: University of Chicago Press.

Dahl, R. (1961) *Who Governs?* New Haven: Yale Unversity Press.

Dahl, R. and Lindblom, C. (1953) *Politics, Economics and Welfare*. New York: Harper and Brothers.

Dahrendorf, R. (1967) *Society and Democracy in Germany*. London: Weidenfeld and Nicolson.

Dalton, R. (1996) *Citizen Politics: Public Opinion and Political parties in Advanced Industrial Democracies*, 2nd Edn. Chatham, NJ: Chatham House.

Dalton, R. and Kuechler, M. (eds) (1990) *Challenging the Political Order: New Social and Political Movements in Western Democracies*. Oxford: Oxford University Press.

Dalton R. and Bürklin, W. (1992) 'Two German electorates?', in Smith, G. and Patterson, W. (eds) *Developments in German Politics*. Basingstoke: Macmillan.

Dalton, R., Flanasan, S. C., Beck, P. A. and Alt, J. E. (1984) *Electoral Change in Advanced Industrial Democracies*. Princeton; Guildford: Princeton University Press.

Dalton, R., McCallister, I. and Wattenberg, M. (2002) 'The consequences of partisan dealignment', in Dalton, R. and Wattenberg, M. (eds) *Parties Without Partisans: Electoral Change in Advanced Industrial Democracies*. Oxford: Oxford University Press.

Dekker, P. (1994) 'Intergenerational ideological change and politics in the Netherlands', World Congress of Political Science, IPSA (unpublished).

De-news@listserv.gmd.de

Denzin, N. (1970) *Sociological Methods: a Sourcebook*. Chicago, IL: Aldine.

Der Spiegel magazine. 20/12/97: 'Stimmung Für Rot-Grün': 35 19/01/04: 'Pangrama': 21.

de Swaan, A. (1973) *Coalition Theories and Cabinet Formation*. Amsterdam, Oxford: Elsevier.

de Toqueville, A. (1990) *Democracy in America I-II*. New York: Vintage Books.

Diaz, V. (1991) *The Church and Religion in Contemporary Spain*. Madrid: Instituto Juan March.

Diekmann, A. and Weick, S. (eds) (1993) *Der Familienzyklus als sozialer Prozeß. Bevölkerungssoziologische Untersuchungen mit den Methoden der Ereignisanalyse*. Berlin: Dunckler und Humblot.

Die Republikaner, (2002) *'Bundesparteiprogramme die Republikaner: Sozial, Patriotisch, Ökologisch'*. München.

Di Palma, G. (1973) *The Study of Conflict in Western Society: A Critique of the End of Ideology*. Morristown: General Learning Press.

Dogan, M. (2000) 'Class, religion, party. Triple decline of electoral cleavages in Western Europe', in Karvonen, L. and Kuhnle, S. (eds) *Party Systems and Voter Alignments Revisited*. London: Routledge.

Downs, A. (1957) *An Economic Theory of Democracy*. New York: Harper and Row.

Doyle, C. (2003) *Collins Dictionary of Marketing*. Glasgow: HarperCollins.

Dunleavy, P. and Husbands, C. (1985) *British Democracy at the Crossroads*. London: Allen and Unwin.

Durkheim, E. (1956) *Education and Sociology*. New York: Free Press.

Durkheim, E. (1979) *Essays on Morals and Education*. London: Routledge.

Duverger, M. (1954) *Political Parties*. New York: Wiley.

DVU (2003) *'Partei-programme: DVU'* München.

Eilders, C., Degenhardt, K., Hermann, P. and van der Lippe, M. (2004) 'Surfing the tide: Social Democracts and Greens stayed on top – casualties among other parties. An analysis of party- and issue-coverage in the national election campaign 2002', in Saalfeld, T. and Lees, C. (eds) *Bundestagwahl 2002: the Battle of the Candidates*. London: Frank Cass.

Eldersfeld, S. (1964) *Political Parties: a Behavioural Analysis*. Chicago: Rand-McNally.

Faas, T. and Maier, J. (2004) 'Chancellor-candidates in the 2002 televised debates', in Saalfeld, T. and Lees, C. (eds) *Bundestagwahl 2002: the Battle of the Candidates*. London: Frank Cass.

Falter, J. (1990) 'The First German Volkspartei: the social foundations of the NSDAP', in Rohe, K. (ed.) *Elections, Parties, and Political Tradition. Social Foundations of German Parties and Party Systems*. Oxford: Oxford University Press.

Falter, J. and Schoen, H. (1999) 'Wahlen und Wählerverhalten' in Ellwein, T. and Holtmann, E. (eds) *Fünfzig Jahre Bundesrepublik Deutschland: Rahmenbedingungen, Entwicklungen, Perspektiven* (PVS Sonderheft 30). Wiesbaden: Westdeutscher Verlag.

Farrell, D. (1996) 'Campaign strategies and tactics', in LeDuc, L., Niemi, R. S. and Norris, P. (eds) *Comparing Democracies*. Thousand Oaks, CA: Sage.

Farrell, D. and Webb, P. (2002) 'Political parties and campaign organisation', in Dalton, R. and Wattenberg, M. (eds) *Parties Without Partisans: Electoral Change in Advanced Industrial Democracies*. Oxford: Oxford University Press.

FDP (2002) *Bürgerprogramme 2002*. Berlin.

Feist, U. and Liepelt, K. (1987) 'Modernisierung zu Lasten der Großen', *Journal für Sozialforschung*, 27, 3/4: 277–95.

Feld, L. and Kirchgässner, G. (2000) 'Official and hidden unemployment and the popularity of the government: an econometric analysis for the Kohl government', *Electoral Studies*, 19: 333–47.

Fiorina, M. (1990) 'Information and rationality in elections', in Ferejohn, J. and Kuklinski, J. (eds) in *Information and Democratic Processes*. Chicago: University of Illinois Press.

Flanagan, S. (1973) Models and methods of analysis', in Almond, G., Flanasan, S. and Mundt, R. J. (eds) *Crisis, Choice and Change: Historical Studies of Political Development*. Boston: Little, Brown.

Flanagan, S. (1982) 'Changing values in advanced industrial society', *Comparative Political Studies*, 14: 403–44.

Flanagan, S. (1987) 'Value change in industrial society', *American Political Science Review*, 81: 1303–19.

Flynn, R. (1983) 'Co-optation and strategic planning in the local state', in King, R. (ed.) *Capital and Politics*. London: Routledge.

Forschungsgruppe Wahlen (1991) 'Gesamtdeutsche Bestätigung für die Bonner Regierungskoalition. Eine Analyse der Bundestagswahl 1990', in Klingemann, H.-D. and Kaase, M. (eds) (1994) *Wahlen und Wähler. Analysen aus Anlaß der Bundestagswahl 1990*. Opladen: Leske und Budrich.

Forschungsgruppe Wahlen. Various datasets 1970–98. Mannheim.

Forschungsgruppe Wahlen (2002) 'Bundestagswahl. Eine Analyse der Wahl vom 22 September 2002'. Mannheim: FGW Nr. 108.

FT Deutschland, 16/10/2002 'Koalitionsvertras Bedentet'; Seite 13.

Gabriel, O. (1997) 'Parteiidentifikation, Kandidaten und politische Sachfragen als Bestimmungsfaktoren des Parteienwettbewerbs', in Gabriel, O., Niedermayer, O. and Stöss, R. (eds) *Parteiendemokratie in Deutschland*. Opladen: Westdeutsche Verlag.

Gallagher, M., Laver, M. and Mair, P. (2001) *Representative Government in Western Europe*. New York: McGraw Hill.

Gamson, W. (1961) 'A Theory Of Coalition Formation', in *American Sociological Review*, 26: 373–82.

Gibowski, W. (1995) 'Germany's general election in 1994: who voted for whom?', in Conradt, P., Kleinfeld, G., Romoser, G. and Soe, C. *Germany's New Politics: Parties and Issues in the 1990s*. Oxford: Berghan.

Gibowski, W. (1999) 'Social change and the electorate: an analysis of the 1998 Bundestagswahl' in Padgett, S. and Saalfeld, T. (eds) *Bundestagswahl '98: End of an Era?* Special issue of *German Politics*, 8, 2: 10–32.

Glaser, J. (1994) 'Back to the black belt: racial environment and white racial attitudes in the South', *Journal of Politics*, 56: 21–41.

Gluchowski, P. and von Wilamowitz-Moellendorff, U. (1997) 'Sozialstrukturelle Grundlagen des Parteienwettbewerbs in der Bundesrepublik Deutschland', in Gabriel, O. *et al.* (eds) *Parteiendemokratie in Deutschland*. Opladen: Westdeutsche Verlag.

Goetz, K. (2003) 'Government at the centre', in Padgett, S., Smith, G. and Paterson, W. (eds) *Developments in German Politics, 3*. Basingstoke: Palgrave.

Goldthorpe, J., Lockwood, D., Bechhofer, F. and Platt, J. (1969) *The Affluent Worker in the Class Structure*. London: Cambridge University Press.

Gotto, K. (1983) 'Zum Selbstverständnis der katholischen Kirche im Jahre 1945', in Albrecht, D., Hockerts, H. G., Mikat, P. and Morsey, R. (eds) *Politik und Konfession. Festschrift für K. Repgen zum 60. Geburtstag*. Berlin: Dunker und Humblot.

Grabow, K. (2001) 'The re-emergence of the Cadre party? Organisational patterns of Christian and Social Democrats in Unified Germany', in *Party Politics*, 7, 1: 23–43.

Grofman, B. (1982) 'A dynamic model of protocoalition formation in ideological *n*-space', in *Behavioural Science*, 27: 77–90.

Gunlicks, A. (2003) *The Länder and German Federalism*. Manchester: Manchester University Press.

Gunther, R. and Diamond, L. (2003) 'Species of political parties: a new typology', in *Party Politics*, 9, 2: 167–99.

Hall, P. (1986) *Governing the Economy*. Oxford: Oxford University Press.

Hall, P. (1989) *The Power of Economic Ideas*. Princeton: Princeton University Press.

Hay, C. (1995) 'Structure and agency', in Marsh, D. and Stoker, G. (eds) *Theory and Methods in Political Science*. Basingstoke: Macmillan.

Hofferbert, R. and Klingemann, H.-D. (1990) 'The policy impact of party programmes and government declarations in the Federal Republic of Germany', in *European Journal of Political Research*, 18: 277–304.

Holzhacker, R. (1999) 'Campaign communication and strategic responses to change in the electoral environment', in *Party Politics*, 5, 4: 439–69.

Hopkin, J. (2002) 'Comparative methods', in Marsh, D. and Stoker, G. (eds) *Theory and Methods in Political Science*, 2nd Edn. Basingstoke: Palgrave.

Hough, D. (2002) *The Fall and Rise of the PDS in Eastern Germany*. Birmingham: Birmingham University Press.

http://speigel.de/wirtschaft

http://www.wahlrecht.de

Huckfeldt, R. and Sprague, J. (1995) *Citizens, Politics, and Social Communication. Information and Influence in an Election Campaign*. Cambridge: Cambridge University Press.

Hülsberg, W. (1988) *The German Greens*. London: Verso.

Hunt, R. N. (1964) *German Social Democracy 1918–1933*. New Haven, CT: Yale University Press.

Ikenberry, G. J. (1988) 'Conclusion: an institutional approach to American foreign economic policy', in Ikenberry, G. J., Lake, D. A. and Mastanduno, M. (eds) *The State and American Foreign Economic Policy*. Ithaca, NY: Cornell University Press.

Ingelhart, R. (1977) *The Silent Revolution: Changing Values and Political Styles among Western Publics*. Princeton, NJ: Princeton University Press.

Ingelhart, R. (1981) 'Postmaterialism in an environment of insecurity', *American Political Science Review*, 75: 880–900.

Ingelhart, R. (1990) *Culture Shift in Advanced Industrial Society*. Princeton, NJ: Princeton University Press.

Inkeles, A. and Smith, D. (1974) *Becoming Modern: Individual Change in Six Developing Countries*. Cambridge, MA: Harvard University Press.

Irish, M. and Prothro, J. (1971) *The Politics of American Democracy*, 5th Edn. Eaglewood Cliffs, NJ: Prentice Hall.

Ismayr, W. (1997) *Der Deutsche Bundestag im politischen System der Bundesrepublik Deutschland*. Opladen: Leske & Budrich.

Iyengar, S. (1991) *Is Anyone Responsible?* Chicago: University of Chicago Press.

Iyengar, S. and Reeves, R. (eds) (1997) *Do the Media Govern? Politicians, Voters, and Reporters in America*. Thousand Oaks, CA: Sage.

Janda, K. (1980) *Political Parties: A Cross-National Survey*. New York: Free Press.

Jeffery, C. (1994) *The Länder Strike Back: Structures and Procedures of European Integration Policy Making in the German Federal System*. Centre for Federal Studies, University of Leicester, Discussion Papers in Federal Studies No. FS94/4.

Jeffery, C. and Savigear, P. (eds) (1991) *German Federalism Today*. Leicester: Leicester University Press: 28.

Jeffery, C. and Collins, S. (1998) 'The German *Länder* and EU enlargement: between apple pie and issue-linkage', in *German Politics* 7, 2: 86–101.

Jeffery, C. and Lees, C. (1998) 'Whither the Old Order? the collapse of the GDR and the 'new' German party system', in Davies, P. and White, J. (eds) *Political Parties and the Collapse of Old Orders*. New York: SUNY Press.

Johnson, N. (1983) *State and Government in the Federal Republic of Germany*. Oxford: Pergamon Press.

Jun, U. (1994) *Koalitionsbildung in den deutschen Bundesländern. Theoretische Betrachtungen, Dokumentation und Analyse*. Opladen: Leske und Budrich.

Kaack, H. (1995) 'Functions of party programmes', in Thesing, J. and Hofmeister, W. (eds) *Political Parties in Democracy*. Sankt Augustin: Konrad Adenauer Stiftung.

Kaase, M. and Klingemann, H-D. (1994) 'The cumbersome way to partisan orientations in a "New" Democracy: the case of the former GDR', in Jennings, M. and Mann, T. E. (eds) *Elections at Home and Abroad*. Ann Arbor: University of Michigan Press.

Katz, R. and Mair, P. (1992) 'The membership of political parties in European democracies, 1960–1990', in *European Journal of Political Research*, 22: 329–45.

Katz, R. and Mair, P. (1995) 'Changing models of party organisation and party democracy: the emergence of the Cartel Party'. *Party Politics*, 1, 1: 5–28.

Katzenstein, P. (1987) *Policy and Politics in West Germany: The Growth of a Semisovereign State*. Philadelphia: Temple University Press.

Kenny, C. (1994) 'The microenvironment of attitude change', *Journal of Politics*, 56: 715–28.

Key, V. (1964) *Politics, Parties, and Pressure Groups*. New York: Crowell.

Key, V. and Munger, F. (1959) 'Social determinism and electoral decision: the case of Indiana', in Burdick, E. and Brodbeck, A. (eds) *American Voting Behaviour*. Glencoe: Free Press.

King, D. S. (1995) *Actively Seeking Work. The Politics of Unemployment and Welfare Policy in the United States*. Chicago: University of Chicago Press.

King, R. (1983) 'The political practice of local capitalist associations', in King, R. (ed.) *Capital and Politics*. London: Routledge.

Kirchgässner, G. (1986) 'Economic conditions and the popularity of West German parties: a survey', *European Journal of Political Research*, 14: 421–39.

Kirchheimer, O. (1966) 'The transformation of the Western European party systems' in La Palombara, J. and Wiener, M. (eds) *Political Parties and Political Development*. Princeton, Guildford: Princeton University Press.

Kitschelt, H. (1986) 'Political opportunity structures and political protest: anti-nuclear movements in four democracies', in *British Journal of Political Science*, 16, 1.

Kitschelt, H. (1989) *The Logics of Party Formation*. Ithaca, NY: Cornell University Press.

Kitschelt, H. (1994) *The Transformation of European Social Democracy*. Cambridge: Cambridge University Press.

Knutsen, O. (1995) 'Party choice', in van Deth, J. and Scarbrough, E. (eds) *The Impact of Values*. Oxford: Oxford University Press.

Koga, K. and Nagatani, H. (1974) 'Voter antagonism and the paradox of voting', in *Econometrica*, 42: 1045–67.

Korpi, W. (1983) *The Democratic Class Struggle*. London: Routledge and Kegan Paul.

Kramer, G. H. (1973) 'On a class of equilibrium conditions for majority rule', in *Econometrica*, 41: 285–97.

Krasner, S. (1988) 'Approaches to the State: alternative conceptions and historical dynamics', in *Comparative Political Studies*, 21: 223–46.

Krehbiel, K. (1988) 'Spatial models of legislative choice', *Legislative Studies Quarterly*, 3: 259–319.

Kropp, S. and Sturm, R. (1998) *Koalitionen und Koalitionsvereinbarungen: Theorie, Analyse, und Dokumentation*. Opladen: Leske und Budrich.

Kühnel, S. and Fuchs, D. (1998) 'Nichtwählen als rationales Handeln: Anmerkungen zum Nutzen des Rational-Choice-Ansatzes in der empirischen Wahlforschung II', in Kaase, M. and Klingemann, H.-D. (eds) *Wahlen und Wählen: Analysen aus Anlass der Bundestagswahl 1994*. Opladen: Westdeutscher Verlag.

Kühr, H. (1982) 'Lokalpartei und Kirche', in Kühr, H. and Simau, K. (eds) *Lokalpartei und vorpolitischer Raum*. Melle: Knoth.

Landman, T. (2000) *Issues and Methods in Comparative Politics: An Introduction*. London and New York: Routledge.

Lane, J.-E. and Ersson, S. (1999) *Politics and Society in Western Europe*, 4th Edn. London: Sage.

Lane, R. (1965) *Political Life: Why and How People Get Involved in Politics*. New York: Free Press.

Langguth, G. (1984) *Der grüne Faktor*. Zurich: Edition Interfrom.

Laver, M. and Budge, I. (1992) *Party Policy and Coalition Government*. London: Macmillan.

Laver, M. and Hunt, B. (1992) *Policy and Party Competition*. New York: Routledge.

Laver, M. and Schofield, N. (1990) *Multi-Party Government: The Politics of Coalition in Europe*. Oxford: Oxford University Press.

Laver, M. and Shepsle, K. A. (1990) 'Coalitions and Cabinet Government', in *American Political Science Review*, 84: 873–90.

Laver, M. and Shepsle, K. A. (1995) *Making and Breaking Governments: Cabinets and Legitimacy in Parliamentary Democracies*. Cambridge: Cambridge University Press.

Lazarsfeld, P., Bereleson, B. and Gaudet, H. (1944) *The People's Choice*. New York: Columbia University Press.

Lazarsfeld, P., Berelson, B. and Gaudet, H. (1968) *The People's Choice. How the Voter Makes up His Mind in a Presidential Campaign*, 3rd Edn. New York: Columbia University Press.

Lees, C. (1995a) *Paradise Postponed: An Assessment of Ten Years of Governmental Participation by the German Green Party*. Institute for German Studies, University of Birmingham, Discussion Papers in German Studies, No. IGS95/4.

Lees, C. (1995b) 'Bringing the PDS into the coalition equation', *German Politics* 4, 1: 150–4.

Lees, C. (1996) 'A watershed election: the Berlin State and City elections of 22 October 1995', *Regional and Federal Studies*, 6, 1: 63–72.

Lees, C. (1998) *Red-Green Coalitions in the Federal Republic of Germany: Models of Coalition Formation and Maintenance*. Unpublished thesis, Birmingham University.

Lees, C. (1999) 'The Red-Green Coalition', Padgett, S. and Saalfeld, T. (eds) *Bundestagswahl '98: The End of an Era*. Special issue of *German Politics*, 8, 2: 174–94.

Lees, C. (2000) *The Red-Green Coalition in Germany: Politics, Personalities, and Power*. Manchester: Manchester University Press.

Lees, C. (2001) 'Coalitions – beyond the Politics of Centrality?' in Padgett, S. and Poguntke, T. (eds) *Continuity and Change in German Politics: Beyond the Politics of Centrality. A Festschrift for Gordon Smith*. Special issue of *German Politics*, 10, 2: 117–34.

Lees, C. (2002) 'Dark matter: institutional constraints and the failure of party-based Euroscepticism in Germany', *Political Studies*, 50, 2: 244–67.

Lees, C. (2005a) 'The limits of party-based Euroscepticism in Germany', in Taggart, P. and Szczerbiak, A. (eds) *Opposing Europe* (Vol. 2). Cambridge: Cambridge University Press.

Lees, C. (2005b) 'Environmental policy: the law of diminishing returns?', in Paterson, W. and Green, S. (eds) *The Semisovereign State Revisited*. Cambridge: Cambridge University Press.

Lees, C. (2005c) 'Political marketing in Germany', in Lees-Marshment, J. and Lilleker, D. (eds) *Political Marketing in Comparative Perspective*. Manchester: Manchester University Press.

Lees-Marshment, J. (2001) 'The product, sales, and market-oriented party: how Labour learnt to market the product, not just the presentation', in *European Journal of Marketing* 35, 9/10: 1074–84.

Lehmbruch, G. and Schmitter, P. (eds), (1982) *Patterns of Corporatist Policy-Making*. London: Sage.

Leiserson, M. (1968) 'Factions and coalitions in one-party Japan', *American Political Science Review*, 68: 770–87.

Lenski, G. (1966) *Power and Privilege: A Theory of Social Stratification*. New York: McGraw-Hill.

Lewis-Beck, M. and Paldam, M. (2000) 'Economic voting: an introduction', *Electoral Studies*, 19: 113–21.

Lijphart, A. (1968) *The Politics of Accomodation: Pluralism and Democracy in the Netherlands*, 2nd Edn. Berkeley: University of California Press.

Lijphart, A. (1971) 'Comparative politics and the comparative method'. *American Political Science Review*, 65: 652–93.

Linz, J. (1967) 'Cleavage and consensus in West German politics', in Lipset, S. and Rokkan, S. (eds) *Party Systems and Voter Alignments: Cross-National Perspectives*. New York: Free Press.

Lipset, S. and Rokkan, S. (1967) 'Cleavage structures, party systems, and voter alignments: an introduction', in Lipset, S. and Rokkan, S. (eds) *Party Systems and Voter Alignments: Cross-National Perspectives*. New York: Free Press.

Loewenberg, G. (1968) 'The making of the German party system: political and socio-economic factors', *Polity*, 1: 86–113.

Lukin, D. and Lightfoot, S. (1999) 'Environmental taxation in contemporary European politics', *Contemporary Politics*, 5, 3: 243–62.

Machnig, M. (1999) 'Die Kampa als SPD-Wahlkampfzentrale der Bundestagswahl '98: Organisation, Kampagnenformen und Erforlgsfaktoren', in *Forschungsjournal NSB*, 12, 3: 20–39.

Mackie, T. and Marsh, D. (1995) 'The comparative method', in Marsh, D. and Stoker, G. (eds) *Theory and Methods in Political Science*. Basingstoke: Macmillan.

MacKuen, M. and Brown, C. (1987) Political context and attitude change', *American Political Science Review*, 81: 471–90.

Maier, J. and Rattinger, H. (1999) 'Economic conditions and the 1994 and 1998 Federal elections', *German Politics*, 8, 2: 33–47.

Maier, J. and Rattinger, H. (2004) 'Economic conditions and voting behaviour in German Federal Elections, 1994–2002', in Saalfeld, T. and Lees, C. (eds) *Bundestagwahl 2002: the Battle of the Candidates*. London: Frank Cass.

Mair, P. and Smith, G. (eds) (1990) *Understanding Party System Change in Western Europe*. London: Frank Cass.

Mair, P. and van Biezen, I. (2001) 'Party membership in twenty European democracies, 1980–2000', *Party Politics*, 7, 1: 5–21.

March, J. G. and Olsen, J. P. (1984) 'The new institutionalism: organisational factors in political life', *American Political Science Review*, 78: 738.

Markovits, A. S. and Gorski, P. S. (1993). *The German Left: Red, Green and Beyond*. Cambridge: Polity Press.

Marsh, D. and Furlong, P. (2002) 'A skin not a sweater: ontology and epistemology in political science', in Marsh, D. and Stoker, G. (eds) *Theory and Methods in Political Science*, 2nd Edn. Basingstoke: Palgrave.

Marsh, D. and Stoker, G. (eds) (1996) *Theory and Methods in Political Science*. Basingstoke: Macmillan.

Maslow, A. (1954) *Motivations and Personality*. New York: Harper and Row.

Matheson, D. (1979) *Ideology. Political Action and the Finnish Working Class: A Survey Study of Political Behaviour*. Helsinki: Societas Scientiarium Fennica.

Metje, M. (1994) *Wählerschaft und Sozialstruktur im Generationswechsel*. Wiesbaden: Westdeutscher Verlag.

Merten, K. (1994) 'Wirkungen von kommunication' in Merten, K., Schmidt, S. J. and Weischenberg, S. (Hrsg) *Die Wirklichkeit der Medien*. Opladen: Leske und Budrich.

Michels, R. (1915) *Zur Sociologie des Parteiwesens in der modernen Demokratie*. Berlin, Leipzig, Stuttgart: Union Deutsche Verlagsgesellschaft.

Miller, W. (1956) 'One-party politics and the voter', *American Political Science Review*, 83: 1125–45.

Miller, W. and Levitin, T. (1976) *Leadership and Change*. Cambridge, MA: Winthrop.

Mintzel, A. (1984) *Die Volkspartei. Typus und Wirklichkeit*. Opladen: Leske und Budrich.

Mueller, D. C. (1996) *Constitutional Democracy*. Oxford: Oxford University Press.

Müller, W. (1996) 'Die Organisation der SPÖ, 1945–95', in Maderthaner, W. and Müller, W. (eds) *Die Organisation der Österreichischen Demokratie*. Vienna: Löcker Verlag.

Müller, W. and Strøm, K. (2003) 'Coalition governance in Western Europe', in Müller, W. and Strøm, K. (eds) *Coalition Governments in Western Europe*. Oxford: Oxford University Press.

Müller-Rommell, F. (1984) 'Die Grünen im Licht von neuesten Ergebnissen der Wahlforschung', in Kluge, T. (ed.) *Grüne Politik*. Frankfurt: Fischer.

Müller-Rommel, F. (1993) *Grüne Parteien in Westeuropa: Entwicklungsphasen und Erfolgsbedingungen*. Westdeutscher Verlag.

Müller-Rommel, F. and Poguntke, T. (1992) 'Die Grünen', in Mintzel, A. and Oberreuter, H. (eds) *Parteien in der Bundesrepublik Deutschland*. Opladen: Leske and Budrich.

Nannestad, P. and Paldam, M. (1994) 'The VP-function: a survey of the lierature on vote and popularity functions after 25 years', *Public Choice*, 79: 213–45.

Nataf, D. (1985) *The Electoral Ecology of Portugal 1976–1983* (unpublished).

Neumann, S. (1956) 'Towards a comparative study of political parties', in Neumann, S. (ed.) *Modern Political Parties*. Chicago: University of Chicago Press.

New York Herald Tribune. Newspaper. Interview with Parlor Maran Niemöller. 14/12/49.

Niedermayer, O. (1995) 'Party system change in East Germany', *German Politics*, 4, 3: 75–91.

Niemi, R. G. (1969) 'Majority decision making with partial unidimensionality', *American Political Science Review*, 63: 488–97.

Niffenegger, P. (1989) 'Strategies for success from the political marketeers', in *Journal of Consumer Marketing*, 6, 1: 45–61.

Noelle-Neumann, E. and Kocher, R. (1993) *Allensbacher Jahrbuch der Demoskopie*. Munich: Saur.

NPD (1999) '*NPD Europaprogramm 1999*', Berlin.

NPD (2002) '*NPD Kurzprogramm 2002*', Berlin.

Odmalm, P. and Lees, C. (2005) 'Getting ethnic questions on the agenda: party formation as a strategy for social movements', *Journal of Social Movement Studies*, Forthcoming.

OECD (1994) *OECD Employment Outlook: July 1994*. Paris: OECD.

Olson, M. (1965) *The Logic of Collective Action: Public Goods and the Theory of Groups*. Cambridge, MA: Harvard University Press.

Orizo, A. (1983) *Espana entre la Apatia y el Cambio Social*. Madrid: Mapfre.

Ostrom, E. (1986) 'An agenda for the study of institutions', *Public Choice*, 48: 3–25.

Padgett, S. (1995) 'Superwahljahr in the new Länder: polarisation in an open political market', in Roberts, G. (ed.) *Superwahljahr: the German Elections in 1994*. Special issue of *German Politics*, 4, 2: 75–94.

Padgett, S. (ed.) (1993) *Parties and Party Systems in the New Germany*. Aldershot: Dartmouth.

Padgett, S. and Burkett, T. (1986) *Political Parties and Elections in Western Germany*. London: Hurst/St. Martins.

Panebianco, A. (1988) *Political Parties: Organization and Power*. Cambridge: Cambridge University Press.

Pappi, F. (1984) 'The West German party system', *West European Politics*, 7: 7–26.

Pappi, F. (1998) 'Political behaviour: reasoning voters and multi-party systems', in Goodin, R. and Klingemann, H-D. (eds) *A New Handbook of Political Science*. Oxford: Oxford University Press.

Pappi, F.-U. (1985) 'Die konfessionale-religiöse Konfliktlinie in der deutschen Wählerschaft: Entstehung, Stabilität und Wandel', in Obendörfer, D., Rattinger, H. and Schmitt, K. (eds) *Wirtschaftlicher Wandel, religiöse Wandel und Wertwandel*. Berlin: Duncker und Humblot.

Parsons, T. (1978) *Action Theory and the Human Condition*. New York: Free Press.

Paterson, W. (1976) 'Social Democracy: the West German example', in Kolinsky, M. and Paterson, W. (eds) *Social and Political Movements in Western Europe*. London: Croom Helm.

Paterson, W. (1987) 'West Germany: between party apparatus and basis democracy', in Ware, A. (ed.) *Political Parties: Electoral Change and Structural Response*. Oxford: Blackwell.

Paterson, W. and Southern, D. (1991) *Governing Germany*. Oxford: Blackwell.

Patzeldt. W. (2004) 'Chancellor Schröder's approach to political and legislative leadership', in Lees, C. and Saalfeld, T. (eds) *Bundestagswahl 2002: the Battle of the Candidates*. London: Frank Cass.

Pennings, P. (2002) 'Voters, elections, and ideology', in Keman, H. (ed.) *Comparative Democratic Politics*. London: Sage.

Pennings, P., Keman, H. and Kleinnijenhuis, J. (1999) *Doing Research in Political Science. An Introduction to Comparative Methods and Statistics*. London: Sage.

Pesonen, P., (1973) 'Dimensions of political cleavage in multi-party systems', *European Journal of Political Research*, 1: 109–32.

Peters, B. G. (1998) 'Political institutions: old and new', in Goodin, R. E. and Klingemann, H-D. (eds) *A New Handbook of Political Science*. Oxford: Oxford University Press.

Popkin, S. (1991) *The Reasoning Voter*. Chicago: University of Chicago Press.

Pridham, G. (1977) *Christian Democracy In Western Germany*. London: Croom Helm.

Pulzer, P. (1975) *Political Representation and Elections in Britain*. London: Allen and Unwin.

Rae, D. and Taylor, M. (1970) *The Analysis of Political Cleavages*. New Haven, CT: Yale University Press.

Rattinger, H. (1995) 'Parteineigungen in Ostdeutschland vor und nach der Wende', in Bertram, H. (ed.) *Ostdeutschland im Wandel: Lebensverhältnisse – politische Einstellungen*. Opladen: Leske und Budrich.

Rattinger, H. (2000) 'Die Bürger und ihre Parteien', in Falter, J., Gabriel, O. W. and Rattinger, H. (eds) *Wirklich ein Volk?* Opladen: Leske und Budrich.

Read, M. and Marsh, D. (2002) 'Combining qualitative and quantitative methods', in Marsh, D. and Stoker, G. (eds) *Theory and Methods in Political Science*, 2nd Edn. Basingstoke: Palgrave.

Rhodes, R. (1988) *Beyond Westminster and Whitehall: the Sub-Central Governments of Britain*. London: Unwin Hyman.

Riesman, D., Denny, R. and Glazer, N. (1950) *The Lonely Crowd*. New Haven, CT: Yale University Press.

Riker, W. H. (1962) *The Theory of Political Coalitions*. New Haven, CT: Yale University Press.

Riker, W. H. (1964) *Federalism: Origin, Operation, Significance*. Boston, MA: Little Brown.

Riker, W. H. (1980) 'Implications from the disequilibrium of majority rule for the study of institutions', in *American Political Science Review*, 74: 432–46.

Riker, W. H. (1982) *Liberalism Against Populism*. San Francisco: W.H. Freeman.

Ritter, G. (1990) 'The social bases of the German political parties, 1867–1920', in Rohe, K. (ed.) *Elections, Parties, and Political Traditions: Social Foundations of German Parties and Party Systems, 1867–1987*. New York: Berg.

Roberts, G. (1997) *Party Politics in the New Germany*. London and Washington: Pinter.

Rogowski, R. (1981) 'Social class and partisanship in European electorates: a re-assessment', *World Politics*, 33: 639–49.

Rohe, K. (1997) 'Entwicklung der politischen Parteien und Parteiensysteme in Deutschland bis zum Jahre 1933', in Gabriel, O., Niedermayer, O. and Stöss, R. (eds) *Parteiendemokratie in Deutschland*. Opladen: Westdeutsche Verlag.

Rokkan, S. (1970) 'Nation-building, cleavage formation and the structuring of mass politics', in Rokkan, S. and Campbell, A. (eds) *Citizens, Elections, Parties: Approaches to Comparative Study of the Process of Development*. Oslo: Universitetsvorlaget.

Rokkan, S. (1970) 'Nation-building, cleavage formation and the structuring of mass politics'.

Rokkan, S. and Campbell, A. *Citizens, Elections, Parties: Approaches to Comparative Study of the Process of Development*. Oslo: Universitetsvorlaget.

Rönsch, H-D. (1980) 'Die Grünen: einmaliges Wahlrisiko oder soziale Bewegung?', *Gewerkschaftliche Monatshefte*, 31: 500–11.

Rosamond, B. (2000) *Theories of European Integration*. Basingstoke: Macmillan.

Rose, R. (1974) *Electoral Behaviour: A Comparative Handbook*. New York: Free Press.

Rose, R. (1991) *Bringing Freedom Back in: Rethinking Priorities of the Welfare State*. Glasgow: Centre for Public Policy, University of Strathclyde.

Rose, R. and Urwin, D. (1969) 'Social cohesion, political parties and strains in regimes', *Comparative Political Studies*, 2: 7–67.

Rose, R. and Urwin, D. (1970) 'Persistence and change in western party systems since 1945', *Political Studies*, 18: 287–319.

Saalfeld, T. (1999) 'Coalition politics and management in the Kohl era', in Padgett, S. and Saalfeld, T. (eds) *Bundestagswahl '98: The End of an Era?* Portland, London: Frank Cass.

Saalfeld, T. (2003) 'Stable parties, Chancellor democracy, and the art of informal settlement', in Müller, W. and Strøm, K. (eds) *Coalition Governments in Western Europe.* Oxford: Oxford University Press.

Sackman, A. (1996) 'The learning curve towards New Labour: Neil Kinnock's corporate party 1983–92, *European Journal of Marketing*, 30, 10/11: 147–58.

Samuelson, K. (1961) *Religion and Economic Activity.* New York: Harper and Row.

Sani, G. and Sartori, G. (1983) 'Polarisation, fragmentation, and competition in Western democracies', in Daalder, H. and Mair, P. (eds) *West European Party Systems: Continuity and Change.* London: Sage.

Sartori, G. (1962) *Democratic Theory.* Detroit: Wane State University Press.

Sartori, G. (1970) 'Concept misinformation in comparative politcs', in *American Political Science Review*, 64: 1033–53.

Sartori, G. (1994) *Comparative Constitutional Engineering: An Inquiry into Structures, Incentives and Outcomes.* New York: New York University Press.

Scammell, M. (1999) 'Political marketing: lessons for political science', in *Political Studies*, 47, 4: 718–39.

Scarbrough, E. (1995) 'Materialist-postmaterialist value orientations' in van Deth, J. and Scarbrough, E., *The Impact of Values.* Oxford: Oxford University Press.

Schäfers, B. (1995) *Gesellschaftlicher Wandel in Deutschland*, 6th Edn. Stuttgart: Enke.

Scharf, T. (1994) *The German Greens: Challenging the Consensus.* Oxford: Berg.

Scharpf, F. W. (1985) 'Die Politikverflechtungs-Falle: Europäische Integration und deutscher Föderalismus im Vergleich', in *Politische Vierteljahresschrift*, 26, 4: 346–50.

Scharpf, F. W. (1988) 'The Joint-Decision trap: lessons from German Federalism and European Integration', in *Public Administration*, 66 (Autumn): 239–78.

Scharpf, F. W. (1997) *Games Real Actors Play: Actor-centred Institutionalism in Policy Research.* Boulder: Westview Press.

Scheuch, E. (1969) 'Social context and individual behaviour', in Dogan, M. and Rokkan, S. (eds) *Quantitive Ecological Analysis in the Social Sciences.* Cambridge, MA: MIT Press.

Schmidt, K. (1990) 'Religious cleavages in the West German party system: persistence and change, 1949–1987' in Rohe, K. (ed.) *Elections, Parties, and Political Traditions: Social Foundations of German Parties and Party Systems, 1867–1987.* New York: Berg.

Schmidt, M. (2003) *Political Institutions in the Federal Republic of Germany.* Oxford: Oxford University Press.

Schmitt-Beck, R. (2003) 'Mass communication, personal communication and vote choice: the filter hypothesis of media influence in comparative perspective', *British Journal of Political Science*, 33: 233–59.

Schmitt-Beck, R., Weick, S. and Christoph, B. (2002) 'The influence of life-cycle events on partisanship: long-term evidence from the German socio-economic panel', paper presented to the 98th Annual Meeting of the American Political Science Assocation, Boston, 29 August–1 September, 2002.

Schmitter, P. and Grote, J. (1997) 'The corporatist sysyphus: past, present, and future', *EUI Working Papers*, SPS No. 97/4. Florence.

Schmitter, P. and Lehmbruch, G. (eds) (1979) *Trends towards Corporatist Interest Intermediation.* London: Sage.

Schneider, F. and Frey, B. (1988) 'Politico-economic models of macroeconomic policy: a review of the empirical evidence', in Willett, T. (ed.) *Political Business Cycles. The*

Political Economy of Money, Inflation, and Unemployment. Durham, NC: Duke University Press.

Schultze, R. (1987) 'Die Bundestagwahl 1987 – eine Bestätigung des Wandels', *Aus Politik und Zeitgeschichte*, B12/87: 3–17.

Schultze, R.-O. (1997) 'Wahlforschung', in Andersen, U. and Woyke, W. (eds) *Handwörterbuch des politischen Systems der Bundesrepublik Deutschland*. Bonn: Bundeszentrale für politische Bildung.

Schumpeter, J. (1943) *Capitalism, Socialism and Democracy*. London: Allen and Unwin.

Semetko, H. and Schoenbach, K. (1999) 'Parties, leaders, and issues in the news', in Padgett, S. and Saalfeld, T. (eds) *Bundestagswahl '98: End of an Era?* London: Frank Cass.

Sennett, R. (1978) *The Fall of Public Man: On the Social Psychology of Capitalism*. New York: Vintage Books.

Shapsley, L. S. and Shubik, M. (1969) 'Pure Competition, Coalitional Power and Fair Division', *International Economic Review*, 10, 3: 337–62.

Shepsle, K. A. (1979) 'Institutional arrangements and equilibrium in multidimensional voting models', *American Journal of Political Science*, 23: 27–60.

Shepsle, K. A. and Weingast, B. R. (1989) 'Studying institutions: lessons from the rational choice approach', *Journal of Theoretical Politics*, 1: 131–47.

Siaroff, A. (2000) *Comparative European Party Systems: An Analysis of Parliamentary Systems Since 1945*. New York, London: Garland Publishing.

Simon, H. (1965) *Administrative Behavior*. Free Press: New York.

Skocpol, T. (1992) *Protecting Soldiers and Mothers: The Political Origins of Social Policy in the United States*. Newbury Park: Sage.

Smith, G. (1979) 'Western European party systems: on the trial of a typology', *West European Politics*, 2, 1: 128–43.

Smith, G. (1986) *Democracy in Western Germany: Parties and Politics in the Federal Republic*. Aldershot: Gower.

Smith, G. (1989) 'A system perspective on party system change', in *Journal of Theoretical Politics*, 1: 349–63.

Smith, G. (2003) 'The "new model" party system', in Padgett, S., Paterson, W. and Smith, G. (eds) *Developments in German Politics*, 3rd Edn. Basingstoke: Palgrave.

Sniderman, P., Brody, R. and Tetlock, P. (1991): *Reasoning and Choice*. London: Cambridge University Press.

SPD (1998) *Arbeit. Innovation und Gerechtigkeit: SPD- Wahlprogramme für die Bundestagswahl 1998*. Bonn.

SPD (2002) *Erneuerung und Zummenhalt -Wir in Deutschland. Regierungsprogramm 2002–2006*. Berlin.

SPD Bündnis'90/Die Grünen (1998) *Aufbruch und Erneuerung – Deutschlands Weg in 21. Jahrhundert*. Bonn.

SPD Bündnis'90/Die Grünen (2002) *Erneuerung – Gerechtigkeit – Nachhaltigkeit: Koalitionsvertrag 2002–2006*. Berlin.

Statistisches Bundesamt. Datasets available at www.destatis.de

Stepan, A. (2001) *Arguing Comparative Politics*. Oxford: Oxford University Press.

Stöss, R. (1976) 'Entstehung und Entwicklung des deutschen Parteiensystems bis 1933', in Staritz, D. (ed.) *Das Parteiensystem der Bundesrepublik*. Opladen: Leske und Budrich.

Sutherland, C. (2001) 'The reinvention of concepts by the Bavarian CSU', in *German Politics*, 10, 3: 13–36.

Swanson, D. and Mancini, P. (eds) (1996) *Politics, Media, and Modern Democracy*. Westport, CT: Praeger.

Talshir, G. (2002) *The Political Idelology of Green Parties: From the Politics of Nature to Redefining the Nature of Politics*. Basingstoke: Palgrave.

Tarrow, S. G. (1994): *Power in Movement: Social Movements, Collective Action and Politics*. Cambridge: Cambridge University Press.

Tawney, R. H. (1938) *Religion and the Rise of Capitalism*. Harmondsworth: Pelican.

Taylor. A. J. P. (1982) *The Course of German History*, 7th Edn. London: Methuen.

Thomassen, J. (1976) 'Party identification as a cross-national concept: its meaning in the Netherlands', in Budge, I., Crewe, I. and Farlie, D. (eds) *Party Identification and Beyond*. London: Wiley.

Thompson, D. (1970) *The Democratic Citizen*. Cambridge: Cambridge University Press.

Tingsten, H. (1955) 'Stability and vitality in Swedish Democracy', *Political Quarterly*, 26: 140–51.

Tóka, G. (1996) 'Parties and electoral choices in east-central Europe', in Pridham, G. and Lewis, P. (eds) *Stabilising Fragile Democracies: Comparing New Party Systems in Southern and Eastern Europe*. London: Routledge.

Truman, D. (1951) *The Governmental Process*. New York: Alfred E. Knopf.

Tsebelis, G. (1990) *Nested Games: Rational Choice in Comparative Politics*. Berkeley, CA: University of California Press.

Tufte, E. (1978) *Political Control of the Economy*. Princeton, NJ: Princeton University Press.

Tullock, G. and Campbell, C. D. (1970) 'Computer simulation of a small voting system', *Economics Journal*, 80: 97–104.

Tuma, N. and Mayer, K. (eds) (1990) *Event History Analysis in Life Course Research*. Madison, WI: University of Wisconsin Press.

Uglow, J. (2002) *The Lunar Men: the Friends who Made the Future, 1730–1810*. London: Faber and Faber.

van Deth, J. and Scarbrough, E. (1995) *The Impact of Values*. Oxford: Oxford University Press.

von Winter, T. (1996) 'Wählerverhalten in den östlichen Bundesländern: Wahlsoziologische Erklärungsmodelle auf den Prüfstand', *Zeitschrift für Parlamentsfragen*, 2: 298–316.

Ware, A. (1987a) *Citizens, Parties, and the State*. Cambridge: Polity Press.

Ware, A. (ed.) (1987b) *Political Parties: Electoral Change and Structural Response*. Oxford: Blackwell.

Weale, A. (1984) 'Social choice versus populism? An interpretation of Riker's political theory', *British Journal of Political Science*, 14: 369–85.

Weale, A. (1992) *The New Politics of Pollution*. Manchester: Manchester University Press.

Weber, M. (1924) *Gesammelte Aufsatze zur Soziologie und Sozialpolitik*. Tubingen: Mohr.

Weber, M. (1962) *Basic Concepts in Sociology*. London: Owen.

Weber, M. (1965) *The Protestant Ethic and the Spirit of Capitalism*. London: Allen and Unwin.

Weingast, B. R. (1998) 'Political institutions: rational choice perspectives', in Goodin, R. E. and Klingemann, H.-D. (eds) *A New Handbook of Political Science*. Oxford University Press.

Weins, C. (1999) 'The East German vote in the 1998 General Election', in Padgett, S. and Saalfeld, T. (eds) *Bundestagswahl '98: End of an Era?*. Special issue of *German Politics*, 8, 2: 48–71.

Weisberg, H. (1999) 'Political partisanship', in Robinson J., Shaver, P. and Wrightsman, L. (eds) *Measures of Political Attitudes*. San Diego: Academic Press.

Wendle, M. (1999) 'Die faszination des "einfachen Denkens." Eine Ideologiekritik der Politischen Ökonomie des "Dritten Wegs" ', in Dörre, K., Panitch, L. and Zeuner, B. (eds) *Die Strategie der 'Neuen Mitte'. Verabschiedet sich der moderne Sozialdemokratie als Reformpartei?* Hamburg: VSA-Verlag.

Whitely, P. (1986) *Political Control of the Macro-Economy*. London: Sage.

Whitely, P. (2005) 'Just the best of a bad bunch? Why politicians are held in low regard', *The Times Higher Education Supplement*, No. 1673 (07/01/05): 19.

Wielgohs, J. (1996) 'Strategies of West German corporate actors in the creation of interest associations in East Germany', *German Politics*, 5, 2: 201–13.

Wiener, A. and Diez, T. (eds) (2004) *European Integration Theory*. Oxford: Oxford University Press.

Wolf, C. (1996) 'Konfessionelle versus religiöse Konfliktlinie in der deutschen Wählerschaft', *Politische Vierteljahresschrift*, 37, 4: 713–34.

Wolinetz, S. (2002) 'Beyond the Catch-all party: approaches to the study of parties and party organisation', in Gunther, R., Montero, J. and Linz, J. (eds) *Political Parties: Old Concepts and New Challenges*. Oxford: Oxford University Press.

Wüst, A. (2004) 'Naturalised citizens as voters: behaviour and impact', in Lees, C. and Saalfeld, T. (eds) *Bundestagswahl 2002: the Battle of the Candidates*. London: Frank Cass.

Yamaguchi, K. (1991) *Event History Analysis*. Newbury Park, CA: Sage.

Zuckerman, A. (1975) 'Political cleavage: a conceptual and theoretical analysis', *British Journal of Political Science*, 5: 231–48.

Index

Printed in the United States
59843LVS00001BC/2